A Comparison of Ancient Near Eastern Law Collections Prior to the First Millennium BC

Gorgias Dissertations

35

Near Eastern Studies 10

A Comparison of Ancient Near Eastern Law Collections Prior to the First Millennium BC

SAMUEL A. JACKSON

GORGIAS PRESS
2008

First Gorgias Press Edition, 2008

Published in the United States of America by Gorgias Press LLC, New Jersey

ISBN 978-1-59333-221-1
ISSN 1935 6870

Gorgias Press
180 Centennial Ave., Suite 3, Piscataway, NJ 08854 USA
www.gorgiaspress.com

Library of Congress Cataloging-in-Publication Data
Jackson, Samuel A.
A comparison of ancient Near Eastern law collections prior to the first millennium B.C. / Samuel Jackson. -- 1st Gorgias Press ed.
p. cm.
Includes bibliographical references and index.
1. Law--Middle East. 2. Law, Ancient. 3. Law--Middle East--History. I. Title.
KL147.J33 2008
340.5'394--dc22
2008018317

The paper used in this publication meets the minimum requirements of the American National Standards.

Printed in the United States of America

For Maya
&
Josiah, Elijah and Layla
Thank you for your patience

CONTENTS

PREFACE

This work grew out of an interest in the application of the comparative method to the Old Testament and some points of disagreement with Malul's and Westbrook's works regarding the comparison of ancient Near Eastern and biblical law. Eventually I decided to remove the Old Testament material from view. The enormity of the secondary literature on biblical law, the myriad issues regarding dating and the relationship between different collections would have taken so long to discuss there would have been little space in the work for comparison. Some virtues did come out of this necessity as the exclusion of the biblical material has enabled the opportunity to test a comparative method without the enormous influence past inclusion of the biblical texts has had on comparative studies. The study of the biblical texts tends to heighten the likelihood of ideological influence and authorial agenda. I hope that the conclusions reached here about comparison, borrowing and culture without such influence may be a useful guide and balance to future attempts at comparison which do include the biblical texts.

Scholars' notions about the Laws of Hammurabi have also had an enormous impact upon the treatment of other law collections, partly due to the greater amount of material available to study this collection. Scholars often prefer to go from the known to the unknown and apply what are supposedly firm conclusions about the Laws of Hammurabi to other collections. In this work there is an attempt to question some of the generally accepted theories about the nature and function of the Laws of Hammurabi and to assert the possibility that the other collections may differ from it.

Setting out to correct or critique is always a dangerous exercise, especially in a doctoral thesis. This one aimed primarily at highlighting and explaining consistent differences in both the framing and content of the various law collections. This was carried out in order to complement the works of Malul and Westbrook, amongst others, as much as to argue against some of their conclusions regarding similarities. It is hoped that this work will provide an alternative to reading the law collections of the ancient Near East as part of a uniform legal culture which was a step towards that of the far superior Greeks and Romans. That is not to say that I do not think there are similarities amongst the law collections of the ancient Near East prior to the first-millennium B.C., nor do I deny that changes took place in legal culture over time. This work was merely designed to fill out the discussion so that the possibility of consistent cultural differences may be reconsidered.

I believe the work is successful in highlighting these consistent differences within the law collections and in correlating them with differences in other areas of culture or literature *e.g.* religion, treaties and historiography. For example, Mesopotamian law collections do not explicitly acknowledge changes, correlating with the notion in Mesopotamia that the correct ways of doing things were handed down from the gods to men in the beginning. In contrast the Hittite law collection does explicitly acknowledge change, correlating with the Hittite tendency to do so in their history writing in order to teach lessons, or in their treaties in order to motivate obedience. The explanations given to account for such differences and their correlations remain speculative and very much open to critique and the proposal of alternatives. It is hoped that the tenuous nature of some of the explanations which are tentatively suggested does not lead the reader or critic to dismiss the firmly founded demonstration that the ancient Near East did not contain a uniform culture. The oft stated "truism" that the various collections freely borrowed material from each other is effectively called into question here. While there is much congruity in terms of the topics covered across the collections (especially amongst those from within southern Mesopotamia), the thesis demonstrates that there is little compelling evidence for specific instances of more substantial literary borrowing within the laws themselves, though it acknowledges some possible cases.

ACKNOWLEDGEMENTS

I owe a debt of gratitude to Dr Noel Weeks, without whom this book would never have come to fruition. I have enjoyed the benefits of years of his teaching on ancient Near Eastern history, historiography, religion and languages, as well as his enormously helpful supervision of this thesis. The concise and thoughtful manner in which he could inspire a path of inquiry, crystallize a series of thoughts, or rip to shreds an unfounded argument has been appreciated by and been of benefit to all of his students and this one in particular. My thanks also go to the library staff at the University of Sydney for their hard work in bringing many books out of storage (having to electronically barcode many of them for the first time) and in tracking down and providing me with my many interlibrary loans. Steve Wiggins', Katie Stott's and George Kiraz' aid and advice with regards to the editing of this work for publication has been much appreciated as has Gorgias' initiative in creating an avenue for the publication of dissertations such as this through the DNES series. Last of all my heartfelt thanks go to my family: to my parents for instilling in me a love of things Old Testament and Near Eastern, and to my wife and children, to whom this book is dedicated, for supporting and patiently putting up with me through the entire process.

1 INTRODUCTION

1.1 INTRODUCTION

Much of the literature on ancient Near Eastern law has attempted to wrestle with issues such as the applicability and purpose of the collections. The issues surrounding the nature, origin and purpose of the ancient Near Eastern law collections are manifold and complex. Though an attempt will be made to tackle them in the course of this study, they will not be the focus of the work. There is a sense where they pose unanswerable questions at times. We simply do not have enough evidence, or at least not the right type of evidence, to be able to answer them for all Near Eastern law collections (perhaps not for any). It will be asserted, however, that to ignore the stated intent of the collections themselves would be a methodological travesty.

What this study will focus on is perhaps more controversial: a comparative look at ancient Near Eastern law collections pre-first millennium B.C.[1] This will inevitably involve some discussion of comparative method, a much maligned and vexed topic. The existence of a number of ill-founded (or un-founded) assumptions which influence research in this area make the project worthwhile, as does the reluctance of most to take up such an endeavor. The publication of the encyclopedic *A History of Ancient Near Eastern Law*[2] and Roth's easily accessible English translation of the Near Eastern law collections[3] has made this task somewhat more feasible, though still quite enormous. The lack of systematic comparison in general is a disturbing trend. With comparison being done on an increasingly smaller scale or as part of a co-operative (or unco-operative as the case may be) venture (collections of articles by multiple authors *etc.*); more room is left for old (or new) assumptions to be left untested (or for selection of those cases where said assumption seems justified).[4] It is quite true that systematic comparison

---

[1] All dates referred to hereafter are B.C. unless otherwise stated.

[2] Raymond Westbrook, ed., *A History of Ancient Near Eastern Law* (2 vols; Handbook of Oriental Studies 72/1; Leiden: Brill, 2003).

[3] Martha Tobias Roth, *Law Collections from Mesopotamia and Asia Minor* (with a contribution by Harry Anger Hoffner, Jr.; Society of Biblical Literature Writings from the Ancient World 6; Atlanta, Ga.: Scholars Press, 1995).

[4] *e.g.* the heavy focus on the laws concerning the goring ox when tackling com-

carries its own set of problems, but this does not make it less worthwhile. All historical research is problematic to a degree.

Much of the avoidance of large scale comparison can be attributed to particularly Eurocentric and anachronistic portrayals of the ancient Near East in the past (unable to think in the abstract *etc.*), the abuses of pan-Babylonism, the controversial issues surrounding comparison with ancient Israel and the development of cultural relativism. Much of it is also due to an ever increasing specialization within the field. Again, one could argue this makes the taking up of this topic all the more worthwhile. The methodological inadequacies of the comparative works contained within collections such as Frankfort's *Intellectual Adventure of Ancient Man*[5] may also have scared some off. The recent resurgence of developmental theories,[6] a renewed in-

---

parative issues, especially from the field of Biblical Studies: Jacob Joel Finkelstein, "The Goring Ox: Some Historical Perspectives on Deodands, Forfeitures, Wrongful Death and the Western Notion of Sovereignty," *Temple Law Quarterly* 46 (1973): 169–290; "The Ox That Gored," *Transactions of the American Philosophical Society* 71 (1981): 1–89; Bernard S. Jackson, *Essays in Jewish and Comparative Legal History* (Leiden: Brill, 1975), ch. 5; Meir Malul, *The Comparative Method in Ancient Near Eastern and Biblical Legal Studies* (Alter Orient und Altes Testament 227; Kevelaer: Butzon & Bercker, 1990), ch. 7; A. van Selms, "The Goring Ox in Babylonian and Biblical Law," *Archiv Orientalni* 18 (1950): 321–30; Reuven Yaron, "The Goring Ox in Near Eastern Laws," *Israel Law Review* 1 (1996): 396–406.

[5] The articles by Henri Frankfort, H. A. Frankfort, John A. Wilson, Thorkild Jacobsen, and W. A. Irwin in *The Intellectual Adventure of Ancient Man: An Essay on Speculative Thought in the Ancient Near East* (Chicago: University of Chicago, 1946). See also Henri Frankfort's *Kingship and the Gods: A Study of Ancient Near Eastern Religion as the Integration of Society and Nature* (Chicago: University of Chicago, 1948). The abuses of the Myth and Ritual school have also contributed to this problem *e.g.* James G. Frazer, *The Golden Bough: A Study in Comparative Religion* (2 vols.; London: Macmillan, 1890), S. H. Hooke, ed., *Myth and Ritual: Essays on the Myth and Ritual of the Hebrews in Relation to the Culture Pattern of the Ancient East* (London: Oxford University, 1933), *The Labyrinth: Further Essays in the Relation between Myth and Ritual in the Ancient World* (London: Macmillan, 1935) and *Myth, Ritual, and Kingship: Essays on the Theory and Practice of Kingship in the Ancient Near East and in Israel* (Oxford: Clarendon, 1958).

[6] Jean Bottéro, "The 'Code' of Hammurabi," in *Mesopotamia: Writing, Reasoning and the Gods* (Chicago: University of Chicago, 1992), 156–84; translated by Z. Bahrani, and Marc van de Mieroop from "Le 'code' de Hammurapi," *Annali della Scuola Normale Superiore di Pisa* 12 (1982): 409–44; Westbrook, "Cuneiform Law Codes and the Origins of Legislation," *Zeitschrift für Assyriologie* 79 (1989): 201–22, and the Axial Age theory which Westbrook refers to *e.g.* the papers in *The Origins and Diversity of Axial Age Civilizations* (ed. Shmuel Noah Eisenstadt; Albany: State University of

terest in comparative method[7] and the lingering notion of a common ancient Near Eastern culture[8] also give this work some current relevance.

Much of this study owes its assumptions and methodology to the work and teaching of Dr Noel Weeks. To an extent this project comes from the seed of an idea sowed in his course on historiography in the ancient Near East and furthered by the recent publication of his work on ancient Near Eastern treaties and covenants.[9]

What this thesis will attempt to do is compare the law collections of pre-first millennium B.C. ancient Near Eastern societies. In doing this we will be looking for consistent differences between cultures, which may give us an insight into how that culture operates or what lies behind aspects of its society. Within the study an eye will be kept on the interaction of different aspects of society with its religious outlook or worldview and political makeup in producing certain ways of doing things (particularly in the field of law). This writer expects to find some consistent distinctions between societies, especially in regard to mode and severity of punishment. There are obviously many theoretical problems raised by such an endeavor. The problem of the applicability of the law collections, their nature, origin and purpose will certainly have to be discussed to some extent. The question of the place of the law collections in scribal curriculum and issues of cultural transmission/borrowing in general will also arise. This inevitably will involve some discussion of form and genre criticism. It will be argued that generally parallels or borrowings are in the eye of the beholder. Such an argument may leave this study open to the charge that the pinpointing of cultural differences is also in the eye of the beholder, let alone their explanation. The collecting of parallels will continue unabated. It is only fitting that an attempt at the description and explanation of cultural differences in the

---

New York, 1986). See also now, *Axial Civilizations and World History* (ed. Johann P. Arnasen, Shmuel Noah Eisenstadt, and B. Wittrock; Jerusalem Studies in Religion and Culture 4; Leiden: Brill, 2005).

7 See for example John Baines and Norman Yoffee, "Order, Legitimacy, and Wealth in Ancient Egypt and Mesopotamia," in *Archaic States* (ed. G. M. Feinman and J. Marcus; Santa Fe, Mex.: School of American Research, 1998), 199–260 or the papers in the collected volume *Order, Legitimacy and Wealth in Ancient States* (ed. J. Richards and M. van Buren; New Directions in Archaeology; Cambridge: Cambridge University, 2000).

8 Westbrook, see notes 12–13 below.

9 Noel K. Weeks, *Admonition and Curse: The Ancient Near Eastern Treaty/Covenant Form as a Problem in Inter-Cultural Relationships* (Journal for the Study of the Old Testament Supplement 407; London: T&T Clark, 2004).

ancient Near East (particularly in the area of law collections) is given an airing as a counterpoint. The claim, put forward by many, that borrowing was so prevalent that there are numerous examples of verbatim copying or translation of laws will be put to the test.[10] The more difficult issues surrounding the pinpointing of stimulus diffusion as opposed to independent invention in a similar society will be avoided due to limitations of space. This work will not focus on contesting the possibility of such stimulus diffusion (which may explain things such as the similarities between law collections in terms of the topics chosen to treat, or even how they are used), but will aim at undercutting the claims of more direct and wholesale borrowing.

In some sense we can see the present study as a balance to the work of those who postulate a common culture within the ancient Near East. While it cannot be denied there are many similarities between societies within the ancient Near East it does scholarship little good if it focuses only on these aspects and ignores the differences. In speaking of all the legal systems referred to in *A History of Ancient Near Eastern Law*[11] Westbrook is able to state, "it is impossible to say of any legal system from any place or in any period within the parameters set by this history, that its laws come from a conceptual world alien to the others."[12] Earlier he phrases it thus, "I would argue that all the ancient Near Eastern systems belonged in varying degrees to a common legal culture . . . they shared a legal ontology: a way of looking at the law that reflected their view of the world and determined the horizon of the lawmaker."[13] Westbrook spends a good portion of his introduction outlining what he sees as the elements common within this legal culture. The work set out here is partially aimed at complementing such an approach, but will inevitably contradict it also.

---

[10] *e.g.* Westbrook, "Biblical and Cuneiform Law Codes," *Revue Biblique* 92 (1985): 248, 252, 256; Norman Yoffee, "Context and Authority in Early Mesopotamian Law," in *State Formation and Political Legitimacy* (ed. R. Cohen, and J. D. Toland; New Brunswick: Transaction Books, 1988), 102; Nicholas Postgate, *Early Mesopotamia: Society and Economy at the Dawn of History* (London: Routledge, 1992), ch. 15 "Laws and the Law," 289.

[11] Which covers the law of the third to the first millennium B.C. within all of Mesopotamia (including Assyria), Hatti, Israel, Egypt and smaller entities such as Ugarit, Nuzi, Alalakh and Emar.

[12] Raymond Westbrook, "The Character of Ancient Near Eastern Law," in *A History of Ancient Near Eastern Law* (ed. Raymond Westbrook; vol. 1; Handbook of Oriental Studies 72/1; Leiden: Brill, 2003), 24.

[13] *Ibid.*, 4. To be fair he does recognize some degree of difference within these systems (especially Egypt).

With this stated purpose in mind this writer is sure any tenuous arguments and explanations put forward here will be criticized by opponents of such an approach. This is to be welcomed, as forced arguments do one's purpose no favors. This being said, an attempt will be made to remain open to cultural parallels, borrowings and literary conventions. To deny these exist at all would be nonsensical. To think one can come up with a definitive methodology with which to pinpoint and explain parallels or differences is equally naïve[14] so the method to be used here will be set out as briefly as possible.

First, an attempt to define the topic to be treated. The term "law collections" here shall be applied loosely. It is not to be taken as a generic identifier of a common Near Eastern text type so much as a useful term for any text from our region and period which contains a collection of legal provisions. This is not to say that each type of text will be treated in the same way; quite the opposite. This writer believes that such a loose definition will help to avoid lulling one into the mindset that what we are dealing with is a uniform type of text and will intensify the readiness to identify individual differences and nuances. To treat a text such as the Sumerian Handbook of Law Forms (SLHF) or *ana ittišu* in the same way as the edict of Ammiṣaduqa (AE) or the Laws of Hammurabi (LH) would be methodologically poor. To deny that these are texts capable of comparison would also be a poor approach. This loose definition is helpful in a number of other ways, not the least of which is that it enables Egypt to become part of the discussion.[15] It gives us a wider base of texts on which to test theories of cultural or textual specificity. Due to the size of the project and the problematic assumptions that would be involved, this study is not necessarily a comparison of the substantive law[16] of these different societies. The large number of legal sources that would have to be covered in such a topic is immense. Even in an encyclopedic work such as *A History of Ancient Near Eastern Law*, each topic is only covered briefly, and this in a volume with many contributors. A comparison of the substantive law would also open up discussion of a number of cultures for whom we do not have law collections as such *e.g.* Ugarit, Nuzi, Alalakh, Emar *etc.* Limitations of space and time have excluded this. Though this severely limits some of the questions

---

[14] *confer* Malul, *The Comparative Method*, chs. 5–6 *e.g.* "There exist objective ways to explain similarities and differences," 83–84.

[15] Through texts such as the Edict of Horemheb, the Nauri Decree, Elephantine Decree *etc.*

[16] By this is meant independently valid, current, and applicable law.

which can be answered (*e.g.* with regard to the relationship between the collections and actual practice) it does allow the time to pursue the main goal of this work.

Again, for the purpose of limitation, ancient Israelite or Old Testament law has been left out of the discussion for the time being.[17] The controversy that would be sparked by the inclusion of Israel in such a work would mean an enormous amount of time would have to be spent covering the secondary literature. The many issues that would be raised, such as dating, the nature of the sources (multiple author, purpose, composition, text history *etc.*) and the agendas involved in the various sides of the arguments would mean much time would be spent dealing with introductory issues rather than the comparison which is the goal of this work. One of the issues thus postponed is the question of whether the Israelite law collections are best compared to other ancient Near Eastern law collections or other covenants and treaties.[18] There are some happy benefits that come from this (along with the disappointments and shortfalls of not including Israel in the work). One of the benefits of this omission is that the agendas and biases concerning comparison of ancient Near Eastern societies with Israel will play less of a role in this work. In this way it is hoped that perhaps a model will be set up with which to do such studies in the future. Another benefit is that methods of comparison with Israel can be indirectly put to the test by comparison within the ancient Near East itself. This work will involve some criticism of the approach that treats the entire ancient Near East as a monolithic cultural unit. This will have implications both for those who see the Near East as a monolithic unit in contrast with Israel[19] and for those who see Israel as merely part of said monolithic unit.[20]

One of the many methodological problems raised by this work hinges on the definition of the terms 'culture' and 'society'. This is especially so for Mesopotamia. When one approaches a comparison of ancient Near Eastern law does one treat Mesopotamia as a cultural unit or look for smaller units within that entity? Is this an unnecessary dichotomy *i.e.* are both possible

---

[17] It is hoped that this work can be used as the basis for a follow up volume comparing Old Testament law with the other ancient Near Eastern law collections.

[18] See Weeks, *Admonition and Curse*. The present writer thinks that comparison with both is a viable possibility.

[19] *e.g.* Moshe Greenberg, "Some Postulates of Biblical Criminal Law," in *Essential Papers on Israel and the Ancient Near East* (ed. F. E. Greenspahn; New York: New York University, 1991), 333–52; repr. from *Studies in Bible and Jewish Religion: Yehezkel Kaufmann Jubilee Volume* (ed. Menahem Haran; Jerusalem: Magnes, 1960), 5–28.

[20] *e.g.* Westbrook, see notes 12–13 above.

and if so how? It is hoped that this study will show that though there are similarities within all Mesopotamian societies and cultures, there are also significant differences. The comparison of the Middle Assyrian law collections should demonstrate this amply. So, again, it seems a loose definition of the terms 'society' and 'culture' will be employed. This should enable this writer to notice both similarities and differences on a number of different levels. It would also be naïve to deny the possibility of cultural development or change over such a long period. Though in most cases the lack of sources enables us to bypass such an issue, it is something we intend to keep in mind.

Perhaps the next issue that should be raised is that of what to compare within these collections. There is debate in many fields as to the benefits and pitfalls of emic vs etic classification.[21] Within the ancient Near Eastern law collections that is less of an issue in practice for we have very few texts which specifically elaborate any classification within the law collections. Regarding emic classification, there are three manuscripts of LH with subject headings.[22] No two of these texts have the same heading in the same place so this writer does not feel the need to be restricted by them as they were not even authoritative within their own context. This is not to say there was no emic classification. Much ink has been spilled over the internal structure of the law collections in arranging the various laws into topics.[23] This is perhaps something we should consider, especially when assessing claims of borrowing. It is generally thought that the laws were not arranged solely on the basis of legal topics as we would think of them. This writer does not feel such emic classifications should limit what we treat as comparable subject matter, though we must keep an eye on the effects of lumping

---

[21] *e.g.* Tremper Longman III, "Form Criticism, Recent Developments in Genre Theory, and the Evangelical," *Westminster Theological Journal* 47 (1985), esp. 55–56.

[22] See Roth, *Law Collections*, 75–76. For bibliographical information regarding editions of these texts see the listings for sources S, r and t on pages 252–53 in the same work.

[23] Barry L. Eichler, "Literary Structure in the Laws of Eshnunna," in *Language, Literature, and History: Philological and Historical Studies Presented to Erica Reiner* (ed. Francisca Rochberg-Halton; American Oriental Series 67; New Haven: American Oriental Society, 1987), 71–84; Herbert Petschow, "Zur Systematik und Gesetztechnik im Codex Hammurabi," *Zeitschrift für Assyriologie* 57 (1965): 146–72; "Zur 'Systematik' in den Gesetzen von Eschnunna," in *Symbolae Iuridicae et Historicae Martino David Dedicatae* (ed. J. A. Ankum, R. Feenstra, and W. F. Leemans; vol. 2; Studia Documenta ad Iura Orientis Antiqui Pertinentia 2; Leiden: Brill, 1968), 131–43. See also the discussions within the various editions of the law collections.

the laws into modern or Roman legal categories.[24] An attempt to understand each law within its collection and society will be made before comparison. The law collections generally follow a seeming train-of-thought structure (elsewhere termed "association").[25] It is not unknown for laws we would consider to be within the same area of law, or at least to demonstrate similar legal principles, to be found nowhere near each other within a collection, and certainly in different places across collections.[26] With this in mind, this writer feels at liberty to construct his own topical classifications to compare across collections and will leave it to the reader to judge whether they are useful.[27]

The lack of sources at our disposal and the gaps within those sources throw up some very serious problems for our work. A classic example is the seemingly disproportionate emphasis the Middle Assyrian law collections have on laws to do with women. If one were comparing the importance of various areas of law across the collections some skewed conclusions could be made. The focus of the first tablet of the Middle Assyrian laws on the topic of women, the accident of discovery that that tablet is the best preserved, combined with the fact our other law collection for the Middle Assyrian period is a group of Harem decrees may explain the apparent overemphasis on women in the Assyrian sources. It is very important to consider the possible gaps in the evidence before making any hasty conclusions. Perhaps a more important example is the lack of a law collection in Egypt on the scale of such collections as we find in Mesopotamia and Asia Minor. Is this due to our lack of sources[28] (particularly acute in Egypt at the best of times) or a difference of outlook within Egypt?[29] These things will need to

---

[24] See already the comment of Reuven Yaron, *The Laws of Eshnunna* (2nd ed.; Jerusalem: Magnes, 1988), 158, n. 94.

[25] *e.g.* by similar terms or subject matter such as Tablet A of MAL which deals with laws to do with women. For discussion of this phenomenon see the articles by Petschow in note 23, or more briefly in the following: Johannes Renger, "Noch einmal: Was war der 'Kodex' Hammurapi-ein erlassenes Gesetz oder ein Rechtsbuch?," in *Rechtskodifizierung und soziale Normen im interkulturellen Vergleich* (ed. Hans-Joachim Gehrke; Script Oralia 66; Series A: Altertumwissentschaftliche Reiche vol. 15; Tubingen: Gunter Narr, 1994), 38; Roth, *Law* Collections, 3–4.

[26] *e.g.* the sex laws of MAL which are bunched together between A 12–24 and then two more are found at A 55–56.

[27] They are vaguely related to Westbrook's distinct areas of law as set out in *History*.

[28] Westbrook, "Character," 5.

[29] John A. Wilson, "Authority and Law in Ancient Egypt," *Supplement to Journal*

be considered during comparisons. It will be best then to attempt to keep comparisons between cultures to topics at least two cultures cover in their collections.

This work shall begin with an introduction to the issues and debates within the study of ancient Near Eastern law and how they have developed and changed. This will also discuss the issue of comparative method more thoroughly before continuing. It will then compare individual topics across cultures *e.g.* punishment, structure of the collections, generic identification and separate legal topics such as theft, murder, rape, adultery *etc.* This will be concluded with the findings of these comparisons, including an attempt to define consistent aspects of each society's (including Mesopotamia as a whole and as smaller units) law collections and possible influences on it *e.g.* political makeup, religious outlook, worldview *etc.*, and the implications for further research both comparatively and in the field of ancient Near Eastern law.

1.2 The Historiography of Ancient Near Eastern Law

The study of ancient Near Eastern law has gone through a number of transformations since the discovery of the stele containing the law collection of Hammurabi in 1901. Many of the older assumptions still have a lingering influence on the field. Before LH was available to modern scholars, the study of ancient Near Eastern law was focused on Egypt and the Old Testament.[30] The tales told by Herodotus and Diodorus of the Egyptian erudition in legal matters and the Egyptian origin of classical law were the sum of our non-biblical information. This focus on Egypt fitted in quite nicely with late 18th and early 19th century Egyptomania on the heels of Napoleon's *Mission de Egypte.* With the discovery of LH the focus shifted to Mesopotamia for the study of the origin of law giving. This was a general shift that was happening with the rise of Assyriology in the mid to late 19th century.[31]

Immediately treated as a source from which to obtain the substantive law of ancient Babylonia, what Roth has termed the "Hammurabi's Gesetz" approach took off.[32] Scholars (and others) wished to know what the Babylonian law was on certain subjects and sought to find out through an analy-

of the American Oriental Society, 17 (1954): 1–33.

[30] Including the study of the Talmud, Mishnah *etc.*

[31] See below on pan-Babylonism.

[32] Martha Tobias Roth, "Reading Mesopotamian Law Cases: PBS 5 100: A Question of Filiation," *Journal of the Economic and Social History of the Orient* 44 (2001): 243.

sis of the law collection and the documents from practice.[33] Many other assumptions played a role in this early stage of the study of ancient Near Eastern law. Evolutionary theories as to the development of human society (and more specifically law) could now be tested to some extent.[34] They did not fare too well, but other developmental theories took their place.[35] Diffusion was also popular, with pan-Babylonism developing during this period.[36] The immediate interest in Hammurabi's laws for scholars of Old Testament law was also immense.[37] Many of these shared an approach based on pan-Babylonism which has greatly influenced the field ever since. Due to a European bias and the assumption that Hammurabi's stele represented substantive law, those interested in comparative law or the history of law often read into Hammurabi's collection models or concepts from Roman or modern law.[38] This again, is a practice not without modern adherents.[39] Form critical arguments also began to play a role in assessing the origin and purpose of the law collection.[40]

---

[33] Most famously seen in the multi-volume *Hammurabi's Gesetz* project. J. Kohler and F. E. Peiser, *Hammurabi's Gesetz* (vol. 1; Leipzig: Pfeifer, 1904); J. Kohler and A. Ungnad, *Hammurabi's Gesetz* (vol. 2; Leipzig: Pfeifer, 1909); *Hammurabi's Gesetz* (vol. 3; Leipzig: Pfeifer, 1909); *Hammurabi's Gesetz* (vol. 4; Leipzig: Pfeifer, 1910); *Hammurabi's Gesetz* (vol. 5; Leipzig: Pfeifer, 1911); Paulo Koschaker and A. Ungnad, *Hammurabi's Gesetz* (vol. 6; Leipzig: Pfeifer, 1923).

[34] *e.g.* that of Henry Sumner Maine, *Ancient Law* (London: John Murray, 1864; repr., Tucson: University of Arizona, 1986).

[35] See the discussion of Raymond Westbrook, "Character," 71–74.

[36] The seminal works of scholars involved in the Babel-Bibel controversy were written in the first decade of the 20th century.

[37] *e.g.* D. H. Müller, *Die Gesetze Hammurabis und ihr Verhältnis zur mosaischen Gesetzgebung sowie zu den XII Tafeln* (Vienna: Hölder, 1903) even translated it into Hebrew and placed it parallel to the Old Testament laws.

[38] *e.g. Hammurabi's Gesetz'* rendering of LH into modern legal form and its division of the documents from practice into modern legal areas, and Müller's, *Die Gesetze Hammurabis*, setting out of the laws next to the Roman Twelve Tables.

[39] *e.g.* Russ VerSteeg, *Early Mesopotamian Law* (Durham, N.C.: Carolina Academic, 2000)

and to a lesser extent Westbrook (see bibliography for some of his works).

[40] *e.g.* Paulo Koschaker in *Rechtsvergleichende Studien zur Gesetzgebung Hammurapis Konigs von Babylon* (Leipzig: von Veit, 1917). See comment by Roth, "The Law Collection of King Hammurabi: Toward an Understanding of Codification and Text," in *La Codification Des Lois Dans L'Antiquité: Actes du Colloque de Strasbourg 27–29 novembre 1997* (ed. Edmond Lévy; Université Marc Bloch de Strasbourg: travaux du centre de recherche sur le Proche-Orient et la Grèce antiques 16; Paris: De Boc-

After some decades scholars began to realize that Hammurabi's collection of laws did not regularly match up with the documents from practice[41] and that they did not cite his collection as an authoritative source for the decision of their case.[42] Some began to question the substantive nature of his document. With the discovery of more law collections from Mesopotamia pan-Babylonism asserted itself again. The discovery of Sumerian law collections such as that of Lipit-Ishtar or Ur-Nammu fuelled the argument for original Sumerian (non-Semitic) civilizational development. The existence of a propagandistic prologue (and epilogue for Lipit-Ishtar) furthered the argument that the purpose of the law collections was not substantive law but royal propaganda.[43] For others the existence of copies of these texts in scribal schools created another line of argument, namely that these were works of Mesopotamian legal science not a code of comprehensive laws directly applicable in the law courts of the society.[44] Still Form Criticism and now Genre Criticism became popular tools to use in assessing background and purpose for the law collections.

A closer look at the development of the historiography of ancient Near Eastern law is warranted at this point. It is worth noting the historical background to some of the changes within the field, the prominent position of LH in the discussion, the influence this has on the treatment of other collections, and the influence of methods from Biblical studies and Roman and modern legal studies on approaches and methodology. The next section will focus on the comparative method itself more specifically.

It has been pointed out by scholars that the early treatment of LH was conditioned by historical context.[45] Scheil gave the title "*Les Lois de code Hammurabi*"[46] to the collection of laws contained on the Louvre stele. This

---

card, 2000), 17.

[41] W. Eilers, *Die Gesetzesstele Chammurabis. Gesetze um die Wende des 3. vorchristlichen Jahrtausends* (Der Alte Orient 31: 3/4; Leipzig: J. C. Hinrichs, 1932).

[42] Benno Landsberger, "Die babylonischen Termini für Gesetz und Recht," in *Symbolae Paulo Koschaker Dedicatae* (ed. Johannes Friedrich, J. G. Lautner, and John C. Miles; Studia Documenta ad Iura Orientis Antiqui Pertinentia 2; Leiden: Brill, 1939), 219–34.

[43] Finkelstein, "Ammisaduqa's Edict and the Babylonian 'Law Codes'," *Journal of Cuneiform Studies* 15 (1961): 91–104.

[44] F. R. Kraus, "Ein zentrales Problem des altmesopotamischen Rechtes: Was ist der Codex Hammurapi?," *Genava* 8 (1960): 283–96; Bottéro, "'Code'".

[45] Renger, "Noch einmal," esp. 27–30.

[46] V. Scheil, *Textes élamites-sémitiques: deuxième série* (Mémoires de la Délégation en Perse 4; Paris: Libraire Ernest LeRoux, 1902).

clearly echoed the '*Code Napoleon*' for the scholar of his day. Initially most scholars treated the collection as a law code, a document with statutory force which collected together the laws of ancient Babylonia. Even after 70 years of scholarship questioning the legal status of the document and assertions that the label 'Code' is anachronistic and inapplicable in the case of LH, there are still many who refer to it with this appellation. In the context of the early twentieth century it was understandable. Apart from the 'Code Napoleon' issued in France in 1804, there were also codes issued in Austria in 1811,[47] Netherlands, Italy, Spain and Portugal also in the 19th century and then Germany in 1900.[48] With the background of these European civil codes emerging at the same time as nationalism and imperialism it is no wonder LH was treated as it was initially. The unification of the various nation states, the rise of imperialism in the 19th century and the connection of this context with the setting forth of law codes suggested a framework for understanding Hammurabi's proclamation of laws. The idea was soon hatched that the 'Code Hammurabi' was set forth as an attempt to unify the law of Babylonia after his expansionary military achievements and administrative reforms.[49] This is an idea that still has many adherents[50] though their number is dwindling.

It is interesting that the three main early critics of LH's legal status were all German speaking.[51] Perhaps it was a European conception of 'Code' that led them to decide LH was not substantive law.[52] Coming from a continental European background with a civil law tradition may have limited some scholar's conceptions of the roles of LH. A civil law[53] tradition, stated simply, involves applying stated principles and interpreting authoritative works on law. This was clearly seen as contrary to Hammurabi's tradition given the casuistic[54] framing of his laws and the lack of citation of

---

[47] *Allgemeines Burgerliches Gestezbuch*

[48] *Burgerliches Gesetzbuch für das deutsches Reich.* The criminal law code had been completed almost simultaneously with unification in 1871.

[49] *e.g.* C. Edwards, *The Oldest Laws in the World* (London: Watts, 1906), 12.

[50] See Renger's discussion of this issue, "Noch einmal," 32–34.

[51] Eilers, Landsberger, and Kraus.

[52] It is also interesting to note Bottéro, "'Code'" who furthered Kraus' position also comes from continental Europe.

[53] As opposed to common law.

[54] *i.e.* conditional (if) clauses in the protasis followed by a conclusion/judgment/verdict in the apodosis *e.g.* If a man does x, then y.

them in the documents from practice.[55] It is interesting that John Miles, an English legal historian, is able to still treat LH as a real piece of legislation in analogy with the Anglo-Saxon common law system.[56] Common law traditions, as opposed to civil law, are based upon the study of precedents, or exemplary cases rather than codified statutes. Common law traditions are seen in most countries colonized by England and in all English speaking countries such as the USA. Though it is not always the case, this writer believes the various national backgrounds and historical contexts of scholars working on ancient Near Eastern law may have affected their works.

A case in point may be Sophie Lafont's theory of subsidiarity in Mesopotamian law.[57] Her theory is that regional customary law may have existed and that the local standards were left to function when thought sufficient. It was only in cases where the local standard was deemed insufficient that it was thought necessary for the highest level of power to intervene. She sees this reflected in the enforcement of Mesopotamian law collections. It is interesting that the issue of subsidiarity has been raised in connection with law as the European Union attempts to develop a theory of law that will accompany national differences within a unified entity.[58]

Earlier we mentioned some of the internal reasons for the questioning of the legal status of LH. These were perceived discrepancies between the laws and the documents from practice, and the lack of citation of the laws in the same documents. Other internal factors which have fuelled this skeptical stance have been: the absence of any specific address to judges in the laws themselves[59] and their non-comprehensive nature.[60] The discovery of a

---

[55] And the lack of legislative influence reflected in the documents.

[56] Godfrey Rolles Driver and John C. Miles, *The Babylonian Laws* (vol. 1; Oxford: Clarendon, 1952), 48.

He makes a similar comparison with MAL. See Godfrey Rolles Driver and John C. Miles, *The Assyrian Laws* (Oxford: Clarendon, 1935), 14.

[57] Sophie Lafont, "Codification et Subsidiarité dans les Droits du Proche-Orient Ancien," in *La Codification Des Lois Dans L'Antiquité: Actes du Colloque de Strasbourg 27–29 novembre 1997* (ed. Edmond Lévy; Université Marc Bloch de Strasbourg: travaux du centre de recherche sur le Proche-Orient et la Grèce antiques 16; Paris: De Boccard, 2000), 49–64.

[58] The links to Hammurabi's imperial context are again not hard to see. I owe the observed correlation between Lafont's theory and the modern context of the EU to Roth, "Hammurabi's Wronged Man," *Journal of the American Oriental Society* 122 (2002): 39, n. 7.

[59] Landsberger, "Babylonischen Termini," 221.

[60] See Renger, "Noch einmal," 35, n. 40.

number of other law collections from the ancient Near East with a similar form and the existence of copies of LH for over a millennium suggested an alternative context for LH. This was the *e₂.dub.ba*, or scribal school. It is an interesting phenomenon in scholarship that when scholars write about ancient scholars they often portray them as they would like to see themselves.[61] This writer cannot help but think that perhaps it was partly due to this desire that the great law collection of Hammurabi was placed squarely within this context. Gone were the days when 'great men' occupied our history books, the law collection of Hammurabi was the collective effort of a group of scholars and belonged to Mesopotamian legal science. Incidentally, it was also seen to be composed, at least in part, with respect to the proper international literature (the earlier law collections of Mesopotamia).[62]

The next development in the scholarly portrayal of LH came with Finkelstein's 1961 article on Ammiṣaduqa's edict.[63] Again one can postulate internal developments within the field of ancient Near Eastern law and an external context which may have led to the thesis presented. With the discovery of the Old Babylonian *mišarum* decrees, there was another reason to question the legal nature and purpose of the law collections. The *mišarum* decrees were not only framed differently, they were both cited and followed in the documents from practice.[64] If this was the case for the *mišarum* decrees,[65] why not for the law collections? The answer for Finkelstein lay in the purpose of the law collections. They were not meant to be legislation. To look for promulgated law in ancient Mesopotamia was an anachronism.[66] For the most part the *mišarum* decrees were temporally specific and retrospective. What then was the purpose of the law collections? The existence of the prologue/epilogue form suggested another alternative. Most of

---

[61] This can perhaps be seen best in many works about Old Testament wisdom literature. Often ideals of modern scholars are imported/highlighted in the ancient wisdom literature: the international, co-operative nature of scholarship, the non-partisan nature of the scholars, their healthy scepticism and humanist inquiry. Those aspiring to a so-called 'ethical monotheism' set on a pedestal in the 19th century have been particularly guilty of this.

[62] Kraus, "Ein zentrales Problem," 293–95.

[63] Finkelstein, "Ammisaduqa's Edict".

[64] At least to some extent. Both Kraus and Finkelstein did question the applicability and legal force of the *mišarum* document also. See Kraus, *Ein Edikt des Königs Ammi-ṣaduqa von Babylon* (Studia et Documenta ad Iura Orientis Pertinentia 5; Leiden: Brill, 1958).

[65] At least part of them. Finkelstein, "Ammisaduqa's Edict," 100–1.

[66] *Ibid.*, 103.

these sections were spent glorifying the achievements of the king. Obviously this was the purpose of the law collections. They were royal propaganda. The collection of laws themselves served to justify the king's claims to be a just king and thereby a rightful ruler. All of this was of course argued on the basis of the sources and the general background of Mesopotamian kingship and law. This writer finds it unlikely to be a coincidence that the suspicion that all was smoke and mirrors and that rather than serving any useful function, the law collections were merely propaganda first found its expression in the 1960s. The background of the beginnings of the social movements, a rise in Marxism's popularity (and in particular Gramsci's notion of hegemony), the arrival of the post-colonial era and a growing distrust of government in the post-McCarthy era all set themselves up as likely suspects for this change in approach, though it would be a braver man than I to single out any one in particular in Finkelstein's case.[67] It is similarly interesting to see the influence of Kuhn and Foucault in Roth's dealings with the same questions in more recent times.[68]

Another set of influences shaping the discussion of the ancient Near Eastern law collections has been the various emphases of the different disciplines weighing into the debate. Those who have written about ancient Near Eastern law collections generally come from three different fields: legal history, Biblical studies and Assyriology. Within the first there are those who bring with them ideas from modern law and those who have cut their teeth on Roman law. The interest of this subject to all is quite obvious though each brings with them a different perspective and set of methodological tools. These fields are by no means exclusive. One could hardly exclude scholars such as Yaron or Westbrook from any of the three. This said there are some general tendencies and influences typical to those from each field. The most general observation, already made by Renger, is that those from a legal background are more likely to treat the various law collections as some form of legislation, or at least a closer reflection of legal realities,[69] whereas those from Assyriology tend to be more skeptical.[70] The reason for this is open to debate.[71] The influence of Roman legal history can be seen

[67] One would assume this was not a cynically conscious decision made by Finkelstein or those who followed him, but the subtle unconscious influence of a change in cultural mood towards such things.

[68] Especially "Reading Law".

[69] See those listed by Renger, "Noch einmal," 28.

[70] Eilers, Landsberger, Kraus, Bottéro, Finkelstein, and Roth to name but a few.

[71] Though we suspect a nagging sceptical empiricism (in terms of the need for

throughout the various debates. The notion of code versus precedent and civil versus common law can be seen as part of the debate over the distinction of *ius* and *lex* (later *Recht und Gesetz*). The terminology used in this sort of debate is borrowed from Roman legal history. Inevitably we try to understand the unfamiliar with reference to the familiar. Many of those who have worked on the ancient Near Eastern law collections have done so out of a prior interest in ancient (read classical) law. As an example Koschaker's higher critical approach to LH, rather than coming from a Biblical studies background, may well have come from his work in Roman law. The Roman law collections such as the *Twelve Tables* and Justinian's *Corpus Iuris Civilis* are from various earlier sources which have been put together.[72] The assumption that LH and the other Near Eastern law collections would be the same has influenced much of the work in the field. For many this assumption has come from a Biblical studies background also.[73] Perhaps someone from a Romanist background will attempt to put to rest the debate over LH's scholarly or legal function by reminding us of the *Digest of Justinian* which was given the honor of having both at the same time. The influence of comparative legal historians has also been felt in the tendency for some to postulate universals within the area of law whether they be linear developments,[74] or deep structures.[75]

---

external verification in the documents for the purpose of the collections) and the influence of Gramsci (and later Liverani-in terms of the default position being one of royal propaganda).

[72] The difference between the two fields of course being that at least some Roman law collections name their sources, *e.g. Digest of Justinian.*

[73] *e.g.* Eckart Otto *e.g.* "Aspects of Legal Reforms and Reformulations in Ancient Cuneiform and Israelite Law," in *Theory and Method in Biblical and Cuneiform Law: Revision, Interpolation and Development* (ed. Bernard M. Levinson; Journal for the Study of the Old Testament Supplement 181; Sheffield: Sheffield Academic, 1994), 160–96 or "Kodifizierung und Kanonisierung von Rechtssatzen in Keilschriftlichen und Biblischen Rechtssammlungen," in *La Codification Des Lois Dans L'Antiquité: Actes du Colloque de Strasbourg 27–29 novembre 1997* (ed. Edmond Lévy; Université Marc Bloch de Strasbourg: travaux du centre de recherche sur le Proche-Orient et la Grèce antiques 16; Paris: De Boccard, 2000), 77–124; Reuven Yaron, *The Laws of Eshnunna.* It must be said that these two are more form critics.

[74] Bottéro, "'Code'". Westbrook *e.g.* "Character," 23 where he "cheerfully admits to being a developmentalist".

[75] Bernard S. Jackson's unique approach. See it spelled out in "History, Dogmatics and Halakhah," in *Jewish Law in Legal History and the Modern World* (ed. Bernard S. Jackson; The Jewish Law Annual Supplement 2; Leiden: Brill, 1980), 1–26.

The weight of Biblical studies has been felt most in the influx of the tools of criticism imported from that field be it form, literary-historical, redaction,[76] or genre criticism or the study of literary structure. Controverisal tools which are regularly criticized within their own field[77] they have somehow managed to exert an influence in our own. For the scholar of Old Testament law, the law collections of the ancient Near East are fodder for explanatory parallels be they of form, genre, social development, *mentalité etc.* The bulk of this work is done in an attempt to situate the Old Testament laws within their broader Near Eastern setting and to import the Near Eastern models in order to interpret the Old Testament-but more will be said on the comparative method in a moment. Whatever the downside of these influences each field brings with it its own insights, questions and approaches which enable the work of critical scholarship to go on debating both new issues and old ones from new perspectives. It is hoped that the application of this author's context, background and motivations will also add to the field. It is also hoped that said writer will be aware of these things and not allow them to unduly influence the arguments and conclusions presented. One of the most encouraging movements within the field is an interest in finding out what the law collections were to the people involved with them themselves *i.e.* their authors, audience (intended and otherwise) and anyone else affected by them.[78] Ideally this work will also help us to understand the ancient Near Eastern law collections in their own settings, both historical and cultural.

Before proceeding to discussion of the comparative method, we would like to discuss another phenomenon in this field: that of the undue prominence of LH. Most of the ink spilt over the issues of the nature, purpose, origin *etc.* of the ancient Near Eastern law collections has focused on this text in particular and assumed that the findings were generally applicable for the other collections[79] (or at least for the other tripartite structured collections such as LL and LU). Though it is possible in theory that we may well find this to be the case, this is hardly something that is safe to assume. There is a general tendency within Assyriology for the first text of its kind

---

[76] *e.g.* Eckart Otto uses all three.

[77] The study of literary structure perhaps being the exception.

[78] Expressed for example in Kraus' groundbreaking article "Ein zentrales Problem," 284.

[79] *e.g.* see Westbrook's statement "Cuneiform Law," 201–2 that "the debate . . . has centered mainly around Codex Hammurabi, but its conclusions are assumed to apply to the codes in general."

or subject matter to forever retain the most important position in scholarship. We have seen this with *Enuma Eliš*. Being the first discovered creation story from Mesopotamia, it came to prominence at the same time as pan-Babylonism and has held its place ever since. LH has shared a similar fate. Immediately hailed as the oldest code of laws in the world,[80] one suspects it has been the subject of more monographs and articles than the rest of the ancient Near Eastern law collections combined. This is due partly to the primacy of its discovery, partly to the publicity afforded it during the Babel-Bibel controversies, and partly to its more complete state of preservation, its greater length and the more impressive monument upon which it was found. None of these things necessarily should lead one to conclude it was more important in its own context than the other law collections. Perhaps it is just the nature of research that we spend more time studying that for which we have better sources.[81] It should be emphasized, however, that the fact that we have more sources with which to study LH and its context does not necessarily mean that we should import those conclusions into the study of other Near Eastern law collections. The same can be said for *Enuma Eliš* in regards to Babylonian religion. There are many who would see this work not as 'The Babylonian Creation Story' as it has been hailed, but as a particularly unique (perhaps aberrant) creation story from Babylon with a very particular context.[82] Vigilance is needed to avoid being caught in such traps. Though there may be obvious similarities between LH and other collections, we must recognize the possibility that LH was atypical or at least special or unique amongst the ancient Near Eastern law collections.[83] To be fair to those who have worked in this field, this writer does not mean to imply that scholars have been completely blind to the differences between collections before. The year after the discovery of MAL in 1920, Koschaker recognized a great difference between it and LH and designated it as a private *Gesetzbuch* of a judge rather than a code of laws.[84] This said,

[80] *e.g.* C. Edwards, *Oldest Laws*. A position LH still holds for some, though erroneously.

[81] As well as LH being the best attested ancient Near Eastern law collection in terms of preservation and number of copies, the Old Babylonian period is particularly rich in other legal material with which to compare it

[82] *e.g.* W. G. Lambert, "The Reign of Nebuchadnezzar I: A Turning Point in the History of Ancient Mesopotamian Religion," in *The Seed of Wisdom: Essays in Honor of T. J. Meek* (ed. W. S. McCullough; Toronto: University of Toronto, 1964), 3–13. Followed by Baines and Yoffee, "Order, Legitimacy, and Wealth," 250.

[83] Done already by Kraus all those years ago in "Ein zentrales Problem," 293.

[84] Paulo Koschaker, *Quellenkritische Untersuchungen zu den "altassyrischen Gesetzen"*

the imbalance of sources, skewed as they are towards the Old Babylonian period, makes it hard to test the theories about LH anywhere else,[85] or to come up with alternative theories. With this in mind it is extremely important we watch for the influence of theories imported from studies of LH when dealing with other sources.

1.3 The Comparative Method

Though we have briefly discussed the aim and method of our study earlier, this writer thinks it important to situate it more clearly amongst the various approaches to the comparative method. There are three main approaches to the comparison of cultures. Simply these are: 1) looking for similarities, 2) looking for differences, and 3) approaches which tend to study the particular, some of which see comparison as violating a society's "*Eigenbegrifflichkeit*".[86] Within the first approach there are various explanations of similarities from parallel development/evolution to historical contact/diffusion/migration, natural laws/universals/human nature *etc.*, common cultural/societal/sociological/environmental setting or racial type and so on.[87] Within the second, differences tend to be explained through differences in the stages of evolution/development or a difference of cultural/societal/sociological/environmental setting or racial type *etc.* There are other explanations including those of chance and coincidence, often used to explain away similarities or differences which contradict one's assumptions. Obviously most scholars would not ascribe to only one approach and explanation though there have been tendencies to favor certain approaches and explanations in different fields and in different periods.[88]

(Mitteilungen der Vorderasiatischen Gesellschaft 26/3; Leipzig: J. C. Hinrich, 1921), 79–84.

[85] For extreme examples take the lack of discovery of a law collection pre-first millennium in Egypt, or the almost total absence of legal practice documents from the Hittite empire.

[86] "conceptual autonomy" *e.g.* Benno Landsberger in his famous article. For an English translation see Benno Landsberger, "The Conceptual Autonomy of the Babylonian World," in *Monographs of the Ancient Near East* (vol. 1, fasc. 4; Malibu: Undena, 1976), 5–15; trans. Thorkild Jacobson, Benjamin Foster, and H. von Siebenthal from "Die Eigenbegrifflichkeit der Babylonischen Welt," *Islamica* 2 (1926): 355–72.

[87] Malul, *The Comparative Method*, ch. 1 classified these explanations broadly into "historical" and "typological" ones.

[88] For a discussion of some of these see William Y. Adams, Dennis P. Van Gerven, and Richard S. Levy, "The Retreat from Migrationism," *Annual Review of*

Often comparative studies have become an excuse for parallel hunting and have resulted in what some have termed "parallelomania".[89] Those who criticize comparative studies of this type have some fuel for their fire. It is quite likely that an understanding of a culture coming only from study of the aspects of it which have parallels elsewhere will be deficient. There have been a number of attempts at a comparative method which takes into account both similarities and differences and attempts to place these within their cultural context.[90] This is one of the goals of this study.

The comparative method in ancient Near Eastern studies has been overshadowed by the study of the Hebrew Bible. Most scholars interested in comparative studies within the ancient Near East want to compare other societies with that reflected in the Hebrew Bible. This has often determined what has been considered worth studying and has heavily influenced which "parallels" would be the focus of scholars' attention.[91] Attitudes towards the Old Testament have often shaped their comparative studies to a significant degree. Some have reacted against this by disavowing comparative studies and calling for the autonomy of Assyriology, Egyptology *etc.* as disciplines separate from the study of the Hebrew Bible.[92] More recently there has been a resurgence of calls in the opposite direction, stressing the importance of studying Israel in its Near Eastern context.[93] It is useful to look at the context in which these debates have raged and situate this work amongst them before proceeding to embark on a comparative study of the ancient Near East.

Perhaps most important for the comparative study of ancient Near Eastern law is the context within which LH was discovered. Though approaches change over time, the initial semblance of ideas at the time of a discovery often have a lingering effect on its later study.[94] Some of these

---

Anthropology 7 (1978): 483–532.

[89] See Samuel Sandmel's discussion of the term in "Parallelomania," *Journal of Biblical Literature* 81 (1962): 1.

[90] *e.g.* Weeks, *Admonition and Curse.*

[91] *e.g.* the goring ox. See note 4 above.

[92] *e.g.* Landsberger, "Conceptual Autonomy".

[93] *e.g.* William W. Hallo, "Ancient Near Eastern Texts and their Relevance for Biblical Exegesis," in *Canonical Compositions from the Biblical World* (ed. William W. Hallo; vol. 1 of *The Context of Scripture*; Leiden: Brill, 1997), xxiii–xxviii.

[94] An example from Egyptology could be the initial rediscovery of Egypt within the context of late 18th, early 19th century anti-clericalism and the lingering influence of the "wicked priest" theories still so prevalent in reconstructions of the political and religious history of ancient Egypt. Another example from Assyriology would

ideas were mentioned briefly in the last section. Those most relevant to this section are pan-Babylonism and the Babel-Bibel debate.

Though discovered slightly too late to be utilized in Delitzsch's first lecture,[95] LH is used in his second.[96] He attempts, through comparison of LH and the laws in the Pentateuch to show which were Israelite, proto-Semitic or borrowed from Babylonia. As is to be expected within Delitzsch's work, he concluded that much was borrowed from Babylonia and that Babylonian law was superior to that of ancient Israel.[97] He stressed the superiority of Babylonian civilization and its non-Semitic (Sumerian) origins.[98] He denied the uniqueness of ancient Israel and searched for dependency. He did all this from the vantage point of anti-Semitism, going as far as claiming that Jesus was not a Jew, but Aryan.[99] After World War I he joined many others in blaming the "Jews" for Germany's poor condition.[100] Unsurprisingly, his approach to LH brought a reaction from those with a more conservative view of the Old Testament. They tended to emphasize differences between Old Testament law and LH, and when they compromised to admit borrowing, they pointed out that what was taken over was still changed and improved. They held, contrary to Delitzsch, that a comparative analysis in proper perspective would "underscore the uniqueness and superiority of the biblical message".[101] They also used LH to argue for the historicity of the Pentateuch, showing that it falsified earlier claims that the period of Moses was too early in history for law to be formulated,[102] and

---

be the rediscovery of ancient Mesopotamia and other Semitic peoples amidst the context of linguistic theories of history in the mid-nineteenth century which portrayed the Semites as originally nomadic peoples (analogous to Arab Bedouin) pouring out of the Arabian desert.

[95] Though he does mention Hammurabi and the highly developed state of ancient Babylonian law in Friedrich Delitzsch, *Babel and Bible: Two Lectures* (ed. with intr. C. W. H. Johns; London: Williams & Norgate, 1903), 35.

[96] *Ibid.*, 184–92, 199–202.

[97] Especially in regards to the position of women. *Ibid.*, 202.

[98] *Ibid.*, passim. See Mogens Trolle Larsen's comments in "The 'Babel/Bible' Controversy and its Aftermath," in *Civilizations of the Ancient Near East* (ed. Jack M. Sasson; vol. 1; New York: Hendrickson, 1995), *e.g.* p. 99.

[99] In *Die grosse Täuschung* as related by Larsen, "Babel/Bible," 105.

[100] See Larsen, "Babel/Bible," 105.

[101] William Rainey Harper, as quoted in Larsen, "Babel/Bible," 103.

[102] See the discussion of König's position in Klaus Johanning, *Der Bibel-Babel-Streit: Eine forschungsgeschichtliche Studie* (European University Studies Series 13: Theology vol. 343; Frankfurt: Peter Lang, 1988), 294. See Johanning's Excursus II

claiming Hammurabi as the Amraphel of Genesis 14.[103] Seeing the same evidence in different hands used for such differing purposes, many within Assyriology reacted by no longer wanting to be a "handmaiden to Old Testament studies".[104] The seminal article to this end was published in 1926.[105]

Landsberger's call to respect the "cultural autonomy" of the Babylonian world has had an enormous influence on Assyriology ever since. There are many, wanting to follow Landsberger's principle, who have steered Assyriology as far from Old Testament studies as possible. Given the continued popular interest in the Old Testament, this has had some unwanted side effects on the funding of the subject and its status in society. Landsberger himself did not shy away from all forms of comparison. In this same article he talks of his empathetic, heuristic method with which he unravels the conceptual world of the Babylonians from within itself.[106] He proceeds to use it to contrast Sumerian and Akkadian thinking.[107] For him, language, or even "*Sprachgeist*", was the key to understanding the conceptual world of a civilization.[108] Interestingly, one of Landsberger's indirect effects on the field was to kill off most comparison and to encourage an increasing specialization within the study of the ancient Near East. Despite this, there were some (perhaps those closer to him) who followed up his heuristic or intuitive method and continued comparative studies. Those involved in Frankfort's *Intellectual Adventure of Ancient Man* were some of the most influential.

Interestingly, the later edition of this study, entitled *Before Philosophy*,[109] did not include a chapter on the speculative thought of the Hebrews. This was included in the original version, possibly due to popular interest rather than the convictions of the authors. There was no way to keep everyone from comparative studies, and no way to abate the popular interest (so important to publishers) in the Old Testament. So while some buried them-

---

in this work for a more thorough description of LH's place within the Babel-Bibel debate.

[103] See *Ibid.*, 291.

[104] Thorkild Jacobson's comment in the introduction to the translation of Landsberger's "Eigenbegrifflichkeit," 4. See note 86 for bibl. details.

[105] Landsberger, "Eigenbegrifflichkeit". Again see note 86.

[106] *Ibid.*, 6.

[107] *Ibid.*, 12–13.

[108] *Ibid.*, 12–15.

[109] Henri Frankfort, H. A. Frankfort, John A. Wilson, and Thorkild Jacobsen, *Before Philosophy* (Harmondsworth: Penguin, 1949).

selves deeper into specialization, these others (Frankfort *et al.*) picked up Landsberger's intuitive method and applied it to a comparative study of the world views of ancient Mesopotamia, Egypt and Israel. The work, however, did reflect the increased specialization of the field in that it was a multi-authored co-operative venture rather than the work of one man. It also displayed Landsberger's conviction that one could use intuition to contrast the cultures of different peoples. On the whole, this work was a reaction to the "Myth and Ritual" school, in particular its form of universalism.

The Myth and Ritual school developed from its evolutionary origins with Frazer and his *The Golden Bough*[110] in the late nineteenth century to a more diffusionist model with Hooke[111] in the early twentieth.[112] Its method was built on assuming similarity and then going about finding it. Frankfort's project was to counter this by contrasting the differences between Mesopotamia and Egypt in particular. One suspects his allegiance to Judaism was a motivating factor in part. Unfortunately, due to his method, based more on intuitive personal insights than sources, this work has not helped the cause of comparative studies and has been seen as an example of its abuse.[113] His geographic determinism also caused him to deny historical change over time within the one society. The geography did not change, so the world view of the society should not either. The application of this assumption led to some of the criticisms that were leveled.[114]

One quickly realizes that the development and application of the comparative method in ancient Near Eastern studies is based very much on scholars' assumptions, particularly their assumptions about the Old Testament, and their assumptions about human nature and civilization. The debate then rages over the extent of the similarity of human nature versus the differences between cultures and those found in developments over time (whether part of a common evolutionary scheme or some idiomatic internal development). On a larger scale this debate is part of the philosophical question of the one and the many. On a smaller scale it is about explaining similarities and differences between the law collections of pre-first millennium B.C. ancient Near Eastern societies. This work will focus on the

[110] Frazer, *Golden Bough*.

[111] Hooke, see footnote 5 above.

[112] This was a general trend in many fields, anthropology in particular.

[113] See the criticisms of Samuel Noah Kramer in his review of *Intellectual Adventure* in *Journal of Cuneiform Studies* 2 (1948): 39–70 and those of M. I. Finley in his review of *Kingship and the Gods* in *Political Science Quarterly* 63 (1948): 275–81.

[114] Finley's review above.

smaller scale comparison at hand. There are some unresolved tensions in the comparative method that should at least be discussed further, if not solved, before proceeding. In order to explore these we will look at the approaches of Talmon, Hallo, Tigay and Baines and Yoffee for the comparative method in general, Greenberg and Jackson for the area of ancient Near Eastern law, and Malul, who writes on both the comparative method in general and ancient Near Eastern law in particular.

As mentioned earlier, most people interested in the comparative method in ancient Near Eastern studies are primarily interested in comparing other societies to ancient Israel.[115] It will be interesting in this study to see whether the systems of comparison set up for this situation work just as well when applied to the Near Eastern civilizations themselves. One of the seminal articles on the comparative method was written by Talmon in 1977.[116] One of the main trends he argues against is that of comparative studies which "deal preponderantly with particular cases of parallels found or assumed to be present in other cultural complexes."[117] He saw the many possible abuses that comparison of this type could perpetrate, and how easy it would be to assert similarity through such an "atomistic approach . . . without reference to the general structure and profile of the overall scale of values and beliefs of the societies involved".[118] He proposed a comparative method which would take account of differences and similarities between societies[119] within the same "historic stream".[120] Distancing himself both from "the comparative approach on the grand scale",[121] and from the atomistic parallel hunting[122] of others, he encourages a "holistic method".[123] In doing so he sides with Landsberger's call to respect the "*Eigenbegrifflichkeit*"

---

[115] Or at least the Hebrew Bible.

[116] Shemaryahu Talmon, "The 'Comparative Method' in Biblical Interpretation-Principles and Problems," *Vetus Testamentum Supplement* 29 (1977): 320–56.

[117] *Ibid.*, 321.

[118] *Ibid.*, 324.

[119] *Ibid.*, 345, 355.

[120] See his explanation of this term in *Ibid.*, 326. He saw it as including "aspects of historical and geographical proximity as well as those of cultural affinity." In encouraging comparison within the historic stream he is similar to Malul, *Comparative Method*, who encourages historical rather than typological comparison, ch. 1.

[121] Talmon, "Comparative Method," 328 *i.e.* evolutionary or diffusionist models or those comparing cultures far removed from each other in an attempt to discover the "fundamental unity of the human spirit". See also pp. 322–24, 356.

[122] *Ibid.*, 343, 356.

[123] *Ibid.*, 328, 356.

of different cultures and the approach of those like Frankfort, Wilson and Jacobsen who attempt to explain individual cultures from the inside with Landsberger's empathetic method rather than those who look for similarity.[124] He emphasizes that there may be similarities between cultures within the same historic stream, but that with this method, by looking at the similarity within the whole cultural complex, one is able to emphasize the "individuality and dissimilarity conferred upon these identified components".[125]

As the title suggested, Talmon's method was set up to be applicable for "biblical interpretation". In siding with Frankfort's statement that "the borrowed features in Hebrew culture, and those which have foreign analogies, are least significant",[126] in asserting the uniqueness of biblical civilization over against the rest of the ancient Near East[127] and in discussing only the use of his method with reference to comparison with the Hebrew Bible, he opened himself to criticisms of double-dealings,[128] of applying his method only to Israel. This writer finds many points of agreement with Talmon's method, but asserts that, to be valid, it should be applied to every society, not just Israel.[129] In the same spirit we have here included the Hittite law collections for study. Too many comparative studies in the ancient Near East make sweeping statements based on comparison with only Egypt and/or Mesopotamia.[130] There are other points within Talmon's method which raise questions and some which have been challenged.

One issue of comparison which we have avoided by the choice of our subject matter is that of the priority of date versus geographical proximity when comparing parallel data.[131] Due to the limitation of our sources to

---

124 *Ibid.*, 328.

125 *Ibid.*, 328.

126 *Ibid.*, 342.

127 *Ibid.*, 355.

128 Such as that of Malul, *Comparative Method*, 51, 157 who thinks Talmon is interested only in understanding phenomena in the wider cultural context for Israel, not the other Near Eastern cultures. If this were the case Talmon's approach could lead to a situation where one respects only the cultural autonomy of Israel while still treating the rest of the ancient Near East as a monolithic block.

129 This is not to say that I agree that Talmon is guilty of double-dealing.

130 *e.g. Before Philosophy* and Baines and Yoffee, "Order, Legitimacy, and Wealth". See Jackson's criticisms of Greenberg for leaving out the Hittites whom he sees as more closely related to Israel, *Essays*, 41.

131 Talmon, "Comparative Method," 325 espouses the priority of date while Malul criticises Talmon as though his method implies what he sees as the "invalid assumption that the biblical corpus is a monolithic and unified work . . . so that one

pre-first millennium B.C. we hope to not have to deal with this question. Leaving out the law in the Hebrew Bible also enables us to dodge this issue for now, as for many, the dating of the legal parts of the Hebrew Bible determines the material with which they are compared.[132] In this way we have also managed to lessen the need to allow for change over time within the one culture.[133]

One of the main challenges to Talmon's holistic method has come from diffusionists or parallel hunters. Those who are interested in determining whether a society borrowed from another only in specific instances are, consciously or unconsciously, fighting against the idea that each aspect of a civilization needs to be understood as part of the whole before it is compared to other civilizations. For example, Malul's work on *The Comparative Method in Ancient Near Eastern and Biblical Legal Studies*, though well aware of Talmon's arguments, and criticizing those who focus only on similarities or differences, implies that the prime task of the comparative historian of ancient law is to ascertain whether or not there is an historical connection between biblical law and that of other Near Eastern societies.[134] The fact that his work, after chapters of theorizing in order to gain a "clear and objective scientific criteria"[135] with which to carry out comparison, uses the fall-back example of the goring ox as its test case, tells us much about his method.

---

may freely resort to any biblical evidence from any genre or period for the elucidation of problems existing in other genres and periods" in *Comparative Method*, 46. A hotbed of debate which we are happy to avoid for now.

[132] *i.e.* if seen as second millennium they could be compared with LH *etc.*, whereas if they are seen as first millennium or even Persian period, they are compared with first millennium collections *e.g.* Morton Smith, "East Mediterranean Law Codes of the Early Iron Age," *Eretz Israel* 14 (1978): 38–43. For extreme examples see Thomas M. Bolin, "History, Historiography, and the Use of the Past in the Hebrew Bible," in *The Limits of Historiography: Genre and Narrative in Ancient Historical Texts* (ed. C. S. Kraus; Mnemosyne: Bibliotheca Classica Batava Supplementum 191; Leiden: Brill, 1999), 113–40 and John Van Seters, *In Search of History: Historiography in the Ancient World and the Origins of Biblical History* (New Haven: Yale University, 1983) who compare biblical historiography with classical antiquarianism.

[133] As mentioned earlier this is a problem with Frankfort's work due to his geographical determinism. The dialectic approach to the law of the Hebrew Bible can be left to a later work also, see discussion in Bernard M. Levinson, ed., *Theory and Method in Biblical and Cuneiform Law: Revision, Interpolation and Development* (Journal for the Study of the Old Testament Supplement 181; Sheffield: Sheffield Academic, 1994).

[134] Malul, *Comparative Method*, 124.

[135] *Ibid.*, 155.

His use of the "safe" case of the goring ox, which most accept as being a borrowing into biblical law, to prove his method works, may help a naïve belief in an objective comparative method, but even with such "safe" cases, there are those who disagree.[136] To assert, as Malul seems to do, that it is only those with some sort of "apologetic" or "pseudorthodox tendencies"[137] who are not objective in this debate is a little ridiculous.[138]

One must admit that it is to some extent an assumption to say that it is to the culture as a whole that one should look for explanation of a phenomenon within a society. There are others who see culture differently. Leach mentions those who see culture "as an assemblage of traits which can be separately compared" in contrast to those who see societies "as systems which can be compared only as wholes".[139] Though this writer sees neither as necessarily true, he leans to the second option. Unfortunately, given the massive amount of detail that would need to be covered in the case of comparison of whole societies it is hardly likely that any one person will ever be able to undertake such a comparison of the cultures of the ancient Near East. Perhaps comparing one aspect of a society may be a working compromise between ideal and pragmatism, so here the written law collections of the ancient Near Eastern societies will be compared. Rather than enter the debate over the usefulness of cultural background in comparative studies in all its details, which could not be done in this work, this model will be offered and it will be left to others to judge its usefulness. It is a minority who would consciously oppose such an undertaking. This writer believes that most merely shy away from such an undertaking themselves due to the risks involved.[140]

To say one will be comparing the law collections of the ancient Near East in their cultural contexts does raise a number of questions. The first has to do with the difficulty of defining these contexts. For example, does one look at LH in the context of Mesopotamia, Babylon, the Old Babylo-

---

136 See the discussion of Jeffrey H. Tigay, "On Evaluating Claims of Borrowing," in *The Tablet and the Scroll: Near Eastern Studies in Honor of William W. Hallo* (ed. Mark E. Cohen, Daniel C. Snell, and David B. Weisberg; Bethesda, Md.: CDL, 1993), 250–55 who mentions scholars who do not see borrowings of Near Eastern material into biblical even in such "safe" cases as Genesis' borrowing of material from *Enuma Elish*, or Ecclesiastes' borrowing of material from *Gilgamesh*.

137 Malul, *Comparative Method*, 160.

138 The fact that Malul focuses his criticisms on those who defend the Old Testament is perhaps testimony to this fact.

139 As quoted in Talmon, "Comparative Method," 336.

140 See discussion in the introduction.

nian period or just Hammurabi's reign? Where does Assyria fit within Mesopotamia? Does one treat the Laws of Lipit-Ishtar (LL) as "Sumerian" law because that is the language it is written in, or does one class it with Babylonian law due to its origins in the dynasty of Isin?[141] What of the relation of the Laws of Eshnunna (LE) to LH?[142] Do we, like many comparative theorists, postulate that the "literary culture" is the most important?[143] Does this mean we lump all the collections together under the rubric of "cuneiform law",[144] or do we still need to understand how a common literary culture was individualized in each society?[145] Should we perhaps look at the general ancient Near Eastern cultural context as determinative and amend differences to become similarities?[146] This writer thinks it is perhaps

---

[141] The issue of the relationship of Sumerian culture to that of Mesopotamia more generally or Babylon and Akkad more particularly has been discussed in the various articles collected in E. Sollberger, ed., "Aspects du Contact Suméro-Akkadien," *Genava* 8 (1960): 241–314. See especially Kraus' famous article "Ein zentrales Problem," and the comments made in conclusion pp. 294–96. Similar problems are mentioned by Tigay, "On Evaluating," 253.

[142] For differing opinions see Jackson, *Essays*, 40 and Yaron, *Laws of Eshnunna.*

[143] *e.g.* Tigay, "On Evaluating", and William W. Hallo, "Biblical History in its Near Eastern Setting: The Contextual Approach," in *Scripture in Context: Essays on the Comparative Method* (ed. C. D. Evans, William W. Hallo, and J. B. White; Pittsburgh Theological Monograph Series 34; Pittsburgh: Pickwick, 1980), 1–26. See esp. p. 2.

[144] As with many before us *e.g.* Paulo Koschaker, "Keilschriftrecht," *Zeitschrift für Deutschen Morgenlandischen Gesellschaft* 89 (1935): 1–39 and "Cuneiform Law," in *Encyclopaedia of the Social Sciences* (ed. E. R. A. Seligman; vol. 9; New York: Macmillan, 1959), 211–9, 263–4; Victor Korošec, "Keilschriftrecht," in *Orientalisches Recht* (ed. B. Spuler; Handbuch der Orientalistik 3; Leiden: Brill, 1964), 49–219; E. A. Speiser, "Cuneiform Law and the History of Civilization," *Proceedings of the American Philosophical Society* 107 (1963): 536–41. Westbrook is even more general, speaking of ancient Near Eastern law as a unit. See notes 12–13 above.

[145] To which most at least pay lip service *e.g.* Malul, *Comparative Method*, 150–51; Tigay, "On Evaluating," 252, 255; Hallo, "Contextual Approach," 8; Talmon, "Comparative Method," esp. 342; John H. Walton, *Ancient Israelite Literature in its Cultural Context: A Survey of Parallels Between Biblical and Ancient Near Eastern Texts* (Grand Rapids, Mich.: Zondervan, 1989), 74–75, 90–91. It should be noted here that some emphasise this in order to emphasise the uniqueness of Israel while others do so in order to continue parallel hunting (and thus emphasise similarity or dependence) despite the differences.

[146] Following Westbrook! See especially his work regarding the difference between laws recording punishments such as death or talio versus those recording

best to leave final conclusions on these matters to a discussion *a posteriori* rather than decide the issue beforehand in an attempt to define an objective *a priori* method. Let it be said that such issues will be kept in mind as comparisons are made and that an eye will be kept on each possible cultural background.

The issue of putting these sources within their cultural context raises an old debate that was heightened within the field of ancient Near Eastern law by the publication of Greenberg's article "Some Postulates of Biblical Criminal Law".[147] In essence, Greenberg's argument was that the apparent differences between criminal law in the Hebrew Bible and that in Mesopotamia were caused by the different ideological principles underlying the different societies. The potential apologetic use of this argument drew criticism from a number of angles.[148] One of the arguments that has arisen is that one cannot draw out underlying societal principles from the law collections due to their casuistic framing.[149] The argument is basically that unless the principles are spelled out by the society themselves, we have no business trying to figure them out.[150] While this writer agrees that it is a difficult task to draw out principles or ideals which are not clearly spelled out,[151] he

---

compensation. Rather than explain the differences culturally or developmentally, he argues that both existed side by side in all cultures, thus erasing any apparent dissimilarity. See for example *Studies in Biblical and Cuneiform Law* (Cahiers de la Revue Biblique 26; Paris: J. Gabalda, 1988), ch. 2. For a critique see Malul's review *Orientalia* 59 (1990): 85–91.

[147] Greenberg, "Postulates". See note 19. For an interesting approach to the more general question of Israelite distinctiveness see Machinist, "The Question of Distinctiveness in Ancient Israel: An Essay," in *Ah, Assyria . . . Studies in Assyrian History and Ancient Near Eastern Historiography Presented to Hayim Tadmor* (ed. M. Cogan and I. Eph`al; Scripta Hierosolymitana 33; Jerusalem: Magnes, 1991), 196–212.

[148] Some were similar to the protests of Finkelstein, "Bible and Babel: A Comparative Study of the Hebrew and Babylonian Religious Spirit," *Commentary* 26 (1958): 436–38 that this sort of comparison violated a true understanding of ancient Mesopotamian culture. See that of Jackson, *Essays*, 30–41. Malul, *Comparative Method*, recognises the usefulness of Greenberg's approach to an extent, see p. 40, n. 6 and p. 46, n. 21, but sees its allegiance to the contrastive method and its apologetic usage as an abuse, *e.g.* pp. 50–51. See also S. Loewenstamm's critique of Greenberg, "The Law of Adultery and the Law of Murder in Biblical Law and Mesopotamian Law," *Beth Mikra* 13 (1962): 55–59.

[149] Primarily argued by Jackson, *Essays*, 32–36, 63, 74, 165.

[150] Jackson, *Essays*, 63 and in more detail in "History, Dogmatics," 11–12.

[151] For example, how does one enter the mind of a civilisation that sentences to death people who sleep with cows, sheep, pigs or dogs, but no punishment for

does not agree with the proposition that it is a fruitless exercise. The fact that the main proponent of the ideal that we should not attempt this is inconsistent in his application[152] and bases his theory on an idiomatic version of Chomskian structuralism[153] enables us to rest easily in our lack of subscription to his theory. One suspects the argument is aimed primarily against those like Greenberg whose arguments have an apologetic use.[154] It is not safe to assume that an apologetic use necessarily equals falsity of method or conclusion. Most who discuss the casuistic nature of the law collections quite freely admit that they are able to be used to extract some form of underlying ideal.[155] The fact that the present study does not include Israel should help alleviate some of the criticisms of its method also. By testing certain methods of comparison used in reference to biblical material solely on other ancient Near Eastern material it is also hoped that this study will help to implement Kitchen's dictum that "methods or principles which are demonstrably false when applied to first-hand ancient Near Eastern data should not be imposed on Old Testament data".[156]

The following discussion will focus on the trend towards comparison solely on the basis of literary context. When LH was first discovered and comparative studies were undertaken, the interest was to compare the actual law of Babylonian society with that of others. Through the many changes

---

those who sleep with horses or mules- HL 187–88, 199–200? For some attempts see Harry Angier Hoffner, *The Laws of the Hittites: A Critical Edition*, (Documenta et Monumenta Orientis Antiqui 23; Leiden: Brill, 1997), 224, 227 or Richard Haase, "The Hittite Kingdom," in *A History of Ancient Near Eastern Law* (ed. Raymond Westbrook; vol. 1; Handbook of Oriental Studies 72/1; Leiden: Brill, 2003), 649 who thinks the key to the difference is that the former are used in rituals while the latter are not.

152 Using underlying societal principles to amend texts even, *Essays*, 98–101.

153 Jackson, "History, Dogmatics," esp. p. 14 where he cites Chomsky's idea of universals. See also his more complete application of this method in *Studies in the Semiotics of Biblical Law* (Journal for the Study of the Old Testament Supplement 314; Sheffield: Sheffield, 2000).

154 See Jackson's criticism of Greenberg, *Essays*, 30–41.

155 See Roth's statement in, *Law Collections*, 7 that the various collections of law "are all products of the cultural assumptions and values of their drafters and copyists". See also her, "Reading Law," where she argues for the law cases as paradigm exemplars used to teach such "standards". Compare Jackson's explicit denial of this in *Essays*, 165.

156 Kenneth Kitchen, *Ancient Orient and Old Testament* (London: Tyndale, 1966), 28.

that have taken place in the field since, most comparisons are now done in an attempt to underscore the literary culture and intertextuality behind the drafting of the written law collections or to define the "genre" so as to have a key to understanding the purpose of the text. This literary emphasis has become so ingrained that few complain when an article on comparative method espousing a "contextual approach" is speaking only of the literary context while excluding any sociological context.[157] This writer is not arguing here that one should not place a written text within its literary context; rather, that this is not enough. The text should be understood first from within itself and secondly within the broader cultural context along with any literary comparison that is attempted. The ideas that the "individual is ineffable"[158] or that "genre is the key to the understanding of the text"[159] are not ones to which this writer subscribes. If the first claim is true one wonders how the first texts were ever written. It is the contention of this writer that the individual literary clues within a text and the actual content of it are what help make meaning rather than the text's relationship to a genre.[160] Therefore we will not concern ourselves overly much with whether or not we are comparing texts of the same genre.[161] Similarly we distance ourselves from Form Criticism and therefore Talmon's well intentioned notion that one should only compare texts which have the same *Form* and *Sitz im Leben*.[162] Form Criticism's shaky foundations in the Romanticist idea of the purity of the original and the simplicity of original form combined with the fact that very few, if any, actual texts seem to fit this ideal[163] makes one wonder about the usefulness of such a tool. The hypothetical reconstruc-

---

157 Hallo, "Contextual Method," 2. But do see Malul's comments, *Comparative Method*, 87–88, about the fact that people do still compare actual life and culture and literary context even though both are accessed mainly through written documents. His call to be clear about which one is comparing should perhaps be heeded. This writer attempts to do both to some extent. While not necessarily dealing with the actual law of the various cultures, it is best attempt to place the literary texts within a cultural context.

158 See discussion of this idea in Longman, "Form Criticism," 50–51.

159 *Ibid.*, 51, 53, 61–63.

160 Longman's approach of mutual elucidation from both the content and genre is similar but this writer believes he places too much emphasis on the role of genre for elucidation. See *Ibid.*, 59.

161 As Hallo, "Contextual Approach," 3 advocates.

162 Talmon, "Comparative Method," 351–52.

163 *i.e.* each text is seen to be a conglomeration of mixed forms from different places in life.

tion of the prehistory of a text as the key to its interpretation based on such a flimsy presupposition will form no part of this work. One wonders at the continuance of this method.[164] Genre criticism has arisen on the back of structuralist literary criticism and the focus on the whole text rather than its individual parts. This is to be welcomed to some extent, but there are problems with an undue emphasis on genre.

The idea that one should only compare texts of the same genre (or form) assumes an unnecessary *a priori*, namely, that the framing of legal material in different "genre" could not reflect cultural differences.[165] To what authority does one appeal to decide genre is most important when comparing two texts? This seems especially problematic as most admit that to borrow genre/form is not necessarily to borrow the ideals or framework of another civilization. Why is it that so many think that form/genre is more likely to be borrowed than content?[166] Is this less offensive to the "*Eigenbegrifflichkeit*" of the borrowing society? Perhaps it is, but the emphasis on comparing texts of the same genre can lead to scholars forcing texts into a generic mould so that they can be compared.[167] Is it not more important to pay attention to what the text actually says while keeping an eye on how it is framed and watching for possible links to other texts? In this sense the shape, function and content of the law collections of the ancient Near East will here be compared. Attention will be paid to the cultural context which the text stems from, not just the literary context. The move from treating LH as substantive law to treating it as a propagandistic text has gone along with the influence of literary interpretation on the field of history and the emphasis on treating written evidence as a "text". Though this has had some fruitful consequences one must not shy too far from treating the texts as some reflection of reality. This said, to some extent this debate is avoided

---

[164] Eckart Otto and Reuven Yaron are perhaps the main scholars working on ancient Near Eastern law who focus on such a method.

[165] *e.g.* Israel's framing of parts of its law within a covenantal framework. But see the discussion of Longman, "Form Criticism," 53–54 who mentions that "a culture-free genre system does not exist".

[166] *e.g.* Jackson, *Essays*, 23 or R. A. F. Mackenzie, "The Formal Aspects of Ancient Near Eastern Law," in *The Seed of Wisdom: Essays in Honour of T.J. Meek* (ed. W. S. McCullogh; Toronto: University of Toronto, 1964), 32 where he states that the "family resemblance which they do show concerns more their form than their substance."

[167] *e.g.* the assumption that most of the law collections were "monumental" inscriptions even though we do not have evidence of this and the forcing of some of the law collections into the tripartite structure of LH.

by focusing on the law collections themselves rather than the actual "law of practice" of the various cultures. As mentioned earlier, this is more to do with the number of sources that would need to be covered (for some collections and the total lack of them in others) in such an exercise rather than a firm position that the law collections do not reflect reality.[168]

Perhaps the next problem which should be addressed is that of identifying a parallel and explaining its significance. This is a problem that plagues comparativists of all kinds. All agree that this is a very difficult task. It is certainly one that is open to the subjective mind of the scholar.[169] Talmon has described the phenomenon thus: "personal inspiration often takes the place of systematic investigation, and impressionistic *déjà vu* insights substitute for the required procedural principles".[170] Even Malul, with his "scientific" criteria for picking a parallel, admits that determining the "direction, nature or type"[171] of it is a more subjective matter. Weeks poses the problems more pertinently: "Does X look similar enough to Y to exclude accidental resemblance and prove historical connection? Whether we ask the question for a literary form or an artistic style we confront the same difficulty. Convincing similarity is in the eye of the beholder."[172] With Weeks, this writer also affirms that the discussion is still worthwhile. An attempt will be made to pick similarities as well as differences and to offer an explanation though, as mentioned earlier, no attempt will be made to identify stimulus diffusion. Though it is quite possible that this form of borrowing lies behind some of the similarities amongst the law collections, there is not room in this work to explore the methodological issues surrounding how one distinguishes stimulus diffusion from independent invention in similar circumstances. This is, of course, a subject worth investigating more fully in the future.

As mentioned earlier we will be comparing the shape, function and content of the law collections. In the conclusion this will be briefly related

---

168 The function of the law collections will be discussed in the next chapter. The difference can be seen between Malul and others who look for literary borrowings (see *Comparative Method*, 93–94, n. 1), versus those like Smith, "Law Codes," who presume an actual legal tradition behind the collections and therefore compare this. Otto is of this latter mould also. Being a form critic, he is certain that a similarity of form must also mean a common background or *Sitz im Leben* as its basis.

169 Again, see Tigay's discussion of differing interpretation of parallels, "On Evaluating".

170 Talmon, "Comparative Method," 344.

171 Malul, *Comparative Method*, 91.

172 Weeks, *Admonition and Curse*, 3.

to a comparison of the world views and cultural makeup of the various societies behind these collections in an attempt to explain the similarities and differences. It should be noted at this point that a cultural determinist point of view is not held by the present author.[173] This would be far too simplistic, as the geographically[174] or racially deterministic[175] comparisons of the past have been. Though points of similarity exist between the approach outlined here and Baines and Yoffee's method spelled out in "Order, Legitimacy and Wealth",[176] this project will not restrict itself to these categories. An attempt will be made to stay open to a range of possible reasons for similarity or difference, ascribing to the possibility of a multi-causal approach.[177] It is expected that this study will show that such deterministic methods are inherently flawed and miss the obvious fact that usually life is more complex.[178] It is also hoped that this complexity will "not blind us to general tendencies".[179]

From at least the time of Aristotle onwards, it has been recognized that History, as a discipline, tends toward the study of the particular. Aristotle saw this as a weakness for history as it could thus not deal very well with the general, the big questions, and was therefore of less use than philosophy or poetry.[180] This said, from Roman times onwards general history has also been written, often in an attempt to give answers to large questions of a philosophical or practical nature. This tension between the accuracy of the particular and the usefulness of the general is one that has been felt

---

173 This approach is criticised, from an anthropological point of view by A. Kuper, *Culture: the Anthropologists' Account* (Cambridge, Mass.: Harvard University, 1999).

174 Frankfort.

175 Delitzsch.

176 Baines and Yoffee, "Order, Legitimacy, and Wealth". This writer finds points of contact with their emphasis on the importance of kingship and ideology as areas of comparison to help understand the cultures of Mesopotamia and Egypt and in their subscription to the idea of cultural differences within the ancient Near East but is less sympathetic to their treatment of all texts as propaganda addressed to the divine or the elite, their emphasis on the concept of order in both societies and their priest vs state dichotomy.

177 Discussed by Adams, Gerven, and Levy, "Retreat," in reaction to migrationism, diffusionism, materialism , evolutionism *etc.* within their own field.

178 Weeks, *Admonition and Curse*, 8–9, 175.

179 *Ibid.*, 176.

180 Aristotle, "The Poetics," in Richard P. McKeon, ed. *The Basic Works of Aristotle.* (New York: Random House; 1941), section 9.

within historiography throughout the ages. Even the man hailed by many as the founder of history's empirical method, Leopold von Ranke, felt this tension and in his old age attempted a "Universal History".[181] This writer also feels this tension in the present study and is wary of the dangers that come with a more general work. As argued earlier, the possible usefulness of such a work, and the myriad of scholars who are capable of correcting errors of detail within it, make it a worthwhile exercise. Due to limitations within our sources, many conclusions must be only tentative. This may limit the usefulness of the study somewhat, and though we generally concur with Boulding that, "It will be a sad day for man when nobody is allowed to ask questions that do not have any answers",[182] it is hoped that the answers offered here will be of some use.

At the end of this introduction the reader can probably tell that this writer has less sympathy with Elton's suggestion that, "a philosophic concern with such problems as the reality of historical knowledge or the nature of historical thought only hinders the practice of history"[183] and more with Butterfield's that, "It matters very much how we start upon our labours".[184]

---

[181] While holding to positions such as the following: "strict presentation of facts, no matter how conditional and unattractive they might be, is undoubtedly the supreme law", he attempted to mesh them with an eye for the universal *e.g.* "It is necessary that the historian keep his eyes open for the general", an historian "will not have preconceived ideas as does the philosopher, but rather while he observes the particular, the course which the development of the world in general has taken will be revealed to him", "It was impossible to remain content with the history of individual nations. A collection of national histories . . . is not what we mean by Universal History", "I have not devoted much space to less significant events; but this has enabled me to pay the greater attention to those of world historical importance", "historians are also mistaken who consider history simply an immense aggregate of particular facts". See the selection from Ranke's works in Fritz Stern, *The Varieties of History: From Voltaire to the Present* (2nd ed., Cleveland: Macmillan, 1970), 54–62.

[182] Quoted in Adams, Gerven, and Levy, "Retreat," 505.

[183] Geoffrey Elton, *The Practice of History* (2nd ed., Oxford: Blackwell, 2002), vii.

[184] Herbert Butterfield, *The Whig Interpretation of History* (London: G. Bell, 1931), 27.

2 COMPARISONS

2.1 SOURCES

2.1.1 Overview

The documents we will be comparing under the rubric of "law collections" are the following:

Reforms of Uru-Inimgina (RU)
Laws of Ur-Nammu (LU)
Laws of X (LX)
Laws of Lipit-Ishtar (LL)
Laws of Rented Oxen (LOx)
Sumerian Laws Exercise Tablet (SLEx)
Sumerian Laws Handbook of Forms (SLHF)
Laws of Eshnunna (LE)
Laws of Hammurabi (LH)
Ammiṣaduqa's Edict (AE)
Middle Assyrian Laws (MAL)
Middle Assyrian Palace Decrees (MAPD)
Hittite Laws (HL)
Edict of Telepinu (ETel.)
Edict of Tudhaliya IV (ETud.)
Edict of Haremhab (EH)
Nauri Decree (ND)
Elephantine Decree (ED)

As one can see we are not too worried about looking at material only from one generic classification. We are interested in comparing works about law from the different cultures of the ancient Near East before the first-millennium B.C. Below is some information regarding these sources.

Reforms of Uru-Inimgina (RU)

Author/Date: Uru-inimgina, last ruler of First dynasty of Lagash. Ruled 2351–2342 B.C.

Texts/Copies:[1] Six copies. Five on clay nails/cones, one on an oval clay plaque. There are supposedly three different versions.[2]

Language: Sumerian.

Laws of Ur-Nammu (LU)

Author/Date: Most likely Ur-Nammu, founder of Third dynasty of Ur, r. 2112–2095 B.C. Some have argued that his son Šulgi was the author due to the mention of military conquests that cannot be firmly ascribed to Ur-Nammu's reign.[3] It is likely the text was written late in the reign of Ur-Nammu. This would go some way to accounting for the lack of reference to these military activities.[4]

Text:[5] Three manuscripts from Nippur, Ur and perhaps Sippar. There is no evidence that this was set up as a stele[6] apart from the reference to the future ruler who effaces the inscription in LX, which may be the conclusion of LU. Wilcke assigns LL a–g (of Roth's edition) to LU also.[7] For ease of reference Roth's edition will be followed here.

---

[1] For English translations and bibliographical information regarding the cuneiform see "Reforms of Uru-inimgina," trans. William W. Hallo (*COS* 2.152:407–8) and Jerrold S. Cooper, *Presargonic Inscriptions* (Sumerian and Akkadian Royal Inscriptions 1; New Haven, Conn.: American Oriental Society, 1986), La. 9.1–9.3, 70–78. Cooper's translations have been followed in this work unless specified otherwise.

[2] See Claus Wilcke, "Early Dynastic and Sargonic Periods," in *A History of Ancient Near Eastern Law* (ed. Raymond Westbrook; vol. 1; Handbook of Oriental Studies 72/1; Leiden: Brill, 2003), 142, n. 6 and Cooper, *loc. cit.*

[3] See discussions of Samuel Noah Kramer, "The Ur-Nammu Law Code: Who Was Its Author?" *Orientalia* 52 (1983): 453–56 and Piotr Steinkeller, "The Administrative and Economic Organization of the Ur III State: The Core and the Periphery," in *The Organization of Power: Aspects of Bureaucracy in the Ancient Near East* (ed. McGuire Gibson, and Robert D. Biggs; 2nd ed.; Studies in Ancient Oriental Civilizations 46; Chicago: Oriental Institute, 1991), 15–33.

[4] Of course, there remains the possibility that these conquests have been exaggerated.

[5] For English translation of this text, LX, LL, LOx, SLEx, SLHF, LE, LH, MAL, and MAPD see Roth, *Law Collections*. For bibliographic information regarding the cuneiform texts, other translations and treatments see pp. 249–54. Roth's translation has been followed in this work for the above collections unless otherwise specified.

[6] Though Bertrand Lafont and Westbrook assume this to be the case. See "Neo-Sumerian Period (Ur III)," in *A History of Ancient Near Eastern Law* (ed. Raymond Westbrook; vol. 1; Handbook of Oriental Studies 72/1; Leiden: Brill, 2003), 183.

[7] Claus Wilcke, "Der Kodex Urnamma (CU): Versuch einer Rekonstruktion,"

Language: Sumerian.

Laws of X[8]

Author/Date: Name of ruler not preserved. This text is possibly the end of LU. Roth dates it to 2050–1800.

Text: Fragmentary text from Sippar.

Language: Sumerian.

Laws of Lipit-Ishtar

Author/Date: Lipit-Ishtar, fifth king of the First dynasty of Isin, r. 1934–1924 B.C. Late in his reign while Larsa is coming into ascendancy.

Text: Most sources from Nippur, R from Kish, N from Sippar. There are more than fifteen mss. a–g perhaps not part of LL.[9] The text is only preserved on tablets[10] though the epilogue refers to the erection of a stele (*na₄*), and Roth asserts that some stone fragments of LL have been identified.[11]

Language: Sumerian

Other: There is possibly a year name recording the setting up of this stele.[12]

Laws of Rented Oxen (LOx)

Date: c. 1800 B.C.

Text: There are nine laws but it is unclear if laws eight and nine are part of the composition. It is witnessed by six supposed student exercise tablets from Nippur.

Sumerian Laws Exercise Tablet (SLEx)

Date: c. 1800 B.C.

Text: Provenance unknown. The tablet has the name of the student Bel-šunu and the number of lines recorded on it, and includes a number of mistakes. On this basis it has been judged a student exercise/copy tablet.

---

in *Riches Hidden in Secret Places: Ancient Near Eastern Studies in Memory of Thorkild Jacobsen* (ed. Tsvi Abusch; Winona Lake, Ind.: Eisebrauns, 2002), 291–333.

[8] For an alternative treatment to Roth's, see Piotr Michalowski and C. B. F. Walker, "A New Sumerian 'Law Code'," in *DUMU.E$_2$.DUB.BA.A: Studies in Honor of Åke W. Sjöberg* (ed. Hermann Behrens, Darlene Loding and Martha Tobias Roth; Occasional Publications of the Samuel Noah Kramer Fund 11; Philadephia: University of Pennsylvania Museum, 1989), 383–96.

[9] See note 7 above concerning Wilcke's reconstruction of LU.

[10] Westbrook refers to them as exercise tablets, "Old Babylonian Period," in *History*, 361.

[11] Roth's comments before her translation of "The Laws of Lipit-Ishtar," in *COS* 2.154: 411.

[12] Roth, *Law Collections*, 23.

The obverse is badly damaged, while there are ten laws legible on the reverse.

Sumerian Laws Handbook of Forms (SLHF)

Date: c. 1700 B.C. Prism.

Text: Provenance unknown. It consists of a mixture of phrases, contractual clauses and laws similar to those of formal collections. It is supposedly written by an accomplished scribe.

Laws of Eshnunna (LE)

Author/Date: Dadusha of Eshnunna. Roth claims a tentative date of c. 1770 B.C. due to the Sumerian date formula which begins the text. Other dates and rulers have been offered.[13]

Text:[14] There are two large tablets which are almost complete, and a third which looks like a student exercise tablet with extracts from the laws.

Language: The text begins with fragmentary date formula/superscription in Sumerian. The rest is in Akkadian. There is no evidence that this collection was set up on a stele.[15]

Laws of Hammurabi (LH)

Author/Date: Towards the end of the reign of Hammurabi, sixth ruler of First dynasty of Babylon, r. 1792–1750 B.C. This is deduced from the list of military achievements in the prologue to the laws and its correlation with other historical evidence such as the Mari letters and year names.

Text:[16] The collection was found on a black diorite stele in Elam. The epilogue mentions that the laws were put on the stele for public display and set up before a statue of Hammurabi, "king of justice" in Babylon within the Esagil temple. Roth claims that fragments from two other stele of LH were also found in Susa.[17] The script and presentation of the stele is archaic. There are dozens of duplicates and extracts of the laws (over 50), including commentaries, references in catalogues, bilingual Sumerian-Akkadian versions, three late OB mss with headings, some copies of only prologue/epilogue *etc.* which range over 1000 years.

Language: Akkadian

---

[13] See the discussion of this and the relevant references in Reuven Yaron, *Laws of Eshnunna*, 20–21.

[14] For an alternative English translation see *Ibid.*

[15] Though this is assumed by Westbrook, in "Old Babylonian Period," 361.

[16] There are an enormous number of translations of this collection into English and many other languages. As mentioned earlier, Roth's translation in *Law Collections* will be followed here unless otherwise specified.

[17] Roth, *Law Collections*, 73.

Ammiṣaduqa's Edict (AE)

Author/Date: Ammiṣaduqa's version of this edict dates from c. 1640 B.C.

Text:[18] AE is the best preserved of the Old Babylonian edicts and shares so many similarities with the other two main texts that this study will not treat them separately. AE has a preamble and 22 paragraphs preserved whereas the Edict of Samsu-iluna (c. 1740 B.C.) has only the date and 3 paragraphs, and that of another Babylonian king[19] is fragmentary, with only 6 paragraphs.

Language: Akkadian, with Sumerian date formula superscribed.

Middle Assyrian Laws (MAL)

Author/Date: The tablets date to the eleventh century during the reign of Tiglath-pileser I, r. 1114–1076. Many scholars see them as copies from c. fourteenth century originals. This would date them to the beginning of Assyria's new found power under Aššur-uballit I. r. 1363–1328.

Text: There are a number of tablets dealing with thematic collections of laws, all of which were found in Aššur. It is not necessarily a single systematic composition *e.g.* there is some duplication of provisions in tablets B and O. The best preserved tablet (A) deals with women and other dependants. There is one duplicate copy of Tablet A from Nineveh which dates to the Neo-Assyrian period.

Language: Akkadian, in the Middle Assyrian dialect.

Middle Assyrian Palace Decrees (MAPD)

Author/Date: This text includes decrees issued by nine-kings. The text was assembled in the time of Tiglath-pileser I. The decrees start with orders from Aššur-uballit I and ends with those of Tiglath-pileser I.

Text: There are nine fragmentary sources from Aššur.

Other: Overlapping laws are not harmonized, just listed in their separate decrees.

Hittite Laws (HL)

Author/Date: The author is unknown. There is some good evidence connecting this text to the early Old Kingdom.[20]

---

[18] For an English translation "The Edicts of Samsu-iluna and his Successors," trans. William W. Hallo, (*COS* 2.134: 362–64). Hallo's translation has been followed in this work unless specified otherwise. For a critical edition and discussion of the texts see F.R. Kraus, *Königliche Verfugungen in altbabylonischer Zeit* (Studia et Documenta ad Iura Orientis Pertinentia 11; Leiden: Brill, 1984).

[19] Possibly Ammi-ditana. r. 1683–1647 B.C.. See Hallo's comments in *COS* 2.134: 362 and Kraus, *Königliche*, 293.

[20] A number of scholars however prefer to date it to the reign of Telepinu,

Text:[21] From Hattusa, at site of royal court of justice. Two tablets: "If a man" and "If a vine". Probably a third tablet, also "If a man", not preserved. Modified parallel text to first tablet: KBo VI 4. Four copies of laws in Old Hittite (1650–1500), rest are Middle Hittite or Neo-Hittite (1500–1180).

Language: Hittite

Other: Has been reworked over time *e.g.* "Formerly . . . now", and the late Parallel Text (PT).

Edict of Telepinu (ETel.)

Author/Date: The Hittite king Telepinu who ruled part way through the Old Kingdom period. This text dates to c. 1500.

Text:[22] There are at least seven thirteenth century copies of the Old Hittite text and two manuscripts of an Akkadian translation.

Language: Hittite.

Edict of Tudhaliya IV (ETud.)

Author/Date: The Hittite king Tudhaliya IV who ruled 1265–1240, during the New Kingdom period.

Text:[23] The Edict is witnessed in one New Kingdom copy.

Language: Hittite.

Edict of Haremhab (EH)

---

based on little more than the fact this king is known to have instituted other reforms. See the discussion of this issue in Itamar Singer's review of Hoffner's critical edition in *Journal of Near Eastern Studies* 60 (2001): 288–89. For the view held here see Singer's review, Alfonso Archi, "Sulla formazione del testo delle leggi ittite," *Studi micenei ed egeo-anatolici* 7 (1968): 54–89 and Franca Pecchioli Daddi, "Il re, il padre del re, il nonno del re," *Orientis Antiqui Miscellanea* 1 (1994): 75–91.

[21] Hoffner, *Laws of the Hittites.*

[22] The English translation followed here is "The Proclamation of Telipinu," trans. Th. P. J. van den Hout (*COS* 1.76: 194–98). For a critical edition see Inge Hoffmann, *Der Erlaß Telipinus* (Texte der Hethiter 11; Heidelberg: Carl Winter, 1984).

[23] An English translation (with transliteration) is given by Westbrook and Roger D. Woodard, "The Edict of Tudhaliya IV," in *Journal of the American Oriental Society* 110 (1990): 641–59. As will be mentioned, this translation is skewed towards a particular reading of this text. The earlier critical treatment of this text should also be consulted, E. von Schuler, "Hethitische Königserlässe als Quellen der Rechtsfindung und ihr Verhältnis zum kodifizierten Recht," in *Festschrift Johannes Friedrich* (ed. R. von Kienle, A. Moortgart, Heinrich Otten, E. von Schuler, and W. Zaumsell; Heidelberg: Carl Winter, 1959), 435–72.

Author/Date: Haremhab, last ruler of the eighteenth or first of the nineteenth dynasty, r. 1323–1295.

Text:[24] Set up on pylon at Karnak.

Language: Similar to the Amarna dialect with its tendencies towards Late Egyptian.

Nauri Decree (ND)

Author/Date: Issued by Seti I, r. 1294–1279.

Text:[25] Set up on stone in Nubia, concerning an estate in Nubia belonging to temple of Osiris at Abydos.

Elephantine Decree of Ramesses III (ED)

Author/Date: Possibly dated to the reign of Ramesses III.[26]

Text:[27] Inscription on a temple block which is part of the quay wall in Elephantine. The text safeguards the temple of Khnum.

Already we can see some differences in the way these various cultures presented legal material. Of course we need to be cautious in playing too much on these differences at this point. There are many problems with our evidence. It is hard to know whether some of the differences we see are accidents of discovery rather than reflections of an actual difference in the place of law within a society's worldview. The most extreme example of this is perhaps the vexed question of the existence of an Egyptian collection of laws comparable to those of Mesopotamia and Hatti.[28] Is our lack of such a document due to the difficulties surrounding the preservation of papyrus or the system of justification around Egyptian kingship?[29] There is also a diffi-

[24] For English translation see William J. Murnane, *Texts from the Amarna Period in Egypt* (Society of Biblical Literature Writings from the Ancient World 5; Atlanta, Ga.: Scholars, 1995), text 108, pp. 235–39. This is based on Jean-Marie Kruchten's critical edition, *Le Decret d'Horemheb:Traduction, commentaire épigraphique, philologique et instutionnel* (Brussels: University of Brussels Press, 1981). For an earlier English translation see Kurt Pflüger, "The Edict of Haremhab," *Journal of Near Eastern Studies* 5 (1946): 260–76. Murnane's translation has been followed here.

[25] For an English translation see William F. Edgerton, "The Nauri Decree of Seti I: A translation and analysis of the legal portion," in *Journal of Near Eastern Studies* 6 (1947): 219–30. This translation does not include the long prologue and epilogue for which see the earlier edition of F. Lt. Griffith, "The Abydos Decree of Seti I at Nauri," in *Journal of Egyptian Archaeology* 13 (1927): 193–208.

[26] We may have an epilogue to this decree which mentions the name of Ramesses III. See Griffith, "Abydos Decree," 207.

[27] For an English translation see Griffith, "Abydos Decree," 207–8.

[28] *e.g.* LH, LE, LU (and LX), LL, MAL, HL.

[29] This is a question we will return to later on.

culty in that the one culture can present law in various forms. This is especially the case if we treat Mesopotamia as a whole. There we have law within the more formal law collections connected to rulers, in decrees, academic treatises, historical inscriptions mentioning reforms, palace decrees, and whatever MAL are! This raises the possibility that we could make too much of the presence or absence of any one of these forms within a culture. Even if we divide Mesopotamia into smaller units we would run into similar problems. There is also the problem of arguments from silence. It is highly unlikely one can have positive evidence of the lack of something. To be able to discuss the lack of something in one culture versus its presence in another, one must resort to arguments from silence. This is always done with hesitation, but is unavoidable to some extent. We can but proceed with these cautions in mind. Perhaps there is much we can still make of the (at least apparent) differences. Our method will be to compare on the basis of the evidence we have at our disposal, not to read in what is expected, and certainly not to alter what we have so it fits expectations.[30] The comparison will focus on the larger, more formal law collections[31] but will include the others in the belief that this will help the study avoid any oversimplification of issues.[32] We shall also test the theory that there is widespread verbatim copying or translation amongst these collections,[33] and Westbrook's theory that: "a large number of the same cases recur in different codes. They are not necessarily presented in the same language, nor do they always have the same solution."[34]

2.1.2 Form

There are a number of issues which are raised through a discussion of the forms[35] within the ancient Near Eastern law collections. Claims are regularly made that it is the form more than the content which is similar in these

---

[30] Our suspicion that the enforcement of a uniform common law of the ancient Near East upon the evidence does it some injustice lies behind this.

[31] LH, LE, LU (and LX), LL, MAL and HL.

[32] See discussion in the introduction, p. 5.

[33] *e.g.* Norman Yoffee, "Context and Authority," 102; Nicholas Postgate, *Early Mesopotamia*, 289.

[34] Westbrook, "Character," 17.

[35] Form here is distinguished from structure. Issues related to the tripartite structure of some law collections and the role of prologue, epilogue, superscription *etc.* will follow shortly. This present section aims to cover merely the significance of casuistic, relative, apodictic forms *etc.* within the law collections.

collections.[36] For some the similarities in form are seen as part of the spread of "cuneiform culture",[37] while others see the similarities as natural ones.[38] There are those who see the differences in form as reflecting a different worldview with regards to the morality of law,[39] some who see the differences as part of developmental change,[40] and those for whom these differences are seen as trivial.[41] Through Form Criticism many issues are raised as to the original source material for the law collections and their *Sitz im Leben*.[42] The origins of the different forms also raise the question of the nature and purpose of the law collections. This aspect of the debate about forms will be left until a later section.[43] The present section will attempt to assess the similarity of forms in these texts and discuss the significance of both general similarities and the differences which do occur.

A description of the forms in the various law collections will be a helpful place to begin. Much of the scholarship regarding forms is based on a distinction between three main forms: conditional (if), relative (any who), and apodictic (do/do not). It is argued here that the distinction between the first two is not always firm, and that it is the influence of the study of Roman law which has led to scholars' attempts to keep such a distinction. A more general distinction between casuistic and apodictic is more feasible

[36] *e.g.* Mackenzie, "Formal Aspects," 32 where he states that the "family resemblance which they do show concerns more their form than their substance." See also Bernard S. Jackson, *Essays*, 23.

[37] Mackenzie, "Formal Aspects," 32; E. A. Speiser, "Cuneiform Law and the History of Civilization," 536–39; Westbrook, "Codification and Canonization," in *La Codification des lois dans l'antiquité: Actes du Colloque de Strasbourg, 27–29 Novembre 1997* (ed. Edmond Levy; Travaux du centre de recherche sur le Proche-Orient et la Grèce antiques 16; Paris: De Boccard, 2000), 35.

[38] See the discussion by Herbert Petschow, "Zu den Stillformen antiker Gesetze und Rechtssammlungen," *Zeitschrift der Savigny-Stiftung für Rechtsgeschichte* 82 (1965): 36–38; Reuven Yaron, "Forms in the Laws of Eshnunna," *Revue Internationale des droits de l'antiquité* 9 (1962): 150.

[39] Mackenzie, "Formal Aspect"; Walton, *Ancient Israelite Literature*, 80–83, 90–91.

[40] This theory is heavily influenced by Daube's theories regarding the development of Roman legal forms in *Forms of Roman Legislation* (Oxford: Oxford University Press, 1956). This model is applied to the ancient Near Eastern collections by Petschow, "Stillformen," and Yaron, "Forms," *e.g.* 150.

[41] Westbrook, "Character," 17: "the approach is always the same."

[42] See the works of Yaron and Eckart Otto in particular for modern proponents of this approach.

[43] Section 2.1.4

though its usefulness can be questioned, especially through an analysis of EH.

The section of RU covering Uru-inimgina's legal reforms is not cast in the casuistic form which is to become common later on. After an account of the abuses which were being perpetrated before his rule, he lists his reforms as past action in the third person.

Each of the provisions in LU begins with the Sumerian *tukum-bi*, "its case". This is certainly a casuistic form. Though this term is usually translated as "if", one could hardly argue that it introduces a conditional clause. The same is the case for LL and all but one of the laws contained in LX.[44] Provision j[45] of LX is cast in the Sumerian equivalent of a relative clause,[46] "A female-weaver who...". It is worth noting that this provision involves the listing of a price. Provision k may be cast similarly but is broken.

The provisions of LOx also all begin with *tukum-bi* as do those of SLEx.[47] The legal clauses and provisions collected in SLHF are diverse in their form. Some are simple statements of past action, possibly recording an action from a case.[48] Others are statements about future action[49] or the present state of affairs. Some are in the more regular casuistic form beginning a protasis with *tukum-bi* describing a possible offence followed by an apodosis making a statement about the consequent action to be taken/punishment to be carried out. Some have a protasis-apodosis form without a relative clause or an initial *tukum-bi*.[50] There are other forms also which look as though they are phrases from contracts or *di-til-la* records.[51]

There are a number of forms in LE. The casuistic form beginning with *šumma* is by far the most common. The term *šumma* is universally translated as "if". In Akkadian the distinction between a conditional and a relative clause would then be distinguishable linguistically, but this writer doubts

---

[44] Which, as we have mentioned earlier, is seen by some as the end of LU.

[45] For the sake of consistency and ease of reference we will follow Roth's numbering where possible.

[46] Formed by the addition of the nominalising particle '*a*' after the verbal root.

[47] Provision 5 seems to be a continuation of provision 4 rather than a completely new paragraph. This may explain the lack of the term at the beginning of this provision.

[48] Be it swearing, validating documents, sounding a horn, having someone killed *etc.*

[49] Whether in the future tense or the desiderative mood.

[50] *e.g.* iv 31–34 which looks like part of a split-protasis or iv 12–14 which merely states a past action and its consequence, "He despised her. He shall . . .".

[51] *e.g.* viii 11–15, vii 34–36, v 45, ii 26–31 *etc.*

that there are significant conceptual differences between these two casuistic forms. There is also some evidence to suggest that the term began as a form of the demonstrative rather than a conditional particle.[52] There are a number of variations of the *šumma* clause.[53] There are four apodictic commands,[54] three of which are negatively formulated, "x shall not…",[55] and one positively, "x shall…".[56] The collection also contains three provisions with the relative construction *awilum ša*, "A man who…".[57] Eleven provisions in LE concern the regulation of price and hire or rates of exchange or interest which are not framed in a casuistic style.

LH is almost completely casuistic in its framing (each clause beginning with *šumma*); even the regulations about price, hire and wage are put into this mould. There are, however, several laws concerning real estate[58] and one about adoption[59] which are framed as third person apodictic commands.

The edict of Ammiṣaduqa has a smattering of all three forms. Six are apodictic,[60] 11 are relative clauses, and 5 are conditional. Within this mixture there is also the combining of the various forms within the one law *e.g.* §3 starts as a relative clause and ends with the apodictic statement, "he may not collect barley…"; §4 begins with a *šumma* clause and ends with a relative clause; §6 begins with an apodictic statement and ends with a conditional clause, "If he duns, he dies."

The Middle Assyrian Laws are almost completely conditional in their form. Three laws are apodictic[61] and one is relative.[62] There is one law framed conditionally which contains a relative clause,[63] and there is the interesting case of law A 40 which begins as an apodictic statement, but then

[52] See the discussion of Mackenzie, "Formal Aspect," 34 and note 8.

[53] The "split-protasis" forms mentioned by Yaron, "Forms," 141–45. We will treat them merely as variant casuistic forms.

[54] LE 15–16, 51–52 (apart from the provisions concerning price and hire).

[55] LE 15–16, 51

[56] LE 52

[57] LE 12, 13, 19

[58] LH 36, 38–40

[59] LH 187

[60] Almost all of these concern the remittance of debt.

[61] A 57–59

[62] F 2

[63] *e.g.* A 41

goes on to a relative clause followed by a conditional one. Many of the laws not from tablet A are too fragmentary to speculate as to their framing.

Mainly conditional again are the Middle Assyrian Palace Decrees. Often, given the fragmentary nature of some of the laws, we are unable to tell if a conditional or relative form was used.[64] There are a number of laws where a mixture of forms may occur.[65] There are some laws which definitely contain relative constructions.[66] Several laws begin with temporal clauses[67] and some contain apodictic statements.[68]

Casuistic framing is most typical throughout the Hittite Laws which generally begin with *takku*. Though most translate this as "if" and treat it as though it introduces a conditional clause, it has been argued that it was in fact a temporal conjunction.[69] Laws 50–52 are relative clauses and 54 and 56 seem to be apodictic. These laws concern rendering of services, as does 55 which records the apodictic declaration of the king within a brief historical narrative. The price laws of 178–185 are framed apodictically (*i.e.* the price of x is y), while that of 186 is a series of relative clauses. Interestingly, while law 48 does not begin with the typical *takku*, its parallel version (PT) does.[70]

The legal and administrative measures set out at the end of the Edict of Telepinu are a mixture of casuistic forms using *takku*, "if" or *kuiš*, "someone, whoever", and apodictic commands of the king.[71] Most provisions include more than one form.[72] The Edict of Tudhaliya IV generally uses the conditional particle *man* or *takku*, though it also employs the relative *kuiš*.

---

[64] *e.g.* § 3

[65] *e.g.* § 1, that of Ashur-uballit I, may contain all three forms. See Roth's reconstruction, *Law Collections*, 197. Also see § 5 which begins with an apodictic statement and ends with several casuistic or relative clauses.

[66] *e.g.* § 7, § 10, part of § 20 (mixed with casuistic clauses also), part of § 21, part of § 23

[67] *e.g.* § 7 *ištu*, "after", § 6 *ki*, "when" or "if" (the latter would make the clause conditional/casuistic rather than temporal, § 8 *ina um*, "on the day when . . .".

[68] § 5

[69] See the discussion of Mackenzie, "Formal Aspect," 34–35 and note 9.

[70] A Neo-Hittite version of the laws which has revised them at points.

[71] *e.g.* § 29 which is framed as a second person prohibitive.

[72] *e.g.* § 28 begins with a command and then a series of conditions introduced by *takku*; § 29 begins with a relative clause introduced by *kuiš* and is followed by a series of commands.

The Edict of Haremhab is traditionally divided into two legal sections: a latter section dealing with administrative reforms and an earlier section dealing with law more properly.[73] In the legal section a conditional framing is more typical while there are also many relative clauses.[74] The supposed conditional form of those clauses introduced by *ir* is not absolute. This particle can also mean "as to" or "concerning" which, while still casuistic, is not necessarily conditional.[75] In the administrative section there are several apodictic declarations, a few relative clauses and a number of sections of historical narrative. The generally casuistic nature of this collection is interesting given its framing as the direct speech/commands of the king.[76]

The section of the Nauri Decree recording the decree of the king to the court has four smaller sections which begin with a list of wrongs to be prevented and are followed by a series of relative clauses which outline the penalties to be meted out for any offenders.

What is the significance of all this? Is it possible to sort through all these texts and forms and come to solid conclusions? The most obvious similarity between all these texts is the preponderance of casuistic forms. A number of the above mentioned texts are almost completely casuistic. For all but EH, ND, RU, EA, ETel. and SLHF,[77] a form argued to be conditional is most common amongst the legal provisions of the collections. What does this show? That a conditional form is a natural way to express a law?[78] Or, given its less frequent use in our two Egyptian texts, do we put it down to the spread of "cuneiform law"?[79] Given its widespread use in Greek, Roman and later law, and its appearance within EH, the former seems more likely. Why then do some texts use only that form, some mix it with others, and some avoid it all together?[80] Does this reflect Daube's model of development from the concrete conditional cases which reflected folk-law to the more general and systematic relative forms, more reflective

[73] See Pflüger's translation, "Haremhab".

[74] There are also some where the text is fragmentary and it is hard to tell.

[75] See Raymond O. Faulkner, *A Concise Dictionary of Middle Egyptian* (Oxford: Griffith Institute, 1999), 24, 145 (*ir* can be the full form of the preposition *r*).

[76] Mackenzie tries to avoid this problem with his statements regarding the administrative rather than legislative function of the Egyptian material and its lack of set juridical modes of expression, "Formal Aspect," 39.

[77] 5 of the 15 collections

[78] Even form critics like Yaron acknowledge this as very likely, "Forms".

[79] See note 37 above.

[80] *e.g.* the later Neo-Babylonian laws which are all relative in form.

of a legal system, and then finally to the apodictic form which comes close to the expression of underlying principles?[81] This model has been argued to hold up in regards to *Keilschriftrechten* by Petschow.[82] The argument rests on shaky grounds. Some argue that the earliest law collections consist almost exclusively of conditional forms, those of the Old to Middle Babylonian period display some sort of mixture of forms, and then the Neo-Babylonian laws consist solely of relative clauses. This is problematic and rests on the determination of *tukum-bi* as a particle introducing a conditional clause. While this writer happily acknowledges *tukum-bi* as one of the many particles introducing casuistically framed laws, he cannot accept it as a conditional form. The fact that our earliest collections are in Sumerian and do tend to have only casuistic forms,[83] says very little. That LH has a preponderance of conditional clauses, though written after LE, which mixes conditional and relative, also argues against this conclusion. There is only one first-millennium B.C. cuneiform law collection available to us, hardly enough to generalize as to developmental principles.[84] Perhaps the snapshot of collections from the second-millennium B.C., displaying various mixtures of all forms should be taken on its own terms, not forced into a developmental mould. Given the fact that most available collections come from this period, one should be wary in declaring this situation to be abnormal. If there were other collections in the first-millennium B.C., perhaps they would also reflect this diversity. This writer argues that one should follow Roth's conclusion that both the supposed conditional and relative clauses are merely variations of a casuistic clause anyway[85] and admit that it is somewhat forced to read a developmental difference into these collections on such a basis. This is especially true when one considers the difficulties involved in defining certain particles as conditional. If collections outside of southern Mesopotamia are included, it is even more difficult to postulate a pattern of development; what we see instead is the plurality of forms available for the structuring of laws.

A similarity amongst the collections is that it is not uncommon for regulations concerning prices, wages, hire *etc.* and/or those concerning the

---

[81] Daube, *Forms of Roman Legislation.*

[82] Petschow, "Stillformen".

[83] Except SLHF.

[84] For our purposes the dating of the law collections in the Hebrew Bible will not be considered here.

[85] Roth, *Law Collections*, 3: "A variation of this casuistic formulation is the relative construction".

ownership of state land and the services to be rendered in return, to be framed differently from the rest of a collection.[86] This said, there is not a uniform way to frame laws concerning prices *etc.* nor those concerning state land. All three forms[87] are used for such laws, there even being diversity within the one collection.[88] Some have suggested that there are different forms for laws concerning economic or administrative matters versus those of a more legal nature, but this does not seem to be borne out by the evidence, especially when one considers that in LH, even these topics were able to be framed in *šumma* clauses.[89]

Theories which postulate a particular *Sitz im Leben* for each form run into the difficulty that most collections contain a mixture of forms. To ask people to assume that each original section of a text was made up of solely one form is to ask them to ignore the evidence to the contrary and instills in them the need to fabricate hypothetical texts.[90] Only four of the texts under consideration here, all Sumerian, live up to such an ideal, LU, LL, LOx and SLEx.[91] One may agree with Yaron that *a priori*: "There is no reason to assume that any one legislator would express his rules in very different ways".[92] Given the evidence that this *was* what legislators[93] had a tendency to do, the onus should be on those whose assumption goes against the evidence.[94] Perhaps there is no reason to assume that any one legislator would

---

[86] *e.g.* the prices within LX (one relative clause), LE (various forms, but not casuistic), Hittite Laws (mostly apodictic, some relative). The prices within LH however are all forced into the casuistic style that dominates the collection. The laws concerning the ownership of state land and services to be rendered in return are framed differently to the rest of the collection in LH (apodictic) and HL (apodictic and relative).

[87] *i.e.* supposedly conditional, apodictic and relative

[88] *e.g.* the variously framed laws concerning prices, wage, hire in LE, or the real estate laws in HL which use all three forms.

[89] Even Yaron, "Forms," admits that the forms used for prices cannot be used to argue for a different origin, 139–40.

[90] See the works of Eckart Otto who, on the basis of his belief in Form Criticism, postulates original texts which all follow the same form and structure.

[91] If LX is the end of LU then this number is further reduced.

[92] Yaron, "Forms," 138.

[93] This term is here used for the sake of contrast, not to imply that these law collections were "legislation" in the modern sense.

[94] *i.e.* though the *a priori* assumption seems reasonable it is proven incorrect *a posteriori* and should thus be abandoned. To force it upon the evidence to the contrary just because it seems reasonable and sensible is the wrong approach according

necessarily want to restrict himself to expressing his rules in only one way, let alone the scribe who actually wrote them up.[95] The fact that the same material can be framed differently across collections, *e.g.* the conditional prices in LH, should make one hesitate to postulate a difference in content as the cause for a difference in form.[96] It is inconsistent to argue that a difference of form in a collection such as LE shows that it is made up of a variety of sources while the uniformity of form within LH shows that the author responsible covered up the variety of sources he used.[97] The assumption that these collections should be made up of a combination of sources which are reflected in different forms is obviously playing a greater role than the evidence in the construction of such a position. As was argued earlier, it is the influence of both the study of sources in Roman law and source critical approaches to the Old Testament which lead to such an approach to ancient Near Eastern law collections.

The idea that offences framed apodictically reflect a moral concern whereas those framed casuistically or in a relative construction reflect only an economic or other amoral concern does not seem to fit the evidence either.[98] This idea has been used as an argument to elevate the Israelite conception of morality onto a higher plane than that of the cultures around them.[99] The argument is that a law which is framed apodictically is forbidden, disobedience is not envisaged whereas a casuistic or relatively formulated law is not forbidden, there are just consequences if one breaks it. While one may agree that an apodictic statement more clearly enunciates moral principles and perhaps states them more forcefully one hesitates to argue that this is always the case. Take the real estate laws of LH and HL as

---

to this writer.

[95] There has been more and more recognition of diversity within scribal practice. One need not assume different scribes each time a word is written differently or a different formula or form is used. Perhaps scribes got bored of uniformity, perhaps they wanted to display their diverse talents, who knows? This writer's theory of best practice is to deal with the text available rather than trying to reconstruct hypothetical originals based on unnecessary and inconsistently applied assumptions.

[96] See also Roth's comments regarding the similarity of content between the Neo-Babylonian Laws and LH despite the difference of form, "The Law Collection of King Hammurabi," 28.

[97] See Yaron, "Forms," 137.

[98] See e.g Mackenzie, "Formal Aspect" and Walton, *Ancient Israelite Literature.*

[99] Especially through a focus on the Ten Commandments/Words and their apodictic framing.

an example. Many of these are framed as apodictic commands. They merely regulate what land can be sold and who has to pay duties or service in return. These are hardly higher moral principles than those concerning rape and adultery in the same collections.[100] Though we rarely have apodictic commands with a second person address in law collections outside of Israel,[101] one also wonders what is to be done with the majority of Israelite laws which are not framed in an apodictic manner. Are these of a lower order of morality?[102]

The idea that Egypt's law was framed apodictically versus the Mesopotamian casuistic framing[103] is difficult to discuss given our lack of a more formal law collection in Egypt. The tendency towards smaller collections contained in edicts or decrees may well explain the perception of a relative preponderance of apodictic commands in Egypt versus those in Mesopotamia. It should be remembered, however, that, though there is a greater sense that the Egyptian material is apodictic due to its framing as the direct commands of the Pharaoh, there were many casuistic forms contained within it. It may be the case that this emphasis on framing law as pharaonic commands is not just the result of the accidents of discovery, but reflects a difference in the Egyptian worldview. This writer does not think it reflects a higher level of morality, rather, a different conception of kingship. Neither EH nor ND are dominated by apodictic forms so the difference is more likely to be found in the framing than the forms used.

What then can be said about the similarities and differences of forms used within the law collections? Little so far, but perhaps more can be said when we discuss the relationship of these forms to the function of the various collections. Thus far the discussion has warned scholars from making much of the forms used in order to reconstruct borrowing channels,[104] original texts, patterns of development or cultural differences. This position

---

[100] One might also look to the regulations concerning prices *etc.* which often tend to be in an apodictic form.

[101] Perhaps this is of more significance, though it is important to consider the second person addresses within Hittite treaties and ETel. 29.

[102] See the many studies on the structure of laws in Exodus and Deuteronomy which see them grouping laws concerning the same commandment (from the Ten Commandments) together *e.g.* Stephen A. Kaufman, "The Structure of the Deuteronomic Law," *Maarav* 1 (1978–1979): 105–58 and A. E. Guilding, "Notes on the Hebrew Law Codes," *Journal of Theological Studies* 49–50 (1948–1949): 43–53. Perhaps this can be taken to imply that these laws are in some sense subsidiary.

[103] Mackenzie, "Formal Aspect," 39.

[104] *e.g.* the spread of cuneiform law.

is supported by Westbrook who, acknowledging the formal differences within the texts, sees them as unimportant, remarking: "the approach is always the same."[105] This writer does not think the variety of forms disproves Westbrook's central contention concerning the unity of ancient Near Eastern law. Let us move on to another topic then.

2.1.3 Framing

The term 'framing' does not refer so much to the literary structure here as to the more general framework affecting the way the laws are presented. A list of the aspects of the collections to be examined will help elucidate what is meant: acknowledgement of change/reform within the laws; the existence of explanations within the laws *e.g.* motive/because clauses or historical information; explicit connection to a ruler; existence and content of a prologue/epilogue (colophon, superscription *etc.*). Basically, this section will attempt to detect anything within the framing of the law collections which may point to a worldview concerning the area of law.[106] Some preliminary observations will be made here. They will be brought together into a more coherent picture in the concluding chapter. This section will only deal with issues of structure where they are seen to bear on the framework in which the laws are put.[107] Issues relating to the nature or purpose of the collections will be dealt with in the next section.

It is a well-known fact that the Hittite law collections, out of all the law collections we possess from the ancient Near East, are the only ones to clearly acknowledge the reform of previous laws, especially HL. Many have

---

105 "Character," 17.

106 Therefore excluding differences of penalty, use of oath, ceremony, or ordeal, what is seen as an offence *etc.* The former and latter will be dealt with in later sections regarding the laws themselves rather than their framing.

107 For some works focusing on the structure of the laws themselves see H. Sauren, "Aufbau und Anordnung der babylonischen Kodizes," *Zeitschrift der Savigny-Stiftung für Rechtsgeschichte* 106 (1989): 1–55; Petschow, "Zur Systematik und Gesetztechnik im Codex Hammurabi," *Zeitschrift für Assyriologie* 57 (1965): 146–72 and "Zur 'Systematik' in den Gesetzen von Eschnunna," in *Symbolae Iuridicae et Historicae Martino David Dedicatae* (ed. J. A. Ankum, R. Feenstra, and W. F. Leemans; Studia Documenta ad Iura Orientis Antiqui Pertinentia 2; Leiden: Brill, 1968), 131–43; Barry L. Eichler, "Literary Structure in the Laws of Eshnunna," 71–84; B. Hruška, "Die innere Struktur der Reformtexte Urukaginas von Lagash," *Archiv Orientalni* 41 (1973): 4–13, 104–32; Korošec, "Sistematika prve hettitske pravne zbirke (KBoVI 3)," *Zbornik znanstvenih razpraw* 7 (1930): 2–12.

seen some of the other law collections as reforming documents.[108] Some have even postulated that they can detect a change in law by comparing laws on the one topic within the one collection.[109] A number of scholars have taken this difference in HL to imply a closer connection between its laws and the laws of practice than other ancient Near Eastern law collections.[110] This is done on the presumption that the changes in the collection must arise as reflections or enactments of changes in the law of practice. Though the latter may well be the case, there is another possible explanation for the difference between the Hittite Laws and the other collections which do not acknowledge legal change in the same manner. It will be argued that RU, atypical for a Mesopotamian collection, also acknowledges change to some extent.

Before these things are discussed, some clarification is needed. While pointing out the difference between HL and the other collections, it is not necessarily implied that the other law collections are not reforming or do not change previously existing laws. This is a possibility, though a contested one. In some of the other collections there is even acknowledgement of a situation where laws were not previously kept.[111] In EH there may even be an indication that some of the laws set forth are new.[112] It is, however, possible that the references in EH imply the re-establishment of old norms which may have fallen out of favor during the Amarna period.[113] No other

---

[108] *e.g.* Driver and Miles, *Babylonian Laws*, vol. 1, 45 regarding LH; the title attributed to Uru-inimgina's document (RU) also implies such a purpose; J. Fleishman on "Legal Continuation and Reform in Codex Hammurabi Paragraphs 168–169," *Zeitschrift für altorientalische und biblische Rechtgeschichte* 5 (1999): 54–65; Hallo on the purpose of AE in *COS* 2.134: 362; Eckart Otto, "Aspects of Legal Reforms and Reformulations," 160–96.

[109] *e.g.* Guillame Cardascia, "La réparation des dommages agricoles dans le Code de Hammurabi," *Revue d'Assyriologie* 79 (1985): 169–80.

[110] *e.g.* Haase, "The Hittite Kingdom," 620.

[111] *e.g.* RU and EH.

[112] See Pflüger, "Haremhab," 267: "commands which My Majesty has newly issued", and, 263: "starting from today, the law shall be applied against him". For the same two phrases Murnane, *Amarna Period*, has similarly (though perhaps implying renewal): "decrees which my Person has made anew", 240 and, in contrast: ". . . still appropriates hides [until] today, let the law be applied against him", 237.

[113] This said, the disruptive and chaotic nature of the Amarna period has been increasingly questioned *e.g.* Mario Liverani, *Three Amarna Essays* (intr. and trans. Matthew L. Jaffe; Monographs on the Ancient Near East vol. 1, fasc. 5; Malibu, Ca.: Undena, 1979).

collection is as explicit as HL in its acknowledgement that an old law has been changed. The existence of such acknowledgements in HL and their absence elsewhere does not necessarily imply that the other collections are therefore less likely to be related to the law of actual practice than HL. It will be argued here that this difference reflects a more general cultural difference between the Hittites, Egypt and Mesopotamia.

This difference is reflected in the historiography and treaty forms of these different civilizations also.[114] Within their royal historical texts, the Hittites, unlike their Egyptian or Mesopotamian counterparts, have a tendency to speak of abuses by previous rulers and the negative consequences which ensued.[115] The Edict of Telepinu is a case in point. Telepinu recounts the bloody and violent squabbles of the past surrounding the throne. He explains that it is these past abuses which have led him to change the succession laws of the Hittite throne.[116] Here we have explicit recognition that the laws of the past were mistaken and have been changed. The Hittite ability to acknowledge past abuses in rulership should perhaps be understood to be connected to their ability to acknowledge a change in law. This writer thinks, with Weeks, that all of this is connected with the Hittite use of history and their system of rule. This will be discussed in the concluding chapter.

Within Mesopotamian historiography it is uncommon to speak of the mistakes of a previous ruler,[117] to acknowledge a defeat[118] or to use history to teach lessons.[119] Atypically, the historiography of Lagash does the latter

---

[114] For the latter see Weeks, *Admonition and Curse.*

[115] See especially the "Plague Prayers of Muršili II," trans. Gary Beckman (*COS* 1.60: 156–60).

[116] He also enacts a number of other reforms, also due to the lessons learned from past mistakes/abuses *e.g.* those regarding the treatment of fortified cities (where rebellion had stemmed from in the past), *COS* 1.76: 198, section 35.

[117] See Esarhaddon's cloaked remarks about Sennacherib's Babylonian policy. This is perhaps as close as they come. English translation available in Daniel David Luckenbill, *Historical Records of Assyria: from Sargon to the End* (vol. 2 of *Ancient Records of Assyria and Babylonia*; New York: Greenwood, 1927), 242–264.

[118] But see the Babylonian chronicles which acknowledge Babylonian defeat in contrast with the Assyrian chronicles which never acknowledge Assyrian defeat. For English translations see Jean-Jacques Glassner, *Mesopotamian Chronicles* (Society of Biblical Literature Writings from the Ancient World 19; Atlanta, Ga.: Society of Biblical Literature, 2004) or Albert Kirk Grayson, *Assyrian and Babylonian Chronicles* (Locust Valley, NY: J.J. Augustin, 1975).

[119] The exception is of course the treaties of Aššur-banipal and the Tukulti-

two.[120] This is connected to its ability to acknowledge legal change, as evidenced in RU. It is here argued that the Mesopotamian conception of institutions and modes of doing things being passed down from the gods to man in the beginning may lie behind their typical unwillingness to acknowledge change, especially in the area of law. If the precepts for law are conceived as having come from the gods in the beginning,[121] then it does the ruler no favors if he claims to change them. Given the Mesopotamian rulers' tendency to shy away from criticism of previous rulers, they are unlikely to mention a situation where the wrong laws were in place. Unlike the Egyptians, they do not even seem to contemplate offering new laws. From what can be gathered from the framing of the Mesopotamian laws in our possession, they conceive of their laws as being applications of the principles of *kittum u mišarum* handed down from the gods to man. In all of the Mesopotamian collections, except RU, there is no acknowledgement that laws have changed. There is some difficulty in discerning exactly what Uru-inimgina is claiming regarding the situation in the past and the relation of his reforms to it.[122] Hallo's translation[123] would seem to fit the more common Mesopotamian practice as it implies that there have been abuses from time immemorial and that Uru-inimgina merely "(re)established the norms

Ninurta Epic. See the discussion of Weeks, *Admonition and Curse*, 41–54. References to these texts can also be found there.

[120] See Cooper, *Presargonic Inscriptions*, 9.4 for a historical account of defeat by Uru-inimgina and see Weeks, *Admonition and Curse*, 17–19 for a discussion of the Lagash treaties.

[121] See the Sumerian King List: Thorkild Jacobsen, *The Sumerian King List* (Chicago: University of Chicago Press, 1939) or the translation of A. Leo Oppenheim (*ANET*, 265–66).

[122] The literature discussing (and demonstrating) the difficulties of interpreting what is being referred to in RU (let alone its relation to actuality) is immense *e.g.* Maurice Lambert, "Les 'réformes' d'Urukagina," *Revue d'Assyriologie* 50 (1956): 169–184; Benjamin Foster, "Social Reform in Ancient Mesopotamia," in *Social Justice in the Ancient World* (ed. K. Irani and M. Silver; Westport, Conn.: Greenwood, 1995), 165–77; I. M. Diakonoff, "Some Remarks on the Reforms of Urukagina," *Revue d'Assyriologie* 52 (1958): 1–15; Dietz Otto Edzard, "'Soziale Reformen' im Zweistromland bis ca. 1600 v. Chr.: Realitat oder literarischer Topos?" *Acta Antiqua Academiae Scientiarum Hungaricae* 22 (1974): 145–56; Claus Wilcke, *Early Ancient Near Eastern Law. A History of its Beginnings: The Early Dynastic and Sargonic Periods* (Sitzungberichte der bayerischen Akademie der Wissenschaften 2003/2; Munich: Bayerischen Akademie der Wissenschaften, 2003).

[123] *COS* 2.152: 407–8.

of old",[124] *i.e.* the way things were supposed to have been done as handed down in the beginning, in order to check these abuses. Hallo's translation runs into problems as a contradiction is implied: the "standards of old" are the problem but the re-establishment of the "norms of old" is the solution. Cooper's translation[125] fits what one would expect from Lagash given its atypical historiography and treaty formulation. He sees the solution to the abusive "conventions of former times" which had been around "since time immemorial" as coming because of Uru-inimgina having "replaced the customs of former times".[126] Though both translations are possible from the Sumerian, Cooper's makes sense of what Uru-inimgina is claiming and links well with the atypical practice of Lagash.

For the Egyptians it is perhaps their conception of kingship which leads to the restraint exercised in regard to criticism of previous practice. The Egyptians generally present their history as unchanging. Though they may at times introduce some new practice, they will never acknowledge that they did away with an old one.[127] The perception of the pharaoh as divine may explain this tendency. If one pharaoh were to question the actions of a previous divine ruler, he may in effect be bringing the whole system of justification into disrepute *i.e.* "If a past divine ruler made a mistake why should we trust this one?" or, "If a past ruler claiming to be divine could make such an error perhaps he was not divine, perhaps the current pharaoh is not either!" Because law is an activity closely associated with the pharaoh, it would possibly be damaging to claim to have reformed or changed a previously existing law. Perhaps the Egyptian conception of Ma'at also plays a role.

For now, what is quite likely is that the Hittite ability to acknowledge wrong practice in the past and change from it in the present may explain the existence of the acknowledgement of change within the Hittite Laws as against the practices of Mesopotamia (with the exception of RU) and Egypt. In the concluding chapter it will be argued that this is connected to the various conceptions of kingship and the mode of rule in these societies. This may have implications for an assessment of the function of the law collections in the next section. It does seem to imply a cultural difference in the framing of the laws of the ancient Near East.

---

[124] *Ibid.*, 407.

[125] Cooper, *Presargonic Inscriptions*, 9.1–9.3.

[126] *Ibid.*, 71.

[127] *e.g.* the move from pyramid building to Sun-temples *etc.*

The existence of motive clauses in Old Testament law has been used to argue for the distinctiveness of ancient Israel's conception of law.[128] Within ancient Near Eastern law there is no parallel within legal material.[129] There is a vaguely related clause within Old Babylonian law; the *aššum* or "because clause".[130] As Roth has observed, this clause is used to repeat the most pertinent section of the case. Her contention, one with which this writer concurs, is that this clause represents some form of punishment rationalization *i.e.* a way to highlight the main factor used to decide the penalty. This type of clause is far removed from those of the Old Testament whose purpose is to motivate obedience. The "because clause" does perhaps indicate a level of reflective legal reasoning not expressed everywhere within ancient Near Eastern law collections. Its restriction to Old Babylonian law collections highlights the fact that law could be framed differently across the cultures and periods of the ancient Near East. In contradiction to the claims of Yaron, the clause does not just reflect the verbose nature of LH in its appropriation of LE,[131] it reflects a wider Old Babylonian convention reflected not only in LH but also in the *mišarum* edicts from the period (*e.g.* AE) and in the documents from practice. It is not only an Old Babylonian convention, however. It is also reflected in documents from practice in Lower Mesopotamia *e.g.* the Ur III period.[132]

Somewhat paralleling their more prevalent use of history to teach lessons, there are some Hittite laws which incorporate some form of explana-

---

[128] *e.g.* Rifat Sonsino, *Motive Clauses in the Old Testament and the Ancient Near East: Biblical Forms and Near Eastern Parallels* (SBL Dissertations Series 45; Chico, Ca.: Scholars Press, 1980) and B. Gemser, "The Importance of the Motive Clause in Old Testament Law," in *Supplement to Vetus Testamentum* 1 (1953): 50–66.

[129] But see Hittite treaties and internal loyalty oaths. For a recent English translation of some of these texts see Gary Beckman, *Hittite Diplomatic Texts* (2nd ed.; Society of Biblical Literature Writings from the Ancient World 7; Atlanta, Ga.: Society of Biblical Literature, 1999).

[130] See Roth, "The Because Clause: Punishment Rationalization in Mesopotamian Laws," in *Veenhof Anniversary Volume: Studies Presented to Klaas R. Veenhof on the Occasion of his Sixty-Fifth Birthday* (ed. W. H. van Soldt, J. G. Dercksen, N. J. C. Kouwenberg and Th. J. H. Krispijn; Publications de l'Institut historique-archéologique néerlandais de Stamboul 89; Leiden: Nederlands Institut voor het Nabije Oosten, 2001), 407–12.

[131] Yaron, *Laws of Eshnunna*, 89–91.

[132] See Nicholas Postgate, *Early Mesopotamia*, 289. Perhaps LE is far enough north to be less influenced by the culture of Lower Mesopotamia. This must be tempered by the fact that MAL A 36 also includes a because clause.

tion or historical detail. HL 49 includes an explanation as to the motivation behind the formulating of the law *i.e.* otherwise the *hipparaš* would do x. This is not, however, simple motivation towards obedience as found in the Hebrew Bible. The inclusion of historical details leading up to the giving of a law is typically Hittite. This is most obvious in ETel. which outlines the past abuses which have led to the need for Telepinu's reforms and uses them as motivation to keep them. HL 55 and ETud. each describe the process leading up to the giving of laws, detailing subjects of the king coming to him as a delegation, and then the king's decision. This very much contrasts with EH's description of Haremhab consulting with himself to give his laws, and neatly parallels the lack of any specific attribution of HL to a king (in that it perhaps demonstrates a less centralized role for the king with regards to law at Hatti).

By far the majority of the law collections dealt with here are explicitly acknowledged as the work of a king.[133] Within Egypt both EH and ND are specifically linked to a king, as is the more fragmentary Elephantine decree. Within Mesopotamia it is only the supposed school exercises LOx, SLEx and SLHF along with MAL which are not specifically connected to a ruler. The HL are also not explicitly connected to a ruler. What significance does this have? One is tempted to see in HL's lack of connection a link to their less centralized form of rule as opposed to that of Mesopotamia and Egypt and thus to postulate a lesser role for the Hittite king in regards to the establishment of law in society. The main obstacle to such a contention is obviously a similar lack of connection in MAL.[134]

It is possible that this obstacle could be removed if it were found that MAL were closer in function to the so called "scribal exercises"[135] from Mesopotamia which also had no explicit royal authorship.[136] The mention

[133] Though in some instances we do not know which particular king *e.g.* the debate surrounding the authorship of LE and LU and the question about whether LX belongs to LU or is a separate collection. See Kramer, "Ur-Nammu". There is also uncertainty as to whether the Elephantine Decree was issued by Ramesses III. All four texts have clear indication that they were nevertheless connected with a specific ruler.

[134] The only section of the collection external to the laws themselves is the appearance of a colophon with a year name at the end of Tablet A. The existence of colophons *etc.* at the end of other tablets of MAL is a possibility due to breaks at the end of each tablet (except perhaps M and O).

[135] *i.e.* LOx, SLHF and SLEx.

[136] See our discussion of this issue in the next section. Westbrook, "Character," 18 sees all collections as associated with rulers as well as having a place in the

of reforms within the Hittite Laws could be used as an argument not to treat them as a scribal exercise or private collection of laws. Earlier it was posited that the lack of explicit mention of reform in Mesopotamian texts possibly reflected cultural rather than functional differences. If this is the case one could not rule out a similar function for MAL to that of HL on the basis of such omission. The existence of explicit royal attribution within MAPD may be due to a difference between the nature and content of this text and MAL. MAPD's context within the royal household and therefore its more immediate connection to the ruler could explain this difference. Another possibility arises which is mere speculation. It is possible that MAL were originally collected in a period before Assyrian imperialism and increased centralization had affected the framing of the law collection. This contention may not be well supported by the evidence given the superscription of tablet A placing our copy in a year during the reign of Tiglath-pileser I (1114–1076). It is a general scholarly consensus that our copies are "eleventh century B.C.E copies of fourteenth-century originals".[137] Though Assyrian society was less centralized and its foreign policy less imperial at this stage[138] it would be somewhat of a stretch to argue that it reflected the Old Assyrian system of rule (and the important role of the council) more closely than the later centralization of the Neo-Assyrian Empire. For now we are left with the possibility that the existence (or lack thereof) of an explicit connection to a king within the law collections may also be related to a cultural difference between the Hittites and Egypt and Mesopotamia. This difference would revolve around the conception of the role of the king with regards to the law.[139] The problematic nature of MAL, without an explicit attribution to a king, may be due to the nature of the copies found or its original production in the fourteenth century, during or before the gradual development of new conceptions of Assyrian kingship. The lack of an explicit attribution does not necessarily imply that the laws were not of royal origin. Of course such an approach would leave this writer open to the charge of basing an argument on the evidence of absence in the case of HL in contrast to ignoring it with regards to MAL.

---

scribal curriculum.

[137] Roth, *Law Collections*, 154 and Sophie Lafont, "Middle Assyrian Period," in *A History of Ancient Near Eastern Law* (ed. Raymond Westbrook; vol. 1; Handbook of Oriental Studies 72/1; Leiden: Brill, 2003), 521.

[138] Especially before the reign of Ashur-uballit I (1363–1328).

[139] The following discussion of the nature and function of the law collections will help elucidate whether this is a likely possibility. The discussion of the laws which mention the king in a later section will also be relevant.

The final aspect of the framing of the laws to be discussed here concerns the prologue and epilogue attached to some of the collections. There is a correlation between the collections which have some form of text attached before or after the legal section of the document and those which attribute its production to a royal source.[140] Again, it is the texts with the supposed school origins which do not have any form of introduction, conclusion, heading, colophon *etc. i.e.* SLEx, SLHF and LOx, nor do MAL[141] and HL. This is of course more than a coincidence as it is these non-legal sections of the collections which tend to mention royal involvement in the production of the text. It is then a question of whether the absence of such a section is merely a difference of structure or whether it reflects a broader worldview concerning the role of the king with regard to the production of law. It is difficult to decide given the fact one must proceed from an argument from silence to argue in this way. There is no evidence to suggest that all collections originally did have a prologue and epilogue. The only ways to argue for a uniform structure for ancient Near Eastern law collections are to severely restrict the collections being looked at[142] or to speculate as to some hypothetical original text with uniform structure as the source material for the diverse collections we have.[143] Neither option attempts to explain the diversity actually extant in the texts available for study. That said there are some obvious similarities among some texts.

It has long been noted that among the ancient Near Eastern law collections, LH, LL and LU share many similarities. One of the most obvious similarities is the form and structure of these collections. The existence of a prologue and epilogue surrounding a collection of casuistically framed laws has led many to see these three collections as belonging to the same tradition of Babylonian legal science. There is certainly much to be said for this idea when one compares the prologues and epilogues of these works. A brief perusal of the three prologues shows many similarities both in themes and phrasing. All three have an opening mention of the granting of kingship

---

[140] It must be said that mention of the king in the title of AE is reconstructed but highly probable.

[141] Though there is a colophon of sorts with a date at the end of Tablet A.

[142] *e.g.* only LL, LH and LU (if one accepts the identification of LX as its epilogue)

[143] *e.g.* Eckart Otto's approach. See bibliography for a list of his works. Even then his definition of a law collection must be restricted to the classic collections: LU, LL, LE, LH, MAL and HL, of which only MAL Tablet A and LOx fit the description of the structure of the original text without doctoring.

by Anu and Enlil to their city deity[144] who then appoints them as king. Each of the prologues mentions the king: establishing justice; eliminating injustice; providing well-being for their people; establishing freedom from enemies or oppression; being loyal to his city; protecting the weak from the strong;[145] doing service to the gods through offerings or temple building. Each of the prologues also ends with the phrase: "At that time", before giving the casuistically formulated laws.[146] The most obvious difference within these prologues is the length of that in LH. Much of this extra space is filled with epithets of Hammurabi developing the above themes in more detail. He spends much time listing his pious acts *e.g.* re/building of temples or the city. These are themes we find in the prologues of both LU and LL also. One theme that is far more highly developed within the prologue of LH, however, is his military prowess. There is not even the hint of claims to be: "the onslaught of the four regions of the world" in LU or LL. Though LU does mention the liberation of cities from Anshan, and LL the liberation of Nippur, Ur and Isin, this is not a major theme in their prologues.[147] For Hammurabi, however, the praise of his military prowess is as prominent as the mention of his pious deeds or good rule. One need not look further than his political context, with him as head of a very large empire won by military conquest, to explain the difference. This military focus is also found in his inscriptions,[148] and is reflected in the heavy emphasis on the curses in his treaty negotiations.[149]

---

[144] Anu's name is broken in LL's prologue but its reconstruction is highly probable.

[145] This theme is not well developed in LL's prologue, but this may be due to the loss of two columns.

[146] Again, this is reconstructed in the break for LL so it is possibly absent. Given the mass of other similar features it is perhaps most likely that this phrase was present originally.

[147] The liberation in LL is possibly akin to the economic liberation of the *mišarum* decrees rather than any military activity.

[148] See *RIME* 4 and specifically those referred to by Marc Van De Mieroop, *King Hammurabi of Babylon: A Biography* (Malden, Ma.: Blackwell, 2005), 124–127.

[149] See Van De Mieroop's description, *Hammurabi*, 21 and Weeks', *Admonition and Curse*, 23–26.

The epilogues of these three collections[150] have only one feature common to all. That is the existence of a curse for any who efface the inscription. This section is again greatly expanded in LH. The epilogue of LL shares some other similarities with LH. Like LH, LL also includes a blessing for him who does not damage the stele he has set up. The epilogues of both also begin with a section declaring the accomplishments of the rulers in accordance with their command from the sun-god to establish justice, set up fair judicial procedure, and to bring well-being to the people. LL again repeats the claim to have gotten rid of injustice, whereas LH mentions how he has put an end to war by annihilating enemies. Again we have a military focus in Hammurabi that is lacking elsewhere. Why do we have this military focus in the prologue and epilogue to a collection of laws? It is possible to relate the giving of the law collection to claims of piety given its relation to a command of a god and its role in exercising good rule over the people of the city. It is more difficult to understand why military conquests make up such a focus. Even though this ought to be admitted, the intimate connection of the actual laws with many sections of the prologue and epilogue of LH, so amply demonstrated by Hurowitz,[151] should make one hesitate before ascribing a lesser role to the laws in the purpose of the text. More about this later. What of the other collections with attachments at their beginning and/or end?

RU does not have a formal prologue, laws, epilogue distinction but there are many similarities to LU, LL and LH in the framing of the reforms it recounts. Uru-inimgina recounts his building works for Nin-Girsu then goes on to describe a situation where injustice was rife. This is followed by the mention of his divine selection for kingship and his establishment of justice at the command of the god. The account of the abuses which were in existence and then rectified share many similarities to those mentioned in the prologue to LU *e.g.* the control of the sea-captains and the misappropriation of sheep. The claims to have established freedom and to have protected the weak also have clear resonance in the prologues of the three col-

---

[150] Assuming LX as LU's epilogue. See discussion above in 2.1.1. For a very different theory as to the epilogue contained in LX see S. J. Lieberman, "Nippur: City of Decisions," in *Nippur at the Centennial* (ed. Maria de Jong Ellis; Rencontre Assyriologique Internationale 35; Philadelphia: Occasional Publication of the Samuel Noah Kramer Fund, 1992), 127–36.

[151] Victor Hurowitz, *Inu Anum Ṣirum: Literary Studies in the Non-Juridical Section of Codex Hammurabi* (Philadelphia: Occasional Publications of the Samuel Noah Kramer Fund, 1994).

lections mentioned earlier (especially to the phrasing of LU). RU ends with the mention of the building of a canal.

The framing of these four collections all reflect a very similar world-view concerning the king's place in regard to the giving of law. They also share some more general aspects of what may be a particularly southern Mesopotamian view of kingship. The laws in each case seem to be given by the king at the behest of the gods. The similarities in the framing of these laws lead this writer to postulate an internal development within southern Mesopotamia regarding how laws were presented. Uru-inimgina makes use of a typical building inscription to recount his judicial activities. Picking up on this idea, the succeeding royal authors of southern Mesopotamian law collections frame their collections within the structure of a building inscription, developing themes both from RU and other building inscriptions regarding kingship and law. If one compares these collections with the building inscriptions of the time there are some interesting similarities. For example, compare the inscriptions of Hammurabi.[152] After a beginning statement concerning the gods granting him kingship we see the phrase, "at that time" as in LH.[153] In the other inscriptions this is used to introduce a narrative of building activities. In LH, the phrase instead introduces Hammruabi's *dinat mišarim*. A similar development seems to lead to the inclusion of military conquests in building inscriptions which later develops into the annal form. Whatever the details of the internal development, it would be a brave scholar who would deny the probability that these texts (RU, LU, LL and LH) were influenced by their predecessors, reflect very similar conceptions about kingship and the law and possibly display an internal development in the structuring of the presentation of the legal achievements of a king. What of the other collections?

LE has a Sumerian superscription at its beginning which, while very different in structure to the prologues of the three collections just mentioned, shares some themes. There is mention of ascension to kingship and the role of the gods Enlil and Ninazu.[154] As with LH, there is also mention of military conquests before the listing of the laws. There is little room on

---

[152] *e.g.* those translated by Douglas R. Frayne in *COS* 2.107: 256–58. More comprehensively see Douglas R. Frayne, *Old Babylonian Period: 2003–1595 B.C.* (The Royal Inscriptions of Mesopotamia, Early Period 4; Toronto: University of Toronto, 1990).

[153] See the use of this phrase in Samsu-iluna's inscriptions also, *e.g.* as translated by Frayne in *COS* 2.108: 258 or *RIME* 4.

[154] Unfortunately the text is a little fragmentary at this point so definite statements as to the significance of this section cannot be made.

the tablet for the king of Eshnunna to have boasted of his piety or role in the establishment of justice in the land. Interestingly, as LU mentions the standardization of weights and measures in its prologue, the superscription of LE is followed by standardized exchange rates for commodities. There is no epilogue for LE though in one copy there is a blank of 6–8 lines where a scribe may have placed a colophon as in MAPD, MAL A or SLEx.

The Old Babylonian edicts also begin with a Sumerian superscription. This merely states that the text is the document of when the king established equity for the land.

The Middle Assyrian Palace Decrees have a specific introduction for each decree (or set of them). This introduction merely mentions the name of the king, his title (*e.g.* overseer or king) and his father's name and title, followed by the statement that he "issued a decree for the/his palace". Though these certainly give us helpful information as to the origin and purpose of the original decrees, these are very different to the prologues of the laws mentioned earlier. There is possibly a colophon at the end of the collection which refers to the whole collection of decrees. It outlines that violating the decrees is a punishable offence and seems to demand the regular proclamation of the decrees.[155] It is possible that, rather than being a colophon, this is a final decree of Tiglath-pileser I. The existence of such a demand within biblical law and Hittite treaties does not help us to decide whether the request to have the decrees read out refers only to Tiglath-pileser's decrees or whether it refers to the whole document. The latter does seem preferable. An eponym year is attached at the bottom of the tablet, dating the text to the reign of Tiglath-pileser I.

The Egyptian texts at our disposal are uniquely framed in that they portray the legal sections of their texts as the direct command of the pharaoh. Though one clearly pictures other decrees as coming from the mouth of the king, none of them explicitly state as much. EH portrays itself as a transcription of the direct speech of the king.[156] It is written in first person as are the prologues and epilogues of RU, LU, LL and LH. These latter texts, however, do not refer to the legal sections as "commands", nor do they address a particular audience as does ND and the Elephantine decree which have a list of officials addressed. ND and the Elephantine decree both contain this brief address, stating that the decree was issued in the

---

[155] Though the text is broken at this point.

[156] *Face principale*, line 13.

royal court to the various officials. This is followed by a statement that "the decree says: His Majesty has commanded . . .".[157]

There are a number of similarities between these texts and those of southern Mesopotamia with the full prologue and epilogue. EH has two introductory sections before the legal and administrative sections. There is also an epilogue of sorts at the end. In the first introductory section Haremhab boasts of having had the throne bestowed upon him, of doing good for the land, bringing it righteousness,[158] expelling injustice and oppression. These are all themes we have seen in the southern Mesopotamian collections we discussed initially. Again, we have a significant difference in this Egyptian text. Whereas in Mesopotamia the king sets forth the laws at the behest of a god,[159] here we are told that Haremhab "took counsel in his heart".[160] It would seem Egyptian law is conceived as coming from the pharaoh in a more direct fashion than in Mesopotamia. Haremhab boasts of traveling through the land, appointing judges of good character and setting forth the laws (*hpw*) for them.[161] The epilogue of EH concludes with an exhortation to heed his commands so as to set the land in order and get rid of the oppression which he has taken to heart. It is self-glorifying. He even wishes himself a long life.

The Nauri decree contains a long prologue and ends with an epilogue of sorts outlining the reason Seti has put forth this decree. He states that he did so as an act of piety towards Osiris so that people will praise the god and in return the god will grant Seti a long life and rule. Similar to the prologues of LU, LL and LH, the long prologue details Seti's appointment to the throne by the gods, praise of them and the listing of pious deeds for them.[162] The Elephantine decree is broken at the end. There is some evidence that its conclusion contained the name of Ramesses III but we know little more than that about it.

Other than these additions to the laws themselves we have a few colophons identifying the scribe who wrote/copied the text *e.g.* SLEx, MAL

---

157 Slightly reconstructed for the Elephantine decree on the basis of ND.

158 Ma'at.

159 Whether the god is understood to provide the laws or just to guard the principles behind them is unclear.

160 Obverse, line 10.

161 Left side (Pflüger, "Haremhab," names this the left side, whereas Kruchten, *Horemheb*, sees it as "*face latérale droite*"), column 4.

162 As mentioned earlier, this long introductory section of ND is not found in Edgerton's edition, but is found in Griffith's, "Abydos Decree".

tablet A, and perhaps MAPD in the break.[163] This tells us very little about the framing of the original text. It just shows us that the collection was thought worthy to be copied for a variety of possible reasons whether academic or practical. It may well reflect a scholarly or school origin of some sort for some texts, but this must be decided on some other basis.

In the framing of these laws then there are a number of features which may be explained as cultural specificities. These range from the Old Babylonian (and lower Mesopotamian) use of the "because clause" to differences which may reflect a different worldview with regards to conceptions of kingship; more specifically the king's role in the production and/or promulgation of law. This may be reflected in things such as the existence and content of additional text before or after the laws themselves,[164] the related question of whether the collection is specifically connected to a ruler; the presence or absence of historical details and perhaps most significantly, the existence of explicit acknowledgement of change within the law collection. To be able to make firmer conclusions about such things it is important to take into account, as far as is possible, the nature and purpose of these various collections. For example, the contention that the Hittite acknowledgement of change within their laws is a reflection of a broader cultural conception would be made less likely if it were found that this feature demonstrated instead that HL were a closer reflection of the law of practice than the collections which did not display such a feature. In a similar vein, the nature of MAL influences the interpretation of the brutality within it. Though it must be said that even if the collection were of a private nature, the laws themselves may well reflect royal rulings of some form. They would thus be connected to kingship, rather than Assyrian culture more generally. This study will now turn to this vexed topic and see what can be made of the data available.

---

[163] Roth, *Law Collections*, 56 thinks that LE may have also had something similar at the end. Numerous copies of LH (Late Old Babylonian and after) also display such a colophon see *e.g.* that in Finkelstein, "A Late Old Babylonian Copy of the Laws of Hammurapi," *Journal of Cuneiform Studies* 21 (1967): 48, as do some copies of the Hittite Laws (all Neo-Hittite or later), see Hoffner, *Laws of the Hittites*, 98 and 160.

[164] Variously termed prologues, epilogues, introductions, conclusions, superscriptions, preambles, colophons *etc.*

2.1.4 Nature, Function and Purpose

2.1.4.1 Introduction

This section aims to assess, as far as is possible, the nature, function and purpose of the various texts under discussion. It was mentioned in the introduction that there has been much literature written on this topic. The law collections dealt with here are generally lumped into three groups. Firstly, there are the more formal law collections (sometimes referred to as codes for ease of reference and distinction from the other texts),[165] then the edicts or decrees[166] and then the texts which are seen to be scholarly exercises or school texts.[167] Most of the discussion as to the nature and function of these texts has focused on LH and assumed or implied that the findings were legitimate for the other formal ancient Near Eastern law collections.[168] This is not a necessary assumption. In our discussion we will attempt to analyze both the traditional classification of these texts and the legitimacy of importing ideas about LH to understand the other formal collections or "codes". It is hoped that this will help to clarify how it is possible to distinguish the different text types and their functions and perhaps also question the simplistic way this has sometimes been presented in the past.

Since the discovery of LH some hundred years ago there have been numerous theories as to the nature and purpose of this text. Theories have been offered which range from seeing LH as: a prescriptive code of laws;[169] a law collection binding on the courts which were given to unify the empire;[170] at once codification and reform;[171] a series of amendments[172] and

[165] *i.e.* LU (and LX), LL, LE, LH, MAL, HL as distinguished from the decrees, edicts and others.

[166] AE, MAPD, EH and ND. RU is sometimes included in this list, *e.g.* by Westbrook, "Cuneiform Law," 214; Westbrook and Woodard, "Tudhaliya IV," 641, n. 3.

[167] LOx, SLEx and SLHF.

[168] *e.g.* Westbrook's statement "Cuneiform Law," 201–2 that "the debate . . . has centered mainly around Codex Hammurabi, but its conclusions are assumed to apply to the codes in general."

[169] Scheil, *Textes élamites.*

[170] Joseph Klíma, "La perspective historique des lois Hammourabiennes," *Compte rendus de l'Académie des Inscription et belles lettres* (1973): 306–7; Edwards, *Oldest Laws*, 12; A. Leo Oppenheim, *Ancient Mesopotamia: Portrait of a Dead Civilization* (rev. ed.; Chicago: University of Chicago Press, 1977), 231.

[171] Koschaker, *Rechtsvergleichende*, 2.

[172] E. A. Speiser, "Early Law and Civilization," *Canadian Bar Review* 31 (1953):

restatements of common law;[173] a reflection of common law with no statutory force;[174] a guide to courts' decisions without having statutory force *e.g.* a private lawbook;[175] an expression of rules for judges rather than individuals;[176] representation of law but not legal reality;[177] a scholarly text/part of Mesopotamian scientific literature;[178] royal apologia[179] or political propaganda;[180] a monumental commemoration of Hammurabi's achievements;[181] originally a training manual for judges appropriated for a political purpose;[182] a collection of the legal decisions of Hammurabi from his role as judge;[183] legislation for new circumstances due to change in society;[184] a

866.

[173] Driver and Miles, *Babylonian Laws*, vol. 1, 45 hold to LH as both amendment and restatement, as does Yaron, "The Nature of the Early Mesopotamian Collections of Laws: Another Approach," in *La Codification des lois dans l'antiquité: Actes du Colloque de Strasbourg, 27–29 Novembre 1997* (ed. Edmond Levy; Travaux du centre de recherche sur le Proche-Orient et la Grèce antiques 16; Paris: De Boccard, 2000), 65–76, Postgate, *Early Mesopotamia*, 289, and Shalom M. Paul, *Studies in the Book of the Covenant in the Light of Cuneiform and Biblical Law* (Vetus Testamentum Supplement 18; Leiden: Brill, 1970), 24–25.

[174] Westbrook, (see any number of his works *e.g.* "Character") though he blends this with other functions *e.g.* he sees LH as a model of good judging and as having its origins in Mesopotamian scientific literature.

[175] Marian San Nicolò, *Die Schlussklauseln der altbabylonsichen Kauf und Tauschverträge* (2nd ed. New introduction and notes by Herbert Petschow; Munich: C. H. Beck, 1974 [1922]), 9–10.

[176] Mackenzie, "Formal Aspect," 36–37.

[177] Eilers, *Gesetzesstele Chammurabis*, 8.

[178] Kraus, "Ein zentrales Problem," 293–95; Bottéro, "Code"; Westbrook, *e.g.* "Character," 17–18, or "Codification and Canonization," 15–36.

[179] Finkelstein, "Ammiṣaduqa's Edict," 103.

[180] *e.g.* Norman Yoffee, "Context and Authority," 107.

[181] Renger, "Noch einmal," 51 and "Hammurapis Stele 'Konig der Gerichtigkeit': Zur Frage von Recht und Gesetz in der altbabylonischen Zeit," *Die Welt des Orients* 8 (1976): 228.

[182] Otto, "Aspects of Legal Reforms," 160–63.

[183] W. F. Leemans, "King Hammurabi as Judge," in *Symbolae Iuridicae et Historicae Martino David Dedicatae* (ed. J. A. Ankum, R. Feenstra, and W. F. Leemans; Studia Documenta ad Iura Orientis Antiqui Pertinentia 2; Leiden: Brill, 1968), 107–29. Kraus, "Ein zentrales Problem," acknowledges this possibility to some extent.

[184] Wilfried G. Lambert, "Morals in Ancient Mesopotamia," *Jaarbericht Ex Oriente Lux* 15 (1958): 187 as followed by Walton, *Israelite Literature*, 87.

means to preserve law as a living tradition[185] *etc.* Some blend a number of these functions,[186] some have given up hope of ever figuring out the nature, function and purpose of LH and the other formal collections in general,[187] while others are so sick of the discussion they have called for scholars to drop it and talk about something else.[188]

The development of some of these ideas was discussed in the introductory chapter. Rather than retrace this development in more detail, what we aim to do here is assess the various arguments in relation to the evidence. Though an analysis of the nature and function of LH has been done before we wish to bring it all together and hopefully add something new to the discussion. Despite the numerous discussions about the function of LH, none of them have been done in the context of comparing the nature and function of law collections across the ancient Near East.[189] Far less discussion has centered on the nature and function of the other law collections. The conclusions drawn from the study of LH seem to hold sway over such discussions. In dealing with each collection this writer hopes to highlight what it is that enables us to judge the nature and function of ancient Near Eastern law collections.

2.1.4.2 Evidence used regarding LH

To begin it may be helpful to outline what kinds of evidence have been brought to bear on this discussion. There are many angles from which scholars have come at the questions surrounding the nature, function and purpose of LH. Within these, arguments have focused on issues such as: the relation of LH to the documents of legal practice (and/or letters of the king regarding juridical matters) from the Old Babylonian period; the form and structure of LH; the existence and content of the prologue and epilogue (including the issue of intended audience and perhaps the relation of these sections to the contents of the laws themselves); the laws' function as

---

[185] Donald J. Wiseman, "The Laws of Hammurabi Again," *Journal of Semitic Studies* 7 (1962):166.

[186] Westbrook.

[187] Roth, "Mesopotamian Legal Traditions and the Laws of Hammurabi," *Chicago-Kent Law Review* 70 (1995): 13.

[188] *e.g.* Paul Eugene Dion, review of E. Levy (ed.), *La Codification des lois dans l'antiquité*, *Journal of the American Oriental Society* 121 (2001): 315.

[189] Except perhaps in some collaborative works, multi-authored volumes or proceedings of conferences *e.g.* Westbrook (ed.), *A History*, and Levy (ed.), *La codification.*

a monumental inscription (including its find place and original setting/s); the existence of copies of LH; the relationship of LH to previous Mesopotamian law collections or other sources; problems in applying the laws/problems of logical consistency within them; the non-comprehensive nature of the laws; the historical context for the giving of the law collection. A study of the nature and function of LH raises most of the issues[190] regarding the nature and function of the other collections. Despite this the present writer feels it is best to start this discussion with an analysis of the edicts/decrees as they compare to LH and the "monumental" law collections.[191] This will enable a questioning of the usefulness of some of the arguments put forward to decide upon the nature, function and purpose of LH. This in turn will stop this writer from importing conclusions made about LH from such faulty argumentation in order to interpret the nature, function and purpose of other collections. The study will then proceed to analyze some of the other evidence used to decide upon LH's nature, function and purpose, followed by an analysis of the other formal law collections and the scholarly texts.

2.1.4.3 Westbrook's definition of edicts/decrees

Westbrook sees a number of distinctive factors within the group of texts which he sees as edicts or decrees.[192] What he sees as the characteristic features of decrees is that they have an actual effect on legal relations,[193] their content is restricted to matters such as debt-release, and economic and administrative reform,[194] and they tend to mention past abuses and the king's correction of them.[195] He contrasts this to the formal law collections which he does not see as having any effect on legal relations and which cover a broader range of topics. Though there is much to commend this theory, there are a number of points of contention. His inclusion of RU within the

---

[190] The Hittite Laws do raise another issue concerning the recognition of legal change within their collection that some have used to argue for a closer relationship between HL and legal practice than the other ancient Near Eastern law collections.

[191] LU, LL, LX. RU will also be discussed.

[192] RU, AE, EH, Edict of Telepinu and Edict of Tudhaliya IV, to which we will add in this discussion ND, ED and MAPD.

[193] Westbrook and Woodard, "Edict of Tudhaliya IV," 641 and Westbrook, "Cuneiform Law," 214–217.

[194] Westbrook and Woodard, "Edict of Tudhaliya IV," 641 and Westbrook, "Character," 15–16 where "constitutional law" is added.

[195] Westbrook and Woodard, "Edict of Tudhaliya IV," 641 and n. 4.

genre of decrees is not accepted by all. There is a fervent debate over the purpose and legal effects of RU.[196] There are many scholars who see this text as royal propaganda in analogy with Finkelstein's Lower Mesopotamian "law codes".[197] Another problem with Westbrook's arguments regarding decrees is that he has read conclusions from the study of AE and the effect of the *mišarum* edicts into the other sources. If one were to try and treat this group of collections as a literary genre there would be even more difficulties, especially given the length of the non-legal sections in texts other than AE.

2.1.4.4 Past abuses as reason for reform?

Let us begin with the point Westbrook makes least of. Though he claims it is "typical" for edicts and decrees to list past abuses or reasons reform is needed, a number of texts in this group do not do so *e.g.* AE and MAPD, or can be interpreted otherwise *e.g.* ND and ED which state that they are set up in order to prevent certain things happening.[198] The monumental law collections also claim to eradicate enmity, violence, injustice *etc*,[199] and are thus not to be distinguished on this basis.

2.1.4.5 Subject matter of edicts and collections fixedly different?

The claim that edicts cover the limited range of topics enumerated above in contrast to the law collections is also questionable. For example, should we accept the claim that because the legal sections of the Egyptian decrees might possibly deal only with offences committed by officials or people in positions of authority that it reflects only an administrative reform? We are not even sure that all the legal clauses of these documents are restricted to abuses of this kind.[200] Given the fact that the law collections also cover similar abuses, what are we to make of such a distinction anyway?[201] While it is true that AE deals solely with measures related to the issuing of a *mišarum* or debt-release decree, ND and ED are addressed to officials and relate to their actions towards a particular estate with links to the royal administra-

---

[196] See the references supplied above in note 122.

[197] *e.g.* Edzard, "Soziale Reformen" and Yoffee, "Context and Authority," 99.

[198] This does not necessarily imply that these were current abuses, though that is possible.

[199] See the later discussion of the non-legal sections of the law collections.

[200] Though it does seem fairly likely.

[201] *e.g.* LH 33–34. To be fair, Westbrook does admit that the formal collections can include the subject matter of the edicts and decrees, "Cuneiform Law," 217.

tion, RU seems to cover economic and administrative reforms, the Hittite texts do not fit so neatly. In both the Edict of Telepinu and of Tudhaliya IV there are sections not relating to economic or administrative matters. For example, the Edict of Telepinu contains provisions for punishments in the case of homicide or sorcery.[202] While the law dealing with sorcery speaks specifically of offenders within the royal family and the law of murder could be linked to Telepinu's recounting of royal assassinations and usurpations surrounding positioning for the throne and his succession reforms, this law is framed as generally applicable. When we come to the Edict of Tudhaliya IV the issue is complicated. Originally there were sections of this text which were seen as similar to those covered by formal law collections. For example, von Schuler treated the text as a law collection parallel to HL which was intended as legislation.[203] This was on the basis of a number of provisions which dealt with topics such as theft and murder. Westbrook will have none of this and has published an alternative translation which squashes these provisions back into the purview of an edict, *e.g.* he forces the law regarding murder and blood-payment into a provision concerning debt-release.[204]

2.1.4.6 Edicts applicable in contrast to collections?

Westbrook's claim that the edicts (in contrast to the formal law collections) had an effect on legal reality is based on the external evidence available that the Old Babylonian *mišarum* decrees had such an effect. For none of these other edicts/decrees do we possess evidence which confirms their applicability in the same way.[205] This similarity has been assumed on the basis of the other similarities between these texts (such as the content). Interestingly, Finkelstein and Kraus argue that AE was not the actual text of the *mišarum* edict but only a guide for officials in its execution.[206] Kraus went even fur-

---

[202] Hoffner is so convinced of their similarity with the formal law collections that he adds these two provisions at the end of his translation of HL in Roth, *Law Collections*, 237–38.

[203] Schuler, "Hethitische Königserlässe," 445.

[204] Westbrook and Woodard, "Edict of Tudhaliya IV," 643.

[205] Though there is of course the evidence of Hittite succession practices after Telepinu and the economic and administrative documents from Lagash. The latter are extremely difficult to use to assess the effect of RU, especially given the difficulties in translation of RU. See the discussion of Foster, "Social Reform". He does raise the possibility that one of Uru-inimgina's reforms can be traced in the sources, 238.

[206] See Finkelstein, "Ammisaduqa's Edict," 92 and Kraus, *Ein Edikt* and see also *Königliche*.

ther pointing out that there was little correlation between the kinds of contracts covered by the edicts and those found in actual documents.[207] Finkelstein argued that the more general pronouncements contained in the texts of the *mišarum* act were "for the most part pious hopes and moral resolve rather than effective law", and he was happy to see such regulations as being incorporated into law collections.[208] It would seem that discerning the applicability of edicts, even the *mišarum* ones, is as problematic as the case of LH. Perhaps it is better to discuss any evidence within the texts themselves as to their intended purpose. It is pertinent at this point to discuss the usefulness of arguments put forward about LH's nature, purpose and function from the basis of its relation to the documents of practice.

As mentioned, one of the reasons LH's legal function has been questioned is the relationship of the legal provisions within it as compared to the documents of practice. Thus far no documents from Old Babylonian legal practice have been found which cite LH as an authority for the decision in their case. Much was made of this by Landsberger in assessing the function of LH.[209] Some have argued for citation of LH in letters.[210] Some have argued for specific references to LH, other decrees or the decisions within other letters on the basis of references to "the words of the stele"[211] or *ṣimdat šarrim*.[212] Veenhof uses such an argument to create numerous Old Babylonian decrees for which we have no other evidence.[213] Given the fact

---

207 Kraus, *Ein Edikt* . See discussion of Finkelstein, "Ammisaduqa's Edict," 94.

208 Finkelstein, "Ammisaduqa's Edict," 102.

209 Landsberger, "Die babylonischen Termini," 221. This observation has been repeated *ad infinitum* in the literature *e.g.* Kraus, "Ein zentrales Problem"; Horst Klengel, *König Hammurabi und der alltag Babylons* (2nd ed.; Darmstadt: Wissenschaftliche Buchgesellschaft, 1992), 184–264; Otto, "Aspects of Legal Reforms"; Renger, "Noch einmal," 35; Niels Peter Lemche, "Justice in Western Asia in Antiquity, or: Why No Laws Were Needed!" *Chicago-Kent Law Review* 70 (1995): 1698.

210 E. Szlechter, "La "loi" dans la Mesopotamie ancienne," *Revue Internationale des droits de l'antiquité* 12 (1965): 55–77; W. F. Preiser, "Zur rechtlichen Natur der altorientalischen 'Gesetze'," in *Festschrift für Karl Englisch* (ed. P. Bockelmann, A. Kaufmann, and U. Klugg; Frankfurt: Main, 1969), 17–36; Leemans, "King Hammurabi as Judge".

211 Hurowitz, *Inu Anum Ṣirum*, 13 mentions the existence of at least 4 such references. They do not seem to match up well with LH.

212 Postgate, *Early Mesopotamia*, 291. See discussion of Renger, "Konig der Gerichtigkeit," 230.

213 Klaas R. Veenhof, "The Relation between Royal Decrees and 'Law Codes'

ṣimdatum can mean "regulation", "decree",[214] "enactment", "laws",[215] or perhaps even just "decision",[216] we should be cautious in our interpretation of what is being referred to. A possible interpretation seems to be that what are being referred to are the other decisions of the king within letters he has sent.[217] That said, we cannot rule out that LH could be referred to by some of these references. Though Hammurabi never refers to his collection as a *ṣimdatum*, LH is referred to as *ṣimdat Ḫammurabi* in a colophon of a late Old Babylonian manuscript.[218]

At least one Old Babylonian letter refers to wages recorded on a stele. The wages referred to are three times that outlined in LH. Some have concluded therefore that LH does not reflect legal reality at the time.[219] Roth has questioned this conclusion, mentioning that LH may have set out minimum wages rather than maximum.[220] Whatever the correct interpretation, we do have evidence that laws set up on a stele could be appealed to in the daily exercise of law.[221] Despite this possibility, some have argued that the reason we do not have citation of LH in the documents of practice was that it was not the practice of the day to cite such collections.[222] If so, one would think the lack of citation could not be used to argue against the legal validity (or at least the reflection of legal actuality) of LH. This has not been

---

of the Old Babylonian Period," *Jaarbericht Ex Oriente Lux* 35/36 (1997–2000): 49–83.

[214] Jeremy Black, Andrew George and Nicholas Postgate, eds., *A Concise Dictionary of Akkadian* (SANTAG 5; Wiesbaden: Harrassowitz, 2000), 338.

[215] Roth, "Mesopotamian Legal Traditions," 21, n. 13.

[216] Bottéro, "Code," 180.

[217] A possibility raised by Veenhof himself, "Royal Decrees," 58. This does not exclude other possibilities. For further discussion of this term see Yaron, *Laws of Eshnunna*, 1988, 121–26 and references there.

[218] Finkelstein, "A Late Old Babylonian Copy of the Laws of Hammurapi," 42–44. Roth, "Mesopotamian Legal Traditions," 21, n. 13. We cannot tell whether this should be construed as a singular or plural *i.e.* "edict", "*fiat*" or "decisions", "laws" *etc.*

[219] R. F. G. Sweet, "On Prices, Moneys, and Money Uses in the Old Babylonian Period" (Ph.D. diss., University of Chicago, 1958), 104–11 as cited by Roth, *Law Collections*, 6, n. 1.

[220] *cf.* Roth, *Law Collections*, 5–7.

[221] See the comments of Roth, *Law Collections*, 7 and Postgate, *Early Mesopotamia*, 291.

[222] *e.g.* Klima, "La perspective," 308 and S. Demare, "La valeur de la loi dans les droits cuneiforms," *Archives de Philosophie de Droit* 32 (1987): 344.

the case. Much has been made of the fact that the documents from practice (contracts) do tend to cite *mišarum* acts.[223] Though Westbrook argues that lack of citation regarding LH does not reflect a difference between it and the actual practice of law, but the absence of legalism (*i.e.* self-conscious reflection on the reasoning behind a decision and the citation of authority for it),[224] he uses the fact that the *mišarum* acts are cited, in contrast to LH, to bolster the argument that LH was not binding on the courts.[225]

In reality, what can this lack of citation tell us about the function of LH?[226] It is not impossible that the lack of citation reflects a Mesopotamian *modus operandi* with regard to their legal system *i.e.* the law collections were not directly referred to in court. This does not necessarily imply that they played no role in the goings on. Its absence may even be due to a concern to keep legal documents brief. We cannot rule out the possibility that the legal cases presented in collections such as LH were discussed in the courtroom or at least influenced the reasoning of the judges in making their decision. It may just be that this reasoning process has not been recorded. Whatever the situation was, it would be unwise to make too many conclu-

---

[223] *e.g.* Westbrook, "Cuneiform Law," 215; Renger, "Noch einmal," 49; Finkelstein, "Ammisaduqa's Edict," 101 argues as much while being careful to distinguish the *mišarum* act itself from the Old Babylonian edicts such as AE which record such an event. H. Olivier, "The Effectiveness of the Old Babylonian Mesharum Decree," *Journal of North-West Semitic Studies* 12 (1984): 108, n. 9 notes that Kraus, *Ein Edikt*, had collected 61 references to *mišarum* enactments to which Edzard had added.

[224] Westbrook, "Codification and Canonization," 40.

[225] Westbrook, "Cuneiform Law," 216 and "Character," 19. It should be said that Westbrook does not see the citation of the *mišarum* acts as a reflection of legalism either. He asserts that the references are to the existence, not the content of such acts. See "Character," 19.

[226] We have not mentioned Veenhof's supposed examples of citation of the prologue and epilogue of LH in two letters, "Royal Decrees", 81–82, due to the dubious nature of such a citation. Veenhof argues that the mention of a concern not to let the strong oppress the weak in one letter and the expression of the idea that Marduk had appointed the king to provide justice in another is evidence that LH could have been cited. He uses this to argue that the reason the laws of LH were not cited was that they were not intended for legal usage. It is quite possible that these two letters are merely appealing to two well known ideological aspects of Babylonian kingship rather than directly quoting LH. The two letters in question do not frame their statements as quotes nor do they directly refer to LH. This writer struggles to see the logic of the argument presented.

sions based on the lack of citation of LH.[227] The economic nature of the *mišarum* acts (perhaps combined with the skewing of our Mesopotamian evidence towards economic and administrative documents and contracts) may also explain the perceived differences in citation practice between LH and *mišarum* decrees. Another possible explanation is that the lack of citation does reflect the lack of influence of LH on practice. This implies very little about the intended purpose of the collection.[228]

There has been an even more fervent debate surrounding the question of whether LH reflects actual legal practice. In an attempt to present Babylonian law on different subjects, the *Hammurabi's Gesetz* project collected the Old Babylonian legal documents from practice and organized them into modern legal topics, as well as presenting a translation of LH. It did not take too long before some questioned how well these two sets of evidence matched up. Eilers in particular argued that LH was at odds with the legal realities of the time and often differed in many respects with the records of actual legal cases.[229] Many scholars since have also analyzed the relationship of LH to these records. A number of different conclusions have been offered. Some see no great distinction between the two sets of evidence. An example is Petschow who argues that LH matches up with these documents.[230] If LH matches up with these documents what would that tell us? Is it merely a reflection of the legal realities?[231] Has it had an effect on legal practice *e.g.* as either reform or prescription of law?[232] Some have attempted to answer this question by comparing documents from before Hammurabi's time to those afterwards. In general it has been found that where LH matches up with the documents of practice, it does so for the periods both before and after its publication. The most famous example is Harris' and others' studies regarding the *naditu* laws.[233] Many have concluded then that

---

[227] See the comments of Renger, "Noch einmal," 35.

[228] See the comments of Lemche, "Justice in Western Asia," 1698.

[229] Eilers, *Gesetzesstele Chammurabis.*

[230] Petschow, "Die §§ 45 und 46 des Codex Hammurapi. Ein Beitrag zum altbabylonischen Bodenpachtrecht und zum Problem: Was ist der Codex Hammurapi?" *Zeitschrift für Assyriologie* 74 (1984): 181–212.

[231] Westbrook, "Cuneiform Law," 204–5.

[232] See Postgate, *Early Mesopotamia*, 291 who finds it difficult to imagine that the codes were simply ignored and did not affect practice.

[233] Rivkah Harris, "The naditu Laws of the Code of Hammurapi in Praxis," *Orientalia* 30 (1961): 163–9 or C. Janssen, "Samsu-iluna and the Hungry naditums," *Northern Akkad Project Reports* 5 (1991): 3–40.

LH was never intended as an influence on the legal realities of Babylonia.[234] Some, however, have argued that they can trace the influence of LH on the legal realities of the day.[235] Petschow's[236] and Yoffee's[237] contrasting positions in regards to LH's relationship to legal practice show that the conclusions based on such studies are not universally accepted. To this we must add several other problems.

Westbrook, who sees LH as reflecting legal reality, but not having a legislative function of any kind, argues that one must not base one's position regarding LH's function on its relationship to the legal documents of the time.[238] With this we agree. There are many problems in the use and interpretation of this evidence to decide upon the purpose of LH. Though the documents may be able to give us some idea of the effects of LH, they do not necessarily give us an insight into the intended purpose of it. An analogy has been offered by Weeks who asks: "Would you be able to discern the driving laws of a country by watching people drive?"[239] If it was found that the laws of Hammurabi's collection were not put into practice, it does not imply that he did not want them to be.[240] It may only record his failure to have his intentions realized. This could be explained a number of ways: opposition to reform based on traditional legal practice; the late date of his collection's publication and the dissolving of his empire not long after his death, the extraordinary or rare nature of many of the cases within his collection *etc.* The fact is, we do not know why the collection was not put into practice and we must look elsewhere again to help us decide upon the nature and purpose of the collection. Roth puts it more forcefully: "Ultimately such questions as Is there any concord between the formal law collections and the transactional contracts? or Is the daily operation of the law

---

234 *e.g.* Finkelstein, "Law in the Ancient Near East," *Encyclopedia Miqra'it* 5 (1968): 588–614, who argues that where LH matches up with the documents of practice it must be seen as a reflection of that practice not an influence on it. Followed by Yoffee, "Context and Authority," 103.

235 See Postgate's discussion regarding the influence of LH on shepherding contracts, *Early Mesopotamia*, 291.

236 LH matches with practice. See note 230.

237 Yoffee, "Context and Authority," 103 following Finkelstein, "Law in the Ancient Near East" where the supposed contradictions lead him to conclude that "Hammurabi never intended that his rules be accorded the status of practical law."

238 Westbrook, "Cuneiform Law," 204.

239 A question asked in his lecture on Hammurabi in the first-year course "Power and Persuasion in the Ancient Near East" at the University of Sydney.

240 Compare the conclusions of Yoffee and Finkelstein above, note 234.

constrained by the rules of the formal law collections? are not really answerable and, moreover, miss the intimate connections between law and society."[241]

She asserts the "independence as well as the independent value of the law collections and the law cases."[242] This said, the fact that the sections, which do seem to match up with legal practice, do so for the period before Hammurabi as well as afterwards may fit well with an explanation based on opposition because of adherence to a traditional legal practice *i.e.* the parts of LH which were reforming were generally ignored.

If such evidence is not able to determine LH's function, we must be careful not to read the conclusions based on this evidence into discussion regarding other collections, especially when such evidence is not available for them. Even in attempting to contrast LH to the Old Babylonian *mišarum* decrees, it has been found that the evidence of documents from practice has limited usefulness.

2.1.4.7 How does one decide the purposes of decrees or monumental law collections? What can the non-legal sections reveal regarding the nature, purpose and function of these texts?

Some scholars make much of the monumental nature of some of the Mesopotamian law collections and the existence of non-legal sections speaking of the actions of the king is used to argue for a propagandistic purpose for these texts as opposed to a legal one.[243] When we turn to the decrees and edicts, there are a number which were also monumental and contained similar non-legal sections. However, these factors are rarely used to argue against the legal intentions of these texts (except in the case of RU). While it may be wise to recognize that the monumental nature of texts such as ND, ED, EH, RU may have given these texts a similar function to other monumental texts,[244] this does not imply that they could not have also served a legal function. Perhaps a warning against the interpretation that a propagandistic or memorializing purpose was specific to monumental inscriptions should be seen in the fact that there is no overt evidence that RU, argued most commonly by scholars to have been mere rhetoric,[245] was ever set up on a stele.[246]

---

[241] Roth, *Law Collections*, 7.

[242] Roth, "Reading Law," 250.

[243] *e.g.* Finkelstein, "Ammisaduqa's Edict".

[244] *e.g.* celebration and memorialising of royal accomplishments.

[245] *e.g.* Diakonoff, "The Rise of the Despotic State in Ancient Mesopotamia," in

Within the non-legal sections of EH there are a number of themes similar to those found in the non-legal sections of the Mesopotamian material *e.g.* the claim to have set forth justice in the land,[247] to have prospered the people,[248] and the concluding wish that people will listen to the laws so that the land will be set in order.[249] He even mentions that the effect of his laws was that people praised his goodness.[250] Despite all these similarities with the monumental laws of Mesopotamia, including its being set up on a stele within a temple, the legal import of EH is rarely questioned. Some have argued that the laws put forth may have had propagandistic value and were aimed at popularizing Haremhab's rule, but they did not question that these laws were meant to be applied.[251]

The Nauri Decree has a very long introductory section full of epithets, the recounting of the divine election of the king, praise of the gods, recounting of pious deeds towards them, and the announcement that he has set a decree to look after the workers of the House of Osiris. He then addresses the decree to the Egyptian royal officials who may have some contact with the estate of Osiris in Cush (Nubia). He lists the offences he is preventing and then lists the laws. The epilogue tells us specifically that the decree was issued as an act of piety towards Osiris so that the god would look after the king.[252] The purposes are clearly stated, protection of the workers of a particular estate of Osiris and a religious purpose seen to give benefits to the king here and now. The Elephantine decree is similar in all extant sections so one would presume a similarity of purpose, though, of course, this may prove unfounded.

The Middle Assyrian Palace Decrees also seem to have a clear cut purpose. Each set of provisions begins with an introduction mentioning the name of the king, his father's name, their title/s and then the statement that the king "issued a decree". Sometimes the decree mentions a specific audi-

---

Ancient Mesopotamia (ed. I. M. Diakonoff; Moscow: Nauka, 1969), 173–203. Edzard "Soziale Reformen," 147. Yoffee, "Context and Authority," 99.

246 The copies we have consist of 5 on clay nails, cones and one on an oval clay plaque. See Wilcke, "Early Dynastic and Sargonic Periods," 142, n. 6. It certainly was an inscription of some sort rather than an internal memo of course.

247 In the prologue to the administrative section in Pflüger's edition.

248 End of section II in admin. sect., in Pflüger's edition.

249 Compare the precatives in LH.

250 End of section II in admin. sect. *cf.* the epilogue of LH and the injunction to the *awilum ḫablum* to praise Hammurabi.

251 *e.g.* Pfluger, "Haremhab," 268.

252 Griffiths, "Abydos Decree," 205.

ence such as "the palace personnel", "the court attendants", "his (the king's) palace", or, in the case of Tiglath-pileser I, "the palace commander of the Inner City, the palace herald, the chief of the water-sprinklers of the Processional Residence, the physician of the Inner Quarters, and the administrator of all the palaces of the entire extent of the country". Both this address and the content of the laws themselves lend weight to the idea these are specific decrees from these kings concerning the internal running of the royal palace/s. The possibility that the colophon of the collection decreed that the rulings should be read out regularly supports the likelihood of their applicability,[253] though the cumulative nature of the rulings from various kings including repetition and overlap may temper this conclusion somewhat.[254]

Through literary analysis of LH, including its structure, solid links have been made between it and contemporary royal inscriptions.[255] This may have implications for its function. Hurowitz' study does seem to imply that LH is unique, though there are certainly still similarities with other texts, especially LL and LU. These results question the idea that the genre of law collection included a tripartite structure.[256] Does this similarity to royal inscriptions imply a similarity of purpose? Is this purpose propagandistic? Some have used the monumental nature of LH, along with its links to contemporary inscriptions, to argue for various purposes for the text. It should be noted here that there is no unanimous agreement among scholars as to the purpose of such monumental inscriptions. Some of the purposes that are thus attributed to LH include: the memorializing of his accomplishments so he is remembered in the future;[257] propaganda for the subject peoples of his empire;[258] propaganda for his own people showing him to be the just king;[259] a self-representation to the gods of his fulfillment of his function as the just king.[260]

---

[253] See Roth, *Law Collections*, 208. See also the end of the Nuzi edict presented in the same work, p. 196.

[254] *Ibid.*, 196.

[255] *e.g.* Hurowitz, *Inu Anum Ṣirum*, 4, 15.

[256] For this opinion see Paul, *Studies in the Book of the Covenant*, 11–42.

[257] Roth, "Mesopotamian Legal Traditions," 17; Renger, "Noch einmal," 50–53; Hurowitz, *Inu Anum Ṣirum*, 103.

[258] Roth, "Mesopotamian Legal Traditions," passim, esp. 18, 24.

[259] Bottéro, "Code," and Kraus, "Ein zentrales Problem".

[260] Finkelstein, "Ammisaduqa's Edict," 103, Roth, "Mesopotamian Legal Traditions," 17, Hurowitz, *Inu Anum Ṣirum*, 30, 61

The relationship between LH and previous law collections has also been used to argue certain things regarding its nature and function. The similarities between the non-legal sections of LH, LL, LU (and LX) and RU have been used to stress the non-legal function of LH and to see it as part of a literary stream or genre or self-aggrandizing royal inscriptions.[261] The similarity of the content of the various law collections has been seen to represent the fact that such texts are examples of legal science (in contrast to legislation) and that various traditional legal problems are dealt with in an academic fashion from culture to culture.[262]

The question has been asked whether the literary context of the scribal school or the monumental inscription determines the function of the law collections, and LH in particular.[263] Our answer is somewhat circumspect in that we think to decide on such questions one should pay closer attention to the content of the laws, specifically their prologue and epilogue, than to its form or structure. Let us now turn to this. What does Hammurabi claim as the purpose for his own collection?

It has long been recognized that Hammurabi's list of epithets in the prologue and achievements in the epilogue refer to his reign in the broadest sense and not merely to his legal achievements, let alone only those accomplished by the setting up of his stele. There are other sections which do directly comment on Hammurabi's role as provider of justice or to the role of the stele itself. It is to these we will look for statements about the purpose of LH. The prologue does not refer specifically to the stele itself, rather it outlines Hammurabi's commission at the behest of the gods. The epilogue then recounts that the commission has been fulfilled in the setting up of the stele (or is at least witnessed by such an act). In the prologue we are told that Hammurabi was named to: make justice in the land; abolish the wicked and evil; to ensure the strong did not oppress the weak; to enhance the well-being of the people; and to illuminate the land. In the last paragraph of the prologue we are also told that Marduk commanded him to provide just ways for the people of the land for appropriate behavior. The statement that Hammurabi established truth and justice and enhanced the well-being of the people follows this command. The laws themselves follow this statement. Surely we are to understand the laws as the fulfillment of this command and the commission Hammurabi was given. The epilogue makes this understanding inescapable.

---

[261] Yoffee, "Context and Authority," 98.

[262] Westbrook, "Codification and Canonization," 43, "Character," 17.

[263] Westbrook, "Character," 19.

The first line of the epilogue tells the reader that these are the just decisions that Hammurabi established which have directed the land along the course of truth and the correct way of life. After a long list of achievements we are told that Hammurabi inscribed his precious words on the stele and set it up: in order that the mighty not wrong the weak; to provide just ways for the waif and widow; to give the verdicts of the land; and to provide just ways for the wronged. This is followed by a wish in the precative that Hammurabi's justice would prevail in the land by the command of Marduk. All of this seems to point towards Hammurabi seeing himself as setting up the model for good judgment in Babylonia. There is no escaping this stated purpose. The flow of LH could be summed up thus: Hammurabi was commissioned by the gods to establish justice *etc.*, the laws and their setting up on the stele have achieved fulfillment of that commission, may they continue to do so. It is in this context that the addresses to the *awilum ḫablum* and the future ruler are to be understood.

The significance of the section of the epilogue addressing the *awilum ḫablum* is highly debated. There are some who, taking the text at face value, see in this section evidence that LH was to be applied in the law courts of Babylonia at the time. The wronged man is to have the stele read out to him so that he can find the relevant provision and have his lawsuit revealed. Some have seen in this an implied address to the judges that they were to look to LH for the verdicts of their cases.[264] Others have made much of the further instruction that the wronged man is then to praise Hammurabi with the formulaic blessing set out on the stele to argue that the praise of Hammurabi is the real purpose in contrast to any legislative function.[265] To this end Martha Roth has even published an article arguing that the wronged man is not someone who has been mistreated or oppressed and has come to the stele looking for legal remedy but someone who has already lost their case, perhaps unfairly, who comes to the stele to be comforted by the fact Hammurabi tried to establish justice.[266] This last argument is very hard for this writer to swallow. Her argument, based on the occurrence of the term *ḫablum* in contemporary records and in two of LH's provisions, is a little

---

[264] Petschow, "Beiträge zum Codex Hammurapi," *Zeitschrift für Assyriologie* 76 (1986): 22 and H. Sauren, "Aufbau und Anordnung," 1–55.

[265] *e.g.* Roth, "Mesopotamian Legal Traditions," 17; "Codification and Text," 41; Renger, "Noch einmal," 31–32; Westbrook, "Cuneiform Law," 203; Yoffee, "Context and Authority," 103.

[266] Roth, "Mesopotamian Legal Traditions," 17; "Codification and Text," 41; "Hammurabi's Wronged Man," 38, 41, 45.

forced. She attempts to limit the wrong being done to: 1) abuse by a person in authority over an underling or, 2) a defendant or plaintiff involved in a case where the undergoing of an ordeal gives the wrong result.[267] This writer would think it highly unlikely that the latter possibility was allowed an airing in Babylonian thought given its connections to the justice of the gods. Roth uses a literary text in which one who has been wronged appeals to the gods as judge and two Old Babylonian letters to argue for the second meaning for "wronged". We certainly agree with Roth that someone who loses a case unfairly can be described as an *awilum ḫablum*. The two cases she presents seem to show this. The problem we have is the attempt to limit the meaning of *ḫabalum* to the two mentioned above. The list of terms given by Roth[268] which can be associated with the verb or its derivatives seem to imply the opposite of her case for such a limited semantic range. She lists terms for murder, villainy, desertion, injustice, affliction, cries for justice *etc.* These terms seem to fit well with a very general meaning for the term *ḫabalum*. CDA gives the translation, "to wrong, oppress".[269] This is how Roth has translated the term also.[270] Despite Roth's arguments for a limited semantic range for the term in this context, it seems the wrong that an *awilum ḫablum* could have suffered could be extremely varied in nature. The examples Roth gives in order to limit the range of the term merely demonstrate that a context is needed to define the wrong more specifically.[271] Interestingly the two letters cited also order that action be taken to correct what has taken place. The addressee is not told to console the victim by taking him to Hammurabi's stele in order to comfort them in the knowledge Hammurabi tried. It is unlikely Hammurabi would think such a wronged man would bless him in such a situation. It is therefore unwise to conclude that the *awilum ḫablum* of LH's epilogue must be a man who has been let down by the justice system, either because of a wrong done to him from above or because he has unfairly lost a case. These two are certainly possibilities given the wide semantic range of the term, but we cannot rule out that the wrong committed against him could have been one of the

---

[267] Roth, "Hammurabi's Wronged Man".

[268] *Ibid.*, 41.

[269] CDA, 98.

[270] *Law Collections*, 133–34.

[271] See Veenhof's comments regarding LH's scribes' infrequent usage of this term: "they prefer rulings on specific cases over formulating general principles," in "Royal Decrees", 62.

many abuses covered by the laws *e.g.* perhaps he could have had his tooth knocked out, or his slave gored by an ox.

Those who would see the wronged man being urged to find the verdict for his case in LH do run into the problem that he is then told, not to take his case before the judges and refer to the judgment of LH, but to calm his heart and to praise Hammurabi with the formulaic blessing on the stele. This has fed arguments that LH was set up to be self-aggrandizing and propagandistic rather than legislative.[272] Perhaps this is an unnecessary and somewhat anachronistic contrast. We do not question that the Assyrian annals record history of some form or another merely because they involve praise of the king's actions. Of course our interpretations of such history should be aware of such an alternative motive, but we do not throw the whole annals out as ahistorical because they are colored by other motives. Why then should we do so with LH? Is it not possible for LH to be self-aggrandizing and legislative at the same time?[273] Here a once popular anachronistic comparison would seem to confirm such a possibility. Did not the *Code Napoléon* play such a dual function (though perhaps more subtly)? Is it really necessary to portray LH as *either* self-aggrandizing *or* legislative in purpose? This said we do not mean to imply that this is legislation in the modern sense of the term. The statements of Hammurabi in his prologue and epilogue do seem to imply that the laws he was setting forth were to have some sort of effect on the running of the judicial system in Babylonia, and that they had in the past.

The address to the future ruler raises similar problems. Hammurabi expresses concern both that the ruler, if he be wise and want to rule his people well, will put Hammurabi's laws into practice and also, that he not deface the inscription in any way or claim Hammurabi's achievements as his own. Hammurabi wishes that the stele will reveal to such a king the tradition/path (*kibsum*), right conduct/way (*ridum*), the judgments and decisions/verdicts of the land (*din/purusse matim*) so that the future king can provide just ways, render judgments, give verdicts, eradicate evil and enhance the well-being of the people. For such a king he wishes a long rule in which they will shepherd the people with justice. The fact that Hammurabi also expresses the concern common to monumental inscriptions that his name and image not be erased, does not mean we should ignore his other

---

[272] *e.g.* Roth, "Codification and Text" and "Hammurabi's Wronged Man," 39.

[273] See Driver and Miles' interpretation, *Babylonian Laws*, vol. 1, 41. They saw the purpose of the *awilum ḫablum* passage with this dual purpose in mind *i.e.* learn the law applicable and praise Hammurabi.

stated intentions. Of course this may imply that Hammurabi had ulterior motives for setting up this stele which may have included a desire for glory and the immortality that comes from being remembered. It should not lead us to exclude all other motives. The fact that the future ruler may have been expected to follow the words on the stele only because they were evidence of wise judgments rather than autonomous law,[274] need not lead us to conclude that Hammurabi did not intend for these laws to be followed both in his own day and in the future.

Though much of the prologue and epilogue speak of the uses of LH with regard to the legal life of Babylonia, we are left with the problem that the text itself addresses only the *awilum ḫablum* and the future king specifically. Surely it is the judges who should be addressed if LH were some form of legislation?[275] This is an understandable objection to LH's legislative purpose. Perhaps at this point we should raise a similar problem for those who would read this text as propaganda or as self-representation to the gods. There is no direct address to either Hammurabi's subjects (apart from the *awilum ḫablum*), whether native or foreign, or to the gods anywhere in his composition. If we are to rule out any judicial function based on the absence of address to the judges, should we not be consistent and rule out a propagandistic purpose based on similar absences? Perhaps such purposes cannot be ruled out. Returning to our question, how are we to reconcile the absence of any address to the judges with the fact that LH sees itself as declaring the relevant case for an *awilum ḫablum* and serving as guide for the legal activities of future rulers? If LH were not binding on the judges what use would it be for the *awilum ḫablum* to approach the court having figured out the relevant case from LH? We cannot really answer this question as there is little evidence to help us do so. There are a number of possibilities. Perhaps the rulings of LH were passed on to judges through some other channel. In the Babylonian judicial system it seems the onus was on the plaintiff to collect witnesses, evidence *etc.* Given this role, perhaps it was expected that the plaintiff, perhaps the *awilum ḫablum*, knew the relevant provision for their case. Again, this is mere speculation. It is unlikely that the legal system in Babylonia worked on the basis of such law collections most of the time. Perhaps it was the knowledge that the legal system would carry on according to tradition that led Hammurabi to not bother addressing the judges. His letters to his administrators do show that he had the

[274] Westbrook, "Codification and Canonization," 40.

[275] A point made long ago by Landsberger, "Die babylonischen Termini," 221–222.

power to make rulings in specific cases and we presume the administrators were to follow such orders in their role as judges so perhaps this explanation does not hold up. That they did not necessarily cite Hammurabi's letters when they did so may give us an interesting check on theories arguing against the applicability of LH due to its lack of citation. Perhaps the question could be resolved if we postulate that the person reading the provision to the *awilum ḫablum* would be a member of the ruling administration. It is possible that it was the judge of the case who would be the most likely person to read out the relevant case. Whatever the situation regarding the applicability of LH for the judges of Babylonia, it seems that if the *awilum ḫablum* were to expect to have his case dealt with as LH set out, it would have to be applicable for the judges as well as for him. As this is the simplest reading of LH we presume it is also the most likely. The fact that the judges did not tend to follow LH or at least did not cite it for their decisions does not tell us very much about the purpose of LH. It may tell us something about the temporary nature of law put forth by a king in Mesopotamia.

Another set of issues arises if we attempt to take seriously LH's claim that the case of the *awilum ḫablum* should be found on the stele. Is Hammurabi claiming that LH is comprehensive? Many commentators have pointed out that it is far from being so. For many this has been one of the key arguments against defining LH as a "code". With this we must agree. LH is certainly not comprehensive in that it does not cover every conceivable case of every conceivable abuse. One could well postulate a situation where an *awilum ḫablum* could come to LH, have it read out and not find his case at all.[276] What significance does this have when considering the nature and function of LH? If it was not comprehensive and did not aim to be it may enable us to stop using the term "code" and perhaps replace it with terms like "restatement", "reform", "law collection", but does it really tell us very much about its purpose? One can see the attraction in doing away with Hammurabi's claim to be putting forth actual law. If one does away with that claim there is no longer a problem regarding the lack of citation of LH, nor with the fact that documents from legal practice may not regularly match up with the provisions in LH, nor with the situation here envisaged that the *awilum ḫablum* may not find the relevant case. The problem is, that to hold such a position one needs to ignore the claims that LH itself makes

---

[276] Thus Westbrook, "Codification and Canonization," 35–36 and Yoffee, "Context and Authority," 103.

whereas surely this should be where we start when looking for the purpose of the collection.

Michalowski has argued against the idea that texts like LH reflect a genre used for Mesopotamian scientific texts.[277] Though he does see them as "scholastic compositions",[278] he sees the monumental origin of LH (along with LL and LU) as setting them apart from the other legal texts found as part of the Mesopotamian scribal curriculum. The relationship of the formal collections to the scholarly compositions will be discussed later. Finkelstein's position has become perhaps the majority stance in regards to the formal law collections with prologue and/or epilogue.[279] He terms these collections "Lower Mesopotamian "law codes"" and asserts that they were "royal inscriptions of the apologia genre" whose purposes were "decidedly not legislative".[280] His argument is based on the fact that the non-legal sections of these texts recount the glorious achievements of the king and his concern for justice within the framework of his divine election and mandate to carry out justice.

Unlike LH, in LU and LL we do not possess a specific address to anyone apart from those in the future who may be in a position to damage the stele. This makes it more difficult to assess the purpose of these collections. Should we attribute the same purpose as in LH to these collections? In LH we had a specific address to the future ruler and the *awīlum ḫablum* which seemed to imply that Hammurabi intended the laws within his collection to affect legal practice. In the case of LU and LL, there are broken sections in the epilogue,[281] but these appear within the curse formula so are unlikely to have contained such an address. If LX be the epilogue of LU, all it seems to have contained is the series of curses for him who effaces the inscription. LL and LU do not contain the purpose and wish clauses of LH which gave us an insight into his intentions in setting up his stele.[282]

---

[277] Michalowski and Walker, "A New Sumerian 'Law Code'".

[278] *Ibid.*, 384.

[279] LU, LL, LH. He was unaware of LX at the time.

[280] Finkelstein, "Ammisaduqa's Edict," 103.

[281] For the sake of argument, we are here assuming that LX represents the epilogue of LU. See Michalowski and Walker, "A New Sumerian 'Law Code'" for discussion. Lieberman's arguments that LX does not represent a royal law collection are unfounded, "Nippur: City of Decisions". See Roth's brief discussion, *Law Collections*, 39, nn. 1–2.

[282] *e.g.* xlvii 59–78 which Roth, *Law Collections*, 133 translates as "In order that the mighty not wrong the weak, to provide just ways for the waif and widow, I have inscribed my precious pronouncements" or the precative forms in the address

All three collections display similarities. The section of LU's prologue where we might expect his divine commission to appear is broken.[283] Like LL, he records part of his fulfillment of such a commission within his prologue, whereas LH leaves this until the epilogue.[284] Both LL and LU, as with LH, claim to have established freedom and justice in the land,[285] LU and LH claim to have stopped the strong oppressing the weak and to have looked after the widow and the orphan.[286] That LL does not claim to have achieved the last two objectives may only be due to the accidents of discovery as over two columns of the prologue are lost. All three collections end with the curse formulae typical of monumental inscriptions.[287] All have a generally casuistic framing.[288] All were probably set up on a stele.[289] All were copied to some extent. Is this enough for us to ascribe a similar purpose to these collections as that claimed for LH? It is certainly enough to make links between the purpose of these collections and the purpose of monumental stele with their concern for posterity. What of the legal import of these collections? LH claims an intention to influence legal practice which most scholars today deny. If these collections do not even claim to have a legal function, should we attribute one to them?

There are some hints in the prologue of LL that his collection may have functioned in a manner similar to LH. The fact that he recounts in the opening section of his epilogue that he has made Sumer and Akkad hold fair judicial procedure, eradicated enmity and violence and made right and

---

to the *awilum ḫablum* and the future ruler. See also the first lines of the epilogue where he states that his *dinat mišarim* have caused the land to seize *ussam kinam u ridam damqam*.

[283] A i 43–74

[284] But do see the last line of LH's prologue.

[285] LU A iii 114–124, C ii 40–51. LL ii 1–15, xxi 5–17, 36–38. LH v 14–24, xlvii 9–58.

[286] LU A iv 162–168, C ii 30–39. LH xlvii 59–64.

[287] Again, presuming LX to have been the epilogue of LU.

[288] If one accepts our earlier broad definition of casuistic as regarding specific cases rather than a definition which would contrast conditional and relative forms. Sumerian *tukum-bi*, "its case" is hardly a conditional particle (in meaning, though of course it may function as such).

[289] There is obviously good evidence for this with LH. LL refers to its being set up as a stele and it is possible some stone fragments have been identified (see Roth in *COS* 2.154: 411). The only evidence that LU was set up on a stele comes from the likelihood that it had an epilogue such as LX which contained the monumental curse formula.

truth shine forth, should perhaps lead one to the conclusion that the laws just enumerated are, at the least, evidence that he has done so. This argument differs in no way from that of those who see the purpose of these collections as royal apologia designed to portray the king's fulfillment of his role as just king. What we are asking is whether this was the only purpose for these collections. With LH we had evidence to the contrary; here we must say we do not. For these texts it seems as though the question of their intended applicability will continue to be decided on the basis of one's presuppositions *e.g.* Otto's ascription to form-criticism and the *Sitz im Leben* of the judge's training causes him to see composite texts, originally arranged by legal topic, which have been taken over for the purpose of royal propaganda.[290] This writer does not feel it necessary to have a form of the laws divorced from their prologue and epilogue for them to have been intended to play a role in the legal life of Mesopotamia. We are cautious in ascribing such an intention given the lack of its expression in the texts themselves, though we would not necessarily deny it.

It has been found that there is a great degree of similarity in the non-legal parts of LH and the other Lower Mesopotamian "monumental" law collections. However, there is also a degree of similarity to the non-legal sections of the Egyptian decrees. Though these sections may add the function of a "monumental inscription" to these works, this does not necessarily deny the possibility that they also played a legal function. This denial is more prevalent in Assyriology than Egyptology when it comes to an analysis of the function of the respective law collections. These non-legal sections, especially in the case of LH, EH, ND and MAPD are most useful to decide upon the purpose of the collections, especially when such a purpose is clearly stated. It would be dangerous to assume a similarity of purpose in LL, LU and LX when it is not stated in such a manner. The content of AE seems to be the best evidence for its purpose. What follows is a discussion of the usefulness of some of the other evidence brought to bear to decide upon the purpose of LH, and other texts.

2.1.4.8 The usefulness of form and the links to Mesopotamian "science"

The contrasting of LH's form to that of the *mišarum* edicts has been used by some to argue for a different function for LH and the other more formal law collections. This argument, to a large extent, depends upon one defin-

[290] Otto, *e.g.* "Aspects of Legal Reforms"; "Auf dem Wege zu einer altorientalischen Rechtgeschichte," *Bibliotheca Orientalis* 48 (1991): 5–13.

ing conditional form as contrastive to relative forms. This is based on the distinction in Roman law between conditional and relative clauses. This distinction does not stand up very well in ancient Near Eastern law (one suspects it is probably unhelpful within Roman law also) as there are few, if any, purely conditional forms. Though one can use the term casuistic with good conscience given the specific case based nature of most legal provisions, one is hard pressed to make a firm distinction between the variously formulated casuistic forms *e.g.* *tukum-bi*, "its case is...", *šumma*, "if/when...", *takku*, a combination of the clause conjunction *ta*, "and then" and the *–aku* ending, "whether/or/if". Though a translation of all these terms with the English word "if" does little damage to their sense, it does give the false impression that the various terms are part of the same grammatical structure. It is worth noting here that none of the edicts or *mišarum* decrees have been found in a school setting as yet.[291]

A number of scholars have seen LH as a collection of the legal judgments of LH in his role as judge.[292] This argument is often based on the evidence of Hammurabi's legal role as reflected in his letters.[293] The specific or casuistic nature of the provisions in LH is used to bolster such an argument.[294] It is seen to reflect the specific cases dealt with by the king in his role as judge while leaving room for some invention of cases also.[295] The use of casuistic forms (whether conditional, relative or otherwise) almost across the board in ancient Near Eastern law collections, including those which are not specifically linked to a king, should perhaps make one hesitate before using this form to argue for the provisions reflecting the legal activity of the king. There are some specific cases where an argument can be made for the process from a specific judgment of Hammurabi in a letter

---

[291] See Michalowski and Walker, "A New Sumerian 'Law Code'," 384.

[292] Leemans, "King Hammurabi as Judge" and to a lesser extent Kraus, "Ein zentrales Problem".

[293] *e.g.* Kraus' collection of the letters to and from Shamash-Hazir, *Briefe aus dem Archive des Shamah-Hazir* (Altbabylonische Briefe 4; Leiden: Brill, 1968).

[294] Yaron, *Laws of Eshnunna*, 107–8. His position here is somewhat more circumspect than his first edition. See *The Laws of Eshnunna* (Jerusalem: Magnes, 1969), 66.

[295] The invented nature of at least some cases has become a generally accepted position from the time of Kraus, "Ein zentrales Problem" onwards. See the comments of Roth, "Reading Law," 48; Postgate, *Early Mesopotamia*, 289; Renger, "Noch einmal," 38–39; Westbrook, "Cuneiform Law," 218–219 and "Character," 18.

to a provision in his law collection.[296] As pointed out by Leemans, the possibility that LH may reflect Hammurabi's actions as a judge does not rule out the conclusion reached by Kraus and others that it is "learned literature", Mesopotamian science, or in the service of propaganda.[297]

The casuistic nature of LH has been used by many to argue for a link between it and Mesopotamian scientific literature in general *e.g.* omen lists, medical texts *etc.*[298] Scholars researching the intellectual history of Mesopotamia have often made much of the concrete nature of such texts with their lists of individual cases.[299] A large number of such scholars have taken this concretization in the presentation of Mesopotamian texts to reflect an inability on the part of the Mesopotamian people to think in the abstract.[300] This idea has been questioned in more recent times. Roth has done so in the area of law by pointing out the usefulness of teaching through concrete examples. She links this approach to Kuhn's notion of paradigm exemplars in order to highlight the ability of concrete cases to teach abstract notions or principles (especially through the arrangement of contrasting examples *e.g.* LH 133–136).[301] If we accept this as the case, then the form of the laws does not rule out a legislative function, though, of course, one different to the civil law of modern times with its declaration of statutes and principles.[302] This will be of relevance when one comes to the problem of the applicability and internal consistency of the laws. For example, some have argued that, as the laws are so specific, there would be enormous trouble applying them in cases where some detail was missing. A famous example is LH 230 where the law states that a builder who builds a wall which col-

---

[296] See Veenhof, "Royal Decrees," 69–72 and Leemans, "King Hammurabi as Judge" for possibilities. See also Westbrook, "Biblical and Cuneiform Law Codes," 260 and Bottéro, "Code," 421.

[297] Leemans, "King Hammurabi as Judge," 129, n. 1.

[298] Landsberger, "Die babylonischen Termini"; Kraus, "Ein zentrales Problem"; Bottéro, "Code"; Finkelstein, "Ammisaduqa's Edict"; Westbrook, "Cuneiform Law," 251–53.

[299] This includes the lexical lists and grammatical texts which teach through lists of individual examples, rather than abstract rules.

[300] *e.g.* Bottéro, "Code," 177–78; Westbrook, "Codification and Canonization," 35–36.

[301] Roth, "Mesopotamian Legal Traditions," 35. The idea that such individual cases can be used to teach more general principles is accepted to some extent by Westbrook, "Character," 18.

[302] *e.g.* Postgate, *Early Mesopotamia*, 289 who sees the ability of such individual cases to portray general principles as an argument for their prescriptive nature.

lapses and kills a man's son will have his son killed. Commentators have ruminated about the problems of applying this law if the builder had no son.[303] Perhaps this is the wrong approach to these collections. Westbrook has postulated "that some of the punishments reflect the scribal compiler's concern for perfect symmetry and delicious irony rather than the pragmatic experience of the law courts."[304] It is unlikely that ancient Mesopotamian law applied these collections in the way we picture statutes being applied these days *i.e.* according to the letter of the law. This does not mean that this law may not have been taken into consideration when its exact details did not apply. At the least, one could imagine it being considered as a model of good judgment in a similar case and therefore having some precedential value.[305] This fits with the claims Hammurabi makes for his collection in its prologue and epilogue.

The casuistic nature and the structure of LH and other collections and their supposed link to other Mesopotamian texts set out in a similar fashion has been used to assess the nature and function of the legal collections. Most commonly the link is made between LH and the omen texts which are seen to be a mixture of historical omens and invented ones which pad out other possibilities.[306] A similar process is then read into LH which is seen to consist of some cases from Hammurabi's role as a judge and some which are invented in order to provide contrasting cases and fill gaps.[307] If this was the case, then we can see the laws within LH as some sort of teaching tool or merely as an intellectual exercise. The function is not decided by such evidence as many possibilities are left open *e.g.* this process was used by Hammurabi to convey most effectively the laws he wanted to be implemented in the land, or at least the model of judging he wanted to be followed; what is presented comes from legal scholars of some sort who studied the problems of the law purely as an intellectual exercise;[308] what was collected was originally the training manual for judges which taught them

[303] *e.g.* Finkelstein, "Ox that Gored," 33–35. There are similar problems applying LH 210 if the offender has no daughter or LH 25 if the fire had gone out.

[304] Westbrook, "Character," 71.

[305] The collection's role as some kind of model for good judgement is generally accepted, even by Bottéro, "Code," 167.

[306] Kraus, "Ein zentrales Problem," 289–90; Bottéro, "Code," 169–77; Westbrook, "Biblical and Cuneiform Law Codes," 253–64.

[307] See previous note.

[308] Often other scholars' summary of the position of Kraus and Bottéro *e.g.* Westbrook, "Cuneiform Law," 201.

how to decide difficult cases by teaching them the principles they should apply through these sets of contrasting cases.[309] All these theories involve a degree of speculation from such evidence. If LH's origins are within Mesopotamian legal science then are we to distinguish it from collections such as LOx, SLHF or SLEx? Has Hammurabi merely appropriated one such collection and given it a new function by adding a prologue and epilogue? Once we start to divide our texts into sections and hypothesize about originals and original functions for which we have little or no evidence our conclusions must be taken with more than a grain of salt.

The Edict of Haremhab raises many problems for those who would use the existence of forms to decide upon the nature, function or purpose of a collection. EH frames itself as direct commands from the king, even though many of the rulings are in a casuistic form.[310] This makes a mockery of the arguments presented above on the basis of the forms within other collections, especially the idea that such a form cannot come from the *Sitz im Leben* of a royal order, but must come from legal science.

Westbrook claims that the structure of LH "made no pretence of being anything but an academic treatise".[311] Perhaps the question we need to ask is whether the structure really tells us very much about the purpose of the collection. The structuring of LH according to the principles of association and extrapolation[312] does not necessarily tell us the function of the text, even though these structural principles may be found in other Mesopotamian texts. Given that scholars seem to give the omen lists and medical texts a practical function it seems a little strange that LH's similarity of form and structure is used to argue that the opposite is the case.[313] Westbrook originally questioned the purely scientific character of the laws based on this similarity with the omen texts which had a practical function.[314] Interest-

---

309 Thus Otto, "Kodifizierung und Kanonisierung," 77–124.

310 So much for the supposed *Sitz im Leben* of this form *cf.* Yaron, *Laws of Eshnunna*, 1969, 66–67.

311 Westbrook, "Codification and Canonization," 39.

312 See discussions of Sauren, "Aufbau und Anordnung"; Petschow, "Systematik Hammurabi"; Bottéro, "Code," 173–77; Renger, "Noch einmal," 38–39 *etc.*

313 Westbrook is aware of this dilemma but offers no solution, merely asserting that LH did not seem to function in such a manner, "Codification and Canonization," 41. See the next footnote for his earlier position. Bottéro was also aware of this contradiction, "Code," 177–79.

314 Westbrook, "Biblical and Cuneiform Law Codes," 253.

ingly, it is only during the reign of two Neo-Assyrian kings[315] that we have evidence of citation of the omen texts. One presumes they were consulted in earlier periods also. It has been conjectured that the reason the citation appears for this brief period is due to an aberrant situation where the omenologists were living away from the palace and had to be consulted via letter rather than orally.[316]

Though there may be a link between LH and the other formal law collections and the concrete nature of other texts such as omens, this evidence cannot be used to decide upon the nature, function or purpose of these texts.

2.1.4.9 Comprehensivity

Some have used the non-comprehensive nature of law collections such as LH to argue that legislation must not have been their purpose.[317] Though we may agree that "it is clear that none attempts to set out a complete law of the land,"[318] we must also agree that "it is not clear what conclusions follow."[319] The fact that the entire law of the land was not contained within LH does not necessarily mean he did not mean for the laws he did present to be followed.[320] Various conclusions have been made around this non-comprehensive nature of LH. Many have argued that no written laws were needed and there must have been some sort of unwritten or common law which guided everyday practice.[321] Some see LH as some sort of confirmation or correction of such a common law and thus keep a legislative function for it.[322] Renger has aptly pointed out that the expectation of comprehensivity is a modern bias and is therefore invalid in determining the function of such a text.[323]

---

[315] Esarhaddon and Aššur-banipal.

[316] Westbrook, "Biblical and Cuneiform Law Codes," 255.

[317] Finkelstein, "Law in the Ancient Near East"; Westbrook, "Character," 20; Yoffee, "Context and Authority," 102.

[318] Roth, *Law Collections*, 4.

[319] *Ibid.*, 4.

[320] However we conceive that.

[321] *e.g.* Lemche, "Justice in Western Asia," 1699.

[322] Cardascia, "La coutume dans les droits cuneiformes," *Recueils de la société Jean Bodin* 51 (1990): 61–69; Driver and Miles, *Babylonian Laws*, vol. 1, 45; Postgate, *Early Mesopotamia*, 289.

[323] Renger, "Noch einmal," 36.

2.1.4.10 Historical context

The historical context has been used to determine the purpose of EH. Coming so soon after the Amarna period, many have seen it as a series of reforms to do away with the abuses of this period, though it is difficult to prove this.[324]

The historical context of the giving of LH has also been called upon to help decide the purpose and function of the text. Many have seen the creation of Hammurabi's empire as creating a need for a unified legal and administrative system. They see LH as being set up all over his empire in order to enforce such uniformity.[325] The fact that a number of the promulgators of the more formal law collections were kings who had recently annexed new territories lends weight to such a theory.[326] Though this is a logical possibility supported by the fact of copies of LH throughout the empire,[327] we do not possess the evidence to be able to decide whether this was the purpose. Hammurabi never states so much in his text. We do not have evidence of the impact of LH in subject areas nor do we have enough evidence to suggest that there was a significant variation in local practice across his empire.[328] It has even been questioned whether such uniformity was needed or desirable for Hammurabi's empire to function.[329] In this context a letter from Hammurabi is cited (AbB 13 10:10ff) where he instructs one of his officials in Emutbalum to treat a case "*kima dinim ša inanna ina Emutbalum iddinnu*", "according to the law/in accordance with the case/decision they currently apply in Emutbalum". Unfortunately this letter does not tell us whether its import is that Hammurabi is happy for his officials to give verdicts in accord with local practice, or, whether it is remind-

---

[324] Pflüger, "Haremhab," 267–68 thinks so, though he is reserved as he finds no direct reference to this in the text.

[325] Edwards, *Oldest Laws*, 12; Klima, "La perspective," 306–7; George E. Mendenhall, "Ancient Oriental and Biblical Law," *Biblical Archaeologist* 17 (1954): 33.

[326] Postgate, *Early Mesopotamia*, 290.

[327] Admitted by Roth, "Codification and Text", 29.

[328] As pointed out by Roth, "Codification and Text", 29; Westbrook, "Cuneiform Law," 204 and Renger, "Noch einmal," 33–34. The only possibilities admitted are the distinction between the inheritance rights of firstborn sons in the north and the south of Mesopotamia, Westbrook, "Cuneiform Law," 204 and sealing practices, as shown by Leemans, referred to by Renger, 33.

[329] Renger, "Noch einmal," 33. Westbrook, "Cuneiform Law," 204.

ing the official to apply the newly enforced royal rulings in contrast to the local practice.[330]

Historical context may raise some possible reasons for the promulgation of a law collection, but cannot be used as evidence by itself.

2.1.4.11 Copies

The fact that the copies of the edicts from Samsu-iluna and Ammiditana seem to have the same provisions, bar several which may have been added by Ammiṣaduqa,[331] may point to the applicability of the provisions. It could then be argued that further provisions were added to deal with the difficulties of enforcement. The updating of the copies of HL are also used to argue for its applicability. This will be discussed later.

The existence of copies of LH can tell us much about its later use but perhaps little about its original intention. The many copies of LH show us that it became a staple of the Babylonian *e$_2$-dub-ba*. There are over 50 copies of LH ranging from complete copies to extracts, lexical commentaries and bilingual versions. Amongst these some copies have subject headings above the laws, and some copies consist of only the prologue and epilogue. This multitude of school versions of LH does show us that it came to serve some sort of scholastic function. The fact that the prologue and epilogue could be copied separately to the laws may tell us that this section was appreciated for its literary excellence or as a model to follow in writing texts which praised the king. The lexical commentaries show us that the text was used to help teach the scribes how to read and write Akkadian. None of this tells us that the original function of LH could not have been legal in nature. Kraus' claim that the copies attest to the literary excellence of LH rather than its legal applicability is an unnecessary contrast.[332] It is certainly feasible that part of the reason LH was passed on was its usefulness in training judges to solve difficult cases, or, perhaps less likely, to teach them the laws of the land. Wiseman has argued that some of the later copies "could point to an Achaemenid or later inquiry into Babylonian precedents."[333] The exis-

[330] See discussion of Veenhof, "Royal Decrees", 78.

[331] See comments of Lieberman, "Royal 'Reforms' of the Amurrite Dynasty," *Bibliotheca Orientalis* 46 (1989): 255 and Olivier, "Old Babylonian Mesharum Decree," 108–109.

[332] Kraus, "Ein zentrales Problem"; Bottéro, "Code," *e.g.* 160. See Renger's comments, "Noch einmal," 51.

[333] Wiseman, "The Laws of Hammurabi Again," 162 (and see reference in note 5).

tence of the copy of LH containing only the non-legal sections should not be used to confirm the suspicion that LH had no legal purpose.[334] It does attest to a non-legal use in later days. It should certainly not be used to reconstruct the textual history of the composition. As Roth has pointed out, we cannot tell whether the distinction between the laws and the non-legal sections of LH was primary or a secondary development.[335] Hurowitz has aptly demonstrated the intimate relationship between the two sections in LH as we have it.[336]

2.1.4.12 Some conclusions thus far

For most of the texts classed as decrees or edicts, their purpose does not seem overly difficult to decide. Perhaps it is this factor, more than anything else, which has led to scholars grouping them together.

The provisions of AE for example all relate to the application of the *mišarum* or debt-release decree. Since at least the time of Bottéro's important article on the subject,[337] it has been generally accepted that the *mišarum* edict was aimed at increasing stability and getting rid of economic disorder, a kind of compression valve to prevent the collapse of the economy. It is now generally accepted that this was done on the basis of perceived need rather than a fixed periodicity.[338] The need for such a decree of release within the Old Babylonian economy and the citation of these decrees in contracts and documents from the time has meant few have questioned the

---

[334] *e.g.* N. Wasserman, "CT 21, 40–42: A bilingual Report of an Oracle with a Royal Hymn of Hammurabi," *Revue d'Assyriologie* 86 (1992): 1–18.

[335] Roth, "Mesopotamian Legal Traditions," 16.

[336] Hurowitz, *Inu Anum Ṣirum*, passim. See his comments on page 7 about the intimate relationship between these two sections and pages 14–15 where he admits the possibility that LH is a form-critically composite work, but asserts that the final form is unified and integrated.

[337] Bottéro, "Désordre Economique et Annulation des Dettes en Mesopotamia a l'époque paleo-babylonienne," *Journal of the Economic and Social History of the Orient* 4 (1961): 113–63.

[338] Contrast Finkelstein's earlier position in "Ammisaduqa's Edict," with that in "Some New Misharum Material and its Implications," in *Studies in Honor of Benno Landsberger* (ed. Hans G. Guterbock and Thorkild Jacobsen; Assyriological Studies 16; Chicago: University of Chicago Press, 1965) *e.g.* p. 243. See discussion of G. Komoroczy, "Zur Frage der Periodizitat der altbabylonischen Misharum-Erlasse," in *Societies and Languages of the Ancient Near East: Studies in Honour of I.M. Diakonoff* (ed. M. Dandamaev and I. M. Diakonoff; Warminster: Aris & Phillips, 1982), 196–205; Lieberman, "Royal Reforms," 255, n. 56.

applicability of such decrees. The most scholars have done is to question the importance of the written form of the decree for the carrying out of its stipulations *e.g.* Lieberman: "Promulgation of the edicts was one way to let individuals know about the king's decisions, but not the only one, and perhaps not the most important."[339]

In general, there seems to be a double-standard of sorts geared towards a propagandistic rather than legal reading of LH. Despite the lack of address to any of Hammurabi's conquered subjects within the laws, numerous scholars have argued for a propagandistic purpose in the context of the establishment of Hammurabi's empire. Given the evidence for literacy rates in the ancient Near East, it is difficult to imagine the content of the inscription being of much use as propaganda, except perhaps towards some of the conquered elite. Despite this, arguments are regularly put forward concerning such a function for LH. For example, Roth reads the first and last laws of the inscription, referring to false accusation of unlawful death and the rebellion of slaves from the perspective of the historical context of Hammurabi's order. She sees the first law as code warning against the accusations being made against Hammurabi for the warfare he has carried out on the now subject cities and the last law as a warning against any form of rebellion from such "enslaved" cities.[340] This is ingenious and in the realm of the possible but finds no evidential support. Yoffee also understands LH as propaganda within his imperial context. He sees LH as portraying Hammurabi's imperial rule as just.[341] The historical context, like so much evidence bearing on the issue of the nature and function of LH, is not enough to decide the issue. The fact that we have no evidence that LH affected the legal practice of his empire does not rule out that this may have been an intention of his just as the lack of address to any subject peoples does not mean that the stele could not have played a propagandistic role. It does seem to be quite a coincidence that most of the law collections were probably promulgated by imperial rulers. Whether this helps us to understand the propagandistic element of the collections or the need for legislation is still open to debate.

Given the uncertain significance of most of the evidence that can be brought to bear to decide on the issue of LH's purpose and function it would seem unnecessary to try and explain away the simplest reading of his prologue and epilogue and its claims that what is being presented will be of

---

339 Lieberman, "Royal Reforms," 258.

340 Roth, "Mesopotamian Legal Traditions," 18–19.

341 Yoffee, "Context and Authority," 107.

use to the *awilum ḫablum* in his case and to the future ruler in deciding the law of the land. We must hold this purpose in tension with the clear links between LH and royal monumental inscriptions. Perhaps the address to the future ruler is here of more importance than the imperial context and our expectation of propagandistic usage.[342] Hammurabi does intend to memorialize his accomplishments. Perhaps this is done through the survival of Ḫammurabi's name due to the existence of the stele and its consultation by future rulers just as the name of rulers was passed down through their building inscriptions being replaced when their palace, temple or canal was rebuilt.

Apart from these two stated purposes we are left with some other possible functions for LH whether it be as some form of propaganda within his imperial context, an attempt at unifying the law within his empire, a proof to the gods that he fulfilled the role for which they elected him, an example of academic legal reasoning, a collection of Hammurabi's decisions from his role as judge with some cases possibly added *etc. etc.*

Whatever the other functions may have been there are two likelihoods to keep in mind. The first is that, whether intended to be applied by the letter of the law (unlikely) or to be used to ascertain the standards or principles that were to be used when making decisions, or merely to cover particularly difficult cases, LH is intended to have some sort of role as a model for successful legal practice and thus to affect its everyday running. This is true whether this intended desire came to fruition or not. While not being codification in the modern sense of the term, and it being difficult for us to decide whether it reflects or attempts to change contemporary practice, LH was, at the least, a collection of examples of decisions which were to be emulated. This can be reconciled with the idea that the document itself may not have become autonomous law.[343] Hammurabi may have been well aware of the fact that his collection may not carry authority after his death, that it would not be cited by judges in the documentation of their legal decisions, that it would not be the sole source of law in the land and would be difficult to enforce throughout the empire. This does not imply that LH was merely an intellectual exercise with no intended consequences. That it

---

[342] See N. K. Weeks, "Assyrian Imperialism and the Walls of Uruk," in *Gilgameš and the World of Assyria: Proceedings of the Conference Held at Mandelbaum House, The University of Sydney, 21–23 July 2004* (ed. J. J. Azize and N. K. Weeks; Ancient Near Eastern Studies Supplement 21; Louvain: Peeters, 2007), 79–90.

[343] As argued by Westbrook, "Cuneiform Law," 220, "Codification and Canonization," 38.

does not look or behave like a modern law collection does not mean its stated intentions are false. An approach is needed which both accounts for the difference between law of this period and modern law and takes seriously the claims made by ancient documents about their own purpose. While we may not exclude some secondary possibilities, we will not elevate them above the purposes for which we have evidence. It would be wisest not to try and fill in too many of the details regarding the nature of the document when we do not have the evidence at our disposal to do so. Sometimes it is better to say we do not know than to force an argument.

Given the enormous amount of material that can be brought to bear on the issue of LH's nature, function and purpose when compared to the other law collections under study here, the hesitancy of our conclusions regarding this issue do not bode well for us being able to decide upon the purpose of the collections not yet treated. That said, we were able to offer a general thesis in this regard on the basis of the claims made by the text itself in the case of LH, EH, ND and MAPD, and hope to be able to do so for these other collections. We found it more difficult to offer a thesis regarding the purpose of the monumental collections due to the lack of a clear statement of purpose within those collections. We will proceed by analyzing the rest of the formal law collections, and the supposed scholarly texts.

2.1.4.13 Other formal collections

Our problem is exacerbated when we turn to the other formal law collections.[344] With these texts we do not have non-legal sections in which to search for a purpose. The laws are not part of a monumental inscription.[345] We cannot say that an intention is expressly indicated in the texts themselves. Nevertheless there is not a scholar who thinks these texts served no intended purpose at all. There are some clues as to the nature and function of these texts.

For MAL we are not even sure we are dealing with one composition. What is generally termed MAL is in fact, a series of tablets, mostly fragmentary, which deal with various topics "rather than a single, systematic, reconstructed, composition".[346] There is some evidence which possibly implies different copyists and/or different dates for the tablets,[347] but it would be

344 LE, MAL, HL.

345 Though Westbrook does see such a function for LE, See "Character," 9.

346 Roth, *Law Collections*, 153. This is a generally accepted conclusion. See Driver and Miles, *Assyrian Laws*, 12.

347 See Driver and Miles, *Assyrian Laws*, 7–9.

unwise to base any theories on orthographic variants within cuneiform.[348] For all but one tablet we have only one copy.[349] The only non-legal section we have from these tablets is the eponym year inscribed at the end of Tablet A. Though this helps us to date the copy of the text, it tells us nothing about its nature.

Some have tried to use the fact that Tablet A deals with offences by or against women to speculate as to the nature of the laws. For example, MAL, along with LOx, are the only collections which approach Otto's postulated original *Vorlagen*. He argued for series of tablets, each dealing with a separate legal topic, which were put together to form the other law collections.[350] The tablets of MAL do seem to be arranged to fit a particular topic. Tablet A deals with laws dealing with women, B and O with fixed property laws (*i.e.* real estate, including inheritance laws), C with movable property laws (including sale and theft), D and E are too fragmentary to tell, both extant laws of F deal with animal herding, J and K are very fragmentary also, but J may cover laws pertaining to public works or royal service and K may deal with credit, L is too fragmentary, M deals with boats (perhaps negligence more generally) and N with quarrels (perhaps personal injury more generally). Unfortunately for Otto's theory, he still feels the need to find interpolations and a mixture of sources for MAL itself. We think it better to deal with the text before us, but what can this arrangement by topic tell us about the sources? Driver and Miles used this arrangement to argue against the idea the laws were similar to a modern code as they thought this should be arranged according to specific areas of law, not offences against women.[351] Both the question of codification and the expectation of certain arrangement principles are anachronisms in the interpretation of these texts in general.

What are we left with to help decide upon the nature and function of these tablets? The casuistic framing, similar to the Lower Mesopotamian collections, suggested to Driver and Miles that they were "clearly enactments which have either been or are intended to be henceforth in force."[352] Others may have seen this same framing as implying merely an academic

---

[348] There are some minor grammatical variations also, but again, one should be cautious not to impose uniformity on a period, or even a scribe.

[349] There is a fragmentary Neo-Assyrian copy of Tablet A and some provisions are duplicated in B and O.

[350] See note 290.

[351] Driver and Miles, *Assyrian Laws*, 12.

[352] *Ibid.*, 12.

purpose for the collection. As they did with LH, Driver and Miles turn to their English common law system to explain the nature of MAL and argue that it "presupposes the pre-existing law and proceeds to alter it".[353] In contrast to this, Cardascia thought the laws were the expression of the unwritten customary law already in place,[354] while Lafont sees them as similar to modern "restatements".[355] The last piece of evidence that has been brought to bear on this discussion is the findspot for the tablets. It is thought that the tablets were found in the gate of Shamash, which would be the normal location for a courthouse.[356] On this basis a number of theories have been offered. Some have seen the texts as a legal library for judges,[357] perhaps part of a royal archive.[358] Others still follow Koschaker's theory that the tablets represent a collection of laws for personal use.[359] In the end we must agree with Roth that we remain uncertain whether the copies we have were collected for royal or private use,[360] and even more uncertain what the original purpose of the texts was.[361]

HL also contain no express statement regarding their purpose. They are not framed by any type of superscription or prologue. Again, the only non-legal sections consist of colophons from the scribes who copied the laws. The colophon on KBo 6.6 has the interesting phrase "Of the father of

---

[353] *Ibid.*, 14.

[354] Cardascia, "La formazione del diritto in Assiria," in *La Formazione del Diritto ne vicino oriente antico* (ed. Aristide Theodorides, Carlo Zaccagnini, Guillaume Cardascia, Alfonso Archi and Reuven Yaron; Rome: Edizioni Scientifiche Italiene, 1988), 55. He contrasts this to the opinion of others that the casuistic nature of the document shows that it stems from the *Sitz im Leben* of actual legal cases.

[355] Lafont, "Middle Assyrian Period," 521.

[356] See the statements of Westbrook, "Character," 9–10 and "Biblical and Cuneiform Law Codes," 255; Ernst Weidner, "Das Alter der mittelassyrischen Gesetzestexte," *Archiv für Orientforschung* 12 (1937/9): 46–54; Cardascia, "La formazione del diritto in Assiria," 55.

[357] Weidner, "Das Alter der mittelassyrischen Gesetzestexte," 46–54.

[358] Westbrook, "Biblical and Cuneiform Law Codes," 255 and "Character," 9–10; Weidner, "Die Bibliothek Tiglatpilesers I," *Archiv für Orientforschung* 16 (1952/53): 197–215.

[359] Koschaker, *Rechtsvergleichende*, 79–84. His argument is based more on the form of the document than its findspot. Followed by many, including Lambert, "Tukulti-Ninurta I and the Assyrian King List," *Iraq* 38 (1976): 85–86, n.2.

[360] Roth, *Law Collections*, 154.

[361] It is generally assumed that these tablets are eleventh century copies of 14th century originals *e.g.* Westbrook, "Character," 10; Roth, *Law Collections*, 153.

His Majesty".[362] Though this may or may not be of use in connecting these texts with the royal administration,[363] it tells us little else. Again, arguments have taken place over the significance of the casuistic nature of the laws, some framing this as evidence of the laws' origins in precedent cases.[364] Archi argues that HL stem from customary law but have been transformed by the addition of palace concerns.[365] Most of the discussion around this collection of laws has centered on the evidence for reform within the texts themselves. This comes in two forms. One is the *karu…kinuna*, "formerly…now" passages which mention the old ruling and the new one. The second is evidenced in the New Kingdom text KBo 6.4 (PT)[366] which covers the same material as the Old Kingdom version of the laws, but has often changed the ruling in some way.[367] This evidence for the reforming or updating of the Hittite Laws has affected the debate about their nature. For example, Westbrook states: "Regular changes to keep abreast of developments in the law would not have been necessary if the text were merely academic."[368] While this may possibly be a useful contrast with the later copying of LH, perhaps showing it was copied due to its literary or academic excellence rather than its legal import, it does not imply that LH itself was not originally intended to influence the law of Babylonia. Our earlier contention that the Mesopotamian scribes' unwillingness to speak of legal reforms (changes to royally promulgated law) in contrast to the Hittite openness to speak of such things should also be taken into consideration when weighing up the impact of these sections of HL on the debate surrounding the nature and purpose of the ancient Near Eastern law collections. This said, the fact that HL does tell us that it was updated/reformed

---

362 Hoffner's translation, *Hittite Laws*, 98.

363 E. Neufeld, *Hittite Laws* (London: Luzac & Co., 1951), 111 discusses the significance of this colophon and argues that it may just represent the fact that a king had this text copied, not necessarily that he instigated its collection. Hoffner's New Kingdom dating of this text would support such an idea, *Laws of the Hittites*, 161.

364 *e.g.* Hoffner in Roth, *Law Collections*, 215. Neufeld, *Hittite Laws*, 110.

365 Alfonso Archi, "La formazione del diritto nell'Anatolia Ittita," in *La Formazione del Diritto ne vicino oriente antico* (ed. Aristide Theodorides, Carlo Zaccagnini, Guillaume Cardascia, Alfonso Archi and Reuven Yaron; Rome: Edizioni Scientifiche Italiene, 1988), 61–76.

366 Parallel text. The term and abbreviation given follows Hoffner, in Roth, *Law Collections*.

367 There are numerous New Kingdom copies of HL which do not show this reforming aspect.

368 Westbrook, "Biblical and Cuneiform Law Codes," 256.

etc. does have some implications for *its* relation to the law of practice. It is highly unlikely that such a text would be updated or mention reforms if it was not intended to bear relation to actual law. Unfortunately for us, though the Hittite Laws themselves are the most copied of the Hittite texts at our disposal, our evidence for Hittite legal practice is extremely poor and we cannot assess the relationship between the two in this way.[369]

Though we can be certain that within HL the reforming paragraphs "may show that the Code is linked to the law in practice", we must concede with Westbrook that "they do not necessarily mean that the Code is the source of the reform mentioned."[370] Though a number of commentators have taken these reforming paragraphs to mean that the laws were the source of the reform,[371] HL could just be a description of the law in practice rather than its prescription or reform.[372] Many have continued to see it as a law book of sorts whether of a private or royal nature.[373] If the evidence for reform in HL merely shows that it is a reflection of current laws or legal standards, an attribute ascribed by most commentators to all law collections to varying degrees,[374] then does this aspect of HL necessarily distinguish its function from that of any other collections?

It is similarly difficult to ascertain the purpose of LE. Depending on which evidence one focuses on, this text has been variously linked to[375] or

---

[369] See comments of Haase, "The Hittite Kingdom," 619.

[370] Westbrook, "Cuneiform Law," 205. See also his discussion of HL 55 in this regard. It ascribes the reform to the king's father.

[371] *e.g.* Haase, "The Hittite Kingdom," 620. Neufeld sees most of HL as a lawbook, but sees the *karu…kinuna* sections as statute, or the prescription of positive law, *Hittite Laws*, 107.

[372] One of Westbrook's main contentions for all the formal law collections of this period.

[373] Marian San Nicolò, "Die Stellung der Keilschrifturkunden in der vorderasiatischen Rechtsentwicklung," *Zeitschrift der Savigny-Stiftung für Rechtsgeschichte* 48 (1928): 37 and *Beiträge zur Rechtsgeschichte im Bereiche der keilschriftlichen Rechtsquellen* (Instituttet for Sammenlignende Kulturforskning 13; Oslo: Aschehoug & Co., 1931), 97; Korošec, "Beiträge zum hethitischen Privatrecht," *Zeitschrift der Savigny-Stiftung für Rechtsgeschichte* 52 (1932): 157. Westbrook, "Biblical and Cuneiform Law Codes," 255 sees it as part of the royal archives because of its location.

[374] *e.g.* Westbrook, description not prescription, "Cuneiform Law," 205. Malul, review of Westbrook *Studies in Biblical and Cuneiform Law*, 85–90, among others, has criticised him for assuming this reflection. Roth sees the collections as a reflection of legal standards of some sort *e.g.* *Law Collections*, 1.

[375] *e.g.* Wesbrook, "Character," 9; Yoffee, "Context and Authority," 100.

separated from[376] the monumental law collections, linked to *mišarum* edicts,[377] seen as a text that stands midway between the two,[378] and could be linked to the scholarly texts also.[379] Unlike MAL or HL, LE contains a short superscription at its beginning. Its mention of the kingship of Eshnunna and military conquests could be seen as a link to the themes of the non-legal sections of the monumental law collections. We possess no evidence that LE was set up as a monument. Our two main witnesses to this text are clay tablets which have sometimes been interpreted as school texts,[380] as private copies of an official inscription,[381] or extracts of some other real law of Eshnunna.[382] Our third witness to the collection has been described as "a student exercise tablet recording extracts from the laws".[383] It seems it is only the superscription that would enable us to distinguish this text from the "scholarly" texts.

In fact, this superscription has been used to link LE to the *mišarum* and other Old Babylonian edicts such as AE.[384] AE also begins with a dated superscription written in Sumerian, in contrast to the rest of the collection which is in Akkadian. The economic focus of some of LE's provisions has also provided material for scholars to make the link between it and these other edicts *e.g.* LE's first provisions deal with prices and rates of exchange. Its later provisions deal with topics more regularly found in the formal law collections.[385] Perhaps this is a slightly false distinction given the fact that

---

376 *e.g.* Michalowski and Walker, "A New Sumerian 'Law Code'," 386.

377 Roth, *Law Collections*, 57.

378 Finkelstein, "Ammisaduqa's Edict," 102–3.

379 *e.g.* all three copies of the text could be interpreted as school copies or exercise texts. See Westbrook, "Biblical and Cuneiform Law Codes," 252 and Roth, *Law Collections*, 58. Eichler, "Literary Structure," 81 links LE to Mesopotamian scholastic tradition on the basis of its structure and presentation of polar cases.

380 Westbrook, "Biblical and Cuneiform Law Codes," 252.

381 *e.g.* Yaron, "Context and Authority," 30.

382 John C. Miles and O. R. Gurney, "The Laws of Eshnunna," *Archiv Orientalni* 17 (1949): 174–88.

383 Roth, *Law Collections*, 58.

384 *e.g.* discussion of Roth, *Law Collections*, 57; Finkelstein, "Ammisaduqa's Edict," 102–3.

385 But see Yoffee, "Context and Authority," 100 who sees LE as slightly different to the monumental collections due to subject matter and arrangement, though he is speaking, at least in part, about the economic measures contained at the beginning of the provisions and the lack of a prologue and epilogue as in the other monumental collections.

AE also deals with non-economic topics, and that the other formal law collections deal with prices and economic measures also.[386] Sometimes the spattering of relative (as opposed to the *šumma* clauses) clauses are used to make links to the edicts or to proclamations in general,[387] at other times it is the apodictic clauses which are used for this purpose.[388] The fact that the relative formulation also turns up in MAL and is but a variation of a casuistic framing should make one a little hesitant to follow this line of argument. The fact that AE does contain a number of *šumma* clauses should have the same effect or perhaps, may make us question any strict distinction between the formal collections and edicts/decrees based on form. Perhaps what an analysis of the nature and function of LE tells us is that such things cannot and should not be hastily decided on the basis of form or genre.

Again, we have a variety of opinions of the text's purpose ranging from those who see the laws as officially promulgated[389] (perhaps linked to the political context of empire again)[390] to those who see it as some kind of private text based on actual law.[391] All agree that the text is non-comprehensive and perhaps has an emphasis on the exceptional.[392]

2.1.4.14 School Texts

Let us now turn to the group of texts which are generally classed as "scholarly" or "school texts".[393] Is the distinction between these texts and the formal law collections a secure one or is the link between these two groups of texts perhaps so strong that we should postulate a school origin for the

---

[386] *e.g.* LH 268–277 and the prologue of LU which speaks of the standardisation of measures, A iii 135–iv 149.

[387] *e.g.* Yaron, *Laws of Eshnunna*, 1988, 106–113.

[388] *e.g.* Finkelstein, "Ammisaduqa's Edict," 102.

[389] Yaron, *Laws of Eshnunna*, 1988, 30; Albrecht Goetze, *Laws of Eshnunna* (Annual of the American School of Oriental Research 31; New Haven: Department of Antiquities of the Government of Iraq and the American Schools of Oriental Research, 1956), 16. Korošec, "Keilschriftrecht," 87.

[390] *e.g.* Goetze, "The Laws of Eshnunna Discovered at Tell Harmal," *Sumer* 4 (1948): 67 for Bilalama (a claim later abandoned by Goetze, *Laws of Eshnunna*). This ruler is no longer seen to be connected to the collection, but a similar imperial context also fits for Dadusha.

[391] Miles and Gurney, "Laws of Eshnunna". Yaron mixes the two, seeing the original as officially promulgated and the tablets we have as private copies, *Laws of Eshnunna*, 30.

[392] *e.g.* Yaron, *Laws of Eshnunna*, 86.

[393] SLEx, SLHF, LOx.

formal collections also? Levinson has stated that texts such as SLHF are "important for the ongoing debate about whether the cuneiform legal collections possessed legislative force or represented scribal reflection on ideal norms."[394] Given the fact that this text has a mixture of law provisions in a framing similar to that of the formal law collections[395] and phrases taken from contractual clauses, perhaps we need to rethink the implications of a link between "scholarly texts" and law collections. Why is it that on the one hand one is happy to see the phrases within SLHF as reflecting the scribal practicing of phrases they may have to write in actual legal contracts, whereas when they copy provisions that may appear similar to those in law collections we are to presume that this is merely an academic exercise and serves no practical purpose? Surely this is no more than an assumption. To then argue for a similar purpose for the formal law collections based on similarity with these texts is certainly false methodology.

Within SLHF, the collection of legal phrases next to provisions like those of the formal law collections need not lead one to the conclusion that this text was merely a scholarly exercise. Surely this text could be seen in the way others have seen LE or MAL, as a private collection of some official for his role in the judicial system. Of course, whether the laws within the collection reflected the common law, some officially promulgated written law collection or the academic musings of the legal scholar we cannot tell.

The text named Sumerian Laws Exercise Tablet by Roth (SLEx) does contain a number of hints that the copy we have comes from a school context. The most solid of this evidence is the fact that the scribe, having written *tukum-bi* mistakenly three times, later writes it out properly three times in succession. Apart from this there is only the fact that the scribe has left a colophon listing the number of lines and his name at the bottom of the tablet to tell us that this may be a school text rather than a promulgated law collection. Does this really tell us anything about the original purpose of the text? LH was copied for over a millennia by scribes who sometimes made mistakes and who may or may not have left a colophon at the bottom of the tablet. For MAL and HL we possess similar colophons also.[396] Does this imply that these texts were also nothing but scribal exercises or does it

---

394 Bernard M. Levinson, review of M.T. Roth (with a contribution by H.A. Hoffner), *Law Collections from Mesopotamia and Asia Minor*, *Journal of Near Eastern Studies* 59 (2000): 119.

395 *e.g.* 15 sections of SLHF begin with *šumma*.

396 And Roth thinks it possible that there was space for one at the bottom of LE, *Law Collections*, 58.

just show us that such texts could be copied whether for legal purposes or for scribal education?[397] SLEx was originally interpreted as a code of laws like that of LH,[398] and it must be said that the subject matter of the collection is quite prevalent in other collections. LOx is quite similar. Like SLEx, the copy of it appears to have come from a school context and its subject matter is commonly covered in other law collections.[399] This raises the possibility that these texts serve a different function to the more formal law collections that circulated independently of them, "and, with its repetitive language and limited subject matter, lent itself to student copying and memorization."[400] But that is all it does and this remains but a possibility. We do not have evidence that this text or SLEx were circulated or memorized. It is quite possible that they reflect the study of different topics taken from other law collections, but it is always possible that they are but copies of formal law collections. They certainly do not necessarily imply that LH, or any other formal law collection, was not intended to have any effect.

2.1.4.15 Conclusions

Is the difference between scholarly acceptance of the applicability of ancient Near Eastern law collections based on an objective difference between decrees and law "codes" as Westbrook would have us believe? The evidence is inconclusive, but the classifications usually given to these texts are a little too rigid and unconvincing at crucial points. The arguments used to ascertain the nature and purpose of these same documents do not hold up when looked at from a comparative perspective as we have offered here. The fact that a document was set up on a stele or some other monument has been used by some to question the legal import of several law collections while other scholars do not see a problem with a monumental text having legal import as well as some other role.[401] The use of external evidence for the

---

[397] Whether in legal thought, literary forms or literacy more generally.

[398] by A. T. Clay, *Miscellaneous Inscriptions in the Yale Babylonian Collections* (Yale Oriental Series Babylonian Texts 1; New Haven: Yale University Press,1915), 18. Clay also translated the Sumerian term *ti-la* as "laws" and rendered lines 2 and 3 of column vi of the reverse as "laws of Nisaba and Hani", whereas Roth renders the same text as part of a dedication of the copy of the text to these deities, *Law Collections*, 45.

[399] See comments of Roth, *Law Collections*, 40.

[400] *Ibid*, 40.

[401] *e.g.* Amélie Kuhrt, *The Ancient Near East: c. 3000–330 BC* (vol. 1; London: Routledge, 1995), 111–12.

citation of laws or the correspondence of documents from legal practice with law collections to decide the import of the latter has been seen to be problematic. The creation of separate generic categories for these law collections has also been shown to be unhelpful when trying to decide upon their nature. Arguments regarding the historical context surrounding the giving of a law collection may offer possibilities as to the reason for a collection's promulgation, but given the problems in dating many of these texts[402] and the difficulty in determining the role they were intended to play, it is difficult to make much use of such arguments. The existence of copies of these texts has been used to say more than it can. The fact that a document may have been copied tells us little about its original purpose. In the end, what we are left with, rather than a rigid distinction between text types, each with a similar nature and purpose, is a continuum of different texts which could cover various topics for various purposes and be formulated and framed in a number of different ways and be copied for multiple reasons. We are left with a number of possibilities regarding the nature, purpose and function of these texts. Where the texts themselves have claimed a purpose we have more right to propose one on this basis. Unfortunately, research regarding one of the few texts which does this, LH, has consisted of scholars explaining away some of the legal purposes which were claimed. Our best evidence for the nature of these texts comes from internal clues within the texts themselves such as Hammurabi's desires regarding his stele's effects on the *awilum ḫablum* or the future ruler and his land and his statements about what it shows he has already achieved in the realm of law, the evidence for reform within HL, the superscription on LE, the non-legal sections on other collections. Perhaps our best evidence for the purpose of MAL came from its supposed findspot in the gate of Shamash. Form criticism tells us nothing unless we concoct an extremely complicated prehistory for all our texts so as to not have to explain the texts we have before us. We found that even after all the evidence that is brought to bear, our conclusions on such matters are far from certain.

One issue which has not been mentioned in much detail has been the actual content of the collections. For the *mišarum* edicts, it is the content of the provisions which enables us to postulate its purpose for economic relief. For MAPD, the content confirms the evidence from the non-legal sections that this text is aimed at the regulation of the internal running of the palace. When we come to discuss other law collections, often the content of the provisions has been seen as unimportant, perhaps reflecting something

---

[402] *e.g.* HL, LU, LE, MAL.

resembling the law of practice or some utopian dream of its reform. For the monumental texts especially, many seem to treat the content as mere window dressing to show that the king was just. Perhaps there is more to it than this and an analysis of the content may be able to tell us a little more about the purpose of the collection. At the least, the content should make one suspect, as the first editors of these texts did, that texts containing collections of legal rulings were most likely intended to effect the practice of law to some extent, whether that be through legislation, the collection of exemplary decisions, or decisions on extreme or difficult cases, past commands or decisions of use to judges *etc*. Perhaps an attempt to reconstruct the society which would be created by the application of the laws within collections would be a helpful step towards understanding their intended purposes. Unfortunately the limitations of space mean that such an undertaking must wait. An analysis of the relation of the content of the provisions of LH to Hammurabi's context in Old Babylonian economy, society and politics and to the non-legal sections of his collection would be useful. This writer suspects that these provisions reflect the society Hammurabi wished to create, or had attempted to create. If this was found to be the case, it may go someway towards explaining the lack of citation of LH and perhaps even its perceived lack of correspondence to the documents from practice. It is possible that the end of his empire, his short lived dynasty and the nature of Mesopotamian law, were the reasons his laws were not put into practice. If one were to find that the effect of putting these provisions into practice would have been the accomplishment of the purposes set out in the non-legal sections of the collection, this may lend weight to the idea that these were intended to be put into practice in some form or another.

The comparisons to this point have dealt with various non-legal aspects of the law collections. The following sections will be comparing the legal material itself. This will focus on the similarity or lack thereof between the laws in topics for which there is comparative material. This will involve analysis of the similarity of the situation or offence outlined, the phraseology and vocabulary employed, as well as the proposed outcome of the case. To some extent a comparison will be made regarding the various penalties for each offence. For the most part this will be left until section 2.7 where a comparative analysis of the penalties across collections will be made. A difference of penalty within laws across collections does not rule out the possibility of borrowing though it can demonstrate the lack of a uniform or common law in the ancient Near East. This writer is attempting to determine whether the parallels are quite general, only involving a surface similarity in terms of the topic treated, or are so close that borrowing is likely.

This is a somewhat subjective exercise as discussed in the first chapter, but worthwhile nonetheless. It is hoped that this more comprehensive comparison will help to discern a more accurate view regarding borrowing than that which comes about through selection only of examples where it is considered highly likely.

2.2 ROLE OF JUDGE AND KING

Amongst the laws which mention the roles of judges and kings there is very little of interest from a comparative perspective. There is some very general evidence which enables some insight into the various roles of judges: investigating claims, hearing/seeing evidence, issuing required documents, granting or withholding permission for certain actions, not allowed to change his judgment as well as some sanctions against dishonesty and penalties against those who do not follow his judgment. Possibly of significance with regards to the nature and purpose of MAL is the fact that this collection makes more mention of judges than any other. This supports the scholarly suspicion that MAL was intended as some kind of judge's private law book, though it hardly proves the point. In keeping with the nature of LH in general (in terms of its size), there is more information in this collection about the activity of judges.

There are two issues which are of interest. The first relates to Westbrook's contention that there is a distinction between the collections he terms edicts or decrees and the more formal law collections with regards to their contents, with the former supposedly dealing mainly with administrative and economic matters. It is interesting to note that within the collections Westbrook terms edicts/decrees, EH is alone in its mention of judges.[403] The second relates to another of Westbrook's contentions, namely, that LE 48 is applicable across the entire ancient Near East *i.e.* that judges decide lesser cases and the king decides capital ones.[404]

> **LE 48** And for a case involving a penalty of silver in amounts ranging from 20 shekels to 60 shekels, the judges shall determine the case against him; however, a capital case is only for the king.

It must be said that there is some evidence supporting the notion that decisions could be passed up the line from judges to the king *e.g.* MAL C 8,

---

[403] To be fair, the Hittite "Instructions to Commanders of Border Garrisons," trans. Gregory McMahon (*COS* 1.84: 221–25) does contain mention of their role as judges *e.g.* section 36.

[404] Westbrook, "Character," 30.

HL 102 and *Hittite Instruction for Border Officials* sect. 36.[405] In none of these cases is there the notion that it is only capital cases that go to the king. HL 102, for instance, states that the theft of 3 talents of wood becomes a case for the king's court. Nowhere else in HL is a theft offence punished by death.[406] Given the fact that the theft of two talents of wood only attracts a six shekel penalty it is quite unlikely that this was a capital case. In the Hittite *Instructions to Commanders of Border Garrisons*, as in Exodus 18, the decisions are passed up the line due to their difficulty rather than their gravity. That the king played a role in judging non-capital cases in Assyria is quite clear from other laws such as MAL B 3 and C 10, and it is possible that the laws regarding sorcery in HL 44b and 111, and that regarding a bull outside its corral in HL 176a were not necessarily capital cases.[407] The abundant evidence of the involvement of Old Babylonian kings in mundane, everyday judgments, as witnessed in the numerous letters between the kings and their officials is also testimony to this.[408] Sorcery is also a case for the king in MAL A 47 (which was possibly a capital case) and in ETel. 50. There is evidence that the king had involvement in capital cases in LH 129, LE 58, and the Hittite sex laws *e.g.* 187–88, 198–200a.

There are two laws which possibly cast some doubt on the idea that capital cases were only for the king. The first is ETel. 49. The law deals with a case of murder. In the context of the document as a whole, it probably relates to murder within the intrigues and political maneuverings around the throne. It is stated that the heir of the murdered man can decide whether the offender is killed or makes compensation. The last line contains a statement about the king which Hoffner translates as: "The king shall have no role in the decision."[409] This would seem to imply that the king was to have no role in a decision regarding a capital case. Van den Hout, staying closer to the original, translates the phrase differently: "For the king (there will be) nothing, however."[410] The import of this last line seems to be that

---

[405] Compare also Exodus 18.

[406] The exception to this is found in HL 126, relating to the theft of a spear from the palace. See the later discussion of this law in the section comparing theft laws where it is argued that the unique severity of this law is probably related to the possible use of such an implement for an assassination attempt.

[407] See later discussion of laws regarding sorcery and the goring ox.

[408] *e.g.* letters to Shamash-Hazir in Kraus, *Briefe Shamash-Hazir.*

[409] Hoffner in Roth, *Law Collections*, 237.

[410] "The Proclamation of Telipinu" (*COS* 1.76: 198).

the king will not benefit financially from whatever compensation is paid,[411] rather than that he plays no role in the decision (though this also seems to be true). There are numerous examples of capital cases within these law collections which do not mention the role of the king in the deciding of the case. MAL A 15 specifically mentions that a capital case, involving accusation of adultery, can be brought to either a judge or a king. Though there is good evidence that cases could be passed up the chain of authority, and that kings often did play a role in deciding capital cases, LE 48 does not seem to have been a uniform rule throughout the ancient Near East.

It is worth noting that the Hittite Laws mention the king's role in judging far more than any other collection. It is possible that this is due to a different role for the Hittite king with regards to the legal system at Hatti as compared to Mesopotamia and Egypt. HL 55 displays an interesting feature unique to the Hittites amongst the collections being compared here *i.e.* a narrative description of events leading up to a legal decision.[412]

2.3 MARRIAGE AND DIVORCE

There are certainly some similarities amongst the laws treating marriage and divorce in the ancient Near Eastern collections, though there are also differences. One area where there is not uniformity is that regarding the requirement of some form of written contract for a marriage to be legitimate. This is seen as a necessary requirement in LH 128, LE 27–28 and LU 11. Each of these laws, however, treats a slightly different situation: LH treats marriage in general; LE treats a similar situation but also the implications such an act has for adulterous offences; LU 11 specifically speaks of widows. MAL A 34 also treats marriage to widows, but contains a ruling very different from the others:

> **MAL A 34** If a man should marry a widow without her formal binding agreement and she resides in his house for two years, she is a wife; she shall not leave.

It seems unlikely that there was any literary borrowing among these given their very different framing and slightly different subject matter. The

[411] Perhaps compare the reduction of fines in HL due to the waiving of the palace share. See the later discussion of this in section 2.7.

[412] See the earlier discussion of this feature in 2.1.3 where it was compared to ETel. and RU and contrasted to the rest of the Mesopotamian and Egyptian collections.

law in MAL also shows that this law was not treated in uniform fashion throughout the ancient Near East. Compare:

> **LH 128** If a man marries a wife but does not draw up a formal contract for her, she is not a wife.

An area where there is more agreement concerns the breaking of marriage negotiations. Prior to the full consummation of marriage, at least within the societies for whom we have cuneiform law collections, there was some form of payment from the groom to his prospective father-in-law. Once this was paid the law treated the couple as married as regards outsiders, but the marriage could still be called off by either party. This situation, the breaking of marriage negotiations after the bridewealth had been paid, is dealt with in a fairly uniform way in the extant collections. The most common law amongst the collections concerns the breaking of the deal by the father-in-law. If this happens, he is to return the brideprice double *cf.* LH 160–161; LE 25; LU 15; LL 29; HL 29. It would be difficult to argue for substantial literary borrowing amongst these laws given the many differences in framing. These laws mention the involvement of a third party. LH 161 and LL 29 forbid the marriage of the betrothed woman to any third party to whom her parents may want to give her, whereas LE 25 and LU 15 do not. HL 28 envisages another situation where another man has run off with the betrothed woman. In this case the man who elopes with the woman is to compensate the groom-to-be. If the father and mother gave the woman to another man, they are responsible for the compensation. There is no hint here that the woman cannot run off with another man, or that the parents cannot give the woman to another man, just that this would be an expensive exercise. Interesting in the Hittite collection is the mention of the father and mother rather than just the father, and also the possibility of the bride-to-be running off with someone else and thus herself abrogating the agreement. LH 159 and HL 30 also cover the situation where the groom-to-be abrogates the agreement. In both cases he forfeits the brideprice. The other collections do not treat this situation. Only the two Sumerian collections mention the son-in-law entering the house of his father-in-law as an action occurring at the time of the payment of the brideprice. Compare this to LE 25 where the husband comes to claim the bride from the house of his father-in-law after the payment has been made.

The situation where one member of the married couple dies before they have children is dealt with in several collections. Both LH 163–164 and LE 17–18 determine that both the bridewealth and the dowry should return to their original households, though they phrase this very differently.[413] MAL A 30–31 deal with this situation slightly differently. MAL A 30 specifies that a woman's father can cancel marriage proceedings in the case where the prospective groom is put in a situation where he has to carry out levirate marriage (*i.e.* an older brother has died leaving a childless widow). If the pending marriage is cancelled by the girl's father the prospective groom's father is able to take back the non-consumable portion of the bridal gift and marriage prestation. MAL A 31 allows a man who has presented the bridal gift to his father-in-law to choose whether he will marry a different daughter or take back non-edibles in the case that his prospective bride dies. HL 193 also specifies levirate marriage in the case of a deceased older brother. HL 27 treats the death of a man's wife quite differently to elsewhere. Her personal possessions are to be burnt and her husband is to keep the dowry if there are no children rather than returning it to his father-in-law.

Divorce of a woman by a man seems to be dealt with differently across the collections. LH 138–139 treats the divorce of a woman who had not borne a man children. If there was bridewealth he is to give her silver to its value and return her dowry to her; if not, he pays her 60 shekels. LE 59 treats the divorce of a woman who had borne a man children. Unfortunately the provision is broken. The man seems to be expelled from the house of his second wife. LU 9, similar to LH 139 sets a price of 60 shekels for divorcing a first-ranking wife, LU 10, 30 shekels in the case of the divorce of a widow. SLHF iv 12–14 also implies that divorce involves some kind of payment. MAL A 37, however, declares that a man who wants to divorce his wife can choose whether or not he wants to give her anything. MAL A 38 states that, if his wife was still living in her father's house, the woman gets to keep the bridewealth and the husband can take back any other valuables he gave her. These laws are difficult to compare, but it seems that the woman gets a tougher deal in MAL than elsewhere. Divorce at the behest of the woman is treated in LH and HL. In LH 141 a woman who wants to leave but appropriates goods, squanders possessions or disparages her husband can be divorced by her husband without receiving any payment, or can be made to reside in her husband's house as a slave woman. LH 142–143 possibly treat a case where a woman wants a divorce. Her case is to be investigated. If she passes the tests then she can take her

---

[413] For discussion about the difficulties involved in LE 18 see Roth, *Law Collections*, 69, nn. 5–6; Westbrook, "A Death in the Family: Codex Eshnunna 17–18 Revisited," *Israel Law Review* 29 (1995): 32–42; Yaron, *Laws of Eshnunna*, 54–55.

dowry and leave; if not she is drowned. The only other mention of divorce at the behest of the wife comes in LH 149. In the case that a woman suffers from disease and her husband has married another, she has the right to either stay and be supported or take her dowry and leave for her father's house. HL 26 by contrast, seems to envisage divorce at the behest of the woman as less problematic. The woman takes some sort of payment for bearing children and the man keeps the land and children.

2.4 PROPERTY AND INHERITANCE

2.4.1 Real Estate

Though there is an abundance of laws treating real estate matters within LH, there are only two topics which have comparable material elsewhere: boundary violations and state land. MAL and SLHF also both treat the topic of common property and its upkeep.

There are laws treating boundary violations in LH d, MAL B 8–10, 12–15, 19–20, HL 168–69 and LU 30. Both LH d and LU 30 deal with the unlawful cultivation of another's uncultivated or neglected field. Unfortunately, much of LH d is broken so they are difficult to compare. The laws in MAL on this topic treat a range of offences from the unlawful incorporation of another's land to the building of structures on it, to the unlawful use of it for cultivation or brick making. None of these laws treat exactly the same topic as LH d or LU 30. MAL B 8 treats the unlawful incorporation of a large area of another's land into one's own border severely, punishing this offence with the removal of a finger. This Assyrian prevalence towards corporal punishments will be further demonstrated in the later discussion of topics related to criminal law. Displaying another cultural peculiarity, the Hittite Laws treating this topic involve some kind of sacrifice and reconsecration of the field. There is many other pieces of evidence demonstrating the peculiarly Hittite focus on ritual and purity aspects of law within their law collections. There is nothing in this material upon which one could base and argument for literary borrowing or a common background of cuneiform legal science.

The same is the case within the laws of LH and HL treating the distribution, upkeep and services due from state land. The most that can be said is that both societies utilized a system similar to the medieval feudal system in the distribution of parcels of state-owned land. The system is better understood for LH and the Old Babylonian period, but the Hittite material is clearly not merely a literary borrowing but reflects the peculiarities of the Hittite administration of such land. The relevant laws in LH deal with soldiers and fishermen who are given land in return for various services/payments. This land cannot be sold or transferred. Within the Hittite laws there is a similarity in that state land is being given to certain people in return for payments/services, but it does not seem to be for the same reasons as in LH. This practice is fairly common throughout the historical records, there being parallels in Egypt and medieval Europe. There are many differences between each system of course, as there is here between LH and HL, but the explication of these differences is not the concern of this work. It is enough to state that the similarities in LH 27–41 and HL 39–42, 46–56 are unlikely to be due to literary borrowing, common legal science or any common ancient Near Eastern culture. That the two systems are not identical and that the drafters of the law collections did not have the same topics in mind is demonstrated by a comparison of LH 26 and 33 with HL 42. LH punishes with death any soldier who hires a substitute to go on a royal campaign in his stead whereas HL 42 is concerned only that a person hired to go on military campaign was paid before they went.

The laws treating the upkeep of common property in MAL B 17–18, O 5 and SLHF iii 18–19 share little in common. The Assyrian laws treat the upkeep of irrigation canals whereas SLHF merely refers to shared responsibility for a common wall.

2.4.2 Inheritance

The inheritance of the dowry after a woman's death is a topic treated in a number of collections. In LH,[414] LL[415] and MAL,[416] the dowry goes to the woman's children. If there are no children, it goes back to her father's household (in LH 163 anyway). In MAL, there is the additional possibility that the husband can "take control of her" and give the dowry to one or more of his sons at his discretion. In HL 27, the dowry is not specifically said to be for the children. If the woman dies in her husband's house, her husband keeps the dowry; if in her father's house, her father seems to keep it. Perhaps there is a distinction here between Mesopotamian and Hittite practice.

There are a number of other laws treating the topic of inheritance in the case of the death of the father/head of the household, including those treating the topic of the upkeep of widows. In LH, unless her dead husband

---

[414] LH 162–64, 167, 172–74.

[415] LL 24.

[416] MAL A 29.

has willed her a portion of his estate,[417] the widow has the choice of remaining in her husband's property and having use of it until she dies[418] or, if her children are still young, she can remarry.[419] The laws in MAL on this topic are more detailed, including situations where the widow is residing in her father's house.[420] MAL A 46 basically sets out the same provisions as those in LH, but does so quite differently and adds a number of possibilities *e.g.* marriage to one of her husband's sons. Though the topic and conclusions are similar, borrowing is hardly proven here.

LH 172–74, 177 deal with the topic of a widow's remarriage and the inheritance issues arising regarding the dowry and the estates of her two husbands. MAL A 28 contains a provision differently formulated from that in LH 177. LH 177 describes the remarriage of a widow with young children and stipulates that the later husband will be entrusted with the estate of her former husband but that it will be inventoried and all of it will pass on to the children of the former husband. MAL A 28 specifies the remarriage of a widow who marries with her former husband's child in her womb. The child can either be adopted into the new household or merely take an inheritance share from his father's estate. Though the two rulings amount to a similar thing, they are approached from different angles and formulated very differently, making substantial borrowing unlikely.

Laws discussing inheritance issues relating to a man's second marriage appear in LH, LL and MAL. LH 167 treats the remarriage of a man after his wife's death. This topic is not treated anywhere else. There are a number of laws which specifically treat a secondary marriage to a slave woman: LH 170–172 and LL 25–26. LH deals with the inheritance of the children from a secondary marriage to a slave which occurs while the first-ranking wife is still alive. If the father declares the children of the slave woman to be "My children", then they divide the estate with the children of the first ranking wife, with the preferential share going to a son of the latter. If the father doesn't declare such a status, the release of the slave woman and her children is secured but they do not inherit. The ruling of LL 25 seems to parallel the second situation outlined above (*i.e.* the children of a slave woman and the slave woman are released from slavery but do not inherit), as set out in LH 171, but does not specify any declaration by the father. LL 26 treats a slightly different situation, namely, a secondary marriage to a slave woman

---

[417] LH 150.

[418] LH 171–72.

[419] LH 177.

[420] MAL A 25–26 and 33.

after the death of the first ranking wife. In this case, the ruling parallels that of LH 170, including the stipulation that a child of the first ranking wife will be the primary heir. It is possible that the drafter of LH knew of these laws and used them in some kind of reformation of inheritance law but this is speculative. Though the rulings of LL 25–26 parallel those of LH 170–71, the situations described in each case are not the same.

The marriage of a male slave to a free woman is best dealt with in this section due to the fact that the main concern of the drafters of the laws on this topic was with the division of property amongst slave, spouse and master. LH 175 states that the children resultant from the marriage of a slave to a free woman will not be claimed as slaves by the slave's owner. LU 5, however, states that such a marriage requires one male child to be placed at the service of the slave's owner.

The Hittite Laws also contain a number of laws treating the marriage of slaves, both to other slaves and to either male or female free persons. None of these parallel the laws treating the marriage of slaves in LH or LU *e.g.* whereas LH 176 and HL 32 treat the division of property in the case of the marriage of a male slave to a free woman, LH does so in the case of the death of one's partner, whereas HL does so in the case of divorce.

Both LH 166 and LL 32 concern the provision of bridewealth for an unmarried son upon the death of his father. Unfortunately, LL 32 is too broken to compare fruitfully. Interestingly, LL 23 also contains a law regarding the provision of a dowry for an unmarried daughter. Again, LH 165 and LL 31 both enable a father to give a special gift to a favored son. It is worth noting that these two sets of parallel laws are placed next to each other, in the same order in both collections. It is not impossible that the drafter of LH had knowledge of LL 31–32, nor is it proven that he did.

There is a possible parallel between LH 180 and LL 22 regarding the inheritance of *naditu*. Both laws specify that a *naditu* will divide the estate as an equal heir. LL 22 connects this to an *ugbabtu* or *qadištu* also, while LH 180 connects it to only cloistered *naditu* or a *sekretu*. LH also specifies that the daughter only has the use of the property which still legally belongs to her brothers, whereas LL makes no such statement. This is likely to be an actual difference rather than a more detailed statement in LH as compared to LL. This author is inclined to this conclusion partly due to the unique statement in LL b that unmarried daughters can inherit their father's estate if there is no male heir. It seems there is a slightly different attitude to female inheritance within this collection, at least as compared to LH.

There is very little to compare again concerning disinheritance. LH mentions disinheritance in three places: LH 158, 168–69. The first law prescribes disinheritance for the son who sleeps with his father's principal wife after his father's death, the latter two describe the process of disinheritance which must be overseen and investigated by judges. HL 171 merely describes the ritual used for disinheritance or reinstatement.

There has been some debate surrounding the existence of a double share for the eldest son in Mesopotamia, some arguing that this was a northern, rather than southern practice.[421] As far as the law collections can bear on this issue, LH 170 prescribes a preferential share and LL 26 determines a primary heir, while MAL B 1 specifically mentions a double share for the eldest son. This material does not seem to decide the issue.

2.4.3 Adoption

There are a number of laws within the topic of adoption which relate to inheritance matters, others to contractual ones, hence its location in between these two topics. The relevant laws on this topic are found in LH 185–94, LE 32–35, LL 20, SLEx 4'–6', MAL A 28 and HL 200b. There are difficulties in comparing these laws given the possibility that a child could be taken for rearing without adoption.[422] At times it is difficult to know which arrangement is in view. For example, contrast LH 185 and LE 32:

> **LH 185** If a man takes in adoption a young child at birth and then rears him, that rearling will not be reclaimed.

> **LE 32** If a man gives his child for suckling and for rearing but does not give the food, oil, and clothing rations (to the caregiver) for 3 years, he shall weigh and deliver 10 shekels of silver for the cost of the rearing of his child, and he shall take away his child.

Is this a contrast or two laws for different situations both protecting the adopter (*i.e.* the child stays with them and payment for services is assured)? This hinges on how the last sentence of LE 32 is read. Is the "he" who takes away the child the father or the caregiver? If the caregiver, then it correlates with LH, if the father, then it is in direct contradiction to it. It is possible these laws are dealing with two different situations also *i.e.* LH treats adoption, LE rearing.

A form of adoption was also employed whereby a young child was taken by a craftsman to learn a trade. This appears to have been done differently in Mesopotamia than in Hatti:

---

[421] See Westbrook, "Cuneiform Law," 204 and note 14 for references.

[422] At least within the Ur III period. See Lafont and Westbrook, "Neo-Sumerian Period," 205.

LH 188 If a craftsman takes a young child to rear and then teaches him his craft, he will not be reclaimed.

LH 189 If he should not teach him his craft, that rearling shall return to his father's house.

LL 20b If a man does not raise the son whom he contracted to raise in an apprenticeship, and it is confirmed before the judges, he (the child) shall be returned to his birth mother.

HL 200b If anyone gives his son for training either as a carpenter or a smith, a weaver or a leatherworker or a fuller, he shall pay 6 shekels of silver as the fee for the training. If the teacher makes him an expert, the student shall give to his teacher one person.

In LH and LL, a child taken by a craftsman to learn a trade is only reclaimed if the craftsman breaks the contract, by failing to teach the trade to the child in LH 189, or failing to raise him in LL 20b. HL 200b, however, seems to set up this training via the payment of fees and a replacement person rather than through an adoption process and seems to imply that the student can go free after such payments. This arrangement is somewhat similar to that in LE 32 above regarding the payments required for the rearing of a child. This material is quite difficult to compare given the uncertainties regarding the arrangements in view, though there are certainly some similarities.

Much of the material regarding adoption finds no parallel in other collections. LH 190–193, treating the abrogation of the adoption contract, do find parallels in SLEx 4'–6'. LH 192–93 employ a technique common to LH and prescribe vicious penalties which are framed to fit the crime. A child reared by a courtier or a *sekretu* will have his tongue cut out if he declares his adoptive parents not to be his father or mother, or his eye plucked out if he decides to return to his biological father's house. In SLEx 4', an adopted child who declares his adoptive parents not to be his parents forfeits his possessions and is sold into slavery. The phrasing of SLEx 4' is close to that of LH 192 though the situation is not identical, and the punishment quite different. If any borrowing has occurred it has had little restriction on the formulation of the law. SLEx 5'–6' are quite different to LH 190–191. In the former laws, adoptive parents who attempt to disinherit their adopted son seem to forfeit their estate.[423] In the latter, if an adoptive father does not deem the adopted son as able to inherit an equal portion of his estate, the child is merely to return to his father's house. If he did deem the

[423] These laws are not well preserved.

adopted son as able to inherit his estate and then changed his mind after having children of his own, the adoptive father is to give him a one third share of the estate (in movables, not property).

2.5 CONTRACT

2.5.1 Loans

One commonality amongst some of these collections with regards to loans is the interest rate. In LH t, LE 18A and LX m–n it is stated that a loan in grain attracts an interest rate of thirty-three and a third percent, while a loan in silver twenty percent. No other collections mention interest rates. This similarity is most easily explained by the common background of these actual interest rates in practice in southern Mesopotamia rather than some kind of literary borrowing or common legal science.

There are two other parallel sets of laws on the topic of loans in LH and LE. LH 49–50 and LE 19 both state, in different ways, that the man who lends grain will not have to do any work to recover it with its interest. LH declares that the owner will take the grain and give it to the merchant, while LE states that the lender will collect his payment at the threshing floor (*i.e.* after the work of harvest is finished). The other similarity is found in LH u and LE 20–21 which, again, both state the same legal principle in different ways *i.e.* that the interest rate on a loan is set according to the commodity borrowed (*i.e.* grain or silver), not by the commodity of repayment. The dissimilarity in the phrasing of these laws argues against substantial literary borrowing. Common practice is the most likely explanation for the similar principle behind these different laws, though, of course, minor literary influence is not ruled out with regards to the selection of subject matter.

A better case for borrowing is found between LX 1 and LH 111. Roth's translation follows:

> **LH 111** If a woman innkeeper gives one vat of beer as a loan(?), she shall take 50 silas of grain at the harvest.
>
> **LX 1** If a woman innkeeper gives one of her vats (of beer on credit) to a man, [she shall receive] 50 silas of grain at the harvest.

There is a great degree of similarity between these two laws, so much so that LH 111 is almost a verbatim translation of LX 1. A number of the same ideograms appear in both laws.

On the whole there is little parallel material regarding loans, though there follows some concerning pledges and distraint. The most striking feature when one compares the laws to do with merchants, loans and trade across collections is the inordinate focus on these topics within LH and AE as compared to other collections.

2.5.2 Distraint

There are a number of similarities between the laws of distraint in LH 114–116 and LE 22–24, but no two laws treat exactly the same situation. LH 114 and LE 22 are similar in that they both treat unlawful distraint; however, LH 114 envisages distraint of a household member while LE 22, of a slave woman. LH 115–116 and LE 23–24 are similar in that they treat the death of a distrainee; however, there are a number of differences. LH distinguishes between a distrainee, lawfully distrained, who dies a natural death (for which there is no penalty) and a distrainee, lawfully distrained, who dies from abuse (in which case talion is implemented if it is the son of a man, or a fine of 20 shekels if it is a slave). LE, however, treats two situations of unlawful distraint where the distrainee dies at the hand of the distrainer. If the distrainee was a slave woman, the offender replaces her with two slave women. If the distrainee was the wife or child of a *muškenum* it is a capital offence. SLHF viii 3–10 also contains a law treating the death of a distrainee. In this law there is no specific mention of fault on the part of the distrainer and the distrainee's death is also linked to her disappearance, escape or illness. The distrainer merely has to compensate for her work quota. It would seem this law presumes the distrainee to be a female slave and is only interested in the economics of her unavailability. The law seems to assume lawful distraint. It is worth noting the use of talion in LH in contrast to its absence in LE, but there is little here to suggest more than a common topic within a similar society. The material regarding distraint in MAL and HL does not parallel material elsewhere. MAL is mainly concerned with the illegal sale of a distrainee though it is worth noting the horrifyingly brutal law A 44 with its list of acceptable abuses which can be meted upon a distrainee.

2.5.3 Deposit and Safekeeping

This topic is dealt with in LH, LE and MAL. There are two pairs of laws in LH and LE which are somewhat parallel:

> **LH 120** If a man stores his grain in another man's house, and a loss occurs in the storage bin or the householder opens the granary and takes the grain or he completely denies receiving the grain that was stored in his house-the owner of the grain shall establish his grain before the god,

> and the householder shall give to the owner of the grain twofold the grain that he took (in storage).
>
> **LE 36** If a man gives his goods to a *napṭaru* for safekeeping, and he (the *napṭaru*) then allows the goods which he gave to him for safekeeping to become lost-even without evidence that the house has been broken into, the doorjamb scraped, the window forced-he shall replace his goods for him.
>
> **LH 125** If a man gives his property for safekeeping and his property together with the householder's property is lost either by (theft achieved through) a breach or by scaling over a wall, the householder who was careless shall make restitution and shall restore to the owner of the property that which was given to him for safekeeping and which he allowed to be lost; the householder shall continue to search for his own lost property, and he shall take it from the one who stole it from him.
>
> **LE 37** If the man's house has been burglarized, and the owner of the house incurs a loss along with the goods which the depositor gave to him, the owner of the house shall swear an oath to satisfy him at the gate of (the temple of) the god Tishpak: "My goods have been lost along with your goods; I have not committed a fraud or misdeed"; thus shall he swear an oath to satisfy him and he will have no claim against him.

These laws cover situations where property which had been given to another for safekeeping has been lost. The second pair of laws both treat the situation where both the depositor's and the safe keeper's goods have been lost. LH 125 treats this as carelessness on the part of the safe keeper who is to replace the goods to the depositor whereas LE 37 states that such a case has no claim. It is possible that LH here envisages some form of negligence on the part of the safe keeper and thus orders the replacement of goods. It is also possible that the drafter of this law had LH 23 in mind which states that stolen property will be replaced by the city to the victim who was unable to recover his goods from the thief. The mention of the safe keeper's duty to pursue the thief combined with the subject matter of LH 126 (a false claim of stolen property to the city) makes the latter quite possible. This would explain LH's harsher treatment *i.e.* the safe keeper can afford to replace the goods to the depositor as he will either recover them from the thief or have them restored by the city authorities. This would also explain the difference in penalty in the first pair of laws. The material in MAL treating deposit and safekeeping is concerned with who is allowed to be responsible for the depositing of household goods with a third party and with the falsification of documents relating to such storage. It does not parallel the material here. It is worth noting LH's unique emphasis on the need for witnesses or written contracts for the depositing of property *e.g.* LH 122–124.[424]

2.5.4 Breach of Contract

This is another topic where there is very little parallel material. In three collections there are laws treating the failure of workers to properly cultivate land entrusted to their care. The relevant laws are LH 41–48, 52, 61–65, LU 32 and LL 8. LH is obviously far more detailed in its description of the various situations and the methods of compensation.[425] LU 32 is similar to LH 44 in that both treat the failure of a man to cultivate uncultivated land and both order a fixed compensation based on land area. LL 8 is different to LH 62–63 in that the man who has been given fallow land in which to plant an orchard and fails to do so is merely required to give it to somebody else whereas in LH compensation is required. The only other laws treating breach of contract either involve damage to property or adoption and are treated in their relevant sections.

2.6 CRIME AND DELICT

2.6.1 THEFT[426]

There are an enormous number of laws concerning theft amongst the collections under discussion here. Laws relating to this topic are by far the most frequent. This makes comparison a difficult task, though it also enables some confidence in any findings given the amount of material with which to test any hypotheses. There are some fairly solid distinctions to be found between the penalties given for theft-related offences in these collections. In general, the death penalty is most common in LH and AE, corporal punishments in MAL and the Egyptian material, and multiple payments in kind in HL. There are certainly exceptions to these rules, as will be shown presently, but they do stand up as broad generalizations. Each collection also reflects its different nature/purpose in the selection of offences

---

424 This seems to reflect a development in legal practice during the Old Babylonian period. See Renger, "Noch einmal," 4.1.2.

425 Note that these laws, along with the laws treating damage to agricultural property have sparked a debate in regards to the origin of the various compensation methods and their consistency within LH. This is discussed to some extent in the later section on damage to property.

426 This term is used here in its broadest sense, including offences such as misappropriation, fraud, robbery, brigandage, looting *etc.*

dealt with, *e.g.* the focus of MAL A on offences involving women and EH on offences by officials. There are a number of topics or tropes which are dealt with in different collections *e.g.* the thief who is caught before the act. Whether this is mere coincidence due to the similarity of the societies reflected in the collections (*e.g.* the prevalence of laws dealing with the theft of ploughs, slaves, oxen *etc.*) or whether it reflects a background of some sort of common legal science or literary culture will be explored.

Problems arise in the comparison of this area of law, beginning with an apparent lack of consistency in the punishments meted out in LH. Some of the penalties in LH involve death, some payment, corporal punishment or servitude.[427] There have been a number of approaches to this problem. Some have argued that the differences reflect historical development or a difference between geographic or ethnic systems.[428] These arguments are merely based on the application of various assumptions in an attempt to explain the differences. Westbrook has applied a different set of assumptions to the same data in an effort to harmonize the theft laws of LH. Though this author would also lean towards an attempt to understand this text which presumes consistency (at least within the text) rather than the mindless compilation of conflicting approaches to theft (whether based on different *Sitze im Leben*, historical periods or geographic/ethnic traditions), he believes that Westbrook's attempts at harmonization go against the most obvious reading of the text at times. Given Westbrook's larger program of demonstrating the essential sameness of ancient Near Eastern law one is suspicious of his arguments here. His arguments go further than merely attempting to identify relevant differences between the laws which may have led to the difference in penalty;[429] he also often explains away the death penalty when it is present and reads in the possibility of other penalties. It is this author's suspicion that the theft laws of LH are harmonizable, at times in the way Westbrook has suggested, but that the more forced arguments of Westbrook come about as he attempts to harmonize the theft laws of LH not merely with each other, but with the theft laws of other ancient Near Eastern collections.

Irreconcilable differences within the theft laws of LH would present problems for the suspicions of this author that one can identify differences

---

[427] According to Westbrook, "Old Babylonian Period," 419–20.

[428] See discussion *Ibid.*, 419.

[429] Though he does do this *e.g.* see our discussion of the contradiction between LH 6 and 8 below.

of attitude towards such offences between cultures.[430] If LH has different penalties for the same offence, the task of substantiating this suspicion is made more difficult. These apparent contradictions also feed the arguments that LH could not possibly have been intended to be referred to by judges when deciding cases and the concomitant argument that its real purpose was more propagandistic, the legal paragraphs merely being window dressing to demonstrate the justice of the king. One must ask whether such propaganda would have been positive if the king presented a confused approach to different legal areas. Some may argue that the analysis of a legal area such as "theft" is a totally modern concept and the ancients may not have seen the contradictions we see when comparing these different laws within LH. The contradictory nature of these laws may also be used to argue that they reflect an origin as past decisions in legal cases, which do not necessarily need to be harmonized. One can see the importance then of an analysis of the theft laws of LH itself before we proceed to a comparison of them with those of other law collections.

2.6.1.1 Theft laws of LH

Many of the laws in LH regarding theft in its various forms prescribe some kind of death penalty.[431] One law which offers the possibility of another form of punishment is LH 8. At first sight it seems to be in direct contrast to LH 6:

> **LH 6:** *šumma awilum makkur ilim u ekallim išriq awilum šu iddak u ša šurqam ina qatišu imḫuru iddak-* If a man steals valuables belonging to the god or to the palace, that man shall be killed, and also he who received the stolen goods from him shall be killed.
>
> **LH 8:** *šumma awilum lu alpum lu immeram lu imeram lu šaḫam u lu elippam išriq šumma ša ekallim adi 30-šu inaddin šumma ša muškenim adi 10-šu iriab šumma šarraqanum ša nadanim la išu iddak*-If a man steals an ox, a sheep, a donkey, a pig, or a boat-if it belongs either to the god or to the palace, he shall give thirtyfold; if it belongs to a commoner, he shall replace it tenfold; if the thief does not have anything to give, he shall be killed.

What is the relationship between these two laws? Both mention the theft of goods belonging to a temple or palace. LH 6 states simply that the

---

[430] Jean Bottéro, "Code," 162–63 sees the theft laws of Hammurabi as contradictory and uses this to argue against its applicability. Bernard S. Jackson, *Essays*, ch. 3 argues similarly to deter scholars from looking for underlying principles.

[431] LH 6, 7, part of 8, 9, 10, 11, probably 13, 14 (really dealing with kidnap), 15, 16, 19, 21, 22, 25, 227.

thief and the receiver of stolen goods will be killed. LH 8 is different in a number of respects. One possible solution to this contrast lies in the distinction between the laws regarding the objects that are stolen. However, one would be hard pressed to argue that the list of objects in LH 8 could not be included under the rubric of *makkuru* in LH 6 which simply means "possession" or "property".[432] It does remain possible that LH 8 provides a list of exclusions from the law in LH 6 *i.e.* when put together the import of the two laws is that the theft of the objects listed in LH 8 from a temple or palace requires a thirtyfold payment whereas the theft of any other (more valuable?) object requires the death penalty. The additional mention of the *muškenum* in LH 8 and its separation from LH 6 leads this writer to question whether LH 8 was intended as a comment on LH 6, though this possibility cannot be ruled out, especially given the fact that *muškenum* does not always refer to a class distinct from an *awilum*.[433]

Another possibility is that LH 8 is a more general elucidation of LH 6. This argument would see LH 8 explicating more fully the process that would lead to the death penalty in LH *i.e.* some form of payment in kind was possible with the death penalty only being enforced when the thief was unable to pay. Westbrook attempts a different harmonization hypothesizing that LH 8 covers the situation where the thief was unaware the property belonged to a temple or palace.[434] This would make some sense of the additional mention of the penalty if the property belonged to a *muškenum*. This approach, however, is nothing more than an educated speculation. It finds no real support in the text. There is another harmonization which finds some support in the text. In contrast to LH 8, LH 6 specifies a penalty for the receiver (who is not mentioned in LH 8) as well as the thief. Perhaps LH 6 envisages an organized theft with a view to disposal whereas LH 8 is simple theft for personal use.

Though the attempts at harmonization outlined above remain possibilities, one cannot rule out another, namely that the two laws are in fact different. Whether this reflects the compilation of two different past cases which are lumped together here, whether one is an updating of the other, or they reflect two different traditions to do with this offence cannot be demonstrated. It seems more likely to this writer that there is some substantial difference between the two offences which explains the difference of pen-

---

[432] *CDA*, 192.

[433] See the discussion of Yaron, *Laws of Eshnunna*, 1988, 132–45 and references to the debate between Kraus, Speiser and Finkelstein.

[434] Westbrook, "Old Babylonian Period," 420.

alty, the distinction between organized theft and simple personal theft being the most cogent. One may object that this approach is not based on the evidence but on an unnecessary assumption *i.e.* that the compiler of such a text (with its stated purpose) would be unlikely to preserve two contradictory laws next to each other. In response to such an objection it is worth examining the other theft-related offences in LH, including those which do not require the death penalty. It will be demonstrated that a lesser offence is in view for these laws than those which do attract capital punishment, or that a particular group is being protected. Given the application of such a principle elsewhere in LH, this writer feels somewhat justified in expecting it here also.

Let us first look at the laws which do require the death penalty. LH 6 and 8 have already been mentioned. There are many other laws within LH which require the death penalty. LH 7 prescribes death for a man who purchases or accepts for safekeeping anything from a man's son or slave without witnesses or a contract. Such a man is labeled a thief (*šarraqum*). The mention of the son or slave seems to imply either that the man is dealing with someone ignorant about the processes of sale whom he can take advantage of, or someone who does not have the authority of the head of household to be selling the goods and thus the transaction amounts to a form of theft from the head of household.

LH 9–13 give an extensive treatment regarding the possession of stolen property. It has already been mentioned in LH 6 that one who receives stolen goods is also considered a thief and is to be killed. Laws 9–13 envisage three possible perpetrators in the case where someone claims to identify his lost property in another's possession. The guilty party is detected by the ability to produce witnesses to: identify the stolen property and/or attest to the possessor's purchase of said goods from a third party (the seller). If the owner cannot produce witnesses to attest that the property in question was his he is to be killed for false accusation in a capital case.[435] If the possessor of the goods cannot produce witnesses to confirm his purchase of the goods from a third party he is to be killed for theft and the owner takes his property. If both parties can produce witnesses then the seller is regarded as the thief and is to be killed. The owner of the stolen property takes his lost property and the buyer will recover what he paid for the goods.

LH 12 interrupts the neat flow of this series of laws. It states: "If the seller should die, the buyer shall take fivefold the claim for that case from the estate of the seller." This law, however, does not cover the case that the

---

[435] LH 11. See our later discussion regarding false accusation laws.

seller was found guilty and put to death. It seems to deal with the situation where the seller was the culprit, was not able to be killed for his crime but died a natural death before the court proceedings. This then would explain the fivefold penalty taken by the buyer from the seller's estate. It may be to compensate for the fact he did not have the satisfaction of having the seller put to death. Commentators have pointed out a problem with this interpretation of LH 12. They ask why the owner of the stolen property is not also entitled to receive this fivefold claim.[436] This writer does struggle to find an answer to this objection but perhaps the satisfaction of having the seller killed is of more importance to the buyer as it was the seller who put him in a position where his life may have been taken for being in possession of stolen goods, whereas the owner of the stolen property just had his stuff stolen.[437]

Westbrook has a radically different interpretation of these laws in general. He argues that the innocent receiver of goods (the buyer) was only liable for a multiple payment of the goods (the multiple being lower than that for theft) and that it was up to him to "recoup his outlay" from the seller.[438] This contradicts what is set forth in LH 10 which prescribes death for the buyer if he can not produce witnesses, and a whole range of laws in LH which prescribe death rather than multiple payment for simple theft. Westbrook cites LH 12 in this context in support of the idea that the buyer has to chase the seller to recoup his outlay. This situation is already covered in LH 9. It is unlikely that LH 12 would merely repeat the same situation with a contradictory ruling. It makes most sense if a separate offence is here in view that hinges on the fact that the seller has "gone to his fate". Hence the approach taken to this law above.

LH 13 has been seen as notoriously difficult to interpret. This writer does not see the problem with reading it as a continuation of the situation in LH 12. The import would most likely be that in the case where the buyer attempted to claim his fivefold penalty and could not produce witnesses he was to bear the penalty of the case (*i.e.* he will pay a fivefold penalty to the deceased seller's estate/heirs). This interpretation seems more likely than one which would see this as a general comment that all parties have six months to bring their witnesses (though of course that principle could be inferred reasoning *per analogiam*) given the framing of the penalty. In contrast to LH 11 where the case would result in the buyer or seller being killed

---

436 Driver and Miles, *Babylonian Laws*, vol. 1, 100–1.

437 For a discussion of different interpretations of this law see *Ibid.*, 98–105.

438 Westbrook, "Old Babylonian Period," 422.

due to the malicious charges of the supposed owner of the stolen property, here the case would merely result in the heirs of the deceased seller having to pay a monetary penalty. In LH 11 the penalty for the false charge is death; in LH 13 it is stated: *aran dinim šuati ittanašši*: "he will continue to bear the penalty of that case." Another difference in the framing of these two laws which confirms our suspicion is found in the respective terms used to describe the offender and his action. In both cases the offender is called a liar (*sar*); in the more serious case in LH 11 the offender is said to have *tuššamma iddi*: "spread malicious charges".[439] Whatever the case, in these laws there is no indication that payment was acceptable instead of the death penalty. To read this into these laws, one must infer it from elsewhere. To infer it from practice is to assume that LH must reflect the documents from practice and to rule out the possibility that it tried to change practice but was not followed. To infer it from other collections requires the assumption of essential sameness and goes against the methodology of this thesis. Neither of these are secure or necessary assumptions.[440]

Other theft laws in LH which state the death penalty for the offence include aiding the escape of,[441] harboring[442] or detaining a slave.[443] Robbery,[444] burglary[445] and looting[446] also receive the death penalty. LH 25 contains a somewhat humorous literary framing. The situation envisaged is that a man who has come to help put out a fire at a neighbor's house and ends up stealing his household possessions, will be thrown into that very fire. Many commentators have wasted precious pages trying to figure out what would happen to the man if the fire had gone out before they managed to capture him *etc.* One suspects that is not how the laws were meant to work; merely being intended to display an equitable judgment in that situation. Reasoning from this law to a situation where the fire had gone out would

---

[439] So Roth, *Law Collections*, 84. Another possible rendering that may not support our case quite as well would be "he has thrown (accused of) might-have-beens". See *CDA*, 411 under *tuša/tušām(a)/tuššamma.*

[440] There has been much work pointing out the differences between LH and the documents of practice in the Old Babylonian period (see the earlier discussions in the introduction and 2.1.4.). Though many question the results of this research, one cannot ignore it completely.

[441] LH 15

[442] LH 16

[443] LH 19

[444] LH 22

[445] LH 21

[446] LH 25

not be rocket science. Old Babylonian law was not viewed in the way modern lawyers view statute. A situation would not have arisen where the accused was able to argue the letter of the law and thus avoid punishment because the fire had gone out. This is a completely modern and, one might argue, aberrant approach to law. The lack of comprehensivity in the law collections under view certainly undercuts any remaining idea that the ancients would have had a problem if they could not find a written law that dealt with the specifics of a case.[447] This was not the function of these law collections. This is not to say that the laws which were written down were not intended to have any application. That is a *non sequitur*.

There are four other laws in LH related to theft which prescribe the death penalty. LH m and n mention something about a merchant and a son of a man and a slave respectively. The provisions are too broken to reconstruct but one wonders whether these laws parallel LH 7, this time specifically for the merchant who would deal with a son or slave instead of the head of the household. LH bb is in a worse state of preservation than these last two. The only part of the provision remaining is the death penalty, *iddak*. The only reason it is mentioned here is that some of the nearby laws treat the fraudulent dealings of merchants or traders. The last law in LH that orders the death penalty for theft-related offences is LH 108. The alewife/woman innkeeper (*sabitum*) who refuses to accept grain for the price of beer and defrauds her customer with incorrect weights is to be thrown into the water *i.e.* drowned. This penalty is quite different from that in LH x. LH x supposedly states that a merchant who gives an interest-bearing loan and either hands out or collects the grain or silver with incorrect weights will only forfeit his loan. The text is fairly broken at this point but the final penalty does not seem to be death.[448] The offence of the *sabitum* is possibly compounded by her refusal to accept payment in grain but it is unlikely this is the reason for the difference in punishment. One wonders whether merchants were protected somewhat in LH given the important

---

[447] Joseph J. Azize has argued against such an approach to law in Mesopotamia, "Assumptions of the Criminal Justice System: Euthanasia and Aboriginal Opposition" (paper presented at the conference Law's Empire, Harrison, B.C., Canada, 26 June 2005).

[448] On A. Poebel's copy, *Historical and Grammatical Texts* (Publications of the Babylonian Section, University of Pennsylvania Museum 5; Philadelphia: University Museum, 1914), col ii, ln 21 of the final verb we have only the '*i*'. This would fit the proposed *itelli*, but would not fit *iddak* which would be written *id-da-ak*. Line 20 is similarly broken with only *i-na mi-* preserved. Driver and Miles' transliteration does not reflect this uncertainty, *Babylonian Laws*, vol. 2, 41, § P.

financial role they played in the Old Babylonian economy.[449] LH y also orders an offending merchant to forfeit what he loaned. LH w prescribes a twofold penalty for a merchant who does not acknowledge the receipt of loan repayments. In another context, this time to do with partnerships between merchants and trading agents, the merchant is to pay a sixfold penalty to the trading agent if he denies the return of the silver he lent to him. In LH 106 the trading agent is only asked to pay a threefold penalty if he denies that the merchant lent him silver. It would seem that the merchant is here fined more heavily as he is the greater of the two parties, fitting in nicely with Hammurabi's claim in the prologue that he set up the stele *dannum enšam la ḫabalim*: "so that the strong may not oppress the weak". The progression from LH 106 through to 108 may be of significance here. The trading agent pays a threefold penalty, the merchant sixfold and the *sabitum* is drowned. Does this just show the haphazard nature of this collection or is this a progression of penalties according to Hammurabi's program of protecting the weak? If the latter is so, can it be reconciled with Hammurabi's seeming protection of the merchant and trading agent from the death penalty for offences which seem very similar to the theft laws which receive the death penalty elsewhere in LH? Another example of this is found in LH 112 where the trading agent only receives a fivefold penalty if he misappropriates any goods consigned to him on his journey. LH 120 and 124 also only prescribe multiple payment for fraudulent behavior. They cover the situation where goods are deposited for safekeeping and are either lost or their receipt is denied. In each case the one storing the goods for the other man only pays a twofold penalty. The distinction in severity in LH cannot be one between the theft of movables and fraudulent economic transactions as will be seen presently.

Another group of people who seem to be protected from the death penalty for theft-related offences are hired workers. It is difficult to discern consistency amongst the laws in LH 253–256. LH 253 orders that a hired man who steals the seed for plowing or the fodder for the cattle will have his hand cut off. For stealing some of the stored grain (again seemingly food for the cattle) he is only ordered to make a twofold restitution in LH 254. In LH 255 the provision states that a hired man who hires out the owner's cattle or who steals the seeds so that there is no crop, will pay 18 000 silas per *iku* of land. Both LH 254 and 255 seem to directly contradict

---

[449] *i.e.* Their role as a middle-man who could turn taxes in kind into silver for the palace *etc.* See Yoffee, *The Economic Role of the Crown in the Old Babylonian Period* (Bibliotheca Mesopotamica 5; Malibu: Undena, 1977); Postgate, *Early Mesopotamia.*

LH 253. There are differences between the various laws which may explain the appearance of different penalties. In LH 253 the hired man misappropriates fodder (*ukullum*) whereas in LH 254 it is the stored grain (*aldum*).[450] LH 253 begins "If a man hires another man to care for his field, that is, he entrusts to him the stored grain (*aldum*), hands over to him the care of the cattle, and contracts with him for the cultivation of the field". The hired man has three areas of responsibility: the stored grain, the cattle and cultivation. LH 254–255 cover offences which show a lack of care for these responsibilities. If he is caught *in flagrante delicto* stealing (*šaraqum*) seed or cattle fodder, his hand is cut off (LH 253). In LH 254 the man is not said to have stolen the grain but to have taken it (*ilqema*). Is there some difference of offence implied here? Does it just cover a situation where he was not caught red-handed? LH 255 may cover a more serious offence where so much seed has been misappropriated that there are no crops. The monetary penalty is extremely high for a hired worker and LH 256 would be applied, *i.e.* death. The wording of this law seems to imply that debt slavery was not an option here.[451]

LH 255 seems oddly formulated given the penalty, on first reading, covers the offence of hiring out the owner's cattle. Why would this offence result in the payment of grain by area of land? This penalty certainly seems suited to the offence of stealing the seed resulting in a lack of crops to be harvested, but not hiring out cattle.[452] The last law in this series, LH 256, has a different punishment again. If the hired worker (of LH 255) is not able to pay he is to be dragged through that field by the cattle. This law, combined with LH 8, is used by Westbrook to argue that payment was always the first option regarding the punishment of theft; it was only in the case the thief could not pay that he was put to death. This argument, as pointed out before, goes against the reading of most of the theft laws of LH which prescribe the death penalty. It must be admitted that we are left with some seeming inconsistencies in not forcing this harmonization upon the evidence.

There are several more laws which also seem to confirm that theft-related offences by hired workers were treated more leniently. LH 259 and 260 prescribe the miniscule punishment of 5 and 3 shekels for the theft of a

---

[450] This term seems to be in apposition with the seed in LH 253.

[451] On this we may be mistaken.

[452] Perhaps they are beasts of burden given that the penalty in LH 256 involves the offender being dragged through the field by the cattle. It is also possible that they were used for treading in broadcast grain.

plough or a clod-breaking plough from the common irrigated area. Perhaps it is the position of the plough that lessens the offence and its status as communal property rather than the likelihood it would have been stolen by a hired worker in this case. LH 265, however, does seem to confirm our suspicion. A shepherd who alters the brands and sells the sheep and/or goats under his care is only required to make tenfold restitution. One does wonder whether a hired shepherd would be in any position to pay such a large fine and whether LH 256 would apply here also, again raising the more general question of which options we can or should read into the various laws.

The final theft-related offence which is penalized merely by a multiple payment is found in LH 126. This law should be read in conjunction with LH 23. Taken together what is implied is that a man who fraudulently claims his belongings have been stolen and that he could not track down the thief, who has had his supposedly stolen property replaced by his city-quarter, will pay it back twofold. This seems a little odd. Why would theft from the city-quarter be treated as a lesser offence? Is Hammurabi again applying his principle of protecting the weak rather than the strong? Is it because the city-quarter is more able to pay? Given the harsh penalty in LH 6 regarding theft from the palace or temple,[453] this law is somewhat surprising in its leniency.

There are two more laws which both prescribe corporal punishment of some kind. LH 226 orders the cutting off of the hand of a barber who shaves off a slave's slave-hairlock without the owner's approval. This is not tantamount to theft in that the barber does not keep the slave but it does cause loss to the owner. LH 194 may not be strictly relevant here and deals with fraudulent conduct rather than theft.

It is quite obvious that there are some difficulties in pinning down a precise attitude towards theft in LH. Amongst the various laws punishments have ranged from twofold to thirtyfold restitution, from two shekels of silver to 18 000 silas of grain per *iku*, from the cutting off of a hand to death in its various forms *e.g.* drowning and being dragged through a field by cattle. In general we were able to suggest explanations for the variations in these laws and do not feel the need to secede to the arguments of those who argue that it is impossible to discern principles behind the laws of Hammurabi.[454]

---

[453] Of course, somewhat mitigated by LH 8.

[454] *e.g.* Finkelstein, "Ammisaduqa's Edict," 98–99 argued against the idea that there was any logical consistency within collections such as LH.

2.6.1.2 Comparison of theft laws

2.6.1.2.1 Penalties

The paragraphs dealing with theft-related offences in Ammiṣaduqa's Edict parallel those in LH very well. The offences in AE are not strictly "theft" but economic misappropriation, including falsifying documents, and not following the *mišarum* edict's regulations for financial gain. The most commonly stated penalty, as in LH, is death.[455] AE 4 prescribes the death penalty for any creditor who does not return a wrongly collected loan repayment. AE 6 orders the same penalty for a creditor who seizes the property of an Akkadian or Amorite to whom he has extended credit (as the debt has been cancelled). AE 18 has the death penalty for a *sabitu* or a merchant who uses a false seal for some kind of economic transaction. In AE 5, a creditor who misappropriates interest by writing up the loan in a falsified form[456] merely has the loan document voided and forfeits what he lent. This is very similar to LH x and y.

AE 7 is similar to LH 8 and 256 in that the death penalty is only prescribed in the case where the offender cannot pay. The law covers a situation similar to AE 5. A creditor has had a loan document drawn up and then claims to have given the loan for some other purpose in order to collect more money. The debtor is to bring witnesses and declare an oath that the document has been changed. The creditor is to pay six-fold. If he can't pay, he dies. This law parallels the penalty in LH 107 for the merchant who does not acknowledge loan payments, though there it is in the context of a loan to a trading agent which is specifically ruled out here. It is difficult to see a real difference between AE 5 and 7. The studies regarding the different versions of the Old Babylonian edicts tend to conclude that when new provisions were added, the old ones were kept. Unfortunately the version from Samsu-iluna's time breaks off before § 5 or § 7 so we cannot tell whether one was added as an update or both co-existed. AE shows that the death penalty could be applied to creditors/merchants in the Old Babylonian period. Does AE 7, like LH 8, imply after all that payment was a possibility, at least at times, rather than the death penalty? Whatever the case, there is still a surface similarity between AE and LH in that the death penalty is that most often stated for theft-related offences. As in LH, in AE there are cases where merchants can give a multiple payment or forfeit their

---

[455] AE 4, 6, 7, 18.

[456] *i.e.* turns the loan into one of the loan types in AE 8 which are not remitted *e.g.* money lent for a trading expedition.

loan (as in LH x) rather than receiving the death penalty. Though there are some difficulties in explaining this, this writer does see a link between these two texts as opposed to the other collections regarding the attitude towards theft-related offences.

The penalty for theft at Eshnunna is difficult to determine. There are several laws which prescribe a fixed payment or replacement of goods.[457] None of these deal with simple theft. For theft-related offences the death penalty is only in view for the thief who is caught in the field or house of a *muškenum* at night,[458] or the guard who allows a burglar to break into the house he is watching.[459] There are two other laws which state "it is he who is a thief"[460] or "the palace shall bring a charge of theft against him".[461] The problem is we do not know what penalty this would mean at Eshnunna. Presumably those who were to read LE would have known what the penalty was but there is no sure way to determine this. LE 50 deals with the theft of property from the palace or a *muškenum* by an official. This law has clear parallels to LH 8, but also to LH 6. One hesitates to read the provisions of LH into LE, however. The differences between the laws would make this a very difficult task anyway. For example, LH 8 has two distinct penalties for whether the property stolen was the property of the palace or of a *muškenum* whereas LE 50 merely states that in either case the palace shall charge the offender with theft. It is not impossible that different penalties could still be given as LE 50 does not state any particular penalty but this seems unlikely. Do we assume a more general similarity between LH and LE and argue that LE also provided the death penalty for simple theft? This would give this law a parallel in LH 6. Given the uncertainty regarding these two laws it would be unwise to use them to compare the penalty for theft.

LU is generally thought not to treat the offence of theft. There is a possible reference to a theft-related offence in LU 2, however. Roth translates the law as follows: "If a man acts lawlessly (?), they shall kill him."[462] The Sumerian term she translates as "lawlessly" is not well attested in its form, but its root is. The term is *sa-gaz-še*. *Sa-gaz* is a well attested term that

---

[457] LE 6, 36, 49 and the first halves of LE 12–13.

[458] LE 12–13

[459] LE 60-the guard is to be buried without a grave at the point where the thief entered the house.

[460] LE 40

[461] LE 50

[462] Roth *Law Collections*, 17.

often seems to refer to the infamous *Ḫapiru*. The term also turns up in a lexical list as an equivalent for Akkadian *ḫabbatum*, "plunderer, bandit", or perhaps more simply, "robber".[463] The ending *šè* can follow the adverbial ending *eš*,[464] or can be some sort of terminative ending. Halloran gives "to rob"[465] or "to commit murder" for the phrase we have here, *sa-gaz . . . aka*.[466] Given that the previous law treated murder, and the root's more common connection to robbery, it is most likely that this is what is in view here. If that is the case, here we have another example of the death penalty for robbery. This is possibly not simple theft, however, but probably implies some kind of assault also, hence the possible extension of meaning to "murder". In LL 5 and SLHF iv 42–v 11the term does seem to mean theft more generally, being applied to someone who has misappropriated a boat.

There is very little material in the Sumerian collections dealing with theft-related offences. LL 9 deals with the case of a man seized in the orchard on his way to steal something, which attracts a 10 shekel penalty and 12–13 deal with the harboring of a fugitive slave which is penalized with the return of an additional slave or a payment of 15 shekels. The only other Sumerian material is found in SLHF iii 10–15 where it is stated that the theft of a boat or pig is penalized by a twofold payment.

The material from MAL A focuses on offences committed by women here as elsewhere. Other tablets treat theft involving different persons. MAL A 1 prescribes that a woman who steals something from a temple shall be punished as the deity instructs. MAL A 3–4 deal with situations involving theft of a wife from her husband's household. A 3 prescribes the death penalty for a woman who steals from her husband's house when he is sick or dead and for the receiver of the stolen goods. In the case where the husband was healthy a lesser punishment is in view. The punishment is at the husband's discretion and will be the same for both his wife and the receiver of the goods.[467] A 4 specifies further that if the receiver of stolen goods was a slave, they shall have their nose and ears cut off and restore the

---

[463] *CDA*, 99, from the verbal root *ḫabatum*, "to rob, plunder". For the use of the logogram SA.GAZ for *ḫabbatum*, see *CAD* 6, 13–14.

[464] *e.g.* John A. Halloran, "Sumerian Lexicon," (version 3.0): 158 [cited 13 January 2005]. Online: http://www. sumerian.org/sumerlex.htm.

[465] With a dative infix. There is not one here.

[466] Halloran, "Sumerian Lexicon," 133. The text reads: *tukum-bi lú-ù sa-gaz-šè in-ak in-gaz-e*: "If a man does *sa-gaz-šè*, they will kill him." This is how Westbrook and Lafont treat the term also, "Neo-Sumerian Period," 220.

[467] Compare MAL A 14–15, 22–23 dealing with adultery.

stolen goods and the husband shall cut off his wife's ears. Added to this is a provision in case the husband does not cut off his wife's ears. If such is the case, they will not cut off the nose and ears of the slave, nor will the slave restore the stolen goods. A 5 deals with a man's wife stealing goods worth over 300 shekels from the household of another man. If the owner of the stolen goods swears that he did not incite the woman to steal the goods the husband can hand over the stolen goods thus ransoming his wife and then cut off her ears. If he refuses to ransom his wife the owner of the stolen goods keeps her and cuts off her nose. A 6 treats a case where a man's wife has placed goods for safekeeping. It is stated that the receiver of the goods shall bear liability for stolen property. This penalty is not abundantly clear but may signify that MAL A 3 is applicable in such a case, implying that the wife and the receiver are in cahoots. MAL C 9 seems to repeat the general substance of this law and the ruling. An extra clause is inserted in that the receiver of the goods for depositing is said to have failed to notify the owner of the goods of their deposit by a lesser household member.[468]

All of the other theft-related offences in MAL are somewhat broken and thus not always completely understood. In general these other laws involve some sort of payment or return of goods combined with a number of blows and performance of the king's service for a fixed period of time. MAL C 2–3 fit this pattern. C 2 treats a situation where a creditor sells his debtor's son or daughter who was living in his house as a pledge. The creditor forfeits the loan, gives something[469] to the debtor, is struck an unknown[470] number of blows and performs the king's service for 20 days. In C 3, if the creditor sold the son or daughter into a foreign land the penalty is increased, at least for the king's service which rises to 40 days. If the person whom he sold into a foreign land dies he is to make full payment for a life.[471]

---

[468] The beginning of this law is broken. A slave is certainly mentioned but which other household member is mentioned is unclear. Roth puts wife, son or daughter as possibilities, *Law Collections*, 185. Roth's translations of the two laws falsely imply the use of different terminology. In A 6 she translates *ina kide taltakan* as "place goods for safekeeping" whereas in C 9 she translates *ina kide šaknat* as "as trust [...] it is deposited". The final statement in both laws that the receiver *šurqa inašši* is translated as "bear liability for stolen property" in A 6 and "be liable for theft" in C 9. Though in each case the translations are fitting, the inconsistency is perhaps unhelpful.

[469] Text broken

[470] Text broken

[471] It is most likely that this refers to some kind of fixed monetary value (*cf.* the

C 4 treats the same situation as C 2, but this time the pledge sold is an animal. The creditor is to replace the animal and the loan stands. If he does not replace the animal the loan is forfeited, the debtor seizes his animal and the person from whom he seized the animal recovers his silver from the person who sold it to him.[472] C 5 treats the theft of animals and their sale to a third party. Unfortunately much of the apodosis of this law is broken off. At the least the offender is to restore the stolen goods. C 6 a–b are too broken to discuss here. C 8 seems to cover a similar situation to C 5, namely the theft of animals. Here the offender is to repay the stolen goods, is struck 50 blows and performs the king's service for an unknown number of days. There is an extra clause in this law in case the theft exceeded a certain value of goods. If it did the offender was to return the goods and the king was to determine his punishment, perhaps implying that capital punishment was a possibility.[473] C 10 is too broken for certain reconstruction but seems to refer to a creditor exaggerating the value of his partner's loan. The creditor is declared a thief and the punishment is again determined by the king.[474] C 11 seems to cover a very similar situation, though a partner (*tappa'u*) is not mentioned, and the additional act of recording the inflated figure is. Most of the penalty is broken but it does include an unknown number of blows.

From Tablet F there are two laws dealing with theft. Though F 1 is a little broken it seems to cover a situation where a man changes the brand of his friend's sheep and steals them. He is assessed 100 blows, has his hair torn out, performs the king's service for a month and returns the value of the sheep.[475] F 2 treats a hired horse herder who sells off the horses under his care without the owner's knowledge. Most of the penalty is broken, but some form of laceration is in view. O 6 briefly mentions theft in a very broken context. Payment in silver and/or lead forms some part of the penalty.

Within MAL then, many punishments contain some combination of corporal punishment, return of goods, and performance of king's service.[476]

---

60 shekels in LH 24 and 198). See the discussion of Driver and Miles, *Assyrian Laws*, 491–92.

472 The text breaks off at this point; presumably this last person is the creditor himself.

473 Compare section 2.2 on laws mentioning the king.

474 Perhaps, though not necessarily implying that capital punishment is a possibility *cf.* MAL A 15.

475 Or the sheep themselves.

476 C 2, 3, 8, 11, F 1.

Those from tablet A, treating offences by women, envisage a number of different punishments[477] though most involve mutilation.[478] Death is only mentioned specifically in one law, A 3, though it may possibly be one of the punishments the deity, king, or husband may have decided upon in A 1, 3, C 8 and 10. It is unclear what penalty is implied by the statement *šurqa inašši* in A 6 and C 9, though it is likely to have been at the discretion of the head of household as in A 3. Some form of corporal punishment, be it blows or mutilation, is present in almost all the theft-related laws of MAL. None offer multiple payments.

The theft laws of HL are extremely numerous and will not all be enumerated here for sake of space. Almost every law concerning theft within HL prescribes a penalty of a fixed payment in silver, grain or in kind (often in multiples). It is difficult to explain why some cases of theft require payment in silver while others demand payment in kind but there are some possibilities. All the theft laws which demand payment in kind[479] occur together from HL 57–70 and each deals with the theft of a farm animal. There are, however, some laws treating the theft of different farm animals that require payment in silver, for example HL 81–85 dealing with the theft of pigs or HL 91–92 regarding bees. One law, HL 102, states that theft of over 3 talents of wood becomes a case for the king's court and one, HL 95,[480] prescribes mutilation for burglary committed by slaves. Not all theft offences by slaves are treated this way, with some merely requiring a payment less than that if the offence were committed by a free man *e.g.* HL 93.[481] The offence where mutilation is in view is more serious than the others, involving burglary of a house rather than simple theft. There is only one law within HL where theft requires the death penalty. HL 126 demands the death penalty if someone steals a bronze spear in the gate of the palace. Given that the theft of other objects belonging to the palace in the same law only require minimal payments in silver, one imagines this provision may be aimed against assassination attempts rather than the act of theft itself.[482] Supporting this suspicion is the care urged in *The Hittite Instruction for*

---

[477] Death and that decided by the deity in A 1.

[478] A 3–5

[479] At least in their formulation.

[480] Compare HL 99.

[481] Compare HL 97.

[482] Hoffner expresses amazement and confusion at this ruling, *Laws of the Hittites*, 204. Haase thinks that perhaps the spear was somehow sacred and cites a funerary ritual in which it is used, "Überlegungen zur erlaubten Tötung eines Men-

the Royal Bodyguard regarding the spears of the guards[483] and the evidence in ETel. that such guards could be involved in assassinations.[484] The harsh penalty in this law stands out quite remarkably from the other theft laws of HL. The threat of assassination would explain this relative severity.

Several of the Hittite laws record a reduction in the penalty for the relevant theft given in the formula *karu . . . kinuna*, "formerly . . . now". HL 57–59 reduce the fine from 30 cattle/horses/sheep to 15; 63 from 15 cattle to 10; 81, 94, 119 and 129 from 40 shekels to 12. In addition HL 92, 101 and 121 also reduce a corporal/capital punishment to a fine. There are also two cases, similar to those seen in LE and MAL, where the HL simply states that a man will be considered a thief. HL 45 treats a man who does not return implements he finds to their owner. In PT XXXV, the penalty implied by this is spelt out as three-fold compensation. HL 86 deals with the failure of a man to return a pig carcass after killing it to protect his food supplies. The penalty of HL 82 may apply. There is also one law which seems to contradict the ruling of others. HL 70 states that the theft of an ox, horse, mule or ass will result in the owner taking it back and the thief giving another two. This contrasts to other laws dealing with the theft of these animals which prescribe 10–15 fold replacement.[485] These phenomena will be discussed more fully in the next section of this work. The Hittite Laws are the only ones to distinguish penalties with regard to whether the theft was committed by a slave or a freeman.

ETud. makes mention of the payment of a field as compensation (*šarnik-*) for theft by a free person,[486] blinding (of the slave) or forfeiture if the theft was carried out by a slave.[487] Blinding is forbidden as a punishment for theft by a free man.[488]

The Edict of Horemhab covers offences by officials in general. Many of these include provisions against theft and misappropriation of goods.

---

schen in der hethitischen Rechtssammlung," *Die Welt des Orients* 27 (1996): 37. Neither Hoffner nor this writer are convinced by this speculation.

483 See especially §§ 2, 10, 42, 53 and 58–59 (concerning a bronze spear). Hans G. Güterbock and Theo P. J. van den Hout, *The Hittite Instruction for the Royal Bodyguard* (Assyriological Studies 24; Chicago: Oriental Institute, 1991) or "Instructions to the Royal Guard (*MEŠEDI PROTOCOL*)," trans. Gregory McMahon (*COS* 1.85: 225–30).

484 See especially §§21, 31–33.

485 HL 58, 63–64.

486 Col. i, lines 9–10.

487 Col. i, lines 11–15.

488 Col. i, lines 16–19.

Various penalties including corporal punishment, exile and forced labor are in view. The relevant laws can be summarized as follows: anyone who takes away the craft of a military man or any other person attempting to deliver dues for the breweries or abattoirs of Pharaoh will have his nose cut off and be sent to Sile; the same punishment applies for anyone interfering with the supply of goods to the harem or of offerings to the gods; the same again applies for officials who requisition *kt*-plants and/or privately owned slaves to help them do so; same again for the uncontrolled looting of hides from peasants, involving their beating and being left poor; a military man who commits a similar offence will be struck one hundred blows, receive five open wounds and will have the stolen hides taken from him.

There are also some clauses stating that a particular offence will now be prosecuted or prevented though a penalty is not always given (*e.g.* VI, VIII), some laws protecting commoners who have had dues stolen, and some provisions whose penalty is unknown due to a break in the text (VII *sm*-herbs). All laws within EH regarding theft-related offences that record a penalty involve some form of corporal punishment. None of them require payment or the death penalty. It must be remembered that these laws are addressing offences by officials rather than the general population.

The theft laws in ND combine corporal punishments, whether beatings, making pierced wounds or the cutting of off ears and nose or multiple payments in kind, with forced labor (including being made into servants of the protected foundation) for various misappropriation offences by officials. For the offence of offering dedicated sacrifices to another deity, impalement is prescribed.[489]

2.6.1.2.2 Other theft comparisons

Apart from being able to compare the different penalties for theft in general, there are a number of similarities within more specific aspects of the theft laws from these collections which enable closer comparison. This follows presently and should enable an assessment, to some extent, of the likelihood of borrowing amongst these laws.

There are many laws across these collections which deal with the theft of the same object. Despite this they are often difficult to compare, perhaps implying a lack of borrowing. There are three collections which treat the theft of a boat. LH 8 specifically deals with the theft of a boat[490] from the palace or a *muškenum*. The penalty is thirty fold replacement if from the pal-

[489] Section II.3.b.

[490] Among other items.

ace, ten fold if from the *muškenum*, and death if the thief cannot afford either payment. The specification of the boat's owner along with the list of other objects contained within LH 8 distinguishes it significantly from the other two laws treating boat theft. LE 6 states that a man who steals someone else's boat through deception shall pay 10 shekels of silver.[491] SLHF iii 10–12 puts it more simply again: "If he steals a boat, he shall double (its value) as compensation."[492] Though the penalties of the last two laws may be similar, one could hardly argue that borrowing had necessarily occurred.

The theft (from the palace or *muškenum* again) of a pig, ox, sheep or donkey is also mentioned in LH 8.[493] Each of these items is mentioned in other collections in different contexts. SLHF iii 13–15 again demands a two fold payment for such a theft. Within HL there are a number of laws treating the theft of different kinds of pigs: HL 81, a fattened pig-12 shekels of silver; HL 82, a pig of the courtyard-6 shekels; HL 83, a pregnant sow-6 shekels plus 50 liters of barley for every 2 piglets inside her; HL 85, a piglet stolen from within its mother-100 liters of barley. In HL 86, a man who kills a pig that had trespassed onto a part of his property where it may have damaged food supplies and does not return it to the owner is said to be "considered a thief". Presumably he would pay the 6 shekels outlined in HL 82. Whatever the case, there is little evidence for any borrowing between these laws either. The laws treating the theft of sheep,[494] oxen,[495] donkeys/mules,[496] and horses[497] display many differences also and are not worth outlining in detail here. Amongst the laws the penalties are different in amount and type, the animals mentioned together in the same law are different in each collection as is the order in which they are mentioned, no two collections mention exactly the same combination of animals *etc.* Very different situations are often in view across the collections *e.g.* selling animals held in pledge, stealing from a palace, misappropriating a trespassing or stray animal, the sale of such a stolen animal *etc.* There is not even a case where laws from two different collections that treat the theft of the same animal do so within the same situation *e.g.* simple theft of the animal from another. The only similarity is that the same animal may be mentioned in

---

491 Presumably he also returns the boat.

492 Thus Roth *Law Collections*, 49.

493 With the same penalty as above.

494 LH 8, 265; MAL F 1; HL 59, 69.

495 LH 8; LE 50; MAL C 5; HL 63, 70.

496 LH 8; LE 50; MAL C 4; HL 70–71

497 MAL C 4–5; HL 58, 64, 70; PT XXXV.

more than one collection. This is hardly resounding evidence for borrowing. This minor similarity of content is hardly surprising given the agricultural nature of the societies within which these laws were produced.

Yaron's argument[498] that LH 8 derives from a combination of SLHF iii 10–15 is unconvincing in the extreme. Especially given the fact LH 8 lists many more objects than the two listed in this section of SLHF.

The theft of a plough is treated in both LH and HL. LH 259 demands a payment of 5 shekels for a plough stolen from the common irrigated area and LH 260, 3 shekels if it is a clod breaking plough. HL 121 demands a similar penalty for the theft of a plough, 6 shekels if the thief is a free man, 3 if he is a slave. There is no mention of a common irrigated area in HL which may be significant. The usual penalty for theft in LH is death. The punishment here in LH is very miniscule and it is difficult to understand why this is the case unless the location within the common area somehow lessens the offence.[499] Interestingly, in contrast, this may be one of the few Hittite Laws which mentions a death penalty (as part of the *karu . . . kinuna* clause).[500]

Bricks are another item mentioned in two collections with a similar penalty, but again, there are a number of differences. MAL B 14 treats a situation where a man makes bricks from someone else's plot. The man is to give triple the plot, has his bricks confiscated, is struck a number of blows and performs the king's service.[501] HL 128 prescribes that the theft of bricks shall result in their two fold return. Along with this the theft of foundation stones and the stele is mentioned. The former is paid back five fold and the latter requires a 2 shekel payment. There are many obvious differences between the two laws that seem to question the significance of the surface similarity of the mention of bricks. Though the penalty is similar, in MAL B 14 the whole "plot" is tripled, whereas in HL 128, it is the bricks that are doubled. As usual, MAL includes blows and king's service as part of the penalty.

Another topic dealt with across collections is theft from the palace. Again there is little support for the notion of a common ancient Near Eastern law on this topic, nor for borrowing across the collections. Within LH

---

498 Yaron, "Early Mesopotamian Collections," 69–70. This writer does agree with his notion that LH contains stiffer sanctions for theft-related offences.

499 More like misappropriation than theft.

500 The penalty is quite broken and is usually reconstructed on the basis of HL 166. See Hoffner, *Laws of the Hittites*, 203.

501 MAL B 15 treats a similar offence but is too broken to mention in any detail.

there are four laws which treat this topic. LH 6 and 8 have been mentioned in detail above, 6 prescribing the death penalty for the theft of objects from the palace or temple, and 8 specifying a number of objects which require thirty fold repayment if stolen from the temple or palace, ten fold if from a *muškenum*. LH 15–16 seems to uphold LH 6 in that the harboring of a slave of the palace or a *muškenum* or aiding their escape is punished with death. Unfortunately for our purposes LE 50 simply states that anyone in a position of authority who seizes a fugitive slave or a stray animal belonging to the palace or a *muškenum* and does not return it within a month will be charged with theft. Not knowing what the penalty for such a charge would be at Eshnunna makes comparison difficult. Though it is possible that the penalties may have been the same, there is no support for this idea in the texts themselves. The one obvious similarity between these laws is the connection of the *muškenum* with the palace. This is most safely explained by postulating a similar role for the *muškenu* at Eshnunna as in Babylonia.[502] HL 126 also deals with the theft of a number of objects from the gate of the palace. The first item mentioned is some form of wooden object[503] for which the penalty is 6 shekels. The theft of a bronze spear from the palace gate requires the death penalty. The theft of a pin/stylus,[504] requiring payment of 25 liters of barley and then the theft of threads from a bolt of cloth, requiring a replacement bolt of cloth are mentioned within this law also. The theft of these two items is not specifically said to have occurred at the gate of the palace. It is interesting that within this law there is the death penalty, and payments in silver, grain and kind. The essence of the provisions in this law is certainly not that theft from the palace deserved death. It may be significant that the exception here occurs for an object which may have been used to harm the person of the king *i.e.* the spear.[505]

The theft of slaves is treated in all but two of the collections which contain laws dealing with theft-related offences.[506] In LH, the penalty for detaining a fugitive slave,[507] for aiding the escape of the slave of the palace

[502] See Kraus, *Vom mesopotamischen Menschen der altbabylonischen Zeit und seiner Welt* (Amsterdam: North-Holland, 1973) for an in-depth analysis of this term.

[503] Perhaps a chair or throne. See Hoffner, *Laws of the Hittites*, 203.

[504] *Ibid.*, 203.

[505] See our earlier proposition that some form of treachery or assassination may have been in mind.

[506] All but three if LU 2 is not accepted as referring to theft.

[507] LH 19

or a *muškenum*,[508] harboring such a fugitive slave even at the herald's proclamation,[509] or misinforming a barber so that he inadvertently removes the slave-hairlock of another's slave,[510] all receive the death penalty. If a barber removes the slave-hairlock without the owner's permission his hand is cut off.[511] LE 40 and 50 which both deal with the theft of slaves, merely state that the offender is a thief. LE 40 treats a man who buys a slave and cannot identify the seller while LE 50 treats the detaining of a fugitive slave of the palace or a *muškenum* by someone in authority for over a month. It is possible that the punishment was death, but LE 49 makes this unlikely: "If a man should be seized with a stolen slave or a stolen slave woman, a slave shall lead a slave, a slave woman shall lead a slave woman." What seems to be implied is that the slave will be returned and another will be given in return.[512] This law is very similar to LL 12, which also shares similarity with LE 50. LL 12 states that a man who detains a fugitive slave for over a month must give another slave in return. The ruling and situation are the same as LE 49 and the time period which the detainer has to return the slave is identical to that in LE 50. It is possible that LL lay before the drafter of LE and was used in this case. It is also possible, given the location of both within Mesopotamia, that each reflects a practice that was common in Mesopotamia.[513] LL 13 adds an extra stipulation that a payment of 15 shekels can be delivered if the offender had no slave to give.

The Hittite Laws regarding this offence also contain some suggestive similarities with LE and LL. HL 20 penalizes the abduction of the male slave of a Hittite, stolen from the land of Luwiya and taken to Hatti, with a 12 shekel payment (very similar to the amount of silver in LL 13). HL 21 covers a situation less offensive to the Hittites, namely the stealing of the male slave of a Luwian. For this latter offence the owner merely takes his slave back and receives no compensation. This law is peculiar to the Hittite laws and their focus on international relations regarding kidnapping in general.[514] Covering a situation more akin to those in LL and LE, HL 24 states that 12 shekels will be paid by "the one at whose hearth the slave-owner" finds their runaway male slave, 6 shekels if the runaway slave was female.

---

508 LH 15

509 LH 16

510 LH 227

511 LH 226

512 See Roth *Law Collections*, 70, n. 26.

513 Perhaps excluding Assyria here.

514 See the next section, 2.6.2.

This unique distinction is qualified by the statement that the offender is paying one month's wages, with the male slave earning more. There is a similarity in penalty here and in LL 13, but it seems the similarity arises for different reasons. In LL 13 the 15 shekels is given in place of giving a slave, not necessarily as the equivalent of a month's wages. The mention of the one month time period again at first seems to suggest common practice or borrowing, but it is slightly different here. In HL 24 there is no mention of how long the slave has dwelt in the house, just that the penalty is equivalent to one month's wages. Interestingly, the version of this law supposedly dated to the Neo-Hittite period, demands the payment of one year's wages: 100 shekels if a male slave, 50 if a female. Though one could argue the closer proximity of date between the Old Hittite version of HL and LL and LE, it seems the amounts are similar for different, unrelated reasons, and the common mention of the one month period is merely coincidental. The link between LL and LE here may, however, be more substantial.

Robbery and/or burglary are punished by death in LH 21–22 and possibly in LU 2.[515] MAL A 3 also prescribes death for theft from a house, but a very specific situation is mentioned. The law deals with theft by a man's wife from his house while he is ill or dead. It is only in this situation that the thieving wife and the receiver of the goods are to be put to death. If the husband is healthy, the punishment is at his discretion. If the wife gave the goods to a slave mutilation of ears and/or nose are in view (MAL A 4). If the man's wife steals from another house the woman also has ears or nose mutilated and may be claimed by the owner of the house if not ransomed by her husband. In contrast to the severity of these laws, HL 94 has a simple fine of 12 shekels for burglary of a house by a freeman,[516] to which seems to be added some other monetary compensation dependent on how much is taken. HL 95 has a lesser monetary penalty of 6 shekels if the offence is committed by a slave, to which is added mutilation of nose and ears. The owner of the slave is to pay some form of compensation dependent on the amount stolen or he forfeits the slave. A simple comparison of LH and HL highlights a general trend, namely the harsh nature of LH in contrast to that of HL. Given the uncertain import of the offence listed in LU 2 it would be unwise to make too much of the similar penalty to LH 21–22.[517] The death penalty in MAL is for a very specific situation that is

---

515 See our earlier discussion of the phrase *sa-gaz-šè in-ak*.

516 Down from 40 shekels formerly.

517 Especially given the possibility that the phrase can mean "to murder". See earlier discussion.

not technically robbery or burglary. The series of laws in MAL A treating theft from houses generally involve mutilation of some form. This mutilation of nose and/or ears is paralleled in the treatment of slaves in HL 95 and also in some of the penalties for theft-related offences in ND. This does not seem to be a common law regarding robbery or theft-related offences that crosses cultures, nor a borrowing. That mutilation happens to those particular body parts is a phenomenon that transcends the ancient Near East. The occurrences of mutilation in legal penalties in the Near East will be discussed more generally in a following section.

One topic that has been seen as a borrowing or part of a common legal culture is that regarding the thief caught before the act. The attention given to this topic, as is the case with the goring ox, stems partly from its existence in biblical law.[518] This topic is taken up in three different Near Eastern collections: LE 12–13, LL 9 and HL 93. Similar in each law is the capture of a man before he has committed an offence. Similar also is the mention of a penalty of either 10 or 12 shekels in each case. It is also a reasonable deduction that each law envisages the man as preparing to commit theft. This is clearly stated in LL 9 and is obvious in the case of HL 93 from the content of the two laws which follow it. LE 12–13, however, are surrounded by laws which treat rates of hire. There are a number of significant differences amongst these laws. It is only LE which distinguishes penalties dependent on whether the offender is seized during daylight or night-time.[519] If seized in the daylight the offender is penalized 10 shekels, if at night the law states "he shall die, he will not live".[520] It is unclear what role self-help is to play here. LL 9 simply prescribes a 10 shekel payment and HL 93 12 shekels if the man caught is free or 6 if he is a slave. There is no

518 Ex. 22:2–3 (22:1–2 in LXX and MT/HB): "If a thief is caught breaking in and is struck so that he dies, the defender is not guilty of bloodshed; but if it happens after sunrise, he is guilty of bloodshed. A thief must certainly make restitution, but if he has nothing, he must be sold to pay for his theft." Note here that the law is set among a number of laws which deal with murder rather than theft. The focus is on whether the householder is guilty of murder if he kills an intruder rather than on the penalty to be paid by the thief (though this is also covered).

519 This being one of the points used to argue a parallel with Ex. 22:2–3. Interestingly the Hebrew in this passage allows the interpretation that what is ruled out is not so much killing a burglar who entered during daylight hours, but going after a night-time burglar to kill him the next morning. The meaning hinges on one's interpretation of the phrase אִם־זָרְחָה הַשֶּׁמֶשׁ עָלָיו lit. "If the sun has risen upon him".

520 *imat ul iballuṭ*. Note that the law does not state that the householder is allowed to kill the intruder, but that the intruder will be punished with death.

indication in these laws that they were only applicable during daylight hours. It is quite possible that the drafter of LE used LL 9 here and embellished it. There are some other differences also. The provision in LE 12 is for a man seized in the field (*eqlum*) of a *muškenum*, LE 13, in the house of a *muškenum*. LL 9 parallels LE 12 in that the thief is seized outside, but is different in that he is seized in the orchard (*kiri*$_6$) of a man (*lu*$_2$). HL 93 parallels LE 13 in its mention of the house as that which is in the offender's sights. Again there are significant differences. In HL 93 the thief is seized before entering the house, whereas in LE 13 the offender is seized inside it. As Tigay[521] has pointed out, borrowing does not necessarily lead to word for word translation or adoption but can include significant differences. If this is accepted then borrowing is a possibility here also. It is possible that the drafter of LE was familiar with LL, adapted it and expanded upon it, as it is possible that the drafter of HL 93 was familiar with LE and adapted and shortened it. This, however, is mere speculation, as is any attempt to hypothesize other unwitnessed sources that the drafters may have relied upon. There remains the possibility that such a situation did make up part of the legal training of the drafters of these collections. That its existence at Isin, Eshnunna and Hatti was due to a common legal training across the entire Near East seems unlikely given the many differences amongst the collections regarding other topics and the differences outlined here. That the drafters of these three collections[522] all thought this topic worth consideration is not enough to demand its diffusion in any form, let alone to be able to specify it.[523]

The last topic amongst the theft-related offences that is treated in a number of collections is that of the seller/purchaser of stolen goods. LH 9–13 treat this topic extensively. There is a clear parallel between LH 10 and LE 40. In both cases, if a person in possession of stolen goods cannot establish the identity of the person whom they claim sold them the stolen goods, they are considered the thief. In LH 10 this means they are killed. The penalty is not specified in LE 40. It is possible that LE 40 was stimulus material for the drafter of LH who greatly expanded on the topic. The implication of LE 40, spelled out in LH 9, is that the seller would be considered the thief if identified. This is the case in MAL C 4–6. In C 4 the offender wrongly sells off an animal taken in pledge, in C 5 the offender may

---

[521] Tigay, "On Evaluating".

[522] As well as that of Exodus 22:2–3.

[523] Nor are the differences here outlined and the general differences between these collections outlined elsewhere enough to comprehensively disprove it in this case.

have stolen the goods[524] and C 6 is too broken to reconstruct the situation. The laws certainly treat a topic similar to LH 9 but do so in a very different framing. Again, earlier material in LE and LH may have been a stimulus but this is difficult to argue. The fact that three different societies have decided someone who sells property that is not theirs is a thief and someone who unknowingly buys such property is not does not demand a diffusionist explanation.[525]

2.6.2 Kidnap

In contrast to the theft laws, there is very little material to compare concerning kidnap. No two of the ancient Near Eastern laws on this topic seem to cover exactly the same situation. LH 14 prescribes death for a man who kidnaps someone's young child. LU 3 prescribes imprisonment and the payment of 15 shekels of silver for a man who either detains, kidnaps or falsely imprisons.[526] The object of this offence does not seem to be mentioned specifically. It is tempting to see LH as prescribing a much harsher penalty as was often the case in the theft laws. It would be unwise to be too dogmatic in this case given the uncertain meaning of LU 3. It may even be possible that what is being described is some form of illegal distraint. It is quite possible that LU 3 describes a lesser offence than that of LH 14 rather than highlighting the harsher penalties of LH. The specific mention in LH 14 that the offence is committed against the child of an *awilum* may support this possibility though the term *mar awilim* could refer to any member of the *awilu* class.

The Hittite laws regarding kidnap cover slightly different situations and seem more interested in relations with their Luwian neighbors than the offence of kidnap itself.[527] As a result these are difficult to compare to LH 14. The Hittite laws cover the abduction of a free Hittite person from Hatti to Luwiya by a Luwian, which is punished with forfeiture of the offender's estate,[528] to the abduction of a Luwian slave from Luwiya to Hatti by a Hit-

524 The text is broken at this point.

525 The modern situation where the purchaser of stolen goods is considered liable for an offence presumes a society where sale is carried out in a different manner.

526 Note the uncertainty of the translation: Roth has "detains", *Law Collections*, 17 while Wilcke has imprisonment, as cited by Lafont and Westbrook, "Neo-Sumerian Period," 221.

527 HL 19–21.

528 Literally "house".

tite which involves no penalty, just the return of the stolen slave. In keeping with the Hittite theft laws, some form of pecuniary penalty is prescribed in contrast to the harsher penalty of LH.

The Egyptian material which, on a surface reading, seems to regard kidnap, is really concerned with the misappropriation of labor from temple estates.[529]

2.6.3 Sex Laws

The similarities in the sex laws of the ancient Near Eastern law collections[530] have been used to confirm the existence of a canon of scholarly scientific problems that supposedly spread with cuneiform writing and to confirm the essential sameness of ancient Near Eastern law.[531] Within this model, the differences between the laws are seen as minimal and due to nothing more than the different literary styles of the individual collections.[532] Though there certainly are many similarities between these laws, the differences are not as slight as claimed. The idea that the similarities can be explained via the common legal background of "cuneiform law" and its canonical legal problems, though a possibility, is hardly demonstrable. The assertion that such a canon was so well known that a collection could mention one or two examples from a given topic and assume knowledge in the reader of the others is a forced argument from an unnecessary assumption, as is any attempt to read the provisions of one collection's laws into another's.[533] Other possible explanations will be given for the similarities and the differences will be allowed to speak. Without manipulation of the evidence uniformity is more difficult to find.

2.6.3.1 Offences Involving Married Women[534]

Many parallels can be found amongst the laws treating adultery in the ancient Near East. These include the mention of certain details such as the seizure of adulterers *in flagrante delicto*, the location of the offence, the coercion or lack thereof of the woman, the case of the absentee husband; the general focus on married women; the treatment of adultery as an offence

---

[529] *e.g.* EH and ND.

[530] At least those regarding adultery and rape.

[531] Westbrook, "Adultery in Ancient Near Eastern Law," *Revue Biblique* 97 (1990): 548.

[532] *Ibid.*, 542.

[533] *Ibid.*, 571.

[534] Including those betrothed or holding status as inchoate wives.

against the husband only and the lack of treatment of a husband's marital indiscretions (unless with a married woman); similarities in the description of the penalty for adultery offences including the principle that the paramour is to be treated as the husband treats his wife and the general possibility of the death penalty for the offence. All of this seems to support Westbrook's model of different collections treating common canonical legal topics. Let us analyze these laws in a little more detail.

A number of laws state that the death penalty is in view for both a man's wife and her paramour involved in adultery. This is specifically mentioned in LH 129, MAL A 13, 15, HL 197–198, and is implied in MAL A 14, 16, 22 and 23. A number of laws mention the death penalty for only one or the other person involved in the adulterous offence: LH 130, 133, LU 6–7, MAL A 12, 14 (implied), 16 (implied), 23, LE 26, 28, HL 197. Often this is due to factors such as lack of knowledge of the woman's marital status or the use of force. There are also several laws which mention the possibility of lesser (or no) penalties whether at the discretion of the husband (LH 129, MAL A 14–16, 22–23, HL 198) and/or the king or judges (LH 129, MAL A 15, HL 198).

Westbrook uses all this material and the several laws which mention the seizure of the couple *in flagrante delicto* (LH 129, MAL A 15, HL 197 and LE 28) to reconstruct *the* law of adultery in the ancient Near East. When all details are taken into account this is not an easy task, nor, according to this writer, one that should be undertaken. Generally the laws which speak of the possibility of death for both wife and paramour seem to envisage a mutual sexual encounter without the involvement of force and probably assume the paramour's knowledge of the woman's marital status. LH 129 does not mention the possibility of force nor of the paramour's cognizance that the woman was married but states that, if seized in the act, they shall be thrown into the water.[535] MAL A 13 comes after an example where a man's wife was raped, implying that this is not the case here, and specifically mentions that the paramour knew that the woman was married. The penalty is death. MAL A 15 shares more parallels with LH 129 in that neither aspect is mentioned, merely the seizure of the couple in the act. The husband is able to kill both parties.[536] HL 197, after detailing two situations where only one party is said to die, dependent on the location (*i.e.* in the mountains or in the

[535] There is also the following clause dealing with the situation where the husband pardons his wife. This will be treated later.

[536] As in LH 129 more follows which will be treated later.

woman's house) of the sexual encounter,[537] merely states that the woman's husband, if he catches them in the act, may kill both of them. There is no repeated detailing of the location or any other factor such as the use of force or the paramour's knowledge. Perhaps it is implied that the second situation was envisaged *i.e.* the husband caught his wife and her paramour in his house. MAL A 14 specifies both location (which may have led to the paramour's confusion regarding the woman's marital status)[538] and whether or not the paramour knew the woman was married. If he knew, he is punished as the husband punishes his wife.

MAL A 16 is difficult to reconcile with the other sex laws of this collection and is thus not treated by Westbrook. The opening protasis of the law is somewhat damaged, and leaves the reader somewhat perplexed as to the situation envisaged. The second protasis, however, is completely preserved and its apodosis prescribes punishment for the paramour identical to that meted out to the woman if he used force. This seems to be a direct contrast to the provisions in MAL A 12 and 23 which specify that there is no punishment for the wife if she was forced. In MAL A 22 also, it seems as though a wife who claims to have been raped is also punished. Again there is the statement that the paramour shall be treated as the woman's husband treats his wife. In this law a man's wife has been the traveling companion of another man. The man has to compensate the woman's husband 7200 shekels of lead regardless of any sexual activity that may have occurred. If the man swears that he did not have sex with the woman this is to be the only penalty. If, however, the man's wife contests his claim and declares that the man did have sex with her he is to undergo the River Ordeal. If he refuses to do so, we are then given the statement regarding the identical penalties for the wife and paramour. It would be difficult to imagine that any woman who knew of such a law in operation would claim this sexual activity had taken place, even if it was rape. Knowledge of such a law could not be presumed, and it would be even more difficult to explain the wife's statement if the sex was mutually entered into. It makes most sense if rape was being claimed, but we cannot be certain. Lafont has offered a solution to the apparent contradiction between MAL A 16 and 22, and 12 and 23.[539] She sees within MAL A 16 a situation where the woman has enticed

[537] The difficulty in seeing only the woman being punished in the second case will be treated later.

[538] *i.e.* the locations mentioned, an inn or the main thoroughfare, may have been the typical haunts of prostitutes.

[539] "Middle Assyrian Period," 556. See also her *Femmes, droit et justice dans l'anti-*

the other man with an embrace or some such act and has subsequently been forced to have sex with him. The woman's willingness to become the traveling partner of another man in MAL A 22 would amount to a similar enticement, both acts perhaps making her somewhat responsible for the subsequent rape in the eyes of the laws' drafter. Though this reconstruction is somewhat tenuous, it does make sense of the data here. This situation is dealt with nowhere else in the ancient Near East.

Thus far then we have little problem in terms of contradictions amongst these laws. In LH 129, MAL A 15 and HL 197 the laws simply state that, if caught in the act of adultery, both partners could be killed. In MAL A 15 and HL 197, the person who catches the offenders and kills them is specifically said to be the husband. This is not the case in LH 129 in which an unspecified plural subject, the ever present "they", binds the couple and throws them into the water. The mention of the husband's ability to allow his wife to live (following directly after this statement) does cause one to hesitate to make very much out of this difference. In general, the lack of mention of the use of force or the knowledge of the paramour regarding the woman's marital status in these three laws could reflect a number of different things. As both these aspects of the offence are regularly mentioned in MAL, their absence in MAL A 15 may be significant and imply that they were not taken into account if the husband killed the couple. Perhaps this was to allow for the rage of the husband at the sight before him. It is also possible that these aspects were presumed to be present. For the other two collections it is more difficult to say, especially given LH's failure to discuss the use of force, the location of the offence or the knowledge of the paramour. There is nothing to suggest any real differences in this aspect of these laws. There are some differences in the description of the process that ensues if the husband chooses not to kill the couple on the spot.

This ensuing role of the husband and the king is described in LH 129, MAL A 15 and HL 198. LH 129 declares that if the husband allows his wife to live then the king will allow the paramour to live also. There is no description of the man bringing the couple for trial. MAL A 15 describes the process in more detail. The husband seizes the man and brings him before the king or the judges. If they find the paramour guilty he will be killed if the husband kills his wife, turned into a eunuch[540] and have his face lacer-

---

quité orientale (Orbis biblicus et orientalis 165; Fribourg: Editions Universitaires, 1999), 163–64.

540 *ša rešen*. For a discussion of this title see Luis R. Siddall, "A Re-examination of the Title *ša reši* in the Neo-Assyrian Period," in *Gilgameš and the World of Assyria:*

ated if the husband cuts off his wife's nose, and have nothing done to him if the husband does nothing to his wife. It seems to be the husband who carries out the penalty on both his wife and the paramour. HL 198 has no mention of a trial or judges but does specify that the husband brings his wife and her paramour to the palace gate.[541] If the husband declares that he does not want his wife to die then the paramour's life is also spared. There is an extra statement that the husband shall also "SAG.DU-*ŠU*$_2$ *waššiyezzi*". Most commentators have treated this as the husband carrying out some action upon the paramour's head whether that be some sort of blow, marking or something else. Tsevat[542] has made the suggestion that this phrase actually refers to the (re-)veiling of the man's wife, symbolic of the continuation of their marriage. This interpretation has been followed by Hoffner in his critical edition.[543] Though this interpretation does seem a little more neat and keeps the symmetry of punishment between the wife and paramour, there is a difficulty in the possessive suffix used which is Akkadian third person masculine singular. Though Hittite does not distinguish gender, a practice which may have led to confusion here, they usually use the correct gender for Akkadian suffixes in the laws.[544] It must be admitted, however, that confusion is possible in this case as the textual witness for this law, KBo 6.26, seems to use the *ŠU* suffix for the feminine on two other occasions.[545] Following from this act upon someone's head the law describes a second option. If the husband has brought the couple to the palace gate but wants both of them to die he declares as much and, the law states, "they shall roll the wheel". The import of this is similarly unclear but seems to suggest some form of judicial ordeal.[546] After this action the king

Proceedings of the Conference Held at Mandelbaum House, The University of Sydney, 21–23 July 2004 (ed. J. J. Azize and N. K. Weeks; Ancient Near Eastern Studies Supplement 21; Louvain: Peeters, 2007), 225–40.

541 Probably the location of the royal court.

542 M. Tsevat, "The Husband Veils a Wife," *Journal of Cuneiform Studies* 27 (1975): 235–40.

543 *Laws of the* Hittites, 226. A change to his earlier position, in Roth, *Law Collections*, 237.

544 *e.g.* HL 20–21, 27, 31, 34, 43, 47b, 48, 50 (pl.), 51, 53, 74, 77 (feminine and masculine singular used appropriately), 95, 99, 100, 106, 171 (feminine) *etc.* For a more complete listing see Hoffner's glossary in *Laws of the Hittites*, 333.There are possibly several examples of the masculine singular suffix *ŠU* being used for the feminine *e.g.* HL 27, 171, 175, 200a.

545 HL 171 and 175.

546 See also "Apology of Ḫattušili III," trans. by Th. P. J. van den Hout (*COS*

is said to either have the couple killed or spared. Though it is a minor difference, it is worth noting that in MAL A 15 the husband had the responsibility for his wife's punishment with the king or judges only being responsible for the penalty given to the paramour in response to the husband's decision regarding his wife's punishment. Here in HL 198 the king is responsible for the punishment of both parties. As mentioned above, LH 129 does not specify that the husband, or anyone else, brings the couple to court. Though there is mention of the possibility that the offending couple are killed on the spot if caught *in flagrante delicto*, and mention of a role for the king in pardoning the paramour if the husband pardons the wife, there is no mention of the husband bringing the case to anyone if he wants both to die. As acknowledged by Westbrook, the king's prerogative to pardon both offenders regardless of the husband's wishes is unique to the Hittite collection.[547]

Westbrook explains the similarities in the laws treating the capture of an adulterous couple in the act as due to the background of a common oral discussion of this canonical legal problem, passed around with the spread of cuneiform scribal schools. He sees three aspects: 1) the killing of the couple on the spot by the husband, 2) bringing the couple to court for the death penalty, and 3) in court again, the husband wanting to pardon only his wife. LH 129, which does not mention any court proceedings, is said to cover the second and third situations. This is a possibility, but is a little forced. It is possible that the unspecified "they" in LH 129 who are to throw the offending couple into the water, refers to whoever may catch the couple in the act and is thus a slight variation from Westbrook's situation 1).[548] Unlike MAL A 15 and HL 197, LH 129 does not specify that it is the husband who catches the couple in the act. The continuing section of this law does, in all likelihood, cover Westbrook's situation 3). MAL A 15 and HL 197–198 cover all three situations with the differences enumerated above regarding the role for the king and the husband in carrying out and deciding upon the penalties. It should also be noted here that MAL A 15 alone envisages a corporal mutilation as punishment here. Given the differences between these laws, slight though they may be, it is unwise to presume their composers knew of original oral solutions to all three situations, let alone

1.77: 200, §4 and note 10).

[547] Westbrook, "Adultery," 556.

[548] Though, of course, the husband could be the unspecified captor and executor of the couple, perhaps with a group of friends.

that they presumed knowledge of these in their reader. This is especially the case when we come to LE 28.

LE 28 focuses on a different legal problem, namely, what it is that defines a woman as a "wife". The end of the law mentions that someone who fits the specifications needed to be a wife "shall die, she shall not live" if caught in the act of adultery.[549] This is another case of adulterers caught *in flagrante delicto.* Given the fact Akkadian does not distinguish feminine and masculine in the third person singular verb, there has been some debate as to the subject of the verbs in the penalty clause. Yaron has argued that one or both verbs could refer to the paramour rather than the woman.[550] This is highly unlikely given the subject matter of the rest of the law and its sole focus on the status of the woman. Though this law does not mention that the paramour will also be killed, it should not be assumed that this was not the case at Eshnunna. What is clear, and tacitly admitted by Westbrook, is that this law does not stem from the supposed canonical legal problem he sees as common to the laws treated above.[551] He does, however, think that it refers to it in passing and presumes knowledge of its other aspects in its readers.[552] Though this writer may agree that the drafters of the law collections may have assumed knowledge of local practice, he does not assent to the notion that this practice was necessarily common to the entire ancient Near East, nor even Mesopotamia. That the paramour would have been killed in the situation mentioned in LE 28 is probable but not demonstrable. To argue, as Szlechter does,[553] that this law definitely refers to the killing of the couple by the offended husband is to say more than the text allows. To assume that the other situations, the husband bringing both to court to be killed or in order to pardon his wife, were known at Eshnunna is no more than that, an assumption. It is not certain that pardoning was possible in the mind of the drafter of LE and it should not be assumed.[554]

MAPD 19, set in the context of the harem, is even more severe than those above in that the death penalty is specified for a palace woman and a

---

[549] Literally, "in the lap of another man".

[550] Yaron, *Laws of Eshnunna*, 284–85.

[551] Westbrook, "Adultery," 553: "CE 28 strictly speaking belongs to a different standard problem, concerning the validity of marriage".

[552] *loc. cit.*

[553] Émile Szlechter, *Les Lois d'Eshnunna* (Publications de l'Institut de Droit Romain 12; Paris: Université de Paris, 1954), 110, 123. As followed by Westbrook, "Adultery," 552.

[554] The same is the case regarding the material in the Biblical law collections.

man who stand by themselves behaving "in a flirtatious manner", or any who do not report such an offence.[555]

Let us now turn our attention to those other laws which only mention the death of one offender. Several of these laws treat the rape of a married woman. In these laws it is only the offending male who is punished while the woman goes free.[556] LU 6, LH 130 and LE 26 share many similar details though they are phrased differently. All treat the rape of a man's inchoate wife.[557] Her status is described in two different ways in the laws,[558] but the same state is in view. The description of the penalty is also slightly different but in all laws, death is prescribed for the offending male. LH 130 specifically states that the woman is to be released, and the lack of mention of any penalty for the woman in LE 26 and LU 6, given the same focus of the laws, implies that none was in view.[559] This may possibly reflect some background of borrowing amongst these three collections. The other collections which mention the rape of a married woman do not specify her status as an inchoate wife, perhaps implying that they did not share this practice, or that their laws did not borrow from the others.

MAL A 12 prescribes that there is no punishment for a woman who is seized along the main thoroughfare and forced to have sex with another man as long as she offers some resistance. The man is to be killed, whether on the spot or after the charges are proved in court. MAL A 23 treats a very specific situation, that of a man's wife who has been taken into the house of a procuress and had sex with another man. If the woman did not know what was intended by the procuress and declares that she was raped by the man, she goes free and both the procuress and the other man are killed. Again, MAL introduces an element of foreknowledge not expressed elsewhere. If the woman knew what was intended her husband punishes her at his discretion and the procuress and the other man receive the same punishment. If the woman did not know what was intended, but failed to de-

---

[555] See Roth, *Law Collections*, 205.

[556] See our earlier discussion regarding the apparent contradiction to this rule in MAL A 16 and 22.

[557] For a description of this state, considered as marriage, see Westbrook, *Old Babylonian Marriage Law* (Archiv für Orientforschung, Beiheft 23; Horn: Ferdinand Berger & sons, 1988), chs. 2–3.

[558] With LU 6 and LH 130 sharing the description of her as a "virgin wife".

[559] The case here is different to that in LE 28 where the law focused solely on the woman's status as a wife and the concomitant implication that had for her if she strayed. Here the focus is on the offence, not a particular party, thus the safety in taking the lack of mention of a penalty for the woman as significant.

clare that she was raped, the husband punishes her at her discretion and the procuress and the other man are killed.[560]

HL 197 treats rape, though it is not certain that a married woman is in view. Here is the law in full: "If a man seizes a woman in the mountains, it is the man's offence, but if he seizes her in her house, it is the woman's offence: the woman shall die. If the woman's husband discovers them in the act, he may kill them without committing a crime." The latter part of the law has been dealt with above. The first case implies that a rape has occurred if the woman was seized in the mountains and that it is only the man who is at fault. Interestingly there is no mention of any penalty for him. If the woman is seized[561] in her house, she is seen to be at fault and will be put to death. These two clauses leave much room for speculation. It is unclear if the woman is married though this seems most likely given the mention of a husband in the final clause. The lack of a penalty specified for the man in the first case is unhelpful. One can presume that the death penalty was also in view for him, with its omission due to the focus of the law on the problem of which party was guilty, but this cannot be proven. A similar problem arises in the second case. The woman is said to be "seized" (*epzi*) in her house, as she was in the mountains. If this verb implies she has been taken against her will, then the mention of punishment for the woman alone is very strange. It is difficult to explain even if the verb simply means "to take" and does not imply the use of force. If the act was consensual and the woman married, it would be hard to explain why there is no punishment for the male specified, especially given the fact a husband is allowed to kill both partners if he catches them in the act. There are a number of possible solutions to this problem. The first is that in the first two cases, punishment for the offending man is implied (most likely to be death) though not specified. The second is that, whether the woman is married or unmarried, the first case treats rape and implies a penalty for the man and the second treats a situation where the woman has seduced the man in some way so that only she is punished. This would parallel LU 7. It is very unlikely that there is no penalty for the man who rapes the woman in the mountains though he has committed an offence, and only the woman was to be punished if the adultery was committed in her house. As mentioned, this writer suspects that the omission of these expected penalties is due to the focus of the law on the problem of which party was guilty, rather than on the punishment due.

---

[560] Not treated as the wife due to their added offence of deceit.

[561] Using the same verb as the previous clause.

The law does not seem to aim to give a comprehensive ruling but to clarify a particular issue.

Apart from HL 197, there are two other laws which mention punishment for the married woman only, LU 7 and MAL A 14. MAL A 14 declares that if a man should fornicate with a man's wife at an inn or in the main thoroughfare, without knowing that she was married, he is not punished. The husband has the right to punish his wife as he sees fit. The mention of the location here is different to that in HL 197. It is not designed to describe a situation where the woman could not have screamed for help in contrast to one where she could, but to demonstrate a situation where the offending male may have been confused as to the woman's marital status.[562] This is explained more specifically later in the law. No other collection of laws mentions this aspect of the offence of adultery. It is thus not safe to assume it elsewhere. This is precisely what Westbrook does when he comes to an interpretation of LU 7. The law reads: "If the wife of a young man, on her own initiative, approaches a man and initiates sexual relations with him, they shall kill that woman; that male shall be released." Though this writer may agree with Westbrook's concern that such a law may have led to problems in practice, the man only having to claim he was seduced to get away with adultery, he does not assent to Westbrook's attempts to solve this problem by importing the details of MAL A 14 into this law. LU 7 does not specify, nor does it necessarily imply that the male in question did not know that the woman was married; merely that it was she who initiated the encounter. Given the unique discussion of such matters in MAL, this writer thinks this an unwise conclusion based on the desire to harmonize these two laws. The laws do not contradict each other, but, on their simplest reading, they do release the male from punishment for different reasons. This would question their common background in an oral discussion of a canonical legal problem. Interestingly though, the treating of LU 7 in this way, does further the possibility that HL 197 deals with an analogous situation. HL 197 stands apart in its detailing of the location to assess the coercive nature of the offence,[563] as MAL does in its unique assessment of the man's knowledge of the woman's marital status or, in MAL A 23, the woman's knowledge of the procuress' plans. LU, LH, LE, MAL and HL all seem to punish only the male offender in the case of the rape of a married

[562] The inn and main thoroughfare being popular places for prostitutes.

[563] Note that MAL A 12's detailing of a location within the city's main thoroughfare is not used to imply that the woman is to be held responsible as it is in Deut. 22:23–24 though both laws detail the woman's duty to resist.

woman.[564] All these collections mention the use of force in their description of the offence, except for HL which merely implies its use by detailing the location. Only MAL A 12 mentions the onus on the woman to resist, though it may be implied also in HL 197's detailing of locations.[565]

There is some debate regarding the circumstances which are described in LH 142–143. Westbrook interprets them as referring to pre-marital infidelity, more specifically, infidelity during inchoate marriage.[566] This is based mainly on the woman's statement to "her husband", *ul taḫḫazanni*, "you shall not take me". The verb *aḫazu* regularly means "to take in marriage, to marry". The background of inchoate marriage does explain how a woman can tell her husband that he cannot marry her. Others have attempted to take the verb as referring to the husband's taking of his wife for sexual relations.[567] Adding to the likelihood of Westbrook's interpretation is the use of the term *sinništum* here for the woman in contrast to *aššat awilim* in LH 141, which treats a situation where a wife wants to divorce her husband. This is hardly definitive, however, given the interchangeability of the terms in LH 133a–b. In LH 141 there is specific mention of the fact that the wife resides in her husband's house, perhaps implying that this was not the case in LH 142–143. The statement that the woman *mussa izerma*, "hates her husband", is a common euphemism for divorce, furthering Westbrook's argument again. Roth's translation of this phrase as repudiation of the husband is somewhat circuitous. In LH 142, if the woman declares that she does not want to go through with the marriage (it still being inchoate), the case goes to court.[568] If she is without fault but her husband goes out and slanders her she takes her dowry and goes to her father's house. This last phrase seems to go against the idea of inchoate marriage as the woman should not be residing in her husband's house during this state, and rules out this element as the distinction between this law and LH 141.[569] The statement in LH 143 that she squanders her household possessions would be a strange inclusion

[564] This statement needs to take into consideration the uncertain import of HL 197 as discussed above.

[565] Compare the fuller description of the import of the location in Deut. 22:23–27.

[566] Westbrook, "Adultery," 570.

[567] Roth translates the phrase, "You will not have marital relations with me", perhaps hedging her bets, *Law Collections*, 108.

[568] Westbrook's translation of *warkassa ina babtiša ipparrasma*, "Adultery," 572 is preferred to Roth's, *Law Collections*, 108.

[569] See Westbrook, *Marriage Law*, 50–53.

if these were not the possessions of her husband's household. The implication would then be that the circumstances being dealt with here concern a married woman who wishes to divorce her husband.[570] Though this would make LH 142–143 very similar to LH 141 there is one key difference: in LH 142–143 it is the wife who wishes to initiate the divorce. The strict regulations regarding this in these laws mirror some of the clauses embedded in Old Babylonian marriage contracts aimed at stopping the woman from divorcing her husband.[571] If there are no circumstances to question the woman's motives for divorcing her husband and there are understandable reasons for it, she takes her dowry and returns to her father's house. This is similar to the provision in LH 138 for a husband who divorces his wife,[572] though here she does not also take the bride wealth. LH 143, which prescribes that the woman is to be cast into the water, treats a situation where there is evidence to suggest questionable motives for the woman's desire for divorce. These include the possibility of promiscuous behavior, as intimated by her description as *la naṣratma waṣiat*, "not chaste/circumspect[573] (but) wayward/going out". It is unclear whether a sexual relationship with another man has been established or is just expected.[574] The further mention of squandering household goods or slandering her husband as criteria for her drowning makes it likely that hard evidence of sexual misconduct was not forthcoming, and her character in general was in question in order to determine her likely motives in asking for the divorce. It is probable that the suspicion of a relationship with another man as motivation for the divorce lies at the heart of the penalty, thus paralleling the general punishment within the ancient Near East for adultery.

---

[570] Thus interpreting the phrase *ul taḫḫazanni* as the woman's declaration to her husband "you will not be married to me". See a further possibility in note 573 below.

[571] Referred to by Westbrook, "Adultery," 559–60.

[572] For no particular reason.

[573] The use of this verb, which can imply the preserving of virginity also gives some backing to Westbrook's position and would equally explain the harsh penalty. It is however, difficult to reconcile with the dwelling of the woman in her husband's house unless it was consummation that she had denied her husband in LH 142 with her declaration *ul taḫḫazanni*. The use of the verb in LH 133b, referring to an *aššatu*, questions a meaning limited to the preservation of virginity.

[574] That it could have been established is possible given its use in LH 133b to describe the entrance of a man's wife into the house of another man. The same penalty applies to the woman in that law as in LH 143.

A law which would be somewhat parallel to Westbrook's interpretation of LH 142–143 is found in HL 28. It specifies that a man who runs off with a betrothed woman without her parents' co-operation will pay the man she was betrothed to whatever he had paid as well as some compensation. If her father and mother were involved they are to compensate the first man. If they do not, they are to separate the girl from her new man. The latter half of this law parallels LH 160–161 closer than 142–143. The first situation where the betrothed woman seems to be the instigator of a new relationship and the canceling of further marriage negotiations would parallel what Westbrook thinks is happening in LH 142–143. The lack of any punishment for the woman in HL 28 would then be a significant difference to the drowning prescribed in LH 143 if there is evidence of another relationship. The calling off of proceedings towards the marriage on account of interest in another man receives no punishment in HL 28 whereas proceedings for divorce on the part of a woman for the same reason results in her drowning in LH 143. The two laws do not directly contradict each other on this understanding.[575] Upon our interpretation there would still be a difference in severity here, though perhaps lessened by the woman's status as betrothed rather than married. There may be a different attitude to the state of betrothal in HL, as other collections do not feel the need to distinguish between the rape of or adultery with a married or betrothed woman.[576]

One more set of laws which should be treated here is that dealing with the question of the wife's obligations in the case of an absentee husband. This question is dealt with in LH 133–136, LE 29–30 and MAL A 36, 45, giving rise to more claims about canonical legal topics. Within these laws one could even argue for a development of legal reasoning from earlier to later. Many of the same elements and the same legal reasoning appear within these laws. LE 29–30 state the case most simply:

> **LE 29** If a man should be captured or abducted during a raiding expedition or while on patrol(?), even should he reside in a foreign land for a long time, should someone else marry his wife and even should she bear a child, whenever he returns he shall take back his wife.

---

[575] Nor would they even under Westbrook's interpretation if it was thought illicit sexual activity was proven in LH 143 but not in HL 28.

[576] Except Deuteronomy 22:22–29, which has the death penalty for both parties in the case of adultery involving a married or a betrothed woman (stoning is specified for the latter) linking this offence to the penalty of fornication before marriage in verse 21.

LE 30 If a man repudiates his city and his master and then flees, and someone else then marries his wife, whenever he returns he will have no claim to his wife.

LH 135–136 parallel these two laws very closely:

LH 135 If a man should be captured and there are not sufficient provisions in his house, before his return his wife enters another's house and bears children, and afterwards her husband returns and gets back to his city, that woman shall return to her first husband; the children shall inherit from their father.

LH 136 If a man deserts his city and flees, and after his departure his wife enters another's house-if that man then should return and seize his wife, because he repudiated his city and fled, the wife of the deserter will not return to her husband.

The drafter of LH has added another element to the question of whether the husband has been detained against his will or has fled, namely; the question of whether there were enough provisions in the man's house for the wife to survive. Thus in LH, two new laws are added in LH 133 and 134. LH 133 declares that if the man is captured and there are enough provisions, his wife shall not enter another's house, and prescribes that if she does so she will be cast into the water; the common penalty for an adulteress in LH.[577] LH 134 declares her right to enter another's house if there are not sufficient provisions. LH 135–136 then repeat the provisions of LE 29–30, but specific to the situation where there were not enough provisions.

MAL A 36 and 45 introduce new elements to this situation and leave others out. The formulation of the laws does not mirror those of LH or LE and the rulings are slightly different. The new elements are the time she is to wait for her husband: 5 years in MAL A 36 if she does not have sons to support her,[578] 2 years in MAL A 45 if her husband is taken as a POW and she has no sons or father-in-law to support her, and the detailing of provisions for her while she waits. In both laws it is mentioned that her husband has not left provisions for her. In MAL A 36 she is free to marry in the sixth year if her husband has not returned and she does not have sons to support her. In this case, the husband has no claim to her upon his return if she remarries, somewhat paralleling the husband who flees his city in LH 136 and LE 30. If the husband was not detained of his own intention he is able to take his wife upon the presentation of a comparable woman to his

[577] As seen in LH 129 and 143.

[578] If she does it seems she is to remain unmarried indefinitely.

wife's current husband (another new element). If her husband had been sent on a mission of the king the wife is to wait indefinitely. Unlike in LH 133, however, the woman is not punished with death if she goes to a second husband before the five years are up. The husband merely has the right to take her and her children upon his return. It should be noted that this situation does not directly parallel LH 133 as in that case the husband had left provisions whereas here he has not done so. The treatment of this topic in MAL then makes it more difficult for the woman to leave her husband, adding further conditions and specifying ways of supporting her. MAL A 45 deals specifically with the situation where the woman's husband has been taken as a prisoner of war. The law demands that she remain loyal to him for two years if she has no provisions from sons or father-in-law. The shorter period is probably due to the lesser likelihood of the husband's return. Most of the law details the various means of support available to her during the two years. If the husband returns after the two years he can take back his wife, but not the children she has with her new husband. Despite the different framing of these laws within MAL, the many similarities amongst these three laws and the ability to hypothesize a unilinear development from LE to LH to MAL makes this writer, though usually skeptical of such claims, admit the possibility that the drafters of these laws took the earlier editions into account or were at least conversant with legal reasoning similar to that contained within them which was furthered in each case. It remains possible that MAL did not build on LE and LH, but it would be harder to claim the independence of LH 135–136 from LE 29–30.

2.6.3.2 Offences Involving Unmarried Women

This topic was far less popular than those dealing with married women, reflecting the primary concern for the laws to protect the rights of the husband and head of the household rather than a woman's. The only laws relevant are found in MAL A 55–56 and SLEx 7'–8'. MAL A 55 is lengthy in its description of offence, conditions and subsequent penalties. Put simply it prescribes that a man who rapes an unmarried virgin[579] living in her father's house will have his wife raped and not returned. It also states that the man will have to pay triple the value of the maiden[580] and will have to marry her

---

[579] Also said to be unbetrothed, further demonstrating the lack of a common canonical problem regarding rape of a married woman in the case of MAL *i.e.* its law parallel to LH 130, LU 6 and LE 26 does not treat a betrothed woman, but a married one.

[580] This writer is unsure what payment this refers to. See Driver and Miles, *As-*

if her father so desires.[581] The principle of talion seems to apply here and a physical punishment, so common in MAL, is again in view. The punishment is beneath that regarding the rape of a married woman, as death is not in view. The law specifies that these stipulations stand no matter where or when the offence took place; specifically mentioning the city and the countryside, the main thoroughfare, a granary, along with night time or festival time. The mention of the first two locations may imply knowledge of their import regarding the girl's resistance as in Deuteronomy 22:23–27. Each of the elements listed could be seen to imply some circumstance bearing on the relative faults of the two parties.[582] The import is that these are not to be taken into account here.

MAL A 56 treats the opposite circumstance, where the maiden has given herself willingly. It is not the case then that A 55 is solely interested in the woman's junior status to absolve her of guilt. The mention of forcible seizure is of great importance in that law. Perhaps it is the establishment of that fact that makes time and location of no importance. In MAL A 56 the man is to swear that he did not force himself upon the maiden. He merely pays triple the value of the maiden while the father treats his daughter as he sees fit. This offence is certainly seen in a more lenient light than adultery.

The only possible parallels to these two laws are SLEx 7'–8'. There is some debate over the meaning of these laws.[583] In both laws it is stated that the deflowering offence was committed in the streets. There is a description of someone's ignorance of something in 7' combined with a declaration of some sort and someone's knowledge of something in 8'. It is the significance of these sections which are debated. Finkelstein[584] argues that what is in view is the parents' contributory negligence to what has occurred and that the laws centre on whether the parents had assented to their daughter's presence on the street. For Finkelstein then, in 7' the parents are ignorant of the fact that their daughter was on the street and she claims to have been

---

syrian Laws, 60–65 for discussion.

[581] He has the right to refuse this and give her to someone else.

[582] The city versus countryside location and its possible import for the girl's ability to resist; the main thoroughfare and the heightened likelihood of the man mistaking the girl for a prostitute; the granary as a place two mutual lovers may hide in to conceal their activities; the girl's being out at night time implying some fault on her part; perhaps the festival atmosphere of loosened morals or extra alcohol consumption.

[583] Roth versus Finkelstein.

[584] Finkelstein, "Sex Offenses in Sumerian Laws," *Journal of the American Oriental Society* 86 (1966): 358, 362–366.

raped. Roth treats the ignorance in 7' as an inability to identify the culprit who then turns himself in and asks to marry the girl. Both agree that the ruling is that the girl may be given to the man as a wife. In 8' Finkelstein has the parents cognizant of the fact their daughter was on the street and the offender declaring ignorance of the woman's status.[585] Roth sees 8' treating a situation where the parents do identify the culprit but he disputes their identification. Both see the law ending with the culprit swearing an oath to back up his statement with no penalty or obligation in view. It is very difficult to decide between these two interpretations on a linguistic basis given the murkiness of the text.[586] This writer dislikes Finkelstein's interpretation that the law would hinge on the contributory negligence of the parents. One would think that their lack of knowledge of the girl's whereabouts may imply bad motives on her part rather than the offending male. The idea that as 7' specifies an obligation for the man to marry the woman while 8' does not that he was at fault in the first instance though not in the second is not a necessary one.[587] Given the extreme difficulties in translating these two laws, one is hard pressed to argue with any certainty that they parallel any other.

Interestingly the Hittite Laws have no provisions dealing with offences involving unmarried women, unless that is the topic of HL 197.[588] Simple fornication, however, was not seen as an offence as is demonstrated in HL 191 and 194 which allow a man to sleep with sisters in different locations if he doesn't know of their relationship or if they are slaves. HL 194 also allows brothers to sleep with the same woman and father and son to sleep with the same slave or prostitute. It is difficult to know if this contrasts to the laws treated above as they specifically treat occasions of deflowering.

2.6.3.3 Offences Involving Slaves

LE 31 and LU 8 treat the same offence; the deflowering of someone else's slave-woman.

> **LE 31** If a man should deflower the slave woman of another man, he shall weigh and deliver 20 shekels of silver, but the slave woman remains the property of her master.

---

[585] Perhaps implying he thought she was a prostitute.

[586] There are numerous problems with both translations, from the inanimate object *b* which each treats as animate to the dispute in line 47 of 7' over the inclusion or exclusion of *nam ad-ni* u_3 *ama-e*.

[587] *e.g.* see the translation of Clay, *Miscellaneous Inscriptions*, 22.

[588] See discussion above.

LU 8 If a man acts in violation of the rights of another and deflowers the virgin slave woman of a man, he shall weigh and deliver 5 shekels of silver.

The laws read very similarly but one could not argue that LE had merely translated the law in LU due to the difference in description. The penalty in LE 31 is four times that in LU 8, perhaps implying the drafter of LU saw this as a lesser offence, perhaps a rise in the price of slaves.[589] LE 31 specifies that the slave remains the property of her master, only implied in LU 8.[590] There is no discussion in LU 8, in contrast to LU 7, regarding the initiation of the liaison. Given the slave's standing as her master's property rather than as a legal person this may have been considered unimportant. Elsewhere, however, there is specification regarding the punishment of slaves, and detailing of offences committed or legal claims made by them.[591] There is a good possibility that the drafter of LE 31 knew of LU 8.

The only other laws dealing with sex offences involving slaves come in HL 194, 196 concerning unpermitted sexual pairings. These will be treated below.

2.6.3.4 Incest and Bestiality

Laws detailing unpermitted sexual pairings are rare in the ancient Near East when compared to those dealing with sexual offences involving married women. HL stands apart from the others in its detailed list of these.[592] This mirrors the comparatively heightened concern in these laws about (ritual) purity. Of the other collections, LH 154–158 are the only laws to treat this topic. LH 155 punishes with drowning a father sleeping with his son's wife after their marriage has been consummated and in LH 157 a son and mother who sleep together after the father is dead are to be burned.[593] LH 155 mirrors the general punishment for adultery in LH, whereas the pun-

---

[589] The price of slaves is 10 shekels of silver (implied) in LU 24; 15 in LL 13; 20 in LH 116.

[590] Surely the offender is not able to acquire a female slave for 5 shekels let alone such an amount including the penalty for the offence.

[591] *e.g.* LH s, 205, 282; LU 25–26; LL 14; HL 31–34, 93, 95, 97, 99, 101, 105, 121, 132–133, 142–143, 170, 172–173, 196.

[592] There is of course the Biblical material also.

[593] The specific mention "after his father's death" in this law and in LH 158 is used to distinguish the severity of offences in the Hittite incest laws *i.e.* it is more offensive for a son to sleep with his father's wives while his father is still alive. LH only deals with those offences after the father has died.

ishment in LH 157 treats the offence as more heinous or polluting. Interestingly, a father sleeping with his daughter is only to be banished in LH 154. A father sleeping with his son's wife before the marriage is consummated has only to give the woman 30 shekels of silver, and restore the property she brought with her from her father's house. This law perhaps lends weight to our interpretation of LH 142–143 above as referring to a completed marriage rather than inchoate status given the lenient penalty here for an adulterous liaison during the inchoate state. It is possible, however, that the committing of the offence by the girl's father-in-law, perhaps having legal responsibility for her at the time, was seen as a mitigating circumstance. The lack of any penalty for the girl is strange unless rape is envisaged. A son sleeping with his father's principal wife (not his mother) is disinherited in LH 158.

The Hittite Laws concerning unpermitted sexual pairings are more detailed and different in a number of respects. In contrast to LH 154, sleeping with your daughter was possibly punished with death in HL 189. The Hittite Laws dealing with sexual offences are all grouped together. The laws treating bestiality state their penalties specifically. Apart from having relations with a horse or a mule, or being set upon by an ox or pig, bestiality is said to be punished with death. The process leading to this is further specified with the offender being brought to the king's court where the king can either kill him or spare his life. In every case of bestiality, including those devoid of the death penalty, the offender cannot approach the king so as not to defile him. HL 200a specifies that he who had sex with a horse or mule cannot become a priest and HL 199 that a substitionary sacrifice of a sheep must take place for a man who was leapt upon by an ox (in sexual excitement) and the ox shall die. The concern is with purity. The incest offences, however, merely state whether the situation detailed is unpermitted, *ḫurkel*,[594] or is not an offence. It is unclear whether the process is the same for these offences as for the bestiality offences (also described as *ḫurkel*). This seems a likely interpretation.

There are some parallels between the laws in HL and LH. The only law which has the same penalty is that concerning incest between a son and his mother in HL 189 and LH 157. Both demand the death penalty; LH specifically requires burning. Within LH 157 there is the specification that this offence occurs *warki abišu*, "after his father", implying that his father is dead at the time of the offence. This statement also occurs in LH 158 re-

---

[594] For a discussion of this term see Hoffner, *Laws of the Hittites*, 224 and the references there.

garding the offence of a son sleeping with his father's principal wife in the case she is not his mother. Within LH there is no mention of the corresponding penalty for these offences if the father was alive. Within HL there are also statements regarding the import of whether certain persons were alive at the time of the offence. In every case the offence is seen to be worse if the person mentioned is still alive. HL 190 for example states that it is not an offence for a man to sleep with his stepmother unless his father is still living. HL 192 allows a man to marry his wife's sister if his wife is dead. It is an offence in HL 195 for a man to sleep with his brother's wife while his brother is alive, whereas he is ordered to take her as a wife if his brother dies in HL 193. It may be presumed from this, and from what one would expect anyway in the case of these offences, that the drafter of LH would also have seen the offences laid out in LH 157–158 as being worse if the man's father were still alive. If this was the case, perhaps they needed no mention, the penalty being obvious.

It should be noted here that, despite the relatively few parallel laws between LH and HL, there are at least two distinctions in penalty. The lenient treatment of incest between a man and his daughter in LH contrasted to its status as *ḫurkel* in HL was mentioned above. Another contrast may be found between LH 158 and HL 190. HL 190 sees no offence if a man sleeps with his stepmother after his father's death, whereas LH 158 orders disinheritance. There are some differences in these laws, with LH 158 specifying that the stepmother was the principal wife of the man's father and had borne him children. This merely shows the lack of dependence between the two collections regarding this topic. One should not try to reconstruct the ancient Near Eastern law of incest by postulating one penalty for the specific situation in LH 158 and another for stepmothers in general from HL 190. From its framing, HL 190 would cover the situation in LH 158 also and the penalties are thus distinct.

Common again to the Hittite Laws is the more frequent mention of offences committed by slaves[595] as is the case in laws concerning murder, damage and theft. As with those laws, the penalty for offences committed by slaves is less than that for others. In HL 196, slaves who do *ḫurkel*, are merely separated and require the sacrifice of a sheep. Within the Hittite Laws also is a reflection of a more general phenomenon whereby offences involving slaves are treated less severely. For example in HL 194 a man can sleep with slave women with the same mother whereas this is *ḫurkel* if done

[595] HL 196. None are mentioned in LH regarding sexual offences.

with free women in HL 191.[596] In the same law a father and son can sleep with the same female slave, whereas from HL 191 and 195 it is to be expected that this would have been *ḫurkel* if a free woman was involved.

One final note regarding the sex laws found in these collections is that prostitution does not seem to be an offence. Certain laws seem to imply its validity *e.g.* HL 194; MAL A 40, 49, 52; LL 27. LL 30 does, however, mention judges banning a young married man from visiting a prostitute and forbids his marriage to the prostitute if he divorces his wife after such an order. The circumstances which would lead to the judges' banning of such a man's visits are unclear in this law, especially when compared to LL 27 which specifies the support of a prostitute who bears the child of a married man. This act does not seem to amount to adultery in the eyes of LL's drafter, nor that of HL or MAL.[597]

2.6.4 False Accusation

There are laws covering this offence only in collections from Mesopotamia.[598] Those who postulate a common law in the ancient Near East see in the provisions in the law collections dealing with false accusation the rule, set out a number of times in LH, that the false accuser bears the penalty that the accused would have suffered were he found guilty.[599] A number of laws follow this rule. The most significant exception to the rule in LH concerns the accusation of sexual infidelity against a woman which is treated with less severity. We will assess whether this was a general trend across collections. There seem to be several exceptions to both rules.

LH 1 provides the death penalty for a false accusation of homicide,[600] witchcraft,[601] theft[602] or any other capital offence.[603] LH 126 declares that a man who claims compensation for lost property from a city-quarter shall pay back 2-fold if it is found he did not lose any property. This law should

---

[596] Unless he does not know of the relationship.

[597] Compare Lev. 19:29; 21:9.

[598] LH, LU, LL, MAL.

[599] Specifically stated in LH 3, 4, 13.

[600] LH 1

[601] LH 2

[602] LH 11 and probably 13 also. LH 13 only states that the false accuser shall be assessed the penalty for the case but as the case deals with theft and is but a continuation of the topic from law 11 it seems safe to assume that the death penalty was in view.

[603] LH 3

be read in conjunction with LH 23. LH 23 states that a man who has had his property stolen can claim it back from the city-quarter where the theft occurred if the thief is not apprehended. The man who falsely claims to have had his property stolen in LH 126 is then possibly returning the compensation given him and paying the same amount again. This would amount to keeping the principle that the false accuser bears the penalty of the case.

The statement of this principle in LH 3 and 4 is repeated in LU 29 and in LL 17. Though these collections are those which are seen to be the most alike, there are enough differences in the formulation of this principle to deny that one had been copied or translated from the other.[604] Hammurabi states the principle three times in different contexts. In LH 3 he states that false testimony involving a capital offence receives the death penalty, while LH 4 states that such an act involving an offence with a pecuniary punishment will lead to the false witness bearing the penalty of the case. LU also has two laws covering false witness in general. LU 28 deals with a witness who is demonstrated to be a perjurer. He is fined 15 shekels of silver. In LU 29 a witness who refuses to take the oath pays the penalty that would be involved in the case. It is difficult to understand the difference between these two laws. The difficulty is heightened in that in the first case the judges seem to be more certain that the man was a false witness as he is said to have been "demonstrated" as such. Another problem is that it would seem a more serious offence to have taken the oath and still borne false witness than to have baulked at the point of swearing an oath, yet it is the second offence which may have borne a higher penalty.[605] Whatever the case, an Akkadian translation of either law would be quite different to the two in LH, though the principle is the same in LU 29 as that outlined in LH. LU 28 seems an exception to the principle in that a straight out penalty is given rather than an amount equal to the penalty of the case. LL 17 also states the principle outlined in LH 3 and 4 though it speaks of someone who accuses without grounds rather than a false witness *per se*. The law states that the false accuser will "bear the penalty of the matter for which he made accusation." Again, the principle seems to be the same, though the wording would not necessarily lead one to assume significant borrowing of

---

[604] This is not necessarily to imply that the scribes or authors of these collections were not aware of their predecessor/s.

[605] *e.g.* if the witness accused someone of the offences outlined in LU 1, 2, 6, 19, 20.

this law by LH nor from LU. Of course, some form of stimulus, association or knowledge cannot be ruled out.

LU 13 could be used to argue that the principle was not upheld in this collection. The law describes an accusation proved false by completion of the River Ordeal by the accused. The accuser only seems to be fined 3 shekels as punishment.[606] Given that we are not sure of either the offence that the undergoer was accused of,[607] nor that the penalty for false accusation in this law was only 3 shekels, it would be unwise to make too much of this law. If the offence were sorcery[608] and the fine only 3 shekels for false accusation this would be a severe reduction of the penalty outlined in LH 2 where the false accuser receives both the death penalty and forfeits his estate to the accused.

The MAL do not overtly state the general principle as do the other collections. It is difficult to decide whether the laws to do with unsubstantiated accusation in MAL are based on the same principle as those in the other collections. The laws in MAL possibly deal with the offence of malicious slander rather than false accusation or testimony regarding a criminal case. MAL N 1 and N 2 deal with accusations of blasphemy and pilfering the temple. They are too broken to comment on in any detail. As we do not know the MAL's penalty for blasphemy or pilfering a temple it would be difficult to decide if the penalty meted for false accusation of such an offence was the same as that for committing it. MAL A 19 deals with an unsubstantiated accusation during a quarrel that another man is sodomized by others. Though MAL A 20 deals with the offence of sodomizing others and penalizes the perpetrator with castration and undergoing sodomy himself, there is no indication that undergoing sodomy was an offence. It is even possible that homosexual rape is the offence which is in view in MAL A 20. Another hint that malicious slander is the offence is to be found in the penalty given for the false accusation in MAL A 19. Apart from receiving 50 blows and doing the king's service for a month and paying 3600 shekels of lead, the man has his hair cut off. This seems designed to humiliate the offender as he has humiliated the man he has slandered. A similar offence

---

[606] But see Roth's notes as to the uncertainty of the text at this point, *Law Collections*, 21–22, n. 12. The law is retained only in source A and the penalty only in source B. There is some doubt as to the correlation of the penalty in source B with the law outlined in source A *i.e.* the penalty may belong to another law.

[607] See Roth again *Law Collections* 21–22, n. 12 *contra* Tikva Frymer-Kensky, "The Judicial Ordeal in the Ancient Near East" (Ph.D. diss., Yale University; Ann Arbor: University Microfilms, 1977), 138–44.

[608] As Frymer-Kensky supposes, "Judicial Ordeal," 138–44.

seems to be in view in MAL A 18 where a man who slanders another by claiming that he can prove that his wife has sex with everyone receives the same set of punishments minus 10 blows.

It was mentioned earlier that a general exception to the rule that a false accuser bears the penalty of the case is found when dealing with accusations of female infidelity. This is seen even in LH which has the most consistent application of this rule in other cases. In LH 127, the penalty for unfounded accusation against an *ugbabtu* or a man's wife is flogging and the shaving off of half the accuser's hair. This seems very similar to the combination of punishments found in MAL A 18 and 19, and again, seems to imply that the offence is one of slander.[609] Perhaps the reasoning behind the law does fit with the general principle that the accuser suffers the ill-effects of their accusation, but it is only the ill-effects upon the husband which are in view *i.e.* the humiliation resultant from the slander. If the woman was found guilty of adultery she may have been put to death at the husband's discretion.[610] It is certainly not the case here that the accuser bears the penalty of the case. One wonders whether this was designed as a way to ensure a vehicle for society to enforce the faithfulness of wives to their husbands. Given that there were no laws governing the infidelity of the husband, this is possibly the case.[611] LH 131 supports this possibility as there is no penalty for a man who accuses his own wife of adultery without proof. The woman is merely required to clear her name by an oath. The husband's slander of his wife does not receive any punishment. LL 33 seems to be similar in that a false accusation that a man's virgin daughter had fornicated only receives a penalty of 10 shekels. It is difficult to assess the relative leniency of this punishment in relation to that for the offence of fornication by a man's daughter as we do not possess any other laws dealing with sex offences in LL.

The situation is demonstrably different, however, in the Laws of Ur-Nammu. LU 14 prescribes the payment of 20 shekels for a man who accuses another's wife of adultery if she is cleared by the River Ordeal. This is actually a harsher penalty than that in LU 28 for demonstrable perjury. One wonders, given the relative infrequency of capital punishment in LU, whether it is possible to tell whether this offence was seen to be against the woman or the husband. It would be difficult to state that this law upheld a

---

[609] One assumes that the offence these women are being accused of is of a sexual nature. This assumption is supported by the subject matter of following laws.

[610] LH 129 or 133b.

[611] The only time a man would be punished for adultery would be when he had slept with another man's wife.

general rule that false accusations against women regarding sexual offences were treated less harshly than other false accusations. If the law is compared to LU 29 this may be seen as the case, but not when compared to LU 28.

MAL A 17 may destroy the idea that it was a general rule that false accusations against women were treated less severely than other accusations *i.e.* less than the penalty of the case. There is an apparent contradiction between it and MAL A 18, however. MAL A 17 seems to prescribe that in the case where a man tells another man that everyone has sex with his wife but has no witnesses, both the man and the other man's wife will undergo the River Ordeal.[612] MAL A 18 seems to cover exactly the same offence[613] but prescribes a different penalty. One wonders how to explain this apparent contradiction. Does it reflect the nature of MAL and perhaps imply that it was a collection of judge's decisions which may have included contradictory ones or does it reflect the Assyrian reluctance to speak of change in law and thus the compiler has presented both the old and new laws next to each other? If so, how could one tell which law was older? It may be tempting to try and explain the apparent differences in these two laws as a result of their place in the structure of the laws. A 17 comes at the end of a series of laws regarding sexual offences whereas A 18 is followed by a law possibly dealing with malicious slander rather than false accusation of a punishable act.[614] Perhaps A 17 was conceived as demonstrating the principles behind sexual offences while A 18 was seen as having a similar role for offences of slander. The inclusion in A 18 of a punishment designed to humiliate, the shaving of hair, supports this contention. Given that the structure of MAL is so loose that a law regarding injury causing miscarriage is interpolated amongst these laws dealing with sexual offences[615] we would be hesitant to argue too forcefully from the structure of the collection. One last possibility is that the difference is to be found in the terms used for the offended party. In MAL A 17 it is merely another man, "*a'ilu*", whereas in A 18 it is a friend/comrade, "*tappa'u*". LH fits the rules stated above but one should

[612] The "they" undergoing the ordeal is not specified and could theoretically be the man and the other man he slandered or even the other man and his wife. See the contrast between this law and LH 132, which only requires the accused woman to undergo the ordeal, above.

[613] Though worded slightly differently *e.g.* A 17 mentions no witnesses whereas A 18 mentions that the man claimed he could prove the charges but was unable to. We see little reason to distinguish these offences.

[614] MAL A 19 deals with the unfounded accusation that a man is sodomised by others.

[615] *i.e.* MAL A 21.

hesitate before claiming that such principles underscored ancient Near Eastern law in general. Both principles are demonstrably contradicted in at least one law and two key laws are too difficult to use to assess the existence of these principles.

2.6.5 Sorcery

Both LH and MAL prescribe the death penalty for sorcery.[616] MAL A 47 does so specifically whereas it is only inferred in LH 2 from the fact that someone who falsely accused someone of sorcery would be killed.[617] When this is combined with the following law that a false accuser will bear the death penalty if he accuses someone of a capital crime the implication is clear that in LH sorcery was a capital offence.

It is less clear what the penalty is for sorcery in HL. A number of laws in HL specify that sorcery is a case for the king, as does ETel.[618] For scholars who see a common law in the ancient Near East this referral to the king's court has been seen to imply that it is a capital offence. Analogy is made with LE 48.[619] This is not necessarily the case here, however. As was mentioned earlier, at least two of the Hittite Laws mention cases for the king which were possibly not capital cases.[620] It is difficult to decide whether the offence of sorcery described in these laws was considered a capital offence. If a common ancient Near Eastern law is assumed then it would be expected that this was the case. There are several more Hittite Laws which complicate matters.

In what is possibly the late version of 44b, PT XXXIV does not order the case to the king's court. This law may not be the most useful, however, as there is no statement that this is a case of sorcery, only the broken mention of the need to make something pure again and to compensate for loss. HL 163 only prescribes compensation in the case where a man's animals die as a result of contact with mud used by his neighbor in some sort of ritual. Again, there is no statement that this is considered sorcery. HL 170 is per-

---

616 LH 2 and MAL A 47 (*kišpum*).

617 The falsity of the accusation is seen to be demonstrated if the accused survived the divine River Ordeal.

618 HL 44b, 111, ETel. 50 (*alwanzatar*).

619 Westbrook, "Character," 30 (at least for HL 111).

620 HL 102 which prescribes the king's court for a man who has stolen 3 talents of wood and 176a which prescribes the same for a case where a bull has been kept outside a corral. For the latter law see our discussion of the famous "goring ox" later.

haps more useful. A free man who speaks another's name while/after killing a snake is only fined 40 shekels. A slave who does so is killed (his master is let off). These last laws, HL 170 especially, may lead us to question the generality of the death penalty for sorcery in the ancient Near East. This conclusion is somewhat tentative, however, as the composer of HL himself saw a difference between HL 170 and those which were cases for the king's court so we should be careful in our equation of these offences. Again, in HL 170 the statement that the offence is "sorcery" is missing. The fact that the Hittite Laws tend to pecuniary penalties may lend support to the possibility that sorcery was not considered a capital case.

The fact that other collections do not mention the offence of sorcery may not tell us anything about their attitudes to this offence. Its absence may be due to the purpose of the collections in the case of the decrees *etc.* or the lack of comprehensivity in other cases.

2.6.6 Murder

Three of our collections begin with laws regarding homicide.[621] There is fervent debate over the similarity, or lack thereof, of the penalties for murder in the ancient Near East. Some laws prescribe some sort of compensation (monetary or otherwise),[622] some prescribe death as the punishment,[623] and some state that both are a possibility.[624] In his attempt to force the laws of the ancient Near East into a monolithic common law, Westbrook states on numerous occasions that the penalty for murder across the ancient Near East was at the discretion of the next of kin and could be either compensation or the death of the offender.[625] This is most difficult when it comes to an honest interpretation of Numbers 35:31, but has its own difficulties within the Near East itself. One could only come to this conclusion by vigorously holding onto the assumption that the laws must be the same. Though there are certainly distinctions made depending on the nature of the homicide (*i.e.* what in modern courts would be broken into degrees of murder or manslaughter), contrary to Westbrook's assertions it is possible that fixed payments are not only given when there are mitigating circumstances or a lesser degree of intent. Upon a face value reading of the laws,

[621] LH, HL and LU.

[622] HL 1–2, 5, 43, 44a.

[623] LH (as implied by the combination of LH 1 and 3) and LU 1.

[624] MAL A 10, B 2 and ETel. 49.

[625] *e.g.* Westbrook and Woodard, "Tudhaliya IV," 654–55; Westbrook, *Studies in Biblical and Cuneiform Law*, 39–71 or "Cuneiform Law," 204.

different punishments are in view for the same offences and compensation is not always an option for murder. Many have previously taken Westbrook and others to task over this issue[626] but it is worth doing so again, this time purely from the perspective of the Near Eastern material itself, outside the purview of debates regarding the biblical law/s of murder.

Two laws which support Westbrook's position are found in the Middle Assyrian Laws. MAL A 10 is slightly broken but seems to state that someone who enters someone else's house and kills someone will be given over to the victim's household who have the opportunity to either kill the perpetrator or demand property from them. There is further mention of the situation that would arise if the victim's household chose to accept compensation but the offender was unable to pay. Unfortunately this section of the law is unreadable. MAL B 2 is very similar. There are some slight differences in that there is no mention of anyone entering a house and the offender is specifically a man who has not yet received his inheritance share. The victim's household or next-of-kin have the right to either kill the offender or to take his inheritance share. The law regarding murder found in the Edict of Telepinu 49 states the case in a similar manner. In this law, the murderer is to be given over to the victim's heir who has the right to either kill them or demand compensation.[627]

These are the only three laws which fit Westbrook's assumed ancient Near Eastern law of murder. The Hittite text *Instructions to Commanders of Border Garrisons*[628] orders that the *auriyaš išhaš* (Akk. *bel madgalti*-"commander of the border post") was to decide serious crimes according to the local practice of the border town.[629] Murder is not specifically mentioned but one would presume it would be covered under "serious crimes". The two possible penalties discussed for such crimes, however, are not the two Westbrook assumes to be applicable across the ancient Near East. In the *Instructions* Arnuwanda states: "In a city in which they are accustomed to execute, let them continue to execute. In a city, however, in which they are accustomed to exile, let them continue to exile."

The Hittite material from HL is different again. In HL 1, the case where someone kills (*kuenzi*) a man or woman in a quarrel[630] is outlined.

---

[626] *e.g.* Malul's review.

[627] The option of ransom payment by a murderer is also witnessed in ETud. IV, col. ii, lines 3–8.

[628] Translated by Gregory McMahon (*COS* 1.84: 221–25).

[629] *Ibid.*, p. 224, Section 35.

[630] As with Hoffner, *Laws of the Hittites*, 17; Fiorella Imparati, *Le Leggi Ittite*

The offender is to bring the body for burial[631] and give 4 persons as substitution.[632] HL 2 describes the same offence in the case where a slave is killed. The penalty is described in the same manner though it is likely only 2 persons are brought as substitution.[633] HL 3 and 4 describe the penalty in the same manner but halve the penalties of 1 and 2 respectively. HL 3 and 4 deal with some kind of separate lesser offence than 1 and 2. Whereas the offender was said to kill (*kuen-*) in laws 1 and 2, in 3 and 4 they merely strike (*walḫ-*) the victim who dies as a result. These laws are usually interpreted to

(Rome: Dell'Ateneo, 1964), 35; Johannes Friedrich, *Die hethitischen Gesetze* (2nd ed.; Documenta et Monumenta Orientis Antiqui 7; Leiden: Brill, 1971), 17; but contra Neufeld, *Hittite Laws*, 1 who has "in anger" and Frederic Hrozný, *Code Hittite provenant l'Asie mineure* (Paris: Paul Geuthner, 1922), 3 who has "*d'intention*". The latter may give the intended significance of the law but is not a direct translation from the Hittite.

[631] The most generally accepted interpretation of the import of the verb *arnuzi* in this context. See Hoffner, *Laws of the Hittites*, 166–67 and his discussion there. The verb generally has the simple sense of "to bring". So *apun arnuzi* would mean "he will bring that one (*i.e.* the dead person)". This would only make sense if it was implied that the dead body was being brought for burial. However the verb can also mean "to replace". In that case *apun arnuzi* could mean "he will replace that one". Some, such as Friedrich have adopted this meaning and have thus seen the following statement *Ù* 4 SAG.DU *pa-a-i* ("he will pay 4 persons", lit. heads) as merely describing how it was that the offender was to replace the dead man. Thus Friedrich's translation, "und (zwar ?) gibt er 4 Personen", *Die hethitischen Gesetze*, 17. Hoffner objects to this interpretation stating that such a description of the replacement would need to be asyndetic (*i.e.* have no intervening conjunction), *Laws of the Hittites*, 167. If we accept Hoffner's claim then we are still left with two options: 1) that the dead body is being brought for burial, or 2) that some other restitutive action is first described, whether the replacement of the dead person with one person or some other kind of understood payment or punishment, as well as the payment of four persons in addition (so perhaps the payment of 5 persons in total). The first option does seem most likely and is perhaps confirmed by HL 5 where the dead merchant is to be brought/replaced only if killed in Hatti (perhaps distance was an issue for burial if it happened elsewhere). This writer is loathe to challenge a pre-eminent Hittitologist such as Hoffner on the intricacies of Hittite syntax.

[632] It is not stated what sort of persons were to be brought, but the most likely interpretation is that slaves were here in view.

[633] The text is broken at this point but on analogy with other punishments regarding offences against slaves in HL one would expect the penalty to be half that of the offence against a free person.

refer to accidental death.[634] This is due to the lesser penalty and also the phrase "*keššaršiš waštai*", "his/her hand sins" which follows the mention of the victim's death.[635] The later version (PT II) of these two laws changes the penalty to a monetary payment of 4(?)[636] and 2 minas.

HL 5 describes the murder of a Hittite merchant. If our text is correct at this point, this offence is treated in a very severe manner in comparison to the offences in HL 1–4. The offender is to pay 100 minas (4000 shekels) of silver,[637] and is to replace the merchant's goods.[638] The late version of this law (PT III) prescribes some payment which is not preserved and the threefold replacement of the merchant's goods. It also adds a law regarding the killing of a merchant (who did not have goods with him) in a quarrel. There is no replacement of persons as in HL 1–4, only the payment of 240 shekels of silver. This is still a very large payment when one compares it to other laws in the ancient Near East. The distinction seems to be between murder for the purpose of theft in contrast to killing in a quarrel. If the killing of such a merchant was only an accident,[639] the penalty is further reduced to 80 shekels. HL 6 prescribes the taking of 3 acres of land from the

---

[634] Thus Hoffner, *Laws of the Hittites*, 170; Hrozny, 4–5.

[635] Comparisons are often made with the law of accidental death in Exodus 21:13 which similarly refers to the perpetrator's hand to describe the accidental nature of the death. It should be kept in mind that the mention of the perpetrator's hand and the preceding strike in 21:12 are the only similarities between the laws. The interpretation of Ex. 21:13 is made easier due to the addition of another agent (*i.e.* God) in (the description of) the death of the victim. The accidental nature of the strike in a similar situation in LH 207 is also much more obvious due to the declaration of the perpetrator (see LH 206).

[636] Again, this section is broken.

[637] It is possible, though unlikely, as suggested by Friedrich, *Die hethitischen Gesetze*, 17, n. 7, that the Old Hittite scribe here made a mistake writing ME (100) for the similar sign for ½ (MAŠ-*mišlum*). This would give us a fine of 60 shekels which would be equivalent to the payment for a life in LH. As Hoffner points out, *Laws of the Hittites*, 170–71, this seems unlikely given the fact this mistake would have to have been either made again or perpetuated in text B also. The same would be applicable for any argument that the scribe confused his minas and shekels (*i.e.* wrote 100 minas for 100 shekels). Unfortunately the late version of this law is of little help (PT III) as this section is broken. PT III does record penalties of 240 and 80 shekels for what seem to be lesser offences though which would lead us to expect a higher penalty for this offence.

[638] On the assumption that the murder was for the purpose of theft which was promptly carried out.

[639] Again, "if his/her hand sins".

owner of a property in a foreign/another city in which a kinsman died. PT IV is slightly different in the situations that it covers. Rather than the dead body being found in another city, it is found on another person's property. The owner of the property is to give his property, house and 60 shekels of silver if the dead person is male. He gives only 120 shekels if the dead person is female. If the body is found in open country then the dead person's heir is to take either persons or payments[640] from any village within a certain radius.

There are several more laws in HL which deal with murder. In two of them there is no penalty in view for the murders committed. HL 37 seems to allow a man who elopes with a woman to kill up to 3 "supporters" (*šardiya-*) who may come after them.[641] HL 38 also allows murder of a *šardiya-* who is struck due to some kind of argument arising from a lawsuit. The status of the *šardiya-* is not abundantly clear in these two laws. It seems that the situations envisaged are seen as having been instigated by the *šardiya-* who is thus not protected.[642]

HL 43 has a different punishment again. The law seems to involve two men crossing a river, one of whom was on an ox. The man on the ox is pushed off and swept away by the current while the other man is carried to safety by holding onto the ox's tail. The punishment for the surviving man is that he is taken as a servant by the dead man's heirs.[643] HL 44a prescribes

---

[640] The law does not specify what is to be taken. It states that the heir shall take *apušpat*, "those aforementioned". It is unclear whether the aforementioned are the payments or the village(rs). Both readings present difficulties. It would be strange if the heir was to take all the villagers of the nearest village. It is equally difficult to see how the heir could take the same payments (Which one/s? Both? From whom? *etc.*).

[641] A strange law indeed. It is possible that the action of the supporters is viewed as vigilante, and thus the negative results which ensue need no legal redress. For discussion of the import of the this law and the final phrase "you have become a wolf" see Jos Weitenberg, "The Meaning of the Expression 'To Become a Wolf' in Hittite," in *Perspectives on Indo-European Language, Culture and Religion: Studies in Honor of Edgar C. Polomé* (ed. Roger Pearson; vol. 1; Journal of Indo-European Studies Monograph 7; McLean, Va.; Institute for the Study of Man, 1991), 189–98.

[642] Perhaps a modern parallel for HL 38 would be a lesser penalty for an enraged driver killing another driver who had exited his car to start a road rage brawl. HL 37 seems to be aimed against vigilante behaviour.

[643] The most likely reading of the law as per Hoffner, *Laws of the Hittites*, 188. It is less likely that the man was pushed off in order for the other man to steal the ox.

that a man who makes a man fall into a fire and kills him will give a son (or a young man) in return.[644]

The material in HL regarding homicide clearly covers more than just the simple case of a man striking a man in order to kill him. Within HL there seems to be a consistent avoidance of the death penalty for murder of any kind.[645] This is in contrast to both ETel. 49 and the *Instructions to Commanders of Border Garrisons* 35. It is possible that Westbrook is correct and that the laws regarding homicide in HL treat offences of a lesser order than that in ETel. 49.[646] Upon a first reading HL 1 does seem to cover willful homicide in contrast to accidental in HL 3. It is possible, however, that the setting in a brawl does lessen the gravity of the offence.[647] HL 44a also seems to be an act of willful murder where capital punishment was not considered, though it is conceivable that this crime was perpetrated accidentally or with less intention to kill than that in ETel. It is more difficult to deal with the law regarding the offence of murdering a merchant in order to steal his goods. This law carries a penalty far above the killing of a man in a brawl (if the text is to be read as it stands), surely deals with willful murder, yet does not mention capital punishment as a possibility. It does seem strange to postulate inconsistencies regarding laws to do with murder within the one society, but this seems to be the simplest reading of the Hittite material. The laws within HL which deal with homicide all seem to penalize the offence with either the handing over of persons or property or with a fixed monetary payment. It seems impossible to construe this difference regarding the treatment of homicide in Hittite Law as some sort of legal development within Hatti over time given the Old Kingdom dating for the original collection and the fact that the laws seem to have been updated in some New Kingdom copies, especially PT. That the death penalty was considered by Telepinu, a king from the Old Kingdom (seen by some to be the author of the reform of the law reflected in the *karu . . . kinuna* passages)

---

644 Note that there is some debate as to who is given. In comparing Hoffner's translation of this law in Roth *Law Collections*, 223, to that in his critical edition, 52, it seems he has changed his mind. In *Law Collections* he translated the law as, "he shall give one person in return", perhaps treating DUMU.NITA as "young man" rather than "son". The reading "son" is far from definite but seems harsh enough to suit the crime committed. It would be strange for the penalty in this law to be less than that in HL 1 unless an accident was in view.

645 Unless HL 37–38 are to be read differently. See discussion above.

646 See Westbrook and Woodard, "Tudhaliya IV," 655.

647 The parallel law LH 207 would seem to support this conclusion but its relevance can only be assumed not demonstrated.

but not by HL for which we have both Old Kingdom and New Kingdom copies is difficult to explain, especially if one assumes that HL reflects actual practice as reflected in its updating. It is possible, given the subject matter of the edict, that Telepinu was considering murder within the royal family, a more heinous offence than simple murder as treated in HL. This is certainly the case in ETel. 31–33 where the death penalty as an option is clearly linked to murder within the royal household. This relative severity of laws to do with the person of the king is paralleled elsewhere at Hatti.[648] Within laws on homicide from Hittite collections there are penalties including capital punishment, ransom fixed by the heir of the deceased,[649] fixed monetary payment, payment of persons (including a son or the offender himself), payment of property and perhaps even exile.

Evidence of a more conclusive nature for our argument against Westbrook's claimed common law for willful murder in the ancient Near East is found in LU 1. The law states: "If a man commits a homicide, they shall kill that man." There is no mention of the possibility of compensation here. To read this law as though compensation or ransom was a possibility is difficult and unnecessary unless one is attempting to construct a unitary common law for the entire ancient Near East. This is not the goal of this writer and so the law will not be read this way.

Though LH does not contain a law directly parallel to that of LU 1, when LH 1 and 3 are read together they do give us enough information to decide what the law of homicide was for Hammurabi. LH 1 states that a man who accuses another man of homicide without proof will be killed. LH 3 states that a man who gives false testimony in a case involving a capital offence will be killed. By implication then, homicide was a capital offence. Of course this does not automatically rule out the possibility of ransom or compensation in the Old Babylonian period, but it may make us question whether that was what Hammurabi intended. The penalties contained within LH are generally quite harsh in comparison to other law collections and in comparison to the documents from practice from Babylonia itself. This leaves open the possibility that, as ransom is not mentioned for him who falsely accused someone of murder, perhaps it was not an option for someone guilty of murder for LH either. LH 210 would seem to support

---

[648] *e.g.* "Instructions for Palace Personnel to Insure the King's Purity," trans. by Albrecht Goetze (*ANET*, 207) where the death penalty is handed out to a servant who failed to strain a hair from the king's drinking water.

[649] The practice of paying ransom or compensation is possibly also reflected in ETud. See note 625 above.

this view. If a man strikes a pregnant woman and kills her he is to be killed. The same is the case in LL e and MAL A 50. None of these mention compensation as an option. Perhaps the lack of the option of compensation for this offence could be due to its more heinous nature given the strike would have resulted in the death of the unborn child also and given the more vulnerable nature of the victim. This solution would be false if these laws covered accidental blows to the pregnant women[650] but it should be remembered that elsewhere within MAL there is mention of the possibility of compensation or the death penalty in the case of murder. If it is not mentioned in MAL A 50 is it to be implied as a possibility from A 10 or is its absence significant? This is a more general question also. When we come to LU 1, do we read the possibility of compensation into it from analogy with MAL A 10 and ETel. 49 or not? Given that there is fairly good internal evidence not to read it into MAL A 50[651] one should be hesitant to read it into LH 210 or LL e, and perhaps also LU 1. It is certainly impossible to read the possibility of compensation into MAL A 53. The woman who aborts her own child is to be impaled dead or alive. The extremely harsh nature of this penalty hardly lends itself to an interpretation which would posit compensation as a possibility. The same is the case with LH 153 which demands that a woman who has her husband killed on account of another man will also be impaled.

Across a number of collections there is mention of killing someone in a brawl or a quarrel. HL 1–2 have been treated above. LH 207 deals with a similar situation *i.e.* the striking of a man in a brawl which causes his death. LH 207 specifically tells us that the death was not caused intentionally. The offender swears "*ina idû la amḫassu*",[652] "I did not strike him knowingly (lit. in/with knowing I did not strike him)". Perhaps this implies that the blow was unintentional[653] (unlikely in a brawl). More likely is the possibility that the blow was struck without the intention to kill. In any case, the offender is to pay 30 shekels. In LH 208, for the same offence against a *muškenum*, the offender is to pay 20 shekels. LE 47A describes a similar situation. In contrast to LH we are not told that the offender struck the man and killed him unintentionally but that, in the course of a brawl (*ina risbatim* as in LH

[650] See the discussion at 2.6.7.2.

[651] Again, see the discussion at 2.6.7.2. where it is argued that MAL in general displays a higher regard for the life of the unborn child than elsewhere in the ancient Near East.

[652] As in LH 206.

[653] As is implied in Roth's translation of the law, *Law Collections*, 122.

206–207), the offender caused the other man to die (*uštamit*). How does one decide whether this offence was intentional or not? The offender is fined 40 shekels in LE, very similar to the amount in LH. Two other cases of negligent homicide receive a 40 shekel penalty in LE (LE 54 and 56) and another is said to be a capital case (*napištum*) which at Eshnunna was then a case for the king to decide. This would seem to imply that the offence in LE 47A was not willful murder or at the least was seen to have occurred in mitigating circumstances. HL 174 is very similar to the situation set out in LE. There is no mention that the blow is unintentional, just that death resulted from men hitting each other. The surviving party is to supply a replacement person (literally "one head"), probably a slave. When one comes back to HL 1–2 can we then safely interpret these laws as dealing with a form of homicide of a lesser gravity than murder? This seems quite likely. The differences between the laws regarding death resulting from a brawl are fairly minimal between LE and LH, with both most likely dealing with an offence less than murder which is penalized by payment of 30 or 40 shekels of silver. HL 1–2 seem to carry a heavier penalty involving the payment of persons, 4-fold for the death of a free man, 2-fold for killing a slave. Does this reflect a different attitude towards this offence at Hatti than elsewhere? There is a possible development within Hittite law as PT has only monetary payment and not substitution.

Death caused by negligence will be dealt with in section 2.6.7.3.

2.6.7 Personal Injury

Within the laws dealing with personal injury in the ancient Near Eastern law collections, there are only a few which do not have a direct parallel in at least one other collection. This is not to say they are all formulated the same way or contain the same penalty. There is a large degree of overlap between the laws on this topic contained within LH, LE, LU and HL. Within this overlap there are some similarities between the arrangement of topics. The relevant laws within MAL are quite different in their focus. LH stands out as the only collection to prescribe talionic or vicarious punishment rather than some form of pecuniary restitution for the offences in view. HL is the only collection to discuss accidental injury specifically, though several collections set the offence within a context which seems to imply reduced guilt *e.g.* a brawl. Some of the more commonly recurring motifs will be treated separately *i.e.* blows causing a miscarriage and the goring ox laws.

2.6.7.1 General

The topics common to the largest number of collections regard the knocking out of a tooth and the breaking of a bone. There are seven laws across four collections dealing with the offence of knocking out someone's tooth. Interestingly there are no two collections with either the same formulation or a matching penalty. For the knocking out of a free man's tooth by a free man LH 200 prescribes the knocking out of the offender's tooth; LE 42, the payment of 30 shekels of silver; LU 22, 2 shekels; HL 7 records that the penalty used to be 40 shekels but is now 20 whereas the updated PT VII takes it down even further to 12 shekels with the condition that at least 2 teeth have been knocked out. It is thus difficult to argue that the penalties were borrowed, especially given that within the Hittite collection, none of the three options mentioned match up with the penalty of any other collection. LU 22 stands out as being a particularly low penalty when compared to the rest, far lower even than PT VII. LH stands out due to its talionic punishment in contrast to the pecuniary measures of the others. Regarding the knocking out of a slave's tooth by a free man: LH 201 prescribes 20 shekels, HL 8, 10 and PT VII, 6. Again, none are the same.

There are paragraphs detailing offences involving the breaking of bones in the same four collections. There is greater divergence in the description of the offence in this case. LH 197 states simply that the offence of breaking (*šeberum*) the bone of a free man is punished by breaking (the same?) bone of the offender. LH 198 details the penalty for the same offence against a *muškenum* (very high at 60 shekels), and LH 199 against a slave (half the slave's value). LE 44–46 outline different offences which result in the breaking of different bones, each with their own penalty. All three use the same verb (*šeberum*) to describe the breaking of the bone. LE 44 puts this in the context of a man knocking down the other man in the street so that his hand is broken (30 shekels). LE 45 seems to continue this same situation, but treats the offence if a foot is broken as a result (again 30 shekels). LE 46, however, deals with a case where the offender has struck (*imhaṣma*) the other man and broken his collar-bone (20 shekels). It may be that LE records specific details (which are unnecessary) due to the origin of these laws from actual legal cases. LH, due to its talionic principles, may have been able to wipe out the unnecessary details and put forth a much simpler law. The process, if there was one, does not always work like this. LE 42 covers offences resulting in the biting off of a nose, the blinding of an eye, the knocking out of a tooth, taking an ear, and slapping a cheek much more economically than the treatment of these offences elsewhere (including in LH).[654] LU 19 also records some detail about the offence leading up to the breaking of some specific kind of bone. The offence involves a club and thus the shattering of the bone seems to be in view.[655] There is quite a high penalty here of 60 shekels (the same as the bone breaking offence against a *muškenum* in LH 198). Given the extremely low penalty within LU for the knocking out of a tooth and the fact that a club is mentioned, perhaps someone's head is the presumed object of the offence. This would make sense of the relatively high penalty. Similar to LE 44–45, HL 11 specifies that the offence regards the breaking of an arm or leg[656] (20 shekels if that of a free man). PT X further specifies that permanent disablement[657] requires the payment of 20 shekels, otherwise 10 shekels is sufficient. HL 12 deals with the same offence against a slave (10 shekels). Again PT XI halves the penalty if permanent disablement does not result.

There are a number of minor similarities between these laws but many differences. There are only two laws which arguably share the same penalty for the same offence, LH 198 and LU 19. LH 198 is specifically an offence against a *muškenum* whereas LU 19 is not. Given the fact that the penalty of LU 19 is 6 times that for the offence of cutting off someone's foot in LU 18, it seems most likely that a particularly important bone must be in view in LU 19. The bone is not specified in LH 198. The only other similarity is found in the specification regarding the hand and feet in LE 44–45 and the laws from HL. This is hardly surprising, these being the bones most often broken to the present day. It would seem that each law is again formulated differently with differing penalties (whether in amount or type *i.e.* LH's talion again).

Regarding the offence of blinding someone, LH 196 of course penalizes the offender by talion, again with lesser monetary payments if the offence is against a *muškenum* or a slave (LH 198- 60 shekels and LH 199- ½ his value respectively). LE 42 penalizes the offence against a free man with 60 shekels. HL 7 states that 40 shekels used to be paid for such an offence but now only 20 is required. PT V states that if the offence is committed in a quarrel 40 will be paid, if it is an accident, only 20. HL 8 prescribes the payment of 10 shekels if the offence is against a slave. PT VI states that if

[654] Nowhere else are all these offences treated in the same law. But do compare HL 7–8 which combine blinding the eye and knocking out the tooth.

[655] As indicated by Roth's translation, *Law Collections*, 19.

[656] Or "hand or foot". See Hoffner's note, *Laws of the Hittites*, 25, n. 33.

[657] Perhaps. Hoffner, *Laws of the Hittites*, 25, expresses some doubt as to the import of the phrase.

the offence is committed in a quarrel 20 will be paid, if it is an accident, only 10. Note that the Hittite Laws originally combined this offence with that of knocking out a tooth, each receiving the same penalty. In PT the two offences are separated and receive very different penalties *i.e.* 12 shekels for knocking out teeth of a free man, 40 for blinding him in PT in contrast to 20 shekels for either offence in HL. The increase in the severity of the penalty for the offence of blinding in PT mirrors its treatment as a more serious offence than the knocking out of a tooth in LH and LE.[658] Again we have differences of penalty and framing with these laws.

The biting or cutting off of a nose was also a law common to three collections. LE 42 prescribed the payment of 60 shekels for biting it off, LU 20 40 shekels for cutting it off. HL 13 has the same as LU 20 for biting off a nose. Strangely the updated version in PT XII increases the penalty to 1200 shekels! The offence against a slave is only mentioned in HL 14 (3 shekels) and its updated PT XIII (600 shekels). It has been conjectured that the extremely high penalties in PT may be due to mistaken writings of mina for shekel.[659] This would reduce the fines to 30 and 15 shekels respectively.[660] Goetze has even suggested emending HL 14 to read 30 shekels instead of 3 in order to see the penalty reduced in both cases. We think it somewhat precarious to make conclusions about the Hittite attitude to such an offence given the uncertainties about the text. It is interesting that the penalty in HL 13 matches with LE 42 and that both specifically mention biting the nose.

Damage to the ear of a free man receives a 30 shekel penalty in LE 42. It is possible that LU 21 covers this offence but neither the object cut off nor the amount of the penalty are preserved. Tearing off the ear of a free person receives a 12 shekel penalty in HL 15 and PT XIV. The same offence committed against a slave receives 3 shekels in HL 16, 6 in PT XV. There are no similarities here between LE and HL bar the offence being treated. Even then LE does not specify what has happened to the ear which is merely listed as one of a number of objects which may be damaged in

---

[658] LH 198, 60 shekels for the eye of a *muškenum* in contrast to LH 201, 20 shekels for the tooth of such a man. LE 42 prescribes 30 shekels for a tooth and 60 for an eye. It is worth mentioning here also the extremely low value put on the tooth in LU 19, 2 shekels.

[659] See discussion of Hoffner, *Laws of the Hittites*, 178 and his reference to Goetze's translation (*ANET*, 189).

[660] Similar to the problem with the Hittite Laws regarding the murder of merchants. See section 2.6.6.

some way within LE 42 whereas HL specifically mentions that it has been torn off and treats the offence in a separate law.

There are several laws relevant here that are treated in only one collection. LU 18 has a 10 shekel fine for cutting of a man's foot, LE 43 a 20 shekel penalty for cutting off someone's finger and HL 9 a 3 shekel fine (down from 6 when the palace used to take their share) for injuring someone's head which is upheld in PT VIII.

HL 10 specifies that injury causing temporary incapacitation requires the offender to provide medical care to the victim, a person to work in their stead until they recover, the payment of 6 shekels of silver upon recovery and the physician's fees also. PT IX changes this law slightly. Rather than the mention of incapacitation it specifies that the injury was to the free man's head (as in PT VIII). Again medical care and a substitute worker are to be provided. Upon recovery the fee paid to the victim is to be 10 shekels and the physician's fee is specified as 3 shekels. There is also a statement that "If it is a slave, he shall pay 2 shekels of silver". Is this the only punishment, a lesser physician's fee or a lesser fee upon recovery? It is difficult to tell. LH 206 bears some relation to these Hittite Laws. It specifies that a man who struck another man in a brawl and injured him unintentionally shall pay the physician's fees. The Hittite laws do not specify any lack of intent on behalf of the offender. LE 47 is similar to LH 206 in that the setting is in a brawl,[661] but the penalty for injuries caused in such a situation is 10 shekels.

Cheek slapping is treated briefly in LE 42 and more fully in LH 202–205. LE 42 merely lists a slap to the cheek amongst its other offences and prescribes a penalty of 10 shekels. LH distinguishes the cheek slapping offence in the following ways: 202, an *awilum* who strikes the cheek of an *awilum* of superior status receives 60 stripes in a public flogging; 203, an *awilum* who strikes the cheek of an *awilum* of equal status pays 60 shekels; 204, a *muškenum* who strikes the cheek of another *muškenum* pays 10 shekels; 205, a slave who strikes the cheek of an *awilum* has his ear cut off. There is consistency within LH that the striking of the cheek of a superior receives a corporal punishment of some sort. That consistency applies to another law regarding the striking of a superior in LH 195 also. Again we have a case where the penalty for an offence by a *muškenum* is the same as the penalty in LE. For a discussion of the import of the laws in LH see Roth's enlighten-

---

[661] Though a different term for brawl (*šigištum*) is used in LE 47 to that in LE 47A and LH 206 (*risbatum*). See Yaron's comments on the uncertainty of the former term's restoration and import in LE 47, *Laws of Eshnunna*, 71.

ing analysis which suggests that, contrary to LE, the offence is treated as insult rather than injury.[662]

There are several laws from different collections which treat a blow of some kind from a person of lower status upon someone their superior. LH 195 states that a child who struck his father will have his hand cut off. LU 26 mentions a slave striking her mistress but the penalty is broken away. MAL A 8 prescribes that a woman who crushes a man's testicle in a quarrel will have a finger cut off. If she somehow damages[663] both testicles it seems her eyes were to be gouged out.[664] In MAL A 7, a woman who lays a hand upon a man is fined 1800 shekels of lead and is given 20 blows. The obvious similarity between the extant laws in LH and MAL on this topic is the involvement of some kind of corporal punishment for this type of offence. It may be, however, that the authors themselves would not have seen these offences as being similar. This author does not think it is necessarily this aspect of the offence which leads to corporal punishment in MAL.[665] Given the preponderance of corporal punishments within LH, MAL and the Egyptian collections when compared to others, perhaps we should look to another explanation. One should certainly not feign the confidence to read a corporal punishment into LU.

The MAL in general have a different focus than the other collections. Most of the laws from this collection dealing with personal injury deal with male/female relations. This has been seen in the two laws above. MAL A 9 then treats the case of a man attacking a woman "like a rutting bull". He also has one finger cut off, demonstrating that the corporal punishment was not given out due to the nature of the previous offences in MAL A 7–8 being committed by an inferior against a superior *i.e.* woman against a man. If the man forces the woman to kiss him, his lower lip is to be cut off. The Middle Assyrian Laws seem to have a series of paragraphs (A 57–59) dealing with abuse allowable from a husband to his wife. MAL A 59 is the only one fairly well preserved. It allows the husband to whip his wife, pluck out her hair, mutilate her ears or strike her without fear of punishment as well

---

[662] Roth, "Mesopotamian Legal Traditions," 24–36 *contra* Yaron, "Early Mesopotamian Collections."

[663] Either in the quarrel or from subsequent infection.

[664] The object of the verb is broken and could be either eyes or breasts. See Roth, *Law Collections*, 193, n. 10.

[665] Especially given MAL A 9 where a man who attacks a woman also receives corporal punishment.

as meting out other punishments written on the tablet.[666] A similar law (A 44), not dealing with women specifically this time, but any Assyrian person being held as a pledge, also allows the creditor to whip, pluck out the hair of or mutilate the ears of the pledge if they are worth less than the value of the loan. It seems that none of the laws from MAL have any parallels elsewhere in the other collections under discussion here.[667]

The laws regarding personal injury can thus be displayed in the table on the following pages:[668]

---

[666] It is unclear what tablet is referred to here. Driver and Miles, *Assyrian Laws*, 292, assume that it refers to the tablet of the laws.

[667] MAL A 8 of course exhibits parallels to Deut. 25:11–12.

[668] Due to a lack of parallels, those in MAL have been left out.

Offence	LH	LE	HL
Blinding: *Awilum*	Blinding	60 shekels	40 shekels (karu) 20 shekels (kinuna)
Muškenum	60 shekels	n/a	n/a
Slave	½ slave's value	n/a	10 shekels
Breaking bone: *Awilum*	Break bone	30 shekels (hand or foot) 20 shekels (collarbone)	20 shekels (arm/leg)
Muškenum	60 shekels	n/a	n/a
Slave	½ slave's value	n/a	10 shekels (arm/leg)
Knocking tooth: *Awilum*	Knock tooth	30 shekels	40 shekels (karu) 20 shekels (kinuna)
Muškenum	20 shekels	n/a	n/a
Slave	n/a	n/a	10 shekels
Cheek slap: *Awilum*>superior	60 stripes	n/a	n/a
Awilum> *Awilum*	60 shekels	10 shekels	n/a
Muškenum>*Muškenum*	10 shekels	n/a	n/a
Slave>Slave	Cut off ear	n/a	n/a
Nose: *Awilum*	n/a	60 shekels	40 shekels
Slave	n/a	n/a	3 shekels
Ear: *Awilum*	n/a	30 shekels	12 shekels
Slave	n/a	n/a	3 shekels
Finger	n/a	20 shekels	n/a
Foot	n/a	n/a	n/a
Head	n/a	n/a	6 shekels (karu) 3 shekels (kinuna)
Incapacitating injury: *Awilum*	Pay physician's fees (accidental)	n/a	medical care person to work phys. fee 6 shekels
Slave	n/a	n/a	n/a

PT	LU	Offence
		Blinding:
40 shekels 20 shekels (accidental)	n/a	*Awilum*
n/a	n/a	*Muškenum*
20 shekels 10 shekels (accidental)	n/a	Slave
		Breaking bone:
20 shekels (arm/leg-permanently disabled) 10 shekels (otherwise)	60 shekels (shatters x bone)	*Awilum*
n/a	n/a	*Muškenum*
10 shekels (arm/leg-permanently disabled) 5 shekels (otherwise)	n/a	Slave
		Knocking tooth:
12 shekels	2 shekels	*Awilum*
n/a	n/a	*Muškenum*
6 shekels	n/a	Slave
		Cheek slap:
n/a	n/a	*Awilum*>superior
n/a	n/a	*Awilum*> *Awilum*
n/a	n/a	*Muškenum*>*Muškenum*
n/a	n/a	Slave>Slave
		Nose:
30 mina[669] (mistake for shekels?)	40 shekels	*Awilum*
15 mina (mistake for shekels?)	n/a	Slave
		Ear:
12 shekels	unknown	*Awilum*
6 shekels	n/a	Slave
n/a	n/a	**Finger**
n/a	10 shekels	**Foot**
3 shekels	n/a	**Head**
		Incapacitating injury:
medical care person to work 3 shkl phys. fee 6 shekels	n/a	*Awilum*
2 shekels	n/a	Slave

669 Note that there are 40 shekels to a Hittite mina. 30 mina is then equivalent to 1200 shekels.

Our comparison of the penalties found that they were the same on only three occasions. Even then, 2 of those included cases where the penalty in LE matched that in LH for an offence against a *muškenum*. This is not surprising and implies little about borrowing. What appears more similar are the topics chosen for treatment within LH, LE, HL and to a lesser extent LU. Even there, however, one would be hard pressed to see a consistent pattern of borrowing. Though in each case, the laws of personal injury are grouped together, it is extremely hard to find a common order to the offences. The order of topics in the collections is as follows:

LU 18-foot, 19-shatter x bone, 20-cut off nose, 21-cut off x (ear?)

LH 196, 198–99-blinding, 197, 198–99-break bone, 200–201-knock tooth, 206-incapacitate

LE 42-nose, eye, tooth, ear, cheek slap, 43-finger, 44-break arm, 45-leg, 46-collarbone

HL 7–8-eye and tooth, 9-head, 10-incapacitate, 11–12-arm/leg, 13–14-nose, 15–16-ear

PT V–VI-eye, VII-tooth, VIII-head, IX-incapacitate, X–XI-arm/leg, XII–XIII-nose, XIV–XV-ear

As one can see, there are some minor similarities which would not incline one to think any collection mirrored the ordering of any other (except of course that of PT and HL for obvious reasons).[670] The similarity in topics covered may just be a reflection of the limited number of body parts which could be injured with those most likely to be injured appearing most frequently. Apart from the difference in order there is also a difference in which topics are combined into the one paragraph. LH combines blinding and breaking bones, LE 42 combines many different body parts, HL combines blinding and knocking teeth while PT and LU do not combine anything. Again there seems to be no argument for borrowing here either. The attempt to argue that certain topics were treated as a result of a common international legal science or literary borrowing seems forced for this topic. Given the lack of parallels in any other area of these laws, all that one could argue was shared was a common interest in which particular body parts should be discussed. Even there one can clearly see that this was by no means uniform, nor could one argue for a consistent borrowing pattern between any of these collections.[671] It is true that in both LH and HL the miscarriage laws follow on from the laws about personal injury. Given the lack of any other common ordering between the two collections this seems

---

[670] Note that even here, where borrowing is certain, the ordering is not exact.

[671] Again, the obvious exception is PT and HL.

insignificant, especially as the topic fits well amongst laws of personal injury. Within MAL, the miscarriage laws are not found near those dealing with personal injury. HL shares much subject matter with the lower Mesopotamian codes, especially LH and LE. This does not necessarily imply borrowing.

2.6.7.2 Miscarriage and Abortion

Laws dealing with miscarriage or premature birth are found across most of the civilizations for which we have law collections in this period.[672] This fact has often been seen as suggestive that there was widespread borrowing of this legal problem throughout the region. Many trace this borrowing into the biblical law in Exodus 21:22, some as far as the classical period.[673] While this writer would not rule out the possibility of such widespread borrowing of what may have been a popular literary/legal trope, one should be hesitant as to what conclusions are drawn from such a possibility. As Tigay has shown, literary borrowing does not necessarily imply that there has been little change made to the material borrowed.[674] If indeed there was borrowing in this case, it certainly cannot be taken to imply a similar attitude towards the offence of causing a miscarriage across all these civilizations.

We will deal with these laws in separate sections. The most common topic deals with the striking of a free woman with some resultant effect on the unborn child.[675] The penalties for such an offence range from 5–30 shekels of silver in the collections other than MAL. In MAL the punishments range from 7200 shekels of lead to 9000 shekels and 50 blows with a month's service for the king to the death penalty. The first two monetary payments in MAL are possibly not too far removed from the 30 shekel payment demanded in LL. It is difficult to assess the relative weight of these punishments given that our evidence for the exchange rates of goods does not allow us to be very precise. However, there is some material which enables a rough estimate. LE 1 states that one shekel of silver was equivalent

---

672 LH 209–214, LL d–f (if accepted as part of LL), SLEx 1'–2', MAL A 21, 50–53, HL 17–18, PT XVI–XVII.

673 Westbrook, "Adultery," 548. Implied in the title of Haase, "De fetu abito sive. Ne se immisceat mulier praegnans rixae inter viros. Vom ungewolten Abgang der Leibesfrucht im altorientalischen und biblischen Bereich," *Zeitschrift für altorientalische und biblische Rechtsgeschichte* 7 (2001): 384–91.

674 Tigay, "On Evaluating," with examples of Gilgamesh material from outlying areas.

675 LH 209, LL d, SLEx 1'–2', MAL A 21, A 50–52, HL 17, PT XVI.

to 180 shekels of copper. It is generally accepted that lead[676] was worth less than copper.[677] This then would leave us with fines with silver equivalences of less than 40 and 50 shekels respectively, perhaps as low as the 30 shekel fine of LL, though it should be remembered that blows and service are additional to this fine. The death penalty does stand out from the others and can possibly be related to a higher view of the value of the unborn child in MAL.

There is some difficulty deciding upon the offence committed and its results in the various laws. For example, there is some debate as to whether LH 209–214 should be connected to the preceding laws 206–208 which deal with unintentional injury caused when two men are fighting. Should we interpret the laws regarding the striking of a pregnant woman as a continuation of laws dealing with an offence in this situation or let them stand more independently within the broader framework of personal injury laws beginning at LH 195?[678] If we do decide on the latter, does that necessarily imply that the strike by the man was intentional?[679] In the other collections there is no indication at all that this offence occurred in the context of a brawl. In HL for example, the mention of personal injury resultant in a brawl comes some fifteen laws previous to those regarding the offence of causing a miscarriage. In others the former law is not present at all.[680] The hypothesis of such a context for LH 209–214 may have been proposed on the basis of assumed similarity with the law of Exodus 21:22.

---

676 The most likely interpretation of *annuku* in these laws. See Roth, *Law Collections*, 192, n. 8 and references. In contrast see Daniel C. Snell, "Methods of Exchange and Coinage in Ancient Western Asia," in *Civilizations of the Ancient Near East* (ed. Jack M. Sasson; vol. 3; New York: Hendrickson, 1995), 1493 and James David Muhly, *Copper and Tin: The Distribution of Mineral Resources and the Nature of the Metals Trade in the Bronze Age* (Hamden, Conn.: Archon, 1976), 241–47; repr. from *The Transactions of the Connecticut Academy of Arts and Sciences* 43 (1973): 155–535 and 46 (1976): 77–136, who translate the word as "tin". The latter interpretation would amount to an enormous fine equivalent to somewhere between 225 and 900 shekels of silver according to Christopher M. Monroe's exchange rates, "Money and Trade," in *A Companion to the Ancient Near East* (ed. Daniel C. Snell; Blackwell Companions to the Ancient World; Malden, Mass.: Blackwell, 2005), 161.

677 See Monroe "Money and Trade," 160.

678 See the discussion of Haase "De fetu abito," 385–388.

679 See *Ibid.*, 387, n. 13 quoting B. Jacob, "who would purposely have struck a pregnant woman?"

680 Unless one wished to see MAL A 8 as an example. This law bears only a vague similarity dealing with a woman crushing a man's testicle in a quarrel.

A question is raised by the laws contained in SLEx 1'–2' as to whether the same offence has been committed across all collections. In SLEx 1' a man who jostles (*zag an-us2*) the daughter of a man (*dumu-munus lú*) and causes her to miscarry/give birth prematurely (*nig-ša3-ga-ni a im-šub-šub*)[681] is fined 10 shekels of silver. In SLEx 2' a man who strikes (*ba-an-sig3*) such a woman and causes the same results is fined 20 shekels of silver. This has led commentators to wonder whether the first offence implies an accidental injury whereas the second is intentional.[682] This seems the most likely conclusion. There is difficulty in interpreting the effects of the blows on the woman and her unborn child also. It is unclear whether miscarriage or merely premature birth is described.[683] In LL d another verb is used to refer to the blow struck by the male offender (*i-ni-in-ra*) and a different expression used for the resultant effects on the woman (*nig-ša3-ga-na šu mu-un-da-an-la2*). This makes it difficult to compare the slightly higher fine of 30 shekels of silver. Perhaps a miscarriage is here envisaged whereas the slightly lower fines for SLEx result from the lesser offences of unintentionally or intentionally striking and causing premature birth. It is interesting that in our three Sumerian laws regarding this topic we have three different verbs to describe the offending blow by the man and two different verbs to describe the resulting effects on the woman and her child. This does not seem to support the idea that this law was passed on verbatim across the law collections of the ancient Near East.

The material in LH and HL is similarly unclear regarding the resulting effects on the woman and her unborn child. LH describes a man who struck (*imḫaṣma*) the daughter of a man (*marat awilim*) and caused her to miscarry/give birth prematurely (*ša libbiša uštaddiši* lit. he caused her to throw that of her insides/womb/middle). By analogy with SLEx 1'–2' we would expect this offence to be intentional. It is possible of course that the context of these laws following LH 206–208 implies otherwise. The penalty imposed in LH 209 is only 10 shekels. This is equivalent to the jostling offence of SLEx 1' and far less than the striking of SLEx 2' and LL d. Though it is possible to see the 10 shekel fine as matching an unintentional blow resulting only in a premature birth, this is not necessarily the case. LH 209 may well describe an intentional blow resulting in miscarriage. If this were

---

[681] The import of the law here is unclear. See Roth's comment: "The Sumerian expression seems to refer to premature rupture of the amniotic membrane." *Law Collections*, 45, n.1.

[682] See Haase, "De fetu abito," 384–85, esp. notes 3–4.

[683] See note 681 above.

the case it could imply a lesser view of the value of the unborn child in LH than the Sumerian material.

The term used in HL 17 is similarly ambivalent. The law possibly prescribes that a man who causes a woman to miscarry (*šarhuwandušša*. . . *peššiyazi* lit. shoves/fells her unborn children/her insides) will pay 10 shekels if she is in the 10th month of her pregnancy and 5 shekels if she is in the 5th.[684] The later versions of the law dispense with the provisions regarding the gestation period of the pregnancy and double the fine to 20 shekels.[685] The section of HL 17 regarding the 10 month gestation period and the payment of 10 shekels is broken but readable. This aspect of the provision would lead us to the conclusion that the offence in view resulted in a miscarriage. It would make no sense for there to be a higher payment closer to full gestation if premature birth were in view. The chances of the child's survival in the case of premature birth would be near impossible in the 5th month whereas it would be much more likely in the final month of gestation.[686] There is some other external evidence regarding the terminology used which supports the idea that a miscarriage is in view.[687]

It is difficult again to decide whether the offence considered is intentional or accidental. There is no setting in a brawl, not even the mention of a separate blow which causes the resulting miscarriage as we have had in the other comparable laws. There is only one verb used to describe the offence in HL, *i.e. peššiyazi*. It is generally assumed that the miscarriage which resulted was caused unintentionally and was the side-effect of an assault on the woman.[688] Whether the assault was intentional or not is unclear. Given the absence of any detail in the law mentioning an assault on the woman, the first assumption may not even hold and we may have here a law concerning willful abortion with a male assistant. This latter possibility is considered less likely by the present author as it is only the person who causes the woman to miscarry who is punished, not both of them.[689] The lack of

---

[684] KBo VI 3.

[685] PT (KBo VI 4) and KBo 6.5 (seen as having the latest orthography and writing of all copies of the laws by Hoffner, *Laws of the Hittites*, 161, n. 378).

[686] For discussion regarding the Hittite reckoning of a pregnancy at 10 months see Hoffner *Laws of the Hittites*, 179 and references and Neufeld, *Hittite Laws*, 137–8.

[687] See Hoffner *Laws of the Hittites*, 179 and the examples cited of the verb meaning "to fell a deer" *i.e.* to kill a deer.

[688] *e.g.* Neufeld, *Hittite Laws*, 137.

[689] This suspicion is supported by the comparative material in other ancient Near Eastern law collections which do not envisage such a situation. The one law regarding abortion does not mention any third-party assistant, only the woman

mention of any blow to the woman is interesting as most law collections dealing with this topic also have a law concerning the results of the assault on the woman herself.[690]

The rulings regarding this topic in MAL seem confusing. To begin with, one of the laws regarding this offence is to be found 29 laws away from the others. MAL A 21 prescribes the penalty of 9000 shekels of lead, 50 blows and one month's performance of the king's service for a man who struck (*imḫaṣma*) the daughter of a man (*marat a'ile*) and caused her to miscarry/give birth prematurely (*ša libbiša ušaṣliši* lit. he caused her to throw/lay down/fell(?) that of her insides/womb/middle). That the verb here implies a miscarriage can be safely inferred from the extremely harsh penalty given in MAL A 53 where the same verb is used for a woman who aborts her own child. The wording of MAL A 21 is very similar to that of LH 209, but far from identical. One wonders whether there is any significance in the choice of verb which refers to the effects of the strike on the unborn child. Both verbs, *nadu* and *ṣala'u* have the general sense "to throw". It would be strange if one was chosen to represent premature birth and the other miscarriage. If we assume that both verbs have the same connotation then it would seem MAL A 21 carries a far harsher penalty for the offence covered than does LH 209. The penalty would possibly be similar to that prescribed by LL d.

Our task of comparison is made complex by the apparent contradiction between MAL A 21 and A 50. The penalty outlined in MAL A 50 is that the man shall be treated as he treated the woman (*ki ša epušušini eppušušu*).[691] The law also states that he will *kimu ša libbiša napšate umalla*. The import of this phrase is contested. Roth translates it as, "he shall make full payment of a life for her fetus".[692] Driver and Miles argued that the verb *malu* could have the sense of "to fulfill", "to make good" or "to compensate" and thus interpreted the phrase to merely be a statement in apposition to the preceding penalty stating that the penalty thus made good the offence against the life or "(thereby) he compensates for the life".[693] They even mentioned the possibility that the phrase could refer to giving a person as

---

causing her own miscarriage: MAL A 53.

[690] *e.g.* LH 210, LL e, MAL A 50. We will come to a discussion of these laws presently.

[691] Though this section is slightly broken the restoration seems fairly certain.

[692] Roth, *Law Collections*, 173.

[693] Driver and Miles, *Assyrian Laws*, 113.

substitute for the life taken.[694] Their argument was basically that the phrase only turned up after another punishment was already given *i.e.* MAL A 50, 52. They did not think it possible that it referred to another penalty. Their arguments regarding this phrase can safely be ignored when one looks at the parallel usage of the verb in MAL A 4[695] and the fact that it is the only penalty for the last situation envisaged in law A 50.[696] There are also more solid internal reasons to treat the phrase as Roth has done, as a separate monetary payment for the life of the unborn child. In MAL A 50 it seems ridiculous that talio would be seen to be carried out if the man was treated as the woman was, *i.e.* struck. This would leave the death of the unborn child unaccounted for, the man merely being repaid for the blow inflicted on the woman. Driver and Miles were aware of this problem and attempted to read the provision of the law as prescribing that the offender's wife would also be struck so as to cause a miscarriage.[697] There is a fair amount of gymnastics involved in order to read the text this way. It would be ridiculous to consider that the law envisaged no penalty for the death of the unborn child given the harsh penalty for abortion in A 53. The simpler reading of the text implies that two offences are in view: 1) the striking of the woman for which the man is struck in return,[698] and 2) causing the death of the unborn child for which payment of a life is made. In regards to the second offence a distinction is made which depends on the gender of the unborn child and the prior existence of a male heir for the woman's husband. If there is no male heir and the unborn child was male then the offender is killed. If the unborn child was female, the penalty is merely the payment of a life.[699]

Can these two laws be reconciled? Both seem to cover the same offence, the striking of a woman resulting in the miscarriage of her unborn child. A 21 prescribes monetary penalty, blows and royal service whereas A 50 prescribes payment of a life or the death penalty as outlined above. Though the laws are not extremely different, 9000 shekels may not be far from the payment required for a life (especially if blows and service are

---

[694] Though they rejected this interpretation. *Ibid.*, 113.

[695] The arguments of Driver and Miles, *Assyrian Laws*, 24–25 notwithstanding.

[696] Extremely unlikely that the phrase refers back to the middle of the law where the man was treated as he treated the other woman.

[697] *Assyrian Laws*, 110.

[698] Or killed if the blow caused the death of the woman. Discussion of this offence follows presently.

[699] See the earlier discussion of the import of this term.

added), one does feel that the laws do contradict each other. One possible way to reconcile the two laws would be to make something of the fact that the female victim is described as a *marat a'ile* in A 21 whereas she is possibly described as an *aššat a'ile* in A 50.[700] Driver and Miles attempt to do just this, even arguing that the first offence was seen to be a criminal offence (*i.e.* against the state) due to the mention of blows and royal service whereas the latter laws in A 50–52 were merely civil offences (*i.e.* against private persons). One does not see how this argument can stand up and this writer suspects that distinctions such as criminal versus civil offences are merely modern importations into the text. Without using this slight difference to reconstruct a scenario that would explain the apparent contradiction between these two laws we are left with no way of doing so. What the contradiction may imply about the nature of the MAL is a little unclear. Did the compiler merely collect past legal decisions on these topics even if they were contradictory? Does one represent an earlier law and one a later? These questions are unanswerable for now. If the latter were the case, it is interesting that the laws are kept separated from each other in the collection and there is no mention that the law has been changed. This would support our earlier contentions regarding the conceptualizations of law and kingship influencing which cultures do and do not mention the updating of laws.[701]

MAL A 51 is difficult to understand. Again we have a man who struck the wife of a man and caused her to miscarry.[702] Here the woman is described as a wife *la murabbita*. The import of the phrase is that the woman does not raise her children. This offence against such a woman attracts the lesser fine of 7200 shekels of lead. It is not abundantly clear why this woman does not raise her children. Driver and Miles supposed that she was physically unable to do so.[703] Others have argued that perhaps she adopted her children out, that the phrase refers to the stage of her pregnancy or an unsuccessful track record in previous pregnancies.[704] None of these seem satisfactory to this writer who wonders whether the reference is to a woman

---

700 This possibility is based on the occurrence of the term *aššassu* in the laws, the traces of the end of the DAM sign then *a'ile* halfway through the law, and the fact that the following law deals with a type of *aššat a'ile* also. It seems quite likely that this term was used at the beginning of the law, but given the fact that these lines are broken, one should be hesitant in making too much from them.

701 See section 2.1.3.

702 Using the same terminology as in A 50.

703 Driver and Miles, *Assyrian Laws*, 115.

704 See *Ibid.*, 114–15.

from one of the classes of priestesses (*qadiltu?*) who were not supposed to have their own children. This may explain the lesser penalty and the lack of talionic retribution for the blow.[705]

A 52 complicates matters even more. Here we are told that even if a man strikes a prostitute and causes the miscarriage of her child he will be struck blow for blow and make payment of a life as in the first half of A 50. There is no further clause regarding the gender of the child and the existence of an heir as in A 50. This is to be expected given the fact that a prostitute would have no husband concerned with an heir. That this offence against a prostitute and her unborn child is treated in this way may imply a higher view of the unborn child (and perhaps women) in MAL than the other collections under comparison. The difficulty with such an interpretation is of course A 51. A 53 seems to support such a conclusion, however. In this law a woman (*sinniltu*) who aborts her own child (*ina raminiša ša libbiša taṣṣili*) will be impaled and not buried, even if she died in the process of the abortion. This is the fiercest penalty in all of MAL, which is notorious for severe corporal punishments. The attitude towards this offence should surely be used to help interpret the other laws regarding caused miscarriages in MAL, as we have done. Such an approach would lead one to see a distinction between the fine of 10 shekels in LH 209 for causing a miscarriage and the possibility that the death penalty would ensue for the same offence in MAL A 50. This is important in a number of respects, one of which concerns the approach of Westbrook and others which postulates a common law in the ancient Near East. As MAL A 53 is the only law which covers the topic of abortion directly, one may be tempted to treat it as *the* law of abortion in the ancient Near East. The distinction between MAL and the other collections regarding the causing of miscarriages should cause one to hesitate in adopting such a position.

The preceding analysis of the laws regarding the causing of a miscarriage should severely question the idea that this law was the same throughout the ancient Near East. It may also question whether the law is found in

---

[705] More about this in the next section. Driver and Miles use this as evidence that the phrase *napšati umalla* was not a separate penalty, but a statement that talion was exacted. Here there is no mention of talion, only a fine and the phrase is missing. From internal parallels however, it seems that the monetary payment is some sort of reduced fine for the miscarriage of the unborn child and there is no mention of any additional penalty for the blow on the woman. It can be asserted that the mention of treating the man as he treated the woman in A 50 and of striking the man blow for blow in A 52, rather than implying the existence of a talionic punishment in A 51 actually highlights its absence.

so many collections because of some form of borrowing. It is possible that the topic could have been passed around in this way, but the variation in formulation[706] and in penalty given should make it clear that this borrowing did not even approach copying or mere translation. It is not even possible in some cases to be sure that the same offence is in view. For example, SLEx seems to make a distinction between what may be an accidental strike and what may be an intentional one which results in the (presumably) unintended consequence upon the unborn child. None of the other collections give us enough information to decide whether the blow to the woman was intentional or accidental; HL does not even mention such a blow. There is also some confusion regarding the consequent effects on the unborn child. In most cases the effect makes most sense as the death of the unborn child. In HL and MAL this is fairly certain. The similarity of term between LH and MAL seems to support such an interpretation there also. In SLEx it seems most likely that the verb refers specifically to premature rupture of the amniotic membrane. Whether this implies miscarriage or merely premature birth is difficult to tell. The lack of an extra clause specifying whether there was any injury to the child, along with the relatively high fine of 20 shekels of silver[707] may imply that miscarriage was also in view here.

In theory there are no real obstacles to treating all these laws as offences which led to miscarriages. What we are then left with is the variation in penalties. 10 shekels is the most common fine for causing a miscarriage being found in LH 209, SLEx 1' and HL 17. Most other penalties do not stray too far from this amount, the Hittite Laws themselves containing penalties from 5 to 20 shekels. LL is slightly higher at 30 shekels though we are hesitant to make very much of this. Apart from MAL A 51, the Middle Assyrian Laws contain higher penalties for this offence, including the death penalty, and treat abortion as a most heinous crime.

All of the collections dealing with this topic except SLEx also mention the same offence against women of lower status. LH 211 treats the offence against a *marat muškenim* (variously translated as "the daughter of a muškenum" or "a woman of the muškenum/commoner class"), and 212 against an *amat awilim* (a slave-woman of a man). The penalty for causing the miscarriage in 211 is 5 shekels, whereas in 213 it is only 2. LL f penalizes the man 5 shekels for causing the miscarriage of a slave woman. This is

---

[706] *e.g.* the three different Sumerian verbs for striking and two for the resultant miscarriage or premature birth, the lack of mention of the blow to the woman in HL, the additional mention of the gestation period in HL *etc.*

[707] Double that of LH 209 and HL 17 and close to that of LL d.

higher than that in LH but represents a similar ratio regarding the offences against slaves with respect to free women as that in LH. The ratio is 1:6 in LL and 1:5 in LH. In HL the ratio is 1:2 in both versions *i.e.* HL 18 prescribes a penalty of 5 shekels in the tenth month as opposed to HL 17's 10 shekels and PT XVII prescribes 10 shekels in comparison to PT XVI's 20. The MAL do not deal with the case of a man causing a slave to miscarry. Interestingly though, MAL A 52 prescribes as harsh a penalty for the offence against a prostitute as against a free woman whereas MAL A 51 prescribes a reduced penalty for the offence against the woman who does not raise her own children. These laws highlight some of the difficulties in asserting a common attitude towards legal topics in the ancient Near East. Which of these laws do we say reflect similar attitudes? Both HL 18 and LL f prescribe a penalty of 5 shekels for causing a female slave to miscarry but the Hittite penalty is ½ that of the offence against a free woman whereas that of LL is 1/6. The ratios of LL f and LH 213 are very similar but the prices of their penalties are different. The most we could say is that the Hittite laws consistently treat the slave's child as closer to the worth of a free woman's child. The updated law in PT XVII is the highest penalty for such an offence in the collections under consideration here. It is interesting to note that the HL does not prescribe a penalty for the offence in the case that the slave woman was in the 5th month of her pregnancy. This may be due to a lesser status for the slave's child.

In most of the collections dealing with this topic there is separate treatment of the blow inflicted upon the woman which caused the miscarriage. This is not the case in HL or SLEx. LH, LL and MAL do deal with this topic. Each collection deals with this topic in a slightly different manner. LH 210 states that if the blow upon the woman results in her death, the offender's daughter will be killed. This is the only law on this topic where vicarious talion is to be applied. LL e simply states that the man himself will be killed. MAL A 50 states the same as LL. This law, as distinct from the other two collections which only prescribe punishment in the case that the woman is killed, also prescribes talionic retribution upon the offending man whether the woman dies or not: "they shall treat him as he treated her". There is a general agreement that if the blow upon the woman causes her death that a life should be taken in return. Perhaps this implies that the strike in view was intentional.[708] The law from MAL is the only one to pre-

[708] It may also have been designed to encourage extra care around women as in the equivalent biblical law in Ex. 21:22. The lack of a context or statement that would imply these blows were accidental makes it difficult to decide.

scribe punishment for striking the woman if she doesn't die. What does that imply? That it is only MAL that deals with an intentional strike? That MAL has a higher penalty for physical injury (to women)? That the others expect the offence against the woman to be covered by the laws regarding striking others? The latter seems problematic as these other laws do not seem to deal with striking women *e.g.* LH 206 if a man strike a man *etc.* The non-comprehensive nature of the laws presented in the various collections makes any conclusion tentative, as does the possibility that the term *awilum* may be generic.

It is only LH which deals with the case of the death of a woman of lower status resulting from the man's blow. It would be unwise to make much of this given the non-comprehensive nature of the law collections and the fact that LH is by far the longest of the preserved collections. It would be unwise to assume that the death of a slave woman was not treated separately in LL because this situation was already covered in law e. The fact that LL distinguishes the penalty for causing the miscarriage of a free woman or a slave would lead us to expect a similar distinction when it came to punishing the results of the blow on the woman herself. Though MAL does not deal with the attack on a slave woman as a separate topic, it would be similarly unwise to treat MAL A 50 as generally applicable to this situation also.[709]

The fact that only HL 77 treats the offence of blows causing miscarriages in animals, making it unlikely to be a borrowing, supports this writer's suspicion that this topic (treating blows to women) exists in various collections possibly due to the fact that it was actually a problem in these societies rather than some status as a canonical legal problem diffused through the scribal schools.

2.6.7.3 Goring Ox/Bull and Negligence Causing Personal Injury

Due to its appearance in the legal material in the book of Exodus, in LH and LE, the so-called "Goring Ox" laws have become a favorite for those wishing to compare the laws of the ancient Near East. Undue focus has been given to this series of laws as opposed to a more comprehensive analysis of borrowing amongst the collections of the ancient Near East. This can quite possibly be explained by the popular appeal of topics which treat material paralleled in the Hebrew Bible. There is certainly a great

[709] Though this may be a possibility, made more plausible by the severity of punishment for the offence against a prostitute in law A 52, it is questionable upon analogy with the lesser punishment for the offence in A 51.

amount of similarity between the laws as they appear in Exodus, LH and LE. Westbrook has postulated this as another of his canonical legal problems common to ancient Near Eastern jurisprudence. He sees several aspects of the law which are to be dealt with, namely: distinctions as to whether the ox gored for the first time or was a known gorer and distinctions as to the object of the goring whether it be a man, a slave or another ox. He presumes all aspects to be known by the drafters of each collection though not all may appear. LH 250 treats the goring of a man, presumably by an ox which was not a known gorer. LH 251 outlines the same case in a situation where the owner knew the ox was prone to goring and had done nothing about it. LH 252 treats the goring of a slave with no distinction regarding the ox's status as a known gorer.[710] LE 53 treats the goring of another ox and LE 54, the same in the case of a known gorer. LE 55, like LH 252, treats the goring of a slave with no distinction. Without the biblical material used to hypothesize a common background for LH and LE, the closest similarity is found between LE 55 and LH 252, with the different prices paid for the slave reflecting the relative prices of slaves elsewhere in the respective collections. The vocabulary used in these laws is not particularly common. In LH 252, the goring of the slave is not mentioned, merely implied from the preceding law, whereas LE 55 restates the goring and the resultant death of the slave. Different verbs are also used for the payment of the silver. LH 250–251 and LE 53–54 mirror each other in that the first law treats a simple case of an ox goring, while the second treats a case involving a negligent owner as the ox was known to be a gorer. In both LH 251 and LE 54, the owner has been notified of the ox's threat by their *babtum*[711] and has failed to do anything about it. There are some differences in phrasing and the difference of the object of the ox's goring between the laws. None of these would discount the possibility that LH's drafter used LE 53–55 as a model of sorts for LH 250–252. However, this is not the only possibility. Perhaps the treatment of the goring of a slave in LH 252, as a direct continuation from LH 251, is meant to specify that this law only treats the case of the goring of a slave by a known gorer. This would then clarify the uncertainty on this point in LE 55 which could be read as covering either situation.

---

[710] Though it does seem to continue on from LH 251 without a break, perhaps implying it only covered the offence of a known gorer.

[711] Roth's inconsistency in translating this term ("city quarter" in LH 251, "ward authorities" in LE 54) is again unhelpful, *Law Collections*, 67, 128.

The material covered in Exodus 21:28–36 certainly helps the case of those who would see some form of borrowing. There are many similarities, especially in terms of the aspects covered. The situations dealt with in LH 250–251, LE 53–54 and that in LH 252 and LE 55 are those treated in Exodus, with the addition of a section treating the loss of an ox or donkey which has fallen into an uncovered pit. The penalty in Exodus is the same in the situations dealt with in LH 250 (no penalty) and LE 53 (value of both oxen divided). The penalty for goring a slave is higher in Exodus (30 shekels), but, similar to LE 55, and perhaps LH 252, there is no specification as to the bull's status as a known gorer. Paralleling LH 252 is the position of the provision regarding the goring of a slave in Exodus as a continuation of the law regarding the goring of a man by a known gorer. There are a number of differences in the penalties in Exodus for the situations treated in LE 54 and, more particularly, that in LH 251.[712] It would be a braver man than this writer who would rule out the possibility that the drafter of this passage in Exodus was aware of the relevant laws in LH and LE. If borrowing was involved, however, it certainly did not mean the wholesale adoption of the rulings and the attitudes behind them, and seems to have only suggested subject matter.

The biblical material has been mentioned here due to its heightened pertinence for the debate regarding borrowing in the case of the goring ox laws. Even if one accepts the possibility of some sort of borrowing from earlier laws in the Exodus material, this does not imply some original material which contained all topics, from which LH chose three, one in common with LE, which chose another two, with Exodus treating all five. It seems more likely that the borrowing went directly from LE to LH, with the possible clarification of the law regarding the goring of a slave in LH, and then the drafter of Exodus treated the topics of both LH and LE. The specific mention in Exodus 21:31 that the same penalty applies whether offence was committed against a man or son or daughter seems to imply knowledge of

---

[712] This writer would argue that the possibility of compensation in this case does not prove Westbrook's hypothesis of a more general rule that death penalties could be exchanged for compensation at the discretion of the next of kin, but rather, can be explained as specific to this case and resulting from the degree of intent involved here *i.e.* the fact that this was negligence rather than intentional homicide. The only opposition to such an interpretation involves the law treating the causing of a miscarriage by an accidental blow in Exodus 21:22–25. The weak and unprotected nature of the object/s of the offence in that case is what leads to the harsher penalty in the opinion of this author.

talionic practice elsewhere and is perhaps a direct contradiction of the provision in LH 230, also treating death caused by negligence.

Given these many similarities it is difficult to rule out the possibility of borrowing. There is some material which suggests that goring bulls or oxen were an actual threat in the societies of the Near East and that this topic was not merely academic. An example is found in HL 176a. The law states that if anyone keeps a bull outside a corral it will be a case for the king's court and the bull will be sold. This may imply that capital punishment was a possibility but this is unclear.[713] The law seems to legislate against a situation where a bull may have been free to roam the streets and harm people or damage property. Another piece of evidence for this general problem in Near Eastern societies is possibly found in a law suit from Nuzi.[714] Though this is the only document from practice that deals with such a situation, this should not necessarily be taken to imply its occurrence was rare. The statement that the topic of the goring ox was, "The favorite textbook illustration of negligence in the law collections of the ancient Near East",[715] may turn out to be true, but its background as a legal problem common to the Near East has not been demonstrated. Though the many similarities between the goring laws in LH, LE and Exodus make this writer very hesitant to rule out some form of borrowing amongst them, the infrequency of such similarity and the possibility that goring animals were a problem in the Near East, as demonstrated in HL 176a and the document from Nuzi, also make him hesitant to rule out the possibility that these laws are independent after all.[716]

The laws concerning the goring ox treat injury to persons, negligence and damage to property. We shall deal with other laws involving negligence leading to personal injury, then move onto other laws dealing with negligence which leads to damage to property, and then onto any remaining laws

---

713 Refer back to the discussion of laws mentioning the king's involvement in 2.2.

714 "The Goring Ox at Nuzi," trans. William W. Hallo (*COS* 3.121, 270). This law may not however deal with the case of an ox goring another ox. It is a lawsuit by an ox's owner against his ox herd, accusing him of having injured an ox. The statement by the neatherd that "his fellow" injured the ox may refer to a fellow ox of the one injured, or another man in some relation to the ox's owner (*e.g.* another worker or a friend). The former does seem more likely.

715 Hallo, (*COS* 3.121, 270).

716 Perhaps a situation parallel to the frequent attestation of common vocabulary in unrelated languages (with no possibility of an etymological relationship or of loaning from one to the other) is to be understood here.

treating damage of property. Apart from the laws dealing with a brawl, there are not many other laws treating injury caused by negligence. This topic is treated in LH 229–231 regarding the shoddy building of a house which collapses and kills someone, and in LH 218–220 regarding the ill effects of a negligent physician. LE 56–58 are also relevant, treating the negligence of the owner of a vicious dog and of a buckling wall. LE 56–57, deal with the vicious dog in exactly the same manner as 54–55 dealt with the goring ox. Even the corresponding penalties are identical. LH 218–220's treatment of physicians is not paralleled anywhere else. It should be noted that the punishment in 218, cutting off the physician's hand, is for either blinding or causing the death of an *awilum*, whereas the punishment for the two offences is distinguished in LH 219–220 when done to a slave. Perhaps the stylistic value of having the offending hand being cut off overruled the usual concern for symmetry. The purely economic offence in LH 219–220, involving slaves, may also explain the difference.

It is worth comparing LE 58 and LH 229–231. Similar to LE 54 and 56, the owner of the buckling wall has been notified by his *babtum* that his property is posing a threat and has done nothing about it. If the wall collapses and causes the death of an *awilum*, the penalty is harsher than that for the negligent owner of the goring ox or vicious dog. As noted by David, perhaps this is because, in contrast to an animal, the wall does not have a will of its own and the owner is thus more directly responsible for the damage it does.[717] The penalty in LE 58 is stated to be *napištum*, "a capital case", "a case involving life" *etc.* It is up to the king to decide whether or not the offender will be killed.[718] The penalty for the shoddy builder in LH 229–231 is similar but phrased differently, involving talionic and vicarious punishment in contrast to LE 58. If a builder builds a house which collapses and kills someone there are different punishments in LH depending on who is killed. LH 229 prescribes death for the builder himself if the head of the household was killed; 230 the death of the builder's son if the son of the head of the household was killed; 231 the replacement of the slave if a slave was killed. This last law shows the attitude towards slaves in these laws *i.e.* they are seen as property.[719]

---

[717] See the discussion of this law in Yaron, *Laws of Eshnunna*, 1988, 300–3.

[718] The phrase *ṣimdat šarrim*, I interpret as merely referring to the fact it is the king's decision rather than necessarily to some written edict to be referred to. See the earlier discussion of this phrase in 2.1.4. and compare the statement in LE 48.

[719] Compare LH 232 which determines that the builder shall replace any damaged property.

2.6.8 Negligence Causing Loss of or Damage to Property

This topic seems to have been one of the more popular amongst the ancient Near Eastern law collections. This is especially true in regards to laws treating injury to rented animals (particularly oxen) and those involving boats. There are also parallel laws treating the negligent shepherd and negligence leading to theft, as well as a host of laws unique to their collection treating other situations where negligence has led to the loss of or damage to property.

Several laws treating loss under the care of the shepherd are found in LH 263–267.[720] Each law that determines negligence on the part of the shepherd requires him to replace whatever was lost.[721] The only law which excuses the shepherd and determines that the owner shall bear the loss is LH 266 in the case of an outbreak of disease or a lion killing the sheep. The shepherd must take some sort of oath clearing himself of any negligent behavior.[722] This last law has a parallel in HL 80, and, to a lesser extent, those laws treating the killing of rented oxen by lions or disease.[723] HL 80 is formulated very differently to LH 266 and is more concerned with the division of the sheep's carcass in the event it is killed by a lion.[724] It seems to assume there is no negligence on the part of the shepherd. It is difficult to argue for borrowing in this case.

The laws concerning damage to rented oxen are immense in number. Their existence in the monumental law collections LH, LL and HL, as well as three collections which are generally classed as "scholarly texts" (LOx, SLEx and SLHF) has been the subject of debate. Many have used this as evidence of the purely academic nature or scholarly origin of the monumental law collections, questioning their practical intent.[725] Though there may be the likelihood that some of the material in the monumental collections is

---

[720] LH 265 is really misappropriation or theft and is somewhat paralleled in MAL F 1–2. See earlier discussion concerning theft laws.

[721] LH 263–264, 267.

[722] As contrasted to the outbreak of the preventable disease for which he is responsible in LH 267.

[723] See below.

[724] The shepherd keeps the wool, the owner the carcass.

[725] *e.g.* Roth, "Scholastic Tradition and Mesopotamian Law: A Study of FLP 1287, a Prism in the Collection of the Free Library of Philadelphia" (Ph.D. diss., University of Pennsylvania, Ann Arbor: University Microfilms, 1979) or "The Scholastic Exercise 'Laws about Rented Oxen'," *Journal of Cuneiform Studies* 32/33 (1980): 142; Levinson, review of Roth, 119.

indeed mirrored in "scholarly texts", this need not determine the function of either set of texts. The possibility of some form of borrowing or common origin is heightened for this group of laws. They are to be found in LH 244–249, LL 34–37, all of LOx, SLEx 9'–10', i 37–ii 2, SLHF vi 11–36, and HL 74–75, 77b–78. There are a number of common situations which recur within these laws. One of these is the situation where a lion may have killed the ox. In each case the law prescribes that it is the owner's loss.[726] Each of these laws prescribes a specific location for the ox when the attack occurred. None of these are the same in any two laws. It is worth comparing HL 75 at this point. This law states that an ox, mule or ass that dies, gets lost or is eaten by a wolf shall be given according to the law. The import of this last statement is a little unclear, as is the beginning statement that the animal has been hitched up.[727] In HL 80, in the case where a shepherd allowed a wolf to eat a sheep he was able to keep the wool and only had to give the carcass to the owner. Is this what is in view here or did the man in HL 75 have to actually replace the lost or dead animal? The latter seems more probable given the fact that this penalty applies to a lost animal also. This would contrast with every other case treating the killing of a hired animal by a wild animal. There is an out clause in HL 75 which is reminiscent of LH 249. The man can swear an oath that the animal "died by the hand of a god". It is unclear what situation this would cover. The mention of replacement of a lost animal in HL 75 is paralleled in SLEx 10'[728] and i 37–ii 2. In both cases the animal is to be replaced. An ox killed while crossing a river is replaced with additional compensation for its hire in SLHF vi 23–31. This law is paralleled in LOx 6, where the value of the ox is paid in silver.[729] The only other reference to a man killing an ox in his care is in LH 245. It prescribes replacement of the ox with a comparable one if the death was caused by negligence or abuse.

There are a host of laws treating the penalty for injuring certain parts of the ox. As was the case with the personal injury laws the same body parts appear repeatedly, with very similar penalties. As was the case with those

---

[726] LH 244, LOx 7–8, SLEx 9', SLHF vi 16–22, 32–36.

[727] Do all these offences have to occur while the animal is hitched up? Compare LOx 7.

[728] Translated differently by Finkelstein, "Sumerian Laws YBC 2177" (*ANET*, 526). Appears to be an ox goring another ox there. This would make more sense, otherwise the same situation seems to be covered in SLEx i 37–ii 2 (unless "lost" does not necessarily mean he can't find it, but can include loss to death *etc.* also, then it perhaps also parallels LH 245 and HL 75 more generally).

[729] LOx 9 may be relevant also but is too broken to tell.

laws, here again there are differences in the phrasing of the laws, the type of penalty in HL and the body parts considered equal and/or treated in the one law in the different collections. Again, this material is best presented as a table. It must be remembered that two relevant laws are broken (LOx 5 and SLHF vi 11–15) and that LOx has a gap part way through.

Offence	LH	LL	LOx	HL
Break Leg	Replace	n/a	?	replace ox or give bad one and 2 shekels silver
Cut Neck Tendon	Replace	n/a	?	n/a
Blind Eye	½ value	½ value	½ value	6 shekels silver
Break/Cut off Horn	¼ value (break)	¼ value (break)	1/3 value (cut off)	replace ox or give bad one and 2 shekels silver (break)
Cut Tail	¼ value	¼ value	penalty broken	n/a
Cut Hoof Tendon	¼ value	1/3 value	¼ value	n/a

The case for borrowing is perhaps stronger here than in the laws of personal injury given the greater similarity in penalties and the higher degree of similarity regarding the body parts covered. HL 78 covers a situation not dealt with in the other laws.

Negligent damage to boats was a popular topic in these law collections also.[730] There is even one case where some form of borrowing or common origin must be surmised. SLHF iv 42–v 11 and LL 5 seem to be identical apart from minor orthographic variations and LL's omission of one verb.[731] Either the scribe of SLHF copied the law from LL or each got it from some other common source. Though it is possible this common source was contracts from practice, given the other material in SLHF, the phraseology,

---

[730] As was its hire or theft *e.g.* LE 4, 6; SLHF iii 10–12, v 37–44; LH 275–277 and 239 (hire of boatman).

[731] Though LL 5 is broken at points, the commonality is so great that one is able to treat them as the same law with a fair degree of certainty. The possibility remains that the penalty in LL 5 was slightly different given the degree of damage at this point.

beginning with *tukum-bi*, makes it likely that SLHF took it from a law collection. LL is the obvious candidate. The laws deal with a topic also dealt with in SLEx 3'; the loss/sinking of a rented boat whose agreed upon route has been violated. In SLHF the renter[732] is to replace the boat and pay its hire in grain. The penalty in LL 5 is not preserved but can be safely assumed to be that of SLHF. The penalty in SLEx 3' is very similar, but seems to only ask for half the boat's hire and this "until" the restoration of the boat, not in addition to its replacement.[733]

The simple sinking of a boat is mentioned in LH 236–238, LE 5, SLHF v 21–26 and perhaps was preserved in the broken provisions of LL 4 and SLEx ii 7–8. In each case the boat is to be compensated for. LH 236 prescribes its replacement and 237 the replacement of any cargo that was lost.[734] LH 238 alone treats a situation where the boat was sunk and is then raised. In that case the offender pays half its value. LE 5 seems to cover the possibility of both the boat and its cargo needing replacement stating that the negligent boatman, "shall restore as much as he caused to sink." SLHF v 21–26 is similar again, specifying replacement of the boat and payment of its hire.[735] The broken passages in SLEx ii 7–8 and LL 4 also seem to require replacement of the boat. The difference in penalty between LL 4 and SLHF v 21–26 may lead us to expect a similar difference between SLHF iv 42–v 11 and LL 5, but the traces do not seem to fit this expectation.[736]

The collision of two boats is treated in LH 240, SLHF v 27–36 and MAL M 1–2. LH 240 assumes that an upstream boat will sink a downstream boat and determines that the master of the former shall replace the boat and property lost of the latter. The latter is to detail his lost property under oath. SLHF seems to assume negligence only on the part of an upstream boat also. If an upstream boat sinks a downstream boat it is to be replaced but the reverse is not the case. Presumably this is due to the comparative speed and maneuverability of the two boats. The lack of mention

---

[732] Or the boatman which the renter may also have had to hire. See Finkelstein, "Sumerian Laws" (*ANET*, 525, n. 2) Compare the two different situations in LH 236–237 *i.e.* the boatman as the hirer, a third party hiring the boat and a boatman.

[733] There is an amount of uncertainty regarding the translation of this penalty, Finkelstein, "Sumerian Laws" (*ANET*, 525, n. 2). Roth displays more certainty in her translation than Finkelstein, *Law Collections*, 43–44.

[734] In this case a third party has hired boat and boatman with the boatman being at fault. The boatman thus has to replace the boat for its owner and the goods to the man who hired him.

[735] It seems this is assumed to be paid already in LH and LE.

[736] It is possible that LL 4 and SLHF v 21–26 are not parallel after all.

of the property on board the boat is in contrast to LH and MAL. MAL M 1 is a little broken and thus difficult to reconstruct. Here there is mention of replacement of the sunken boat and its property being replaced but the circumstances leading to the incident are unclear. This law may parallel those treating the simple loss of the boat itself but the mention of someone's shout to clear a passage may imply that collision with another boat is in view. Perhaps the situation envisaged is a boat drifting from upstream whose captain has attempted to clear other boats out of the way. There is difficulty in interpreting which boat has sunk and who is to pay the penalty. The last statement that the boatman not swearing an oath need not restore the goods confuses the issue further.[737] MAL M 2's context is clearer but part of the penalty is broken. An upstream boat or a boat crossing the river sinks another boat. It seems likely that the boat and any property on board would be replaced.

These laws again show a similarity of topic among the Mesopotamian collections. Given the (almost) verbatim copying of LL 5 in SLHF, it is interesting that other parallels are not of the same ilk. If there was widespread borrowing, at least among the Mesopotamian collections, why do we not get this word for word copying elsewhere? It is interesting that it occurs in a "scholarly text". Perhaps this was a scribe's exercise. This would explain the copying of a passage from LL 5, but not the variation from other parallel laws, including others dealing with boats. SLHF v 12–20 also contains a unique law dealing with some damage to the boat. It is possible that the other sections of SLHF with parallels in LL which display variation from it, were copied from elsewhere or involved a degree of invention on the part of the scribe. The unique nature of this rare verbatim copying raises a number of questions concerning the discernment of borrowing and borrowing practices without necessarily giving any answers. Tigay's work regarding the comparative method and his examples of loose copying of subject matter in regards to the Gilgamesh epic are pertinent at this point. Here there is the possibility that the drafter of SLHF could borrow topics from other documents in a number of different ways. The sections that are not copied verbatim[738] seem to defy attempts to classify them as borrowing or independ-

---

[737] As does Roth's translation, "the boatman against whom they do not swear an oath by the life of the king shall not turn back (from taking the oath)", *Law Collections*, 189. Theophile J. Meek's translation, "The Middle Assyrian Laws" (*ANET*, 188) is very different. There are a number of difficulties in translation here. Roth's translation implies the boatman is somehow the indirect object of the swearing.

[738] At least not from any source available to us.

ent invention, let alone specifying the degree, direction or avenue of borrowing. The similarity of subject matter is again worth noting.

Flooding of a neighbor's field due to negligent behavior is treated in LH 53–56, LU 31 and SLHF iv 35–41. There has been much debate surrounding the laws in LH as they specify different methods for assessing the relevant penalty *i.e.* replacement of lost grain, delivery of grain according to nearby yields or a fixed measure of grain per area. Some commentators have argued for different practices of assessing such agricultural offences, whether due to different societal practice or development over time, which have somehow been mixed together in LH.[739] There are possible ways to harmonize these laws, as demonstrated by Westbrook.[740] It is possible that LH 55–56 are merely explications of the general rules set out in LH 53–54. There are then two systems of reckoning loss that make most sense as being dependent upon the agricultural season, with LH 55 occurring close to harvest time and LH 56 just before or after planting.[741] If the flooding occurs close to harvest time, it is possible to assess the damage by looking at the comparative yields of nearby fields. If close to planting then this would be a difficulty and a fixed measure is to be used instead. The two laws which parallel these in LH each use one of these systems. LU 31 uses a fixed measure and SLHF iv 35–41 the yield of neighbors. Interestingly, SLHF seems to put the offence sometime after the harrowing of the land, perhaps close to planting.[742] It is possible that the drafter of LH was aware of these two possible means of assessment and drew on both of them to set up a more comprehensive system that would make it easier to assess any damage done a significant time before harvest, but after work had been started on the fields. It is also possible that both methods were in operation.

Negligence in the upkeep of land could be seen as making it easier for a thief to break into a neighbor's house. This is seen in LH e and LL 11. In LH e, the man who fails to reinforce a scalable wall (after a warning) over which a thief breaks into his neighbor's house, or who fails to work an uncultivated plot is to replace any stolen goods. LL 11 prescribes the same compensation for the man who has neglected his fallow land after a warning, again resulting in his neighbor's property being stolen. The mention of

[739] Cardascia, "La reparation".

[740] "Cuneiform Law," 206–13.

[741] Indicated by the mention of the water carrying away the work the neighbour had done.

[742] Not ruling out some time near harvest either.

the neighbor's request that the man do some sort of fortification work is reminiscent of the wall in LH e.

There are a number of other laws, mainly in LH and HL, treating negligence leading to damage of property which are unique to their collection.[743]

2.6.9 Non-Negligent Damage to Property

The Hittite Laws treat this topic far more extensively than any other collection and thus contain many laws unique to it.[744] There are two topics treated in HL which are found elsewhere: the cutting down of another's tree, and damage caused to another's produce by unlawfully grazing sheep. LH 59 and LL 10 are almost identical:

> **LH 59** If a man cuts down a tree in another man's date orchard without the permission of the owner of the orchard, he shall weigh and deliver 30 shekels of silver.
>
> **LL 10** If a man cuts down a tree in another man's orchard, he shall weigh and deliver 20 shekels of silver.

The difference in price may represent the relative costs of trees in the two periods. LH is slightly more detailed in its specific mention of the type of orchard and the lack of permission from the owner but the latter is surely assumed in LL. Borrowing is a definite possibility here. HL 104 and 113 treat quite similar offences. HL 104 specifies two tree types which may have been cut down with some form of payment in silver demanded. HL 113 treats the cutting down of a vine. This is dealt with differently. The offender keeps the cut-down vine and gives its owner a new vine. They seem to swap when the old vine recovers. It is possible that HL 104 was somehow inspired by LH 59 or LL 10. Little more can be said except to note again the relatively more frequent tendency in the Hittite Laws for replacement in kind rather than payment in silver or grain. Further highlighting the similarity of topics across collections, RU mentions officials cutting down the trees of the poor and carrying off the fruit.

LH 57–58 and HL 107 share in common a shepherd allowing sheep to graze on another's produce without permission and a penalty fixed by land area. All other details are different. HL 107 adds a provision in a case where

---

743 LH 225, 227, 231–33; HL 106, 163–65 and 60–62 (the latter perhaps treating ignorance more than negligence); LE 60.

744 HL 86–90, 98–100, 105, 109, 166–69.

the land the sheep were allowed into was bare. This offence only attracts a 3 shekel payment.

2.7 PENALTIES

It is the contention of this thesis that a comparison of these law collections will serve to highlight some systematic differences. A comparison of the penalties, especially those in laws treating what modern jurists may term criminal law, enables these differences to be discerned more easily than is the case from most other aspects of the laws. Apart from this comparison across collections, an attempt will be made to analyze the diachronic changes within HL in this section.

2.7.1 Corporal

What is most striking in a comparison of penalties across these collections is the relative frequency of corporal punishments in Assyrian and Egyptian collections. Around 30–40% of laws in MAL and MAPD contain a corporal penalty.[745] In EH there are only three laws which record a corporal punishment. This may seem fairly minimal, but given that there is only one alternative penalty actually recorded in part B,[746] and one more in part C (the death penalty),[747] its occurrence is relatively frequent. This is also the case in the Nauri Decree with 11 out of the 16 provisions containing corporal punishment. LH also contains a number of laws with corporal punishments, but as a percentage it is a fairly infrequent penalty. There are only 15 such laws out of the 282 recorded. Within the Sumerian material there are 1 or 2

745 This is a rough figure and would actually be higher if other variables were taken into account such as laws in which the penalty is broken or the numerous occasions within MAPD where it is simply stated that it is a punishable offence. The number would be far higher if it were found that this also implied a corporal punishment.

746 See the end of B.I where the official in the wrong is to do the work of the underling he oppressed. Other laws have their penalty broken away, merely mention that an inquiry shall be opened in the case of suspicion of an offence (B.VI), state that no penalty is required, or contain the confusing phrase *m mi.t.t* ("accordingly", "in a fitting way", or "likewise"). At times this seems to imply that the penalty will be the same as that of the preceding provision, at others this is difficult to tell. See Pflüger, "Haremhab," 262, n. 41.

747 Part C mostly records administrative re-organisation rather than laws with penalties attached.

laws with such a penalty.[748] In Hittite material there are only 5 laws with such a penalty, each of which is reserved specifically for slaves.[749]

The most obvious similarity between MAL, MAPD, EH, ND and LH is that all were produced during a period of imperialism. Though one could argue that the kingdoms of Ur, Isin and Eshnunna were also expansionary, they do not approach the imperial nature of the societies behind the aforementioned collections. The level of brutality in the Assyrian collections, what has been termed their "calculated frightfulness",[750] brings to mind the gratuitous nature of many of the later Assyrian royal annals. For example, take these passages from Aššur-naṣirpal II (883–859):

> "I cut off their heads and formed (therewith) a pile. . . . I razed, destroyed and burnt the cities which lay within the mighty highlands. . . . Bubu, son of Babua, son of the city ruler of the city Ništun I flayed in the city Arbail and draped his skin over the wall."[751]

> "I erected a pile (of bodies) in front of his gate; I flayed as many nobles as had rebelled against me and draped their skins over the pile; some I spread out within the pile, some I erected on stakes upon the pile, and some I placed on stakes around the pile. I flayed many right through my land and draped their skins over the walls. I slashed the flesh of the eunuchs."[752]

> "I burnt many captives from them. I captured many troops alive: from some I cut off their arms and hands; from others I cut off their noses, ears and extremities. I gouged out the eyes of many troops. I made one pile of the living and one of heads. I hung their heads on trees around the city. I burnt their adolescent boys and girls."[753]

---

[748] LU 25 which is fairly mild, only involving the scouring of a mouth with salt. LU 26 may have contained a similar punishment given the similarity of subject matter, but it is broken.

[749] This number excludes those references to corporal punishments in the *karu . . . kinuna* sections of HL, and assumes that the final provision of ETud. IV has theft by a slave in view. This last contention is based on an expectation of internal consistency with the other laws within this collection (see Col. I, lines 11–18) and may turn out to be incorrect. The others are HL 95, 99 and 173b.

[750] Lafont, "Middle Assyrian Period," 553.

[751] Translation from Albert Kirk Grayson, *Assyrian Rulers of the Early First Millennium BC* (vol. 1; Royal Inscriptions of Mesopotamia, Assyrian Periods 2; Toronto: University of Toronto Press, 1991), txt. A.0.101.1, pp. 197–98.

[752] *Ibid.*, 199.

[753] *Ibid.*, 201.

The gruesome nature of the Assyrian annals is, however, a development around the end of the second, beginning of the first millennium B.C. Some have explained its late appearance as due to the Assyrian campaigning against the Aramaeans.[754] The existence of similarly gruesome penalties within the Assyrian law collections makes it likely that the representation of violent consequences punishing misbehavior was a common Assyrian practice.[755] The minimal evidence linking MAL to royalty makes it more difficult to argue strongly for a link to the royal ideology of Assyria but some possibilities present themselves. A formula at the end of MAL A dates our copy to the reign of Tiglath-pileser I (1114–1079). The evidence for tracing this and the other tablets back to the fourteenth century is inconclusive.[756] With Tiglath-pileser I Assyrian imperialism and its representation in royal texts develops significantly. It is possible that MAL do date to this period. The collection of MAPD is firmly dated to his reign also though it clearly contains decrees from the fourteenth century. Corporal punishments are ascribed to decrees from Aššur-uballit I onwards in this text so a date for MAL in the fourteenth century is not impossible for MAL either. Given the fragmentary nature of our evidence, it is difficult to judge whether this preponderance of corporal punishments reflects the actual legal practice of the Assyrians or is specific to the law collections. Our inability to determine the private or royal function of MAL also hinders such analysis. MAPD, however, are firmly linked to Assyrian royalty. The brutality of the penalties contained within this collection is mirrored in MAL so is unlikely to be due merely to its context within the running of the harem, so infamous for political intrigues. There is a firm link between the brutality in the Assyrian law collections and the later representation of brutality in the annals. Perhaps this Assyrian representation of violent punishment meted out for misbehavior could only be voiced within the inscriptions once a certain level of imperial power was achieved and the annalistic form had developed further whereas internally this could happen earlier. Our evidence for such representation in Assyria dates firmly during a long period of imperial expansion, begun with Aššur-uballit I.

---

[754] A. Leo Oppenheim, *Ancient Mesopotamia*, 163. Similarly Postgate, *Early Mesopotamia*, 287, notes an increased severity in the oaths used by the Assyrians after the period of conflict with the Aramaeans.

[755] Whether this was used as propaganda to deter such misbehaviour, whether such rebelliousness was seen as deserving harsh penalties, or there was some other explanation will not be explored here.

[756] Based on attempts to date the script and language, neither of which are able to give narrow dates.

The brutality within EH and ND is also firmly fixed within a period of imperial expansion, and again, finds striking parallels with Egyptian royal inscriptions. Though the Egyptian inscriptions do not record acts of brutality as regularly as the later Assyrian ones, there is much similar material *e.g.* Thutmose III and Amenhotep III record the collecting of the severed hands of the enemy in their inscriptions;[757] Amenhotep II the hanging of defeated princes on the walls of cities,[758] and the cutting off of the heads of enemy chiefs.[759] Seti I's inscriptions contain gruesome descriptions of battle also: "making them carcasses in their valleys, overturned in their blood";[760] "his heart is satisfied at seeing blood, he cuts off the heads of the rebellious-hearted, he loves an hour of battle more than a day of rejoicing . . . He leaves not a limb among them."[761]

Merneptah and Ramesses III speak of carrying off the hands and phalli of defeated chiefs,[762] and Ramesses III of killing the wife and children of his enemies.[763] There is little surprise that these references occur during the peaks of imperial expansion in the Egyptian New Kingdom period. The increasing militarization of Egypt, and in particular, the throne, seems a likely catalyst for this element of the inscriptions of this period. It parallels the brutality of the punishments in EH and ND quite well. Several documents from practice record brutal measures being used more generally in Egyptian legal proceedings *e.g.* the beating of witnesses.[764] It must be remembered that these sources are generally written by royal officials and often involved the king himself.[765]

---

[757] James Henry Breasted, *Ancient Records of Egypt* (vol. 2; Chicago: University of Chicago Press, 1906; repr., Urbana: University of Illinois Press, 2001), 185, 187, 216, 341.

[758] *Ibid.*, 313

[759] *Ibid.*, 319. See also Seti I in Breasted, *Ancient Records of Egypt* (vol. 3; Chicago: University of Chicago, 1906; repr., Urbana: University of Illinois, 2001), 79.

[760] Breasted, *Ancient Records of Egypt*, vol. 3, 47.

[761] *Ibid.*, 52.

[762] *Ibid.*, 248–49, 255–56. Breasted, *Ancient Records of Egypt* (vol. 4; Chicago: University of Chicago, 1906; repr., Urbana: University of Illinois, 2001), 23, 30, 31, 66.

[763] Breasted, *Ancient Records of Egypt*, vol. 4, 61.

[764] See Ellen Dailey Bedell, "Criminal Law in the Egyptian Ramesside Period" (Ph.D. diss., Brandeis University, 1973), 82–83.

[765] *e.g.* the trials regarding harem conspiracy (though Ramesses III boasts of not being involved in these trials-see Bedell, "Criminal Law," 23–24) and tomb robberies. See John A. Wilson's translation, "Results of a Trial for Conspiracy" (*ANET*, 214–16) or Robert K. Ritner's, "The Turin Judicial Papyrus" (*COS* 3.8: 28–30) for

LH is also written during a period of imperial expansion. The relative infrequency of corporal punishments within LH is mirrored by the lack of brutality within the historical inscriptions of the period. This writer postulates that the relative infrequency of these punishments is due to a different conception and justification of kingship in Southern Mesopotamia as opposed to that in Assyria. The existence of some corporal penalties within LH does reflect the more severe nature of LH's penalties in general when compared to other Southern Mesopotamian collections and may be, at the least, partly due to the imperial context.[766]

It is thus possible to explain the uneven distribution of corporal punishment within the law collections of the ancient Near East as due to more general cultural differences combined with the influence of an imperial context.

2.7.2 Capital

The data regarding the death penalty is a little harder to compare if one merely looks at the percentage of such punishments within each collection. Though even here, the Hittite, and to a lesser extent the Sumerian, collections, contain a smaller percentage of capital cases than those written in Akkadian. The Hittite laws stand out containing only 10 cases out of 200 laws. Out of these 10 cases, 6 treat unpermitted sexual pairings, a topic treated rarely and briefly elsewhere. The Egyptian collections posit the death penalty on far fewer occasions than corporal: once in EH out of the 5 extant penalties and twice in ND's 16. Though the comparison of these percentages yields only minor differences apart from HL, it is worth comparing the offences which warrant the death penalty in the various collections. The Egyptian material is difficult to compare. Out of the three penalties, the offence for one is broken. The two extant offences treated are the offering of animals dedicated to the foundation of Osiris to another temple and the violation of justice by an official acting as a judge. Only the latter has any parallel in other collections. The penalty here in EH is harsher than that in LH 5 where the judge loses his position and pays twelvefold the claim of the case.

---

the former and T. Eric Peet, *The Great Tomb-Robberies of the Twentieth Egyptian Dynasty: Being a Critical Study, with Translations and Commentaries, of the Papyri in which these are Recorded* (2 vols.; Oxford: Clarendon, 1930) for the latter.

[766] There are some parallels in Hammurabi's inscriptions. For example, see his mention of breaking necks in the inscription referred to by Van De Mieroop, *King Hammurabi*, 124–27.

A comparison of the remaining material is slightly easier. There are some general similarities. Among the collections capital punishment is generally reserved for sexual offences involving married women,[767] murder,[768] robbery/burglary,[769] witchcraft[770] and incest.[771] This is not to say that these offences were treated in the same way across all collections. For example we discussed earlier that, though burglary/robbery received the death penalty in LH and LU, it only attracts a small fine in HL 94–95; murder is similarly treated more leniently in HL, being penalized with replacement or monetary fines;[772] MAL includes an unborn child as a possible victim of murder in opposition to the other collections; witchcraft is only mentioned in two collections and within HL the death penalty is clearly given only for slaves:[773] incest laws appear only in LH and HL and contradict at points. LH, being the longest of the collections, unsurprisingly contains a number of offences that attract the death penalty that are not dealt with elsewhere *e.g.* kidnap,[774] abuse of juniors by a military officer,[775] a tavern woman not dealing with criminals[776] and a violation by a *naditu.*[777] Similarly unique is MAPD's prescription of the death penalty for swearing abuses on three occasions,[778] LE 60's death penalty for a negligent guard, MAL A 47 and MAPD 19's punishment for not reporting certain capital offences, and HL 173a's for rejecting the judgment of a magistrate. In these cases there is nothing to compare across collections. The theft laws are different however. LH and AE have the death penalty for theft-related offences[779] in con-

---

767 LH 129–30, 133b, 143, 153, 155; LE 26, 28; LU 6–7; MAL A 12–16, 22–23; MAPD 19; HL 195a, 197–98.

768 LH 1 (by extension), 153, 229; LE 24, 58; LU 1; MAL A 10, 50, 53, B 2.

769 LH 21–22; LE 12–13; LU 2 (see earlier discussion of this law).

770 LH 2 (by extension); MAL A 47; HL 170.

771 LH 157; HL 189, 191, 195.

772 ETel. 49 does envisage the death penalty but this is likely due to the specific context of the edict which implies that the victim would be from the royal line.

773 HL 170. If a free man commits the same offence he is merely fined 40 shekels.

774 LH 14

775 LH 26, 33–34.

776 LH 109

777 LH 110

778 MAPD 10–12.

779 Including misappropriation, contractual fraud *etc.*

trast to all other collections.[780] Much of the material in HL covers theft-related offences yet the death penalty occurs only once and seems to be connected to the threat of assassination rather than the theft itself.[781]

A comparison of the death penalty across these collections shows LH and AE, the two Old Babylonian collections, to be more severe than the other Mesopotamian collections and HL. The relative frequency of the death penalty within Akkadian collections more generally needs to be tempered by the fact of MAL's focus on women and thus on sex offences involving married women. Though it is difficult to posit an explanation for this difference, it does correlate with the precarious economic set up of Old Babylonian society. This would tie in to the special treatment of merchants observed elsewhere in this study.[782]

Adding to LH's prevalence in regards to the death penalty is a similar frequency in the specification of the mode of execution. Such specificity adds to the harsh nature of the laws of Hammurabi. Eleven times LH details the mode of execution e.g. being cast into the water;[783] being dragged through a field; burning;[784] hanging;[785] and impalement.[786] Four of these are connected to theft-related offences.[787] None of the capital cases in the Sumerian collections are so specific. LE 60 mentions that the negligent guard will be buried without a grave and HL 173a specifies the decapitation of one who rejects a magistrate's judgment.[788] Four of the twenty Assyrian capital cases contain specific descriptions as do two out of the three Egyptian ones. The prevalence of these specific descriptions roughly reflects the distribution of corporal and capital punishment within the collections but it

[780] With the following exceptions: robbery/burglary offences as mentioned above; MAL A 3 which uniquely treats theft by a wife from her sick husband and HL 126 which deals with theft of a spear from a palace (which was earlier posited to be linked to treason of some form).

[781] HL 126-see notes 483-4 above and discussion amongst section 2.6.

[782] 2.5 and 2.6.1.

[783] LH 108, 129, 133b, 143, 155, 256.

[784] LH 25 (where a looter is cast into the fire which he was supposed to help put out), 110, 157.

[785] LH 21. From the root *alalum* meaning "to suspend" rather than hanging with a noose in the modern sense. See CDA, 11.

[786] LH 153

[787] LH 21, 25, 108 and 256.

[788] HL 121 and 166 also specify modes of execution but these are part of a *karu . . . kinuna* clause and will be dealt with later.

seems unwise to press this point too far. On the whole it seems to reflect the methods of the drafter of LH in general as will be discussed presently.

2.7.3 Talionic, Vicarious, and Equivalent

LH, MAL and ND stand alone in their use of vicarious penalties,[789] LH and MAL in the employment of talion.[790] The status of LH and MAL is similar in regards to penalties framed so as to fit the crime (this last category will be easier to grasp when examples are given below). This heightened concern to "make the punishment fit the crime" is most prevalent in LH,[791] though it is certainly reflected in MAL.

The laws of talion are famously expressed within the personal injury laws of LH treating offences against an *awilum* by an *awilum*.[792] In contrast to all other collections treating this topic,[793] LH has the injury returned upon the offending party *e.g.* LH 196 "If an *awilum* should blind the eye of another *awilum*, they shall blind his eye."[794] As with the contrast between capital punishment and compensation, Westbrook contends that the difference between a talionic penalty and payment is not real.[795] Though this may have been remotely possible in practice, the difference in framing is both real and explainable, as it was in the case of capital punishment. This tali-

---

789 For the purposes of this work more general vicarious laws such as those in which a family member can be sold into slavery or given over as a result of the head of the household's transgression will not be treated here. This section will focus on those vicarious penalties in which some form of corporal or capital punishment is in view as it is here that cultural differences are discernable.

790 Except perhaps for LU 3 which seems to order imprisonment for some kind of illegal detainment. Under talion we will not treat laws with the death penalty for murder or laws which punish property offences with replacement or twofold return. Talion is here treated only in the cases where the penalty prescribed is to have the offence meted out to the offender in return. Though the death penalty for murder may fit this definition, this aspect of the laws has been treated in detail elsewhere.

791 This practice of Hammurabi's is witnessed in a comment by Rim-Sin of Larsa, "You throw the slave into a kiln, because he threw a boy into the oven." AbB 9.197. Translation follows Van De Mieroop's in *Hammurabi*, 109.

792 This writer includes LH 127, which prescribes the shaming of someone guilty of baseless slander, among the talionic laws.

793 Which prescribe some form of monetary payment. See above. Note that MAL does not treat this topic.

794 See also LH 197 and 200.

795 Westbrook, "Cuneiform Law," 204 and *Studies*, 45–77.

onic approach to injury laws within LH seems to be the reasoning behind some of the vicarious laws also *e.g.*

> **116** If the distrainee should die from the effects of a beating or other physical abuse while in the house of her or his distrainer, the owner of the distrainee shall charge and convict his merchant, and if (the distrainee is) the man's son, they shall kill his (the distrainer's) son; if the man's slave, he shall weigh and deliver 20 shekels of silver; moreover, he shall forfeit whatever he originally gave as the loan.
>
> **210** If that woman (a pregnant woman struck in a brawl) should die, they shall kill his daughter.
>
> **230** If it should cause the death of a son of the householder, they shall kill a son of that builder.

There are several laws in MAL which are talionic also. In MAL A 50 and 52 a man who strikes a pregnant woman is struck in return. MAL A 18–19 prescribe the shaming of an offender who slanders his companion. MAL A 20 particularly adds to the violent penalties depicted within these laws:

> **A20 If** a man sodomizes his comrade and they prove the charges against him and find him guilty, they shall sodomize him and they shall turn him into a eunuch.[796]

As in LH, there is also a law that combines a vicarious penalty with the principle of talion; MAL A 55 prescribes that a man who rapes the daughter of another man will marry her (if her father allows it) and will have his wife raped and taken by the girl's father.[797]

Amongst the vicarious laws of LH and MAL it is fairly clear that the family and slaves of the head of the household could pay for his offence but the reverse was not the case.[798] That the whole household of the offending head could be punished is evidenced also in ND. On two occasions an offence by an official includes the giving of his family to the work of the temple estate.[799] On another the offending official is to have Osiris hunt down and destroy both him and his family.[800]

---

[796] Again, for a discussion of the term *ša reši* see Siddall, "A Re-examination of the Title *ša reši* in the Neo-Assyrian Period."

[797] It is possible that MAL A 24 involves vicarious punishment but this author thinks it more likely that the offender's wife is seen to be complicit in the offence.

[798] See especially MAL A 2 and 32. See also LH 117–119, 151–152.

[799] As serfs. ND II.B.2.b, II.B.3.b.

[800] ND VI B.

Interestingly, ETel. denies the possibility of vicarious punishment.[801] Though it is in the specific case of treasonous offences by a prince, the statement that the prince's family are not to be punished for his crime is opposed to the principle behind those vicarious laws of LH, MAL and ND. It is also consistent with the Hittite tendency to avoid the more gratuitous framing of their penalties as opposed to LH, MAL and Egypt, as can be seen from the above comparison of corporal and capital punishment.

The bane of many a legal historian in the decades following LH's rediscovery and one of the favorite pieces of evidence for those who argue for LH's propagandistic rather than legal purposes, has been those laws in which the penalty seems specifically formulated to fit the crime. Numerous are the historians who have ruminated over the problem of applying LH 25 if the fire in the house from which the offender had looted had gone out, just as they struggled with the application of the vicarious laws, for example, in the case that the offender in LH 116 or 230 had no son, or he in 210 no daughter.[802] From this some have moved towards the opinion that such laws were not intended to have actual application to the practice of law in Old Babylonia.[803] Though this author would not go so far, one must admit that the most these laws could do in such a situation would be to serve as a guide to encourage an equitable punishment. This is not to say that we ignore the fact that LH frames its laws in such ways far more prominently than other collections, with MAL trailing just behind. In contrast with all the other collections treated in this study HL only contains two such laws and these are mentions of punishments which have been done away with.[804] LU and LE each have one such law, with LU's far from severe:[805]

> **LU 25** If a slave woman curses someone acting with the authority of her mistress, they shall scour her mouth with one sila of salt.

> **LE 60** [If] a guard is negligent in guarding [a house], and a burglar [breaks into the house], they shall kill the guard of the house that was broken into [...], and he shall be buried [at] the breach without a grave.

---

[801] *e.g.* §§ 31–32.

[802] See section 2.1.4., note 303.

[803] See the earlier discussion in chapter 1.

[804] Part of *karu . . . kinuna* clauses in HL 92 (exposure to bee sting for theft of bee hives) and 166 (torn apart by ploughing oxen for impure agricultural practice). More will be said about the diachronic changes with HL shortly.

[805] Compare the treatment of offences against those in superior position in LH 192–93, 205 and 282.

Within the Assyrian material there are four such penalties:[806]

MAL A 8 If a woman should crush a man's testicle during a quarrel, they shall cut off one of her fingers. And even if the physician should bandage it, but the second testicle then becomes infected(?) along with it and becomes .... or if she should crush the second testicle during the quarrel-they shall gouge out both her [...]-s.

MAL A 9 If a man lays a hand upon a woman, attacking her like a rutting bull(?), and they prove the charges against him and find him guilty, they shall cut off one of his fingers. If he should kiss her, they shall draw his lower lip across the blade(?) of an ax and cut it off.

MAPD 10 [Ninurta-apil-Ekur, overseer,] son of Eriba-Adad, himself also overseer, issued a decree for his palace: (Any royal women), either the king's wives or other women [of the palace, who ...] fight among themselves and in their quarrel blasphemously swear by the name of god, he shall [(not)] enter; they shall cut the throat of the one who cursed,(?)] the god Ashur; in their quarrel she shall not satisfy the claim.

Within LH there are 9:

21 If a man breaks into a house, they shall kill him and hang(?) him in front of that very breach.

25 If a fire breaks out in a man's house, and a man who came to help put it out covets the household furnishings belonging to the householder, and takes household furnishings belonging to the householder, that man shall be cast into that very fire.

192 If the child of (*i.e.*, reared by) a courtier or the child of (*i.e.*, reared by) a *sekretu* should say to the father who raised him or to the mother who raised him, "You are not my father," or "You are not my mother," they shall cut out his tongue.

193 If the child of (*i.e.*, reared by) a courtier or the child of (*i.e.*, reared by) a *sekretu* identifies with his father's house and repudiates the father who raised him or the mother who raised him and departs for his father's house, they shall pluck out his eye.

194 If a man gives his son to a wet nurse and that child then dies while in the care of the wet nurse, and the wet nurse then contracts to care for another child without the consent of his (the dead child's) father and mother, they shall charge and convict her, and, because she contracted

---

[806] Two in MAL A 9. That in MAPD may only reflect the offence by coincidence given the differing penalties for similar offences in the following decrees.

to care for another child without the consent of his father and mother, they shall cut off her breast.

195 If a child should strike his father, they shall cut off his hand.

218 If a physician performs major surgery with a bronze lancet upon an awilu and thus causes the awilu's death, or opens an awilu's temple with a bronze lancet and thus blinds the awilu's eye, they shall cut off his hand.

253 If a man hires another man to care for his field, that is, he entrusts to him the stored grain, hands over to him care of the cattle, and contracts with him for the cultivation of the field-if that man steals the seed or fodder and it is then discovered in his possession, they shall cut off his hand.

256 If he (one who had hired out cattle or stolen seed so that crops were not produced in the field) is not able to satisfy his obligation, they shall have him dragged around through that field by the cattle.

Again this distribution is roughly equivalent to that found regarding corporal punishments and this author postulates that such framing is linked to a more general severity within MAL and LH. Given the small amount of material from Egypt, the difference in subject matter and audience, little harm is done to the theory presented here by the absence of such a framing within ND or EH though the possibility is raised that this was a peculiarly Mesopotamian phenomenon.

This author does not think it worthwhile attempting to compare the other penalty types in such a systematic fashion given the mass of material. In skirting this topic difficult issues such as the compensatory or punitive nature of such penalties will be avoided, as will issues regarding the textual certainty of the enormously high fines regarding offences against merchants in HL. It may be worth noting that the extremely high manifold replacements prescribed in ND (up to one-hundred-fold) are seen nowhere else, the closest parallel being the thirty-fold of LH 8. This may say something about the nature of ND and its purpose and envisaged implementation but it would be unwise to push this argument too far. An observation which is worth noting is that HL has the highest percentage of laws with simple replacement or substitution; laws which often attract higher penalties in other collections. This supports the contention made here that HL were less severe with their punishments in general. Another general difference to note is the distinction in penalty for offences dependent on the victim's gender in HL in contrast to all other collections.

2.7.4 Diachronic Analysis of HL

The diachronic analysis of HL is complicated by the debates surrounding the usefulness of typological analyses of both the Hittite language and script for dating texts.[807] The lack of any firm evidence for dating the collection makes conclusions as to the reasons for the changes within it somewhat speculative. There are at least three stages reflected within HL, namely the two represented by the *karu* . . . *kinuna* clauses and that of PT. Korošec adds three stages prior to the *karu* . . . *kinuna* changes according to his assumptions about legal development.[808] This writer does not adhere to these assumptions. It is, however, possible to note differences between manuscripts of HL itself. An analysis of these differences is most useful in the first series (*i.e.* laws 1–100) given the lengthier textual witnesses in KBo 6.2,[809] which Hoffner argues is in Hittite Old Script,[810] and KBo 6.3,[811] which he argues is in a New Kingdom script. The existence of text C for this series, argued to exhibit the latest script, and its relation to HL and PT can also be discussed. Some mention will be made of differences in the second series[812] but the more fragmentary nature of the textual witnesses, PT's restriction to material from the first series, and the errors contained within manuscript 'p', make such an undertaking more difficult.

The *karu* . . . *kinuna* clause appears 22 times within HL.[813] On two occasions the provision in the *kinuna* clause is too broken to reconstruct the difference to that in the *karu* clause.[814] For the most part there is a reduction of penalty from the *karu* clause to the *kinuna*. Hoffner displays this adequately in Table 1 of his critical edition.[815] The reader is referred to this

---

[807] Especially the case concerning the historical texts linked to an Arnuwanda or Tudhaliya placed by some in the early fourteenth century BC (for archaisms in language) and others to the thirteenth (for neat historical progression). See the discussion of Weeks, *Admonition and Curse*, 57; Trevor Bryce, *The Kingdom of the Hittites* (Oxford: Oxford University Press, 1998), 414–15 and references therein.

[808] See Haase, "The Hittite Kingdom," 623.

[809] Hereafter termed 'A' following Hoffner, *Laws of the Hittites*, 160.

[810] Hoffner, *Laws of the Hittites*, 160.

[811] Hereafter termed 'B' following Hoffner. All textual witnesses to HL will hereafter be referred to by their sigla *apud* Hoffner, *Laws of the Hittites*, 160–64.

[812] Certainly those including *karu* . . . *kinuna* clauses.

[813] Across 24 different laws according to Hoffner's numbering system due to the continuation of the clause over 54–55 and 166–167.

[814] HL 91, 122.

[815] Hoffner, *Laws of the Hittites*, 6.

table. In most cases the reduction is fifty percent, though four reflect a seventy percent reduction and one a reduction of one-third.[816] In two cases, HL 9 and 25, the reduction is specifically linked to the king's palace waiving its share of the fine:

> **HL 9** If anyone injures a person's head, they used to pay 6 shekels of silver: the injured party took 3 shekels of silver, and they used to take 3 shekels of silver for the palace. But now the king has waived the palace share, so that only the injured party takes 3 shekels of silver.
>
> **HL 25a** [If] a person is impure in a vessel or a vat, they used to pay 6 shekels of silver: the one who is impure pays 3 shekels of silver, and they used to take 3 shekels for the [king]'s house. **25b** But now the king has [waived] the palace's share. The one who is impure only pays 3 shekels of silver. The claimant shall look to his/her house for it.

It is unclear whether the other reductions were due to the same reform. Some may reflect a change in the value of silver or other commodities but this is unclear.[817] They seem to reflect a more general reduction in the severity of penalties from previous times as seen in the abandonment of several penalties involving corporal/capital punishment. In three cases theft laws, once penalized with corporal or capital punishments, are reduced to mere fines:

> **92** [If] anyone steals [2] or 3 bee hives, formerly (the offender) would have been exposed to bee-sting. But now he shall pay 6 shekels of silver. If anyone steals a bee-hive, if there are no bees in the hive, he shall pay 3 shekels of silver.
>
> **101** If anyone steals a vine, a vine branch, a..., or garlic, formerly [they paid] one shekel of silver for one vine, one shekel of silver for one vine branch, one shekel of silver [for one *karpina-*, one] shekel of silver for one clove of garlic. And they shall strike a spear [...] .... [Formerly] they proceeded so. But now if he is a free man, he shall pay 6 shekels [of silver]. But if he is a slave, he shall pay 3 shekels of silver.
>
> **121** If some free man steals a plow, and its owner finds it, he (the owner) shall put [(the offender's) neck] upon the ... (a part of the plow?), and [he shall be put to death(?)] by the oxen. This is how they

---

816 Hoffner's table includes one law, HL 119, as reflecting a fifty-two percent reduction but this is an error. The table lists a reduction from "25?:12," *Ibid.*, 6. In his transliteration and translation of this law however, Hoffner has "40 shekels" as the most likely penalty in the *karu* clause, *Ibid.*, 109–110. This is then a seventy percent reduction.

817 See Hoffner's comments, *Ibid.*, 6–7.

> proceeded formerly. But now he shall pay 6 shekels of silver, and he shall look to his house for it. If it is a slave, [he shall pay] 3 shekels of silver.

There is another law, incidentally one which highlights the peculiarly Hittite concern with ritual purity in its law collection,[818] where capital punishment has been reduced:

> **HL 166** If anyone sows (his own) seed on top of (another man's) seed, they shall place his neck on a plow. They shall hitch up [tw]o teams of oxen: they shall turn the face of one in one direction and of the other in the other direction. The man will be put to death, and the oxen will be put to death. The party who first sowed the field shall reap it for himself. This is the way they used to proceed. **HL 167** But now they shall substitute one sheep for the man and 2 sheep for the oxen. He shall give 30 loaves of bread and 3 jugs of ... beer, and re-consecrate (the land?). And he who sowed the field first shall reap it.

Though it is unclear exactly what the penalty was in former times in HL 101 and 121, the punishments are clearly corporal or capital in nature, in contrast to all other Hittite theft laws. Laws 92, 121 and 166 fit into the category discussed above of laws in which a harsh punishment is made to fit the crime. It was argued that the prevalence of corporal and capital punishment and the framing of harsh punishments made to fit the crime, were most prevalent within Assyria, Egypt and LH. It was proposed that the imperial and centralized nature of these societies may have contributed to this. The penalties of HL were contrasted to these more gruesome punishments. What then to do about these laws? The fact that they have been done away with in HL supports the theory presented here that the presentation of harsh punishments in law collections can be generally connected with more centralized and imperial societies. However, the mention of its earlier existence makes it difficult to push that theory in this case. It was noted in regards to the Assyrian material, that MAL is not necessarily connected to Assyrian kings, and that it may, and MAPD certainly does, date to a period before imperialism has progressed very far (though centralization may have). This raises the possibility that there may be a more general cultural difference that lies beneath the prevalence of Assyria's depiction of brutality. This may possibly be the explanation here also.

---

[818] MAPD 7 is the one exception. The lack of its expression in law collections does not imply that ritual purity *per se* was not of concern within other ancient Near Eastern societies.

There is some debate as to the dating of the promulgation of the Old Hittite version of HL. Many have ascribed this to Telepinu on little more basis than the fact that there is other evidence of his initiation of reform.[819] Others have concluded that the mention of the "father of the king" in HL 55 and the colophon to D,[820] combined with the geographic references within the laws,[821] must date the text to the reign of Mursilis I. The argument is not decided but the weight of evidence seems to be on the side of those who would date the reforms of *karu . . . kinuna*, and most likely the collection/promulgation of the rest of HL, to the reign of Mursilis I. If this is the case, then it is most likely that the stage of law reflected by the *karu* clause refers to that in place before the beginning of the Hittite Old Kingdom. A different cultural origin for these more gruesome laws would then be a possibility. This makes more sense of the changes, given our ability to link such gruesome penalties to specific cultures elsewhere, than hypothesizing an early Hittite practice which changed over time. Whether this earlier practice is to be attributed to the Hattic culture or elsewhere is speculative. Given the links which can be made between this lack of gruesomeness and severity within HL and the different way in which the Hittites ruled their empire,[822] this author thinks it unlikely that this earlier stage of law dates back to the Kussaran dynasty as Anitta already rules his empire in a manner similar to that of the later New Kingdom.[823] The references to the "palace share" in HL 9 and 25 and to exemptions in 51, 54–55 are not problematic for the contention regarding the date of the *karu* stage as there are numerous references to pre-Old Kingdom Anatolian palaces.[824]

---

[819] Namely the *Edict of Telepinu*. This is Hoffner's argument in Roth, *Law Collections*, 214, and Haase's, in "The Hittite Kingdom," 623.

[820] *e.g.* Archi, "Sulla formazione," 58–59 and Pecchioli Daddi, "Il re," 75–91.

[821] B. J. Collins, "§ 54 of the Hittite Laws and the Old Kingdom Periphery," *Orientalia* 56 (1987): 136–41.

[822] Weeks observed a similar correlation between their use of history within their treaties and their imperial practice as compared to general Assyrian practice, *Admonition and Curse*.

[823] *i.e.* through independent vassals, which he claims to have helped. See "The Proclamation of Anitta of Kuššar," trans. Hoffner (*COS* 1.72: 182–84) and the description of Bryce, *Hittites*, 38–41.

[824] For example see Bryce, *Hittites*, 29 or Mogens Trolle Larsen, *The Old Assyrian City-State and its Colonies* (Copenhagen Studies in Assyriology 4; Copenhagen: Akademisk, 1976), 154–56, 245.

Another aspect of change from *karu* to *kinuna* seems to be the reduction of exemptions from some form of *corvée e.g.* HL 51, 54–55. This merely reflects a change in policy which has been incorporated into the collection. The *karu* period here, like that for the reduced fines (as opposed to the scrapped corporal/capital penalties), may possibly refer to an earlier period of the Old Kingdom rather than the period before it.[825] Nevertheless, the latter is also feasible, especially given the possibility that such exemptions are now being revoked due to the incorporation of territory into the Hittite realm. One law which seems problematic for the theory presented here, at least in Hoffner's translation, is HL 54. Here there is mention of "chariot warriors" in a *karu* clause.[826] The ideogram which Hoffner translates as chariot warrior is KUŠ$_7$ in Hoffner's transliteration.[827] This ideogram stands for Akkadian *kizu*, "animal trainer"[828] which cannot be ruled out in this context. "Chariot warrior" is a possible meaning for this ideogram according to Rüster and Neu,[829] however, they also give "squire", "groom" or "servant" as possibilities.[830] Given the options available for this ideogram and the likelihood *karu* refers to a pre-Hittite period, it is not necessary to translate it with "chariot warriors".

---

[825] Hoffner, in Roth, *Law Collections*, 214 argues that the *karu* period definitely refers to the early Old Kingdom. This is based on his dating of the reforms to the reign of Telepinu.

[826] Hoffner, *Laws of the Hittites*, 66.

[827] *Ibid.*, 65.

[828] René Labat, *Manuel d'épigraphie Akkadienne* (6th ed.; Libraire Orientaliste Paul Geuthner: Paris, 1988), sign 212 on page 121 and CDA, 163.

[829] Christel Rüster and Erich Neu, *Hethitisches Zeichenlexikon: Inventar und Interpretation der Keilschriftzeichen aus den Boğazköy-Texten* (Studien zu den Boğazköy-Texten 2; Wiesbaden: Harrassowitz, 1989), 333: "*Wagenlenker*".

[830] "*Knappe*", "*Pferdeknecht*" and "*Diener*". *Ibid.*, 333.

KBo 6.4, Hoffner's Parallel Text (PT), supposedly dates to the New Kingdom period and reflects a later stage of Hittite Law than the OH version of HL. The most common difference between HL and PT is an increased fine in the latter:

PT II-80 shekels	HL 4-bringing for burial and one person
PT IV-all the offender's land and 40 shekels	HL 6-100 *gipeššar* land
PT V-40 shekels	HL 7-20 shekels
PT VI-20 shekels	HL 8-10 shekels
PT IX-medical care, replacement person to work, 3 shekel physician fee, extra 6 shekel payment	HL 10- medical care, replacement person to work, 6 shekel physician fee
PT XV-6 shekels	HL 16-3 shekels
PT XVI-20 shekels	HL 17-10 shekels
PT XVII-10 shekels	HL 18-5 shekels

There is at least one law which lessens the penalty,[831] and four in which it is the same.[832] There are many provisions within PT that are too broken to compare meaningfully, and one which is difficult to place as a parallel to HL.[833] These changes seem to merely be updates which are possibly due to economic circumstances of some sort and are similar to the price-fixing changes one would expect to happen over time. There are other changes which occur with these however.

There is not merely a change of price in the development from HL to PT. For example, in the personal injury laws, an extra element is added. A distinction is made in PT X and XI as to whether the injury inflicted had permanent or temporary results. This distinction was obviously not helpful

---

[831] The penalties in PT VII are less than those in HL 7–8. That in PT III may be less than HL 5 but this author hesitates to admit such given the ridiculously high penalties in the latter law *i.e.* 4000 shekels of silver for killing a merchant. The opposite is the case for PT XII–XIII and HL 13–14 where the penalties in the former seem to high *i.e.* 30 and 15 mina may be a mistake for shekels in which case the penalty would be slightly lower. For discussion see Hoffner's commentary, *Laws of the Hittites*, 170–71.

[832] PT VIII and HL 9; PT X and HL 11; PT XI and HL 12; PT XIII and HL 14.

[833] *i.e.* it is not certain that PT XXXIV parallels HL 44b.

in many of the other personal injury laws covered by PT *e.g.* the cutting off of an ear/nose or the knocking of a tooth is obviously permanent. In a number of laws the distinction, made in several laws in HL, between accidental and intentional injury, is extended to other topics.[834] The distinction made in HL 17–18 as to the gestation period of the unborn child which is killed is done away with in PT XVI–XVII. The arrangement of the topics is slightly different. For example, in HL 7–8 the blinding and knocking out the teeth of a free man are treated together, followed by the same offences against a slave. The two offences share the same penalty when against a victim of the same status whereas in PT V–VII these topics are separated, treating the blinding of a free man and slave and then the knocking out of their teeth, with separate penalties for the two offences. The topics parallel to those treated in PT XXXII–XXXIII are treated before those in PT XXX–XXXI in HL. The same is the case for those in PT XXXVIII and XXXVI–XXXVII. Within PT there is more consistency regarding the ratio of punishment for offences against slaves in relation to those against free men *e.g.* PT XII–XV create a ratio of 1:2 for these offences as against the uneven ratios in HL 13–16. There is also a case where a clause is added regarding the penalty for an offence committed against a slave, where HL discussed only its perpetration against a free person *e.g.* PT IX vs HL 10. There are also two cases where a distinction is made in PT between offences against free women in contrast to men when they had been treated equally in HL.[835] On another occasion PT specifies an extra condition and a threefold compensation for theft while HL had merely stated that the offender was "considered a thief". The laws regarding *luzzi* and *šahhan* are also covered by PT. There is little change within these laws apart from the substitution of the terms *luzzi* and *šahhan*,[836] and free man and TUKUL-man.[837] This may reflect a change in policy towards these holdings or a looseness of terminology. There is also one case, similar to the changes from *karu* to *kinuna*, of cancellation of exemption.[838] This author does not think it wise to offer an explanation for these changes other than to point out that they seem to include more than mere price fixing, and less than the changes from corporal/capital punishment to mere fines reflected in the *karu* . . . *kinuna* clauses of HL.

---

[834] PT V–VI.

[835] PT II and IV in contrast to HL 3–4 and 6.

[836] PT XXXVII–XXXIX

[837] PT XXX

[838] PT XXXVI

The same can be said for the differences within the various texts of HL itself. To begin, it seems wise to analyze Hoffner's claim that text C reflects the same stage of law as PT.[839] The material from C covers only 20 laws. It is only possible to compare it to PT for 9 of these.[840] Out of these 9 laws, there are only two occasions where C agrees with PT in contrast to the earlier recension of HL.[841] There are 5 occasions where the opposite is true *i.e.* C agrees with the earlier recension witnessed in A and B in contrast to PT.[842] There is one occasion where all three are the same,[843] and one where C agrees with neither recension.[844] This evidence would seem to suggest that C represents a stage of law somewhere between that represented in B and PT. There are two occasions where C, along with B, adds material to A,[845] two where C adds material to both,[846] and one where the material presented is fairly different to both.[847] There are also some other minor textual variants within C that contrast to A and B.[848]

C is not the only witness to HL (apart from PT) which exhibits differences to the Old Hittite version represented by A. There are a number of occasions where the supposedly New Kingdom witness B displays variants to A. Two were mentioned above regarding cases where B reflects the updates of C in contrast to A. Some changes are minor vocabulary differences

---

[839] Hoffner, *Laws of the Hittites*, 6.

[840] HL 9, 11 or 12, 13–18, 45. The other material covered in C: HL 10, 26–30, 41–44 and 46, is broken for either PT or C, or is not covered by PT.

[841] HL 17–18 in contrast to PT XVI and XVII (as witnessed in B as A does not cover these sections due to breakage).

[842] HL 9, 13–14, 16 and 45.

[843] HL 15

[844] Col. I, lines 10–11. This seems to be a parallel variant of HL 11. C has a penalty of 6 shekels in contrast to A and B which have 20 and PT X which has 20 if the injury is permanent, 10 if it is temporary. Hoffner thinks the first section of this part of C is a parallel to HL 11 but the penalty of 6 shekels he sees as a variant of the penalty in HL 12, the scribe of C having skipped a line, *Laws of the Hittites*, 25, n. 32. This is possible given the fact C is missing a law here. In HL 12, A and B's penalties are broken but seem to be 10 shekels, PT XI has 10 if the injury is permanent, 5 if it is not.

[845] HL 42 and 44b.

[846] HL 28a and 43. See Hoffner, *Laws of the Hittites*, 37–38 (esp. nn. 93–97) and 52 (esp. nn. 160–61).

[847] HL 26

[848] For example, see HL 28a. For references see note 841 above.

e.g. HL 39.[849] Others, such as HL 24 seem to reflect an updated approach to a topic. HL 24 specifies a penalty of one month's wages (12 shekels for a male, 6 for a female) for someone who harbors a fugitive slave. In B, this penalty is raised to one year's wages (100 shekels for a male, 50 for a female). Though it is possible both may reflect *per diem* rates, lessening the difference between them, the monetary amounts have still changed slightly. In HL 56, B has changed the duties required as part of public service.[850] In HL 98, A records compensation for the goods destroyed after a house is set on fire. B declares that there is no compensation for the goods, only the house.[851] With B, as with L, there are some minor changes amongst the real estate laws relating to šahhan, luzzi and TUKUL which again, as in the case of PT, may reflect looseness of terminology or changes in policy.[852] There are some occasions in which L agrees with A in contrast to B.[853] These changes are fairly minimal, generally reflecting the addition of details to avoid uncertainty[854] and perhaps some slight changes in a few laws. The last variant worth mentioning is that in witness X for HL 7. It is worth displaying all variant versions of this law:

> **HL 7 (A and B)** If anyone blinds a free person or knocks out his tooth, they used to pay 40 shekels of silver. But now he shall pay 20 shekels of silver, and he shall look to his house for it.
>
> **PT V** (=late version of 7) If anyone blinds a free man in a quarrel, he shall pay 40 shekels of silver. If it is an accident, he shall pay 20 shekels of silver.
>
> **HL 7 (X)**[855] . . . [No]w [he shall pay] 10 shekels of si[lver…]

Within this law then there is a difference between *karu* and *kinuna*, displaying the common 50% reduction, an increase in PT as well as the addition of extra criteria. X stands out as a reduction of the fine represented by the *kinuna* stage. The possible mention of *kinuna* in X, in contrast to PT, makes one suspect that X either represents a stage in between B and C/PT, or reflects a scribal error. In the two following laws, HL 8–9, the only other

---

849 See Hoffner, *Laws of the Hittites*, 46, n. 140. See also HL 71.

850 *i.e.* it has left out the ice procurement recorded in A.

851 Of course this may be a scribal error.

852 B: HL 47a. L: HL 40

853 *e.g.* HL 39.

854 *e.g.* HL 42 and 44b.

855 See Hoffner, *Laws of the Hittites*, 21 and Haase, "Regelt § 9 der hethitischen Rechtssammlung eine leichte Leibesverletzung?" *Bibliotheca Orientalis* 19 (1962): 115.

material available from X, the penalty is not preserved for this witness. This makes any conclusions as to the date or nature of this text speculative.

The variants among the witnesses to the second series of laws, HL 101–200, are fairly minor being mainly slight differences of detail *e.g.* types of animals listed in HL 180. There is little that can be said about these differences given the fragmentary nature of most of the witnesses and the fact that p, exhibiting the bulk of the variants, seems to contain errors.[856] For the purposes of this study we are little interested in grammatical and orthographic variants. The reader is referred to the relevant sections of Hoffner's critical edition.

The differences reflected within the various witnesses to HL demonstrate the uniquely Hittite tendency to reflect the updating of laws within its law collections. This updating is reflected in the differences between *karu* and *kinuna* and those from the earlier recension of the laws to PT. There are some general trends discernible in the changes within each stage supporting the idea that the latter also reflect more than mere textual variants.[857] Within other witnesses it is also possible to discern actual differences of law most probably also reflecting changes of law between the period of writing the Old Hittite copy in A, and the Parallel Text (PT). This is most clearly seen in witnesses B and C. Unfortunately, given our lack of external or internal evidence to date these texts or the changes recorded by them, any attempted explanation for them is no more than an educated speculation. This writer suspects that the stage of law reflected by the corporal and capital punishments of former times, done away with by the Old Hittite version, reflects a period before the onset of the Old Kingdom or the Kussaran dynasty and thus the practice of a culture with a different worldview. The difficulties involved in explaining the changes within HL due to the lack of evidence are also found in attempts at diachronic analysis of other collections, especially those in the Hebrew Bible.

---

[856] *e.g.* HL 191, after the definition of an offence as *hurkel*, p adds "it is not an offence".

[857] This fact is accepted generally for the changes between *karu* and *kinuna* given the clear mention of change within the laws.

3 CONCLUSION

This thesis set out to compare the pre-first millennium B.C. ancient Near Eastern law collections. The application of the method for this comparison, as set forth in the opening chapter, has yielded a number of new conclusions and questioned some widely held views regarding these collections. The comprehensive and systematic comparison undertaken here has highlighted how overstated is the position that there is good evidence for widespread borrowing amongst the ancient Near Eastern law collections. It has also drawn attention to some of the limitations of form and genre criticism. One of the goals of this thesis was to act as a corrective to the theory of a common ancient Near Eastern culture, specifically in regards to the area of law. The detailed comparisons of numerous aspects of these collections have amply demonstrated the fallacy of this assumption. More than that, this study has described and explained many of the differences between the collections on the basis of differing contexts, be they cultural, political or otherwise. The comparative nature of this thesis also enabled a broader perspective from which to analyze the vexed question of the nature, function and purpose of these law collections. The following will briefly set out some of these results. This will be followed by the implications these results and the method used here have for future research, specifically that regarding the subjects of ancient Near Eastern or biblical law, or comparative studies in the field of ancient Near Eastern history in general.

3.1 WAS THERE A COMMON LEGAL CULTURE AND/OR WIDESPREAD BORROWING?

In the opening chapter we discussed some of the difficulties faced in trying to answer a question such as this. Given the fact that this thesis has focused solely on the written law collections from the ancient Near East to the exclusion of the documents from practice, the answer given here to the first question is not necessarily applicable to the actual practice of law within the societies of the ancient Near East. The many differences between the law collections and the suspicion that they are related to actual legal practice to some extent make it possible that some of the conclusions found could be applicable to actual practice also. Within this focus there are difficulties of explanation when similarity is found. Studies such as those of Tigay have shown that borrowing does not necessarily lead to wholesale adoption, mere copying or translation.[1] This makes the task of identification of borrowings quite difficult when it comes to law collections as, theoretically, a law collection may have borrowed a law from another collection yet have changed the framing, phrasing, form and the penalty.[2] All one would be left with would be a vaguely similar subject matter. This difficulty was encountered numerous times. For example, in the laws treating injury, whether to people or animals, there was a great similarity of topic in terms of the objects of injury. It was impossible to decide whether this was simply due to the nature of the offences being described *i.e.* there are only a certain number of body parts which could be injured and only a finite number of ways to injure them in the societies producing the collections. The similarity of the animals mentioned in these laws could be explained as due to the similarity of the agricultural societies producing the collections which covered this topic. The same problems arise in an attempt to treat the overlap across collections in terms of which items were mentioned in theft laws. Similar societies have similar things which could be stolen. The general correspondence across collections concerning what was seen to be an offence, especially in the section on "criminal law", may be explained as due to a common culture, a similar societal make-up, a common human nature or natural law *etc.* There seems to be no objective way to decide upon such things. Due to limitations in space, this work has not attempted to formulate a methodology for exploring the issues of whether stimulus diffusion is more likely in these specific examples, as opposed to independent invention in similar societies. One suspects that it is the modern focus on intertextuality and genre, arising out of structuralism, which has led some scholars to start from the basis of such surface similarities and argue for literary borrowing. Others have been influenced in another direction and have taken the position that a common "scientific" legal culture spread with the cuneiform language. These assumptions have been criticized in this thesis as unnecessary starting points.

The comparison of the distribution of forms within these collections raised a number of problems for those who would wish to use these as an aid to the origin of various sections of a text. The biggest problem was caused by EH which included conditional clauses which were phrased as first person commands. This argued against the *Sitze im Leben* scholars have proposed for conditional, relative and/or apodictic clauses. A number of

---

[1] Tigay, "On Evaluating".

[2] As Westbrook, "Character," 17, in fact argues to some extent.

collections demonstrated the possibility of using a number of different forms within the one document. If the drafters of these collections were happy to do so, the onus is on the form critic to demonstrate that the original drafter of an unwitnessed text would have composed a text with a pure, original form. There was a general similarity in that a casuistic framing, including conditional and relative clauses, was most common. LH demonstrated the possibility of framing almost any topic within a casuistic clause. The evidence did not seem to fit well with the assertion of some that an apodictic framing was linked to a higher view of morality. This writer finds it highly unlikely that a similarity of form is needed across two collections for borrowing to have occurred, and even less likely that the widespread use of various casuistic forms must be explained as due to any form of borrowing. This can only be done through the hyper-diffusionist model of Westbrook and others who would postulate the spread of such a form from Mesopotamia to Greece and Rome and onwards to later Western civilizations. It seems simpler to acknowledge the fact that there are a finite number of ways for any culture to express their laws.

There were some parallels among these collections which bear outlining. It must be admitted that among the cuneiform collections there was a greater degree of similarity in terms of subject matter. This similarity was heightened if one excluded the Hittite and Assyrian material and those collections deemed to be edicts or decrees. Is this so surprising that one needs to posit direct borrowing amongst these collections? Though it is a possibility, the similarity of the cultures and societies of Lower Mesopotamia in general may well give a background to explain many of the supposed parallels. This said, the geographic, linguistic and cultural closeness of these societies also makes borrowing of some kind an altogether more likely possibility.

A greater number of parallels were found amongst the so-called "formal law collections" than across all. It was difficult to assign this to an explanation based on genre. It was also difficult to pin-point systematic commonalities in the usage of form or structure within these "formal" collections or to divine systematic differences to other collections such as edicts and decrees. The main difference between edicts/decrees on the one hand and the "formal collections" on the other, seemed to be subject matter, and even here there was much overlap *e.g.* price fixing in formal collections such as LH and LE, annulment of economic duties in HL, criminal topics in ETel. and ETud. *etc.*

Within the Lower Mesopotamian collections containing non-legal sections there was much thematic overlap, some overlap in phrasing, but few parallels in regard to ordering. A structural development within Lower Mesopotamia from RU to LU to LL to LH was posited as a possibility. LH stood out from these other collections in its emphasis on his military achievements. This was seen to fit nicely within the context of his imperial conquests. Of the themes shared amongst these collections the concern that a future ruler not efface the inscription is a general one in ancient Near Eastern inscriptions and cannot be seen as due to borrowing specifically from any other law collection. The other themes which are shared, such as divine election, the establishment of freedom *etc.* may be due in part to literary borrowing, but all reflect a similarity in worldview common to southern Mesopotamia. The non-legal sections of other collections were very different to these and displayed the possibility of diversity. For example, LE's superscription shares some themes with the non-legal sections of the monumental law collections above, but also shared similarities with the superscriptions common to Old Babylonian edicts. There were some general parallels across collections which contained a non-legal section, including those in Egypt. The lengthier non-legal portions, often termed prologues and epilogues, were uniformly connected to the actions of the king who boasted of his achievements.

A very high degree of similarity was found amongst the laws on the topics of damage to rented oxen and boats. This heightened evidence for parallel material coincided with some of the subject matter of the so-called "scholarly" or "school texts". Despite the parallels in topic, body parts of the oxen to be injured, and even penalties in some cases, it is hard to decide whether a common practice or literary borrowing is more likely, or even whether this is again, merely a topic with finite possibilities treated by similar societies. There is a fair amount of difference in phrasing across all the collections outlining this topic, and HL shows a lower degree of similarity than the Lower Mesopotamian collections display amongst themselves.[3] In the case of damage to boats, treated in LL, SLHF, SLEx, LH and MAL, the laws in MAL stood apart from the others, again displaying the higher degree of similarity amongst the Lower Mesopotamian collections. One set of laws in LL and SLHF seemed to be identical, almost word for word. There was only one other case of such verbatim similarity.[4] This is somewhat problematic. If this word for word copying was possible, why is it not more frequent? Perhaps its existence in a school text from almost the same period as the more formal collection, in close geographical proximity and in the same

[3] LH, LL, LOx, SLEx, SLHF.

[4] LX l and LH 111.

language goes some way to explaining its existence here. However, there are no other word for word borrowings from LL in SLHF apart from this one. The other example, that of LX 1 and LH 111, again occurs between two texts close in proximity both geographically and temporally. It is possible that the existence of such direct borrowings, though few in number, should make one more open to the possibility of stimulus diffusion, or lesser borrowings, seen in such things as similarity of subject matter.

Numerous other topics showed a degree of similarity. For the most part this was fairly general and related only to the topic treated. In many cases, though the general topic was similar, the focus of the "parallel" laws or the exact situation treated were quite different, let alone the particular phrasing used or the penalty given. As mentioned above, most of the closer parallels that were found were amongst Lower Mesopotamian collections, and very few of these were close enough to demand an explanation on the basis of borrowing. This is not to say that exact parallels were rife even here. There were numerous differences amongst these collections on every topic. Though the parallels were most common here, there was not so much material common between any two collections to be able to firmly state that any collection had borrowed from any other to any great extent. Rather there were isolated cases of similarity across a number of these collections. In most cases, this similarity was only found across two or three collections. MAL displayed significant differences to rulings within Lower Mesopotamian collections on many occasions *e.g.* marriage law concerning the need for a contract, divorce, inheritance, the absentee husband, miscarriage and abortion *etc.* HL displayed a number of minor similarities to other collections *e.g.* a vague similarity in topic, but regularly contained laws with very contradictory rulings to other collections and was rarely treating exactly the same topic. Some of the differences that were found amongst these collections will be outlined below. The prevalence of similarity within Lower Mesopotamia as opposed to Assyrian, Hittite or Egyptian collections fits with this writer's initial suspicion that cultural differences would permeate the law collections. There is good evidence for the spread of cuneiform learning to Egypt *e.g.* the Amarna archive, yet few argue for wide scale borrowing by Egypt from Mesopotamia. One wonders why this is claimed so quickly when it comes to other cultures, especially ancient Israel and Judah, for whom there is little concrete evidence of cuneiform scribal schools.

3.2 Systematic Differences and their Explanation

Apart from the many different rulings, the differences in arrangement, phraseology and vocabulary, and the unique topics (or at least focuses within a topic) covered, within the framing and penalties of these collections there were a number of consistent differences. Contextual explanations for these differences are possible and their acceptability is bolstered by similar differences in other text types *e.g.* historical texts and treaties. The main contexts which can be used to explain these differences are culture and society/politics. Personal contexts are also a possibility.

The Hittite collections exhibit a number of peculiarities which can be associated with the culture and make-up of Hittite society and their political practice. These have parallels in the way the Hittites wrote history and framed treaties. The Hittite law collections, more than any other, stood apart in that they acknowledged change in the law. This was seen in HL both within individual texts *e.g.* *karu. . . kinuna* clauses, the publication of PT, and also across the various copies of the text. These changes involved more than mere price fixing and included changes from corporal punishments to monetary ones as well as the addition of new aspects to laws. This acknowledgement of change was also seen in ETel. with its outlining of past practice and the new implementation of succession rules. Along with this willingness to acknowledge change, in the Hittite collections there was a willingness, not found elsewhere, to give details of the situation leading up to the giving of a specific law or to give an explanation of the purpose of the law.[5] This was seen in HL 49 and 55, ETel. and ETud. All of this parallels nicely with the Hittite use of history elsewhere. The Hittites, in contrast to most, acknowledge mistakes by previous and current kings and mention bad things which happen to them. This seems to be part of their general approach to historiography in which they use history to teach lessons and to motivate obedience. The long prologues to their treaties, outlining the good the Hittite king had done for the vassal in an attempt to motivate obedience is almost without parallel in the ancient Near East.[6] Weeks has argued that this particular use of history which needs to include positive and negative details in order to teach lessons, can be seen to be linked to the lesser degree of centralization at Hatti.[7] This aspect of Hittite kingship is also reflected in ETud.'s and HL 55's description of the process leading up to the giving of laws. Each of these details subjects of the king coming to him as a delegation and being involved in the production of the law set forth. Contrast this to centralized Egypt and EH's description of Haremhab consult-

[5] The "because clauses" of LH do not compare at all as discussed earlier.

[6] Apart from the prologues to covenants in the Hebrew Bible and the treaties of Esarhaddon and Aššur-banipal. See Weeks, *Admonition and Curse*.

[7] *Ibid.*, *e.g.* 176–77.

ing with his own heart to produce the laws he sets forth. The lack of any specific attribution of HL to a king may be of significance here also, but that is not certain.

Another aspect of HL which sets it apart from other collections is its concern with ritual purity, especially in regards to the person of the king. This is seen in a number of laws and is reflected in the king's great role in the cult at Hatti.[8] Interestingly, in regard to purity laws, HL has far harsher penalties for incest than LH. This is in contrast to a comparison of penalties in HL and LH regarding criminal law topics, with HL usually containing penalties far beneath its Mesopotamian counterparts. Perhaps this highlights the relative import of ritual purity at Hatti.[9] MAL displays a difference to all other collections in its higher view of the value of the unborn child in its laws concerning miscarriages and abortion.

The only other collection to acknowledge change in the law was RU. It is worth noting that Lagash, like the Hittites, employed a historiography to teach lessons. In *Admonition and Curse* Weeks has also made some links between the existence of treaties involving Lagash, and those of the Hittites in contrast to Assyria and Egypt.[10] This supports the argument presented here that such acknowledgement reflects a difference in historiography and perhaps society or culture.

The differences in punishment within these collections were also found to parallel certain aspects of the cultures behind them. This was seen most clearly in the use of corporal punishment in the Assyrian and Egyptian collections.[11] The brutal punishments in MAL, MAPD, EH, ND and ED very much parallel the uniquely gruesome nature of the historical inscriptions of Assyrian and Egyptian imperialism. LH also contained a number of corporal and brutal punishments, though far fewer on average than the Assyrian and Egyptian collections. This was possibly due to Hammurabi's imperial context and associative brutalization. It parallels the emphasis on the curse in Hammurabi's treaty negotiations with Mari.[12] The Lower Mesopo-

---

[8] For example Mursilis II mentions taking care of religious festivals before going on campaign, "The Ten Year Annals of Great King Muršili II of Ḫatti," trans. Richard H. Beal (*COS* 2.16: 82–90), Year 4, page 86.

[9] This is paralleled in the harsh penalties found in "Instructions for Palace Personnel to Insure the King's Purity," trans. by Albrecht Goetze (*ANET*, 207).

[10] Weeks, *Admonition and Curse*, ch. 1 and conclusion.

[11] It should be remembered that the corporal and brutal punishments within HL have been argued to be from a pre-Hittite period as all of them, apart from those to be meted out upon slaves, are within *karu* clauses.

[12] See Van De Mieroop, *King Hammurabi*, 21. As opposed to historical argument

tamian cultural background perhaps tempered this somewhat in the case of LH. Vicarious punishments were found in LH, MAL and ND, talionic ones in LH and MAL, the mode of death was graphically specified mostly in LH and MAL and capital punishment was most rife in these same collections also. In terms of capital punishment, the Old Babylonian collections, LH and AE, were the only two to punish theft with the death penalty. This paralleled the great concern within these collections in regards to economic matters, including the activities of merchants. This correlates with the nature and structure of Old Babylonian society, specifically its economic structure.

This greater degree of brutality in the punishments of Egypt and Assyria parallels their historical inscriptions as mentioned above. It is difficult to decide whether this is to be connected with Assyrian culture in general or specifically with the period of empire. In Egypt this is also difficult to decide given our meager evidence for law in any period other than the New Kingdom. Given the changes in historiography which accompany the first intermediate period in Egypt *e.g.* acknowledgement of problems and failure, one would suspect that the severity of punishments would also change. There seems to be a loose correlation between centralization and brutality of punishments. This is seen most clearly when contrasting the Hittite collections with those of Assyria and Egypt. This contrast again fits a contrast in historiography and in the use of treaties. It is rare for the Assyrians to motivate obedience through history in their treaties. In most periods they tend to avoid treaties. Motivation to obedience is on the basis of fear rather than benefit in most extant treaties as seen in the emphasis on curses rather than the historical prologues of the Hittites. Egypt in almost all periods also eschews the use of treaties and does not motivate obedience through history of deeds done for the benefit of their allies. The one Egyptian treaty which is extant portrays the might of the Egyptian king forcing the Hittite king to plead for mercy.[13] Assyrian and Egyptian foreign relations are much more authoritarian and motivated by fear rather than thankfulness or the discernment of benefit. This parallels the lack of explication within Assyrian and Egyptian laws and the harsh nature of the penalties. LH shares some of these aspects with Assyria and Egypt but to a far lesser degree. The brutality

---

used for motivation.

[13] Treaty between Hattušiliš III and Ramesses II. For English translation of the two versions see John A. Wilson, "Treaty Between the Hittites and Egypt" (*ANET*, 199–201) and Albrecht Goetze, "Treaty between Hattusilis and Ramses II" (*ANET*, 201–3) or Beckman, *Diplomatic Texts*, 96–100 (which only treats the Egyptian version of the treaty *i.e.* that found in Hatti and written in Akkadian).

of some of the punishments within LH is not paralleled in Hammurabi's inscriptions which fit well into the typical Mesopotamian inscriptions of the time.

The Egyptian centralization in the person of the king is seen in the framing of its law collections as the first person commands of the Pharaoh. This writer thinks, despite the anecdotal evidence for some form of written law in Egypt, that this sole focus of power in the person of the Pharaoh combined with his divine status and the unwillingness of Egyptian royal historiography to acknowledge change or defeat may explain the non-existence of a law collection in Egypt on par with those cuneiform collections from elsewhere. Though this writer finds a number of points of disagreement with the intuitive method of Wilson and Speiser, he believes that their focus on the framing of Egyptian kingship may well be the way to begin an explanation for this anomaly, particularly the possibility that the idea of a law independent from Pharaoh was anathema.[14] This would neatly parallel the almost complete non-existence of evidence for Egyptian vassal treaties.

The harsh nature of MAL may be due in part to the isolated nature of the Assyrian king.[15] This may have led him to project the devious nature of the harem, the seat of many a conspiracy, and the perceived need for harsh discipline within it to the broader society. Some would argue for a geographic determination of the harshness of Assyrian culture and point to the later empires of the Abbasids and Saddam Hussein.[16] This writer thinks it more likely to be the similar context of empire rather than the geography which was a factor here.

These systematic differences between the law collections of the ancient Near East and the ability to connect them to differences in regards to historiography, treaty framing and existence and conceptions of kingship should certainly make one hesitate before ascribing a common culture to the ancient Near East. Questions of the priority of contexts do arise, however. Within this thesis it has been noted repeatedly that there is a higher level of similarity within Mesopotamia, particularly Lower Mesopotamia. This is borne out in a number of different aspects of these collections as outlined above. Within Mesopotamia, however, Assyria stands out as different quite often. LH also displayed a number of differences *e.g.* focus on economic

---

[14] Wilson, "Authority and Law," esp. p. 6; Speiser, "Cuneiform Law," 540.

[15] See N. K. Weeks, "Assyrian Imperialism and the Walls of Uruk."

[16] This writer has only had this theory communicated to him verbally, not seen it in print.

factors, harsher framing including its treating of theft as a capital offence, the particular framing of its drafter in terms of equivalent penalties *etc.* The material written in Sumerian, if RU is excepted, displayed very few differences in terms of framing or penalties and shared much without necessarily having borrowed from each other regularly. This is not necessarily due to a difference of Sumerian culture, however. LL for example is often seen as part of the Old Babylonian rather than Early Dynastic or Ur III periods of Sumerian rule. Many have written on the dangers and difficulties of attempting to distinguish Sumerian from Akkadian culture.[17] This writer will not attempt such a program either. The distinctions that have been discovered in this work lend themselves to explanation on the basis of culture, society, politics and personality, but not race. The hopelessly mixed nature of the population of Mesopotamia would make such an approach to the material untenable. There are firm links between the Lower Mesopotamian collections which may be due to their situation within the same cultural sphere. There are differences within this which are associated with factors such as societal make up and the context of empire in the case of LH, and the different use of history at Lagash for RU. MAL share more aspects within broader Mesopotamia than do HL or Egypt, which shares almost nothing with the other collections.

3.3 Reflections on the Nature, Function and Purpose of the Collections

The analysis of the evidence used to decide upon the nature, function and purpose of these law collections demonstrated its inconclusive nature. It was argued that the most useful material to attempt to decide on such issues was the stated intentions within the collections themselves. This was particularly applicable to LH which contained numerous statements regarding Hammurabi's desired outcomes which were to result from the setting up of his stele. Addresses within the text, whether those of LH to the future ruler or the *awilum ḫablum*, or those in the Egyptian collections or MAPD to royal officials, were also quite useful. Other than this material the actual content of the collections, whether the boasting of the non-legal sections or the

[17] *e.g.* those collected in the various articles collected in E. Sollberger, ed., "Aspects du Contact Suméro-Akkadien," *Genava* 8 (1960): 241–314. See especially Kraus' famous article "Ein zentrales Problem," and the comments made in conclusion pp. 294–96 or his *Sumerer und Akkader, ein Problem der altmesopotamischen Geschichte* (Amsterdam: North Holland, 1970). Similar problems are mentioned by Tigay, "On Evaluating," 253.

laws themselves, and superscriptions, colophons *etc.* gave some clues. Most of the evidence brought to bear to decide these issues *e.g.* documents from practice, form, genre, connection to scribal schools, the existence of copies *etc.*, was found impotent, despite the forced arguments of some.

In general, most internal contradictions which scholars had seen within individual collections were found to be non-existent or explainable.[18] MAL A 21 and A 50 were perhaps exceptions. The distance kept between these two laws gave a possible link to the contention of this writer that the Mesopotamian collections, and especially the Assyrian ones, were not happy to acknowledge change within the law. The proximity of MAL A 17 and 18 which also seem to disagree would temper this conclusion somewhat.

LH's undue influence on scholar's opinions[19] regarding the topic of the nature, function and purpose of other collections was noted. Given the ability of this thesis to demonstrate significant cultural differences in the framing of law collections in the ancient Near East it is hoped that this will be avoided in the future.

This writer contends that an attempt to reconstruct the societies which would result from the application of the laws within each collection would be a useful aid to understanding their purposes.[20] This approach was underutilized in this study due to limitations of space. The Old Babylonian economic focus in LH and AE was noted, however.

3.4 IMPLICATIONS FOR FURTHER RESEARCH

This study has a number of implications for the study of ancient Near Eastern law (including that of the Hebrew Bible) and comparative approaches to ancient Near Eastern and biblical studies. The most important conclusion to come out of the research presented here is that similar societies can exhibit a fair degree of similarity while allowing room for significant differences. These differences cannot be uniformly explained as due to just one context whether cultural, historical, political or personal. The focus of the present thesis was the laying out of differences accompanying both cultural and historico-political contexts. It is hoped that this will act as a corrective

[18] *e.g.* the agricultural laws of LH.

[19] Especially considering the indeterminate nature of most of the evidence used to construct its nature, function and purpose.

[20] Or at least the aspects of the societies reconstructable from the topics covered in the collections. For an example of this approach as applied to the economic implications of the laws in the Hebrew Bible see Neil M. Soss, "Old Testament Law and Economic Society," *Journal of the History of Ideas* 34 (1973): 323–44.

to the theory that there was a uniform culture in the ancient Near East which developed at the same rate everywhere.

Another possibility raised by the material here presented is that the comparison of texts with similar content but different genre can be fruitful. It is also hoped that the approach adopted here with its greater focus on content as opposed to form or genre will be found useful elsewhere. It was found difficult to explain the diachronic changes within HL without any specific statements regarding the date or purpose of such changes within the text itself. This problem was exacerbated by the lack of any objective criteria to firmly date the various copies of the text. I hope to test the conclusion reached in this work that similar content within different genre can be fruitfully compared by comparing the collections of the Hebrew Bible within their various formulations, including those within a covenant, to those presented here.

There are a number of more specific implications that this study has for future research. Many of the cultural specificities attributed to the Hittite law collections *e.g.* the including of more historical information and explanation, the ability to acknowledge change, the concern with purity within law collections treating other topics *etc.*, find parallels with the law within the Hebrew Bible. Weeks has fruitfully compared Hittite treaties and the covenants of the Hebrew Bible on the basis of other similarities. Rather than postulating borrowing one way or the other, his explanation for the similarity rested partly on the lesser degree of centralization in the two societies. In the future this writer hopes to bring the law collections of the Hebrew Bible into this discussion and apply the method used here to see what conclusions can be made. One difference which comes to mind between the Hittite and Israelite collections is the relative prevalence of corporal and capital punishments in the latter. In this thesis it has been argued that this may be related to the lack of centralization at Hatti as compared to the collections of Assyria and Egypt. This writer suspects that a phenomenon similar to that found in the one area in which the Hittites did outstrip their Near Eastern counterparts in the severity of punishment, laws regarding purity, may explain this oddity when it comes to Israel also. This would confirm the suspicion presented here that focus on a sole context, in this case political structure, is too simplistic to account for the complexity of the evidence.[21] It is thought that by leaving Israel out of this discussion thus far this work has managed to demonstrate the falsity of many of the ap-

[21] In this vein, see Kuper's critique of the similarly deterministic approach to social constructivism, *Culture*.

proaches taken to the study of ancient Near Eastern and biblical law, and comparison in general, and that it has freed the way for a new approach to these topics. Perhaps this will aid Kitchen's hope that methods which are demonstrably false when applied to areas other than Israel will not be applied to Israel.[22] This study has shown that an attempt to explain phenomena from within a text's context before appeal to comparative material is both workable and productive. The method of trying to understand laws within their own cultural connections before imposing understandings derived from other cultures should be applied to biblical law also.

Two particular areas which I think could benefit from comprehensive comparative studies using the method employed here, and that of Weeks regarding treaties, are the historiography and the kingship of the ancient Near Eastern cultures.[23] Such studies would also offer an alternative to current research which imports modern typological models to explain the data.[24] A more subjective study, which may be of use, would include a comparison of the relationship of the differences found between societies in these diverse areas of their civilization with their general religious and moral conceptions, or what may be termed their "worldviews". This would need to include openness to the influence of other contexts upon the operation of these societies.

---

[22] Kitchen, *Ancient Orient and Old Testament*, 28.

[23] Some work has been done in these areas already, but not in the comprehensive, systematic and comparative way envisaged by this writer.

[24] *e.g.* models drawn from anthropology or ethnography regarding the operation of complex societies, or the importation of models drawn from modern textual propaganda to interpret ancient texts.

BIBLIOGRAPHY

Adams., William Y., Dennis P. Van Gerven, and Richard S. Levy. "The Retreat from Migrationism." *Annual Review of Anthropology* 7 (1978): 483–532.

Archi, Alfonso. "La formazione del diritto nell'Anatolia Ittita." Pages 61–76 in *La Formazione del Diritto ne vicino oriente antico*. Edited by Aristide Theodorides, Carlo Zaccagnini, Guillaume Cardascia, Alfonso Archi and Reuven Yaron. Rome: Edizioni Scientifiche Italiene, 1988.

———. "Sulla formazione del testo delle leggi ittite." *Studi micenei ed egeo-anatolici* 7 (1968): 54–89.

Arnasen, Johann P., Shmuel Noah Eisenstadt, and B. Wittrock, eds. *Axial Civilizations and World History*. Jerusalem Studies in Religion and Culture 4. Leiden: Brill, 2005.

Azize, Joseph J. "Assumptions of the Criminal Justice System: Euthanasia and Aboriginal Opposition." Paper presented at the conference Law's Empire. Harrison, B.C., Canada, 26 June 2005.

Baines, John, and Norman K. Yoffee. "Order, Legitimacy, and Wealth in Ancient Egypt and Mesopotamia." Pages 199–260 in *Archaic States*. Edited by G. M. Feinman, and J. Marcus. Santa Fe, Mex.: School of American Research, 1998.

Beckman, Gary. *Hittite Diplomatic Texts*. 2nd ed. Society of Biblical Literature Writings from the Ancient World 7. Atlanta, Ga.: Society of Biblical Literature, 1999.

Bedell, Ellen Dailey. "Criminal Law in the Egyptian Ramesside Period." Ph.D. diss. Brandeis University, 1973.

Black, Jeremy, Andrew George and Nicholas Postgate, eds. *A Concise Dictionary of Akkadian*. SANTAG 5. Wiesbaden: Harrassowitz, 2000.

Bolin, Thomas M. "History, Historiography, and the Use of the Past in the Hebrew Bible." Pages 113–40 in *The Limits of Historiography: Genre and Narrative in Ancient Historical Texts*. Edited by C. S. Kraus. Mnemosyne: Bibliotheca Classica Batava Supplementum 191. Leiden: Brill, 1999.

Bottéro, Jean. "The 'Code' of Hammurabi." Pages 156–84 in *Mesopotamia: Writing, Reasoning and the Gods*. Chicago: University of Chicago Press,

1992. Translated by Z. Bahrani, and Marc van de Mieroop from "Le 'code' de Hammurapi." *Annali della Scuola Normale Superiore di Pisa* 12 (1982): 409–44.

———. "Désordre Economique et Annulation des Dettes en Mesopotamia a l'époque paleo-babylonienne." *Journal of the Economic and Social History of the Orient* 4 (1961): 113–63.

Breasted, James Henry. *Ancient Records of Egypt.* Vol. 2. Chicago: University of Chicago Press, 1906. Repr., Urbana: University of Illinois Press, 2001.

———. *Ancient Records of Egypt.* Vol. 3. Chicago: University of Chicago Press, 1906. Repr., Urbana: University of Illinois Press, 2001.

———. *Ancient Records of Egypt.* Vol. 4. Chicago: University of Chicago Press, 1906. Repr., Urbana: University of Illinois Press, 2001.

Bryce, Trevor. *The Kingdom of the Hittites.* Oxford: Oxford University Press, 1998.

Butterfield, Herbert. *The Whig Interpretation of History.* London: G. Bell, 1931.

Cardascia, Guillame. "La coutume dans les droits cuneiformes." *Recueils de la société Jean Bodin* 51 (1990): 61–69.

———. "La formazione del diritto in Assiria." Pages 51–60 in *La Formazione del Diritto ne vicino oriente antico.* Edited by Aristide Theodorides, Carlo Zaccagnini, Guillaume Cardascia, Alfonso Archi and Reuven Yaron. Rome: Edizioni Scientifiche Italiene, 1988.

———. *Les Lois Assyriennes.* Paris: Le Cerf, 1969.

———. "La place du talion dans l'histoire du droit pénal a la lumière des droits du Proche-Orient ancien." Pages 169–83 in *Mélanges offerts à Jean Dauvillier.* Toulouse: Université des sciences sociales de Toulouse, 1979.

———. "La réparation des dommages agricoles dans le Code de Hammurabi," *Revue d'Assyriologie* 79 (1985): 169–80.

Clay, A. T. *Miscellaneous Inscriptions in the Yale Babylonian Collections.* Yale Oriental Series Babylonian Texts 1. New Haven: Yale University Press, 1915.

Collins, B. J. "§ 54 of the Hittite Laws and the Old Kingdom Periphery." *Orientalia* 56 (1987): 136–41.

Cooper, Jerrold S. *Presargonic Inscriptions.* Sumerian and Akkadian Royal Inscriptions 1. New Haven, Conn.: American Oriental Society, 1986.

Daube, David. *Forms of Roman Legislation.* Oxford: Oxford University Press, 1956.

Delitzsch, Friedrich. *Babel and Bible: Two Lectures.* Edited with an introduction by C. W. H. Johns. London: Williams & Norgate, 1903.

Demare, S. "La valeur de la loi dans les droits cuneiforms." *Archives de Philosophie de Droit* 32 (1987): 335–46.

Diakonoff, I. M. "The Rise of the Despotic State in Ancient Mesopotamia." Pages 173–203 in *Ancient Mesopotamia*. Edited by I. M. Diakonoff. Moscow: Nauka, 1969.

———. "Some Remarks on the Reforms of Urukagina." *Revue d'Assyriologie* 52 (1958): 1–15.

Dion, Paul Eugene. Review of E. Levy (ed.), *La Codification des lois dans l'antiquité*. *Journal of the American Oriental Society* 121 (2001): 314–15.

Driessche, J. van den. "A propos de la sanction de l'homicide et dommages corporels dans le code d'Hammurabi." *Akkadica* 13 (1979): 16–27.

Driver, Godfrey Rolles, and John C. Miles. *The Assyrian Laws*. Oxford: Clarendon, 1935.

———. *The Babylonian Laws*. 2 vols. Oxford: Clarendon, 1952.

Edgerton, William F. "The Nauri Decree of Seti I: A translation and analysis of the legal portion." *Journal of Near Eastern Studies* 6 (1947): 219–30.

Edwards, C. *The Oldest Laws in the World*. London: Watts, 1906.

Edzard, Dietz Otto. "'Soziale Reformen' im Zweistromland bis ca. 1600 v. Chr.: Realitat oder literarischer Topos?" *Acta Antiqua Academiae Scientiarum Hungaricae* 22 (1974): 145–56.

Eichler, Barry L. "Literary Structure in the Laws of Eshnunna." Pages 71–84 in *Language, Literature, and History: Philological and Historical Studies Presented to Erica Reiner*. Edited by Francisca Rochberg-Halton. American Oriental Series 67. New Haven: American Oriental Society, 1987.

Eilers, W. *Die Gesetzesstele Chammurabis. Gesetze um die Wende des 3. vorchristlichen Jahrtausends*. Der Alte Orient 31, 3/4. Leipzig: J. C. Hinrichs, 1932.

Eisenstadt, Shmuel Noah, ed. *The Origins and Diversity of Axial Age Civilizations*. Albany: State University of New York Press, 1986.

Elton, Geoffrey. *The Practice of History*. 2nd ed. Oxford: Blackwell, 2002.

Faulkner, Raymond O. *A Concise Dictionary of Middle Egyptian*. Oxford: Griffith Institute, 1999.

Fensham, F. C., "Widow, Orphan and Poor in Ancient Near Eastern Legal and Wisdom Literature." *Journal of Near Eastern Studies* 21 (1962): 129–39.

Finkelstein, Jacob Joel. "Ammisaduqa's Edict and the Babylonian 'Law Codes'." *Journal of Cuneiform Studies* 15 (1961): 91–104.

———. "Bible and Babel: A Comparative Study of the Hebrew and Babylonian Religious Spirit." *Commentary* 26 (1958): 431–44.

———. "The Goring Ox: Some Historical Perspectives on Deodands, Forfeitures, Wrongful Death and the Western Notion of Sovereignty." *Temple Law Quarterly* 46 (1973): 169–290.

———. "A Late Old Babylonian Copy of the Laws of Hammurapi." *Journal of Cuneiform Studies* 21 (1967): 39–48.

———. "Law in the Ancient Near East." *Encyclopedia Miqra'it* 5 (1968): 588–614.

———. "The Ox That Gored." *Transactions of the American Philosophical Society* 71 (1981): 1–89.

———. "Sex Offenses in Sumerian Laws." *Journal of the American Oriental Society* 86 (1966): 355–72.

———. "Some New Misharum Material and its Implications." Pages 233–46 in *Studies in Honor of Benno Landsberger.* Edited by Hans G. Guterbock and Thorkild Jacobsen. Assyriological Studies 16. Chicago: University of Chicago Press, 1965.

Finley, M. I. Review of Henri Frankfort, *Kingship and the Gods. Political Science Quarterly* 63 (1948): 275–81.

Fleishman, J. "Legal Continuation and Reform in Codex Hammurabi Paragraphs 168–169." *Zeitschrift für altorientalische und biblische Rechtgeschichte* 5 (1999): 54–65.

Foster, Benjamin. "Social Reform in Ancient Mesopotamia." Pages 165–77 in *Social Justice in the Ancient World.* Edited by K. Irani and M. Silver. Westport, Conn.: Greenwood, 1995.

Frankfort, Henri. *Kingship and the Gods: A Study of Ancient Near Eastern Religion as the Integration of Society and Nature.* Chicago: University of Chicago Press, 1948.

Frankfort, Henri, H. A. Frankfort, John A. Wilson, and Thorkild Jacobsen. *Before Philosophy.* Harmondsworth: Penguin, 1949.

Frankfort, Henri, H. A. Frankfort, John A. Wilson, Thorkild Jacobsen, and W. A. Irwin. *The Intellectual Adventure of Ancient Man: An Essay on Speculative Thought in the Ancient Near East.* Chicago:University of Chicago Press, 1946.

Frayne, Douglas R. *Old Babylonian Period: 2003–1595 B.C.* The Royal Inscriptions of Mesopotamia, Early Period 4. Toronto: University of Toronto, 1990.

Frazer, James G. *The Golden Bough: A Study in Comparative Religion.* 2 vols. London: Macmillan, 1890.

Friedrich, Johannes. *Die hethitischen Gesetze.* 2nd ed. Documenta et Monumenta Orientis Antiqui 7. Leiden: Brill, 1971.

Friedrich, Johannes. "Reinheitsvorschriften für den hethitischen König." *Mitteilungen der Altorientalischen Gesellschaft* 4 (1928–29): 46–58.

Frymer-Kensky, Tikva. "The Judicial Ordeal in the Ancient Near East." Ph.D. diss. Yale University. Ann Arbor: University Microfilms, 1977.

Gemser, B. "The Importance of the Motive Clause in Old Testament Law." *Supplement to Vetus Testamentum* 1 (1953): 50–66.

Glassner, Jean-Jacques. *Mesopotamian Chronicles.* Society of Biblical Literature Writings from the Ancient World 19. Atlanta, Ga.: Society of Biblical Literature, 2004.

Goetze, Albrecht. *Laws of Eshnunna.* Annual of the American School of Oriental Research 31. New Haven: Department of Antiquities of the Government of Iraq and the American Schools of Oriental Research, 1956.

———. "The Laws of Eshnunna Discovered at Tell Harmal." *Sumer* 4 (1948): 63–102.

Grayson, Albert Kirk. *Assyrian and Babylonian Chronicles.* Locust Valley, NY: J.J. Augustin, 1975.

———. *Assyrian Rulers of the Early First Millennium BC.* Vol. 1. Royal Inscriptions of Mesopotamia, Assyrian Periods 2. Toronto: University of Toronto Press, 1991.

Greenberg, Moshe. "Some Postulates of Biblical Criminal Law." Pages 333–52 in *Essential Papers on Israel and the Ancient Near East.* Edited by F. E. Greenspahn. New York: New York University Press, 1991.Reprinted from *Studies in Bible and Jewish Religion: Yehezkel Kaufmann Jubilee Volume.* Edited by Menahem Haran. Jerusalem: Magnes, 1960, 5–28.

Greengus, Samuel. "Redefining 'Inchoate' Marriage in Old Babylonian Contexts." Pages 123–39 in *Riches Hidden in Secret Places: Ancient Near Eastern Studies in Memory of Thorkild Jacobsen.* Edited by Tsvi Abusch. Winona Lake: Eisenbrauns, 2002.

Griffith, F. Lt. "The Abydos Decree of Seti I at Nauri." *Journal of Egyptian Archaeology* 13 (1927): 193–208.

Guilding, A. E. "Notes on the Hebrew Law Codes." *Journal of Theological Studies* 49–50 (1948–1949): 43–53.

Güterbock, Hans G. "Authority and Law in the Hittite Kingdom," *Authority and Law in the Ancient Orient.* Journal of the American Oriental Society Supplement 17(1954): 16–24.

Güterbock, Hans G. and Theo P. J. van den Hout. *The Hittite Instruction for the Royal Bodyguard.* Assyriological Studies 24. Chicago: Oriental Institute, 1991.

Haase, Richard. *Einfuhrung in das Studium keilschriftlicher Rechtsquellen.* Wiesbaden: Harrassowitz, 1965.

———. "De fetu abito sive. Ne se immisceat mulier praegnans rixae inter viros. Vom ungewolten Abgang der Leibesfrucht im altorientalischen und biblischen Bereich." *Zeitschrift für altorientalische und biblische Rechtsgeschichte* 7 (2001): 384–91.

———. "The Hittite Kingdom." Pages 619–56 in *A History of Ancient Near Eastern Law.* Edited by Raymond Westbrook; Vol. 1; Handbook of Oriental Studies 72/1; Leiden: Brill, 2003.

———. "Kapitaldelikte im Hethititschen Recht." *Hethitica* 7 (1987): 93–107.

———. "Regelt § 9 der hethitischen Rechtssammlung eine leichte Leibesverletzung?" *Bibliotheca Orientalis* 19 (1962): 114–16.

———. "Überlegungen zur erlaubten Tötung eines Menschen in der hethitischen Rechtssammlung." *Die Welt des Orients* 27 (1996): 36–44.

Hallo, William W. "Ancient Near Eastern Texts and their Relevance for Biblical Exegesis." Pages xxiii–xxviii in *Canonical Compositions from the Biblical World.* Edited by William W. Hallo. Vol. 1 of *The Context of Scripture.* Leiden: Brill, 1997.

———, ed. *Archival Documents from the Biblical World.* Vol. 3 of *The Context of Scripture.* Leiden: Brill, 2002.

———, ed. *Canonical Compositions from the Biblical World.* Vol. 1 of *The Context of Scripture.* Leiden: Brill, 1997.

———. "Biblical History in its Near Eastern Setting: The Contextual Approach." Pages 1–26 in *Scripture in Context: Essays on the Comparative Method.* Edited by C. D. Evans, William W. Hallo, and J. B. White. Pittsburgh Theological Monograph Series 34. Pittsburgh: Pickwick, 1980.

———, ed. *Monumental Inscriptions from the Biblical World.* Vol. 2 of *The Context of Scripture.* Leiden: Brill, 2000.

Halloran, John A. "Sumerian Lexicon." Version 3.0. Cited 13 January 2005. Online: http://www. sumerian.org/sumerlex.htm.

Harris, Rivkah. "The naditu Laws of the Code of Hammurapi in Praxis." *Orientalia* 30 (1961): 163–9.

Hoffmann, Inge. *Der Erlaß Telipinus.* Texte der Hethiter 11. Heidelberg: Carl Winter, 1984.

Hoffner, Harry Angier. "Incest, Sodomy and Bestiality in the Ancient Near East." Pages 81–90 in *Orient and Occident. Essays presented to Cyrus H.*

Gordon on the occasion of his sixty-fifth birthday. Kevelaer: Butson & Bercker, 1973.

———. *The Laws of the Hittites: A Critical Edition*. Documenta et Monumenta Orientis Antiqui 23; Leiden: Brill, 1997.

———. "On Homicide in Hittite Law." Pages 293–314 in *Crossing Boundaries and Linking Horizons: Studies in Honor of Michael C. Astour on His 80th Birthday*. Edited by G. D. Young, Mark W. Chavalas and R. E. Averbeck. Bethesda, Md.: CDL, 1997.

Hooke, S. H., ed. *Myth and Ritual: Essays on the Myth and Ritual of the Hebrews in Relation to the Culture Pattern of the Ancient East*. London: Oxford University Press, 1933.

———, ed. *Myth, Ritual, and Kingship: Essays on the Theory and Practice of Kingship in the Ancient Near East and in Israel*. Oxford: Clarendon, 1958.

———, ed. *The Labyrinth: Further Essays in the Relation between Myth and Ritual in the Ancient World*. London: Macmillan, 1935.

Hrozný, Frederic. *Code Hittite provenant l'Asie mineure*. Paris: Paul Geuthner, 1922.

Hruška, B. "Die innere Struktur der Reformtexte Urukaginas von Lagash." *Archiv Orientalni* 41 (1973): 4–13, 104–32.

Hurowitz, Victor. *Inu Anum Ṣirum: Literary Studies in the Non-Juridical Section of Codex Hammurabi*. Philadelphia: Occasional Publications of the Samuel Noah Kramer Fund, 1994.

Imparati, Fiorella. *Le Leggi Ittite*. Rome: Dell'Ateneo, 1964.

Jackson, Bernard S. *Essays in Jewish and Comparative Legal History*. Leiden: Brill, 1975.

———. "History, Dogmatics and Halakhah." Pages 1–26 in *Jewish Law in Legal History and the Modern World*. Edited by Bernard S. Jackson. The Jewish Law Annual Supplement 2. Leiden: Brill, 1980.

———. *Studies in the Semiotics of Biblical Law*. Journal for the Study of Old Testament Supplement 314; Sheffield: Sheffield, 2000.

Jacobsen, Thorkild. *The Sumerian King List*. Chicago: University of Chicago Press, 1939.

Janssen, C. "Samsu-iluna and the Hungry naditums." *Northern Akkad Project Reports* 5 (1991): 3–40.

Johanning, Klaus. *Der Bibel-Babel-Streit: Eine forschungsgeschichtliche Studie*. European University Studies Series 13: Theology vol. 343. Frankfurt: Peter Lang, 1988.

Kaufman, Stephen A. "The Structure of the Deuteronomic Law." *Maarav* 1 (1978–1979): 105–58.

Kitchen, Kenneth. *Ancient Orient and Old Testament*. London: Tyndale, 1966.

Klengel, Horst. *König Hammurabi und der alltag Babylons.* 2nd ed. Darmstadt: Wissenschaftliche Buchgesellschaft, 1992.

Klíma, Joseph. "Einige Bemerkungen zur Bedeutung der 'nicht-juristischen' Bestandteile der altbabylonischen Gesetzwerke." *Journal of Juristic Papyrology* 5 (1951): 161–86.

———. "La perspective historique des lois Hammourabiennes." *Compte rendus de l'Académie des Inscription et belles lettres* (1973): 297–317.

———. "Das politische Profil der altmesopotamischen Herrscher im Lichte der Prologe und Epiloge ihrer Gesetze." Pages 209–24 in *Festschrift Lubor Matouš.* Edited by B. Hruška and G. Komoroczy. Vol. 1. Budapest: Eötvös Loránd Tudományegyetem, 1978.

———. "Zur Gesellschaftlichen Relevanz der Hammurapischen Gesetze." Pages 174–95 in *Societies and Languages of the Ancient Near East: Studies in Honor of I.M. Diakonoff.* Edited by M. Dandamaev and I. M. Diakonoff. Warminster: Aris & Phillips, 1982.

Kohler, J., and F. E. Peiser. *Hammurabi's Gesetz.* Vol. 1. Leipzig: Pfeifer, 1904.

Kohler, J., and A. Ungnad. *Hammurabi's Gesetz.* Vol. 2. Leipzig: Pfeifer, 1909.

———. *Hammurabi's Gesetz.* Vol. 3. Leipzig: Pfeifer, 1909.

———. *Hammurabi's Gesetz.* Vol. 4. Leipzig: Pfeifer, 1910.

———. *Hammurabi's Gesetz.* Vol. 5. Leipzig: Pfeifer, 1911.

Komoroczy, G. "Zur Frage der Periodizitat der altbabylonischen Misharum-Erlasse." Pages 196–205 in *Societies and Languages of the Ancient Near East: Studies in Honor of I.M. Diakonoff.* Edited by M. Dandamaev and I. M. Diakonoff. Warminster: Aris & Phillips, 1982.

Korošec, Victor. "Beiträge zum hethitischen Privatrecht." *Zeitschrift der Savigny-Stiftung für Rechtsgeschichte* 52 (1932): 156–169.

———. "Le Code de Hammurabi et les droits antérieurs." *Revue internationale des droits de l'antiquité* 8 (1961): 11–27.

———. "La codification dans le domaine du droit Hittite." *Revue internationale des droits de l'antiquité.* 4 (1957): 99–100.

———. "Keilschriftrecht." Pages 49–219 in *Orientalisches Recht.* Edited by B. Spuler; Handbuch der Orientalistik 3. Leiden: Brill, 1964.

———. "Sistematika prve hettitske pravne zbirke (KBoVI 3)." *Zbornik znanstvenih razpraw* 7 (1930): 2–12.

———. "Todesstraffe in der Entwicklung des hethitischen Rechtes." Pages 199–212 in *Death in Mesopotamia.* Edited by B. Alster. Compte Rendu Rencontre Assyriologique Internationale XXVIe. Mesopotamia Copenhagen Studies in Assyriology 8. Copenhagen: Akademisk, 1980.

Koschaker, Paulo. "Cuneiform Law." Pages 211–9, 263–4 in *Encyclopaedia of the Social Sciences*. Edited by E. R. A. Seligman. Vol. 9. New York: Macmillan, 1959.

———. "Keilschriftrecht." *Zeitschrift für Deutschen Morgenlandischen Gesellschaft* 89 (1935): 1–39.

———. *Quellenkritische Untersuchungen zu den "altassyrischen Gesetzen"*. Mitteilungen der Vorderasiatischen Gesellschaft 26/3. Leipzig: J. C. Hinrich, 1921.

———. *Rechtsvergleichende Studien zur Gesetzgebung Hammurapis Konigs von Babylon*. Leipzig: von Veit, 1917.

Koschaker, Paulo, and A. Ungnad. *Hammurabi's Gesetz*. Vol. 6. Leipzig: Pfeifer, 1923.

Kramer, Samuel Noah. Review of Henri Frankfort *et al.*, *Intellectual Adventure of Ancient Man*. *Journal of Cuneiform Studies* 2 (1948): 39–70.

———. "The Ur-Nammu Law Code: Who Was Its Author?" *Orientalia* 52 (1983): 453–56.

Kraus, F. R. *Briefe aus dem Archive des Shamah-Hazir*. Altbabylonische Briefe 4. Leiden: Brill, 1968.

———. *Ein Edikt des Königs Ammi-ṣaduqa von Babylon* (Studia et Documenta ad Iura Orientis Pertinentia 5; Leiden: Brill, 1958).

———. "Ein zentrales Problem des altmesopotamischen Rechtes: Was ist der Codex Hammurapi?" *Genava* 8 (1960): 283–96.

———. *Königliche Verfugungen in altbabylonischer Zeit*. Studia et Documenta ad Iura Orientis Pertinentia 11. Leiden: Brill, 1984.

———. *Sumerer und Akkader, ein Problem der altmesopotamischen Geschichte*. Amsterdam: North Holland, 1970.

———. *Vom mesopotamischen Menschen der altbabylonischen Zeit und seiner Welt*. Amsterdam: North-Holland, 1973.

Kruchten, Jean-Marie. *Le Decret d'Horemheb:Traduction, commentaire épigraphique, philologique et instutionnel*. Brussels: University of Brussels Press, 1981.

Kuhrt, Amélie. *The Ancient Near East: c. 3000–330 BC*. 2 vols. London: Routledge, 1995.

Kuper, A. *Culture: the Anthropologists' Account*. Cambridge, Mass.: Harvard University Press, 1999.

Labat, René. *Manuel d'épigraphie Akkadienne*. 6th ed. Libraire Orientaliste Paul Geuthner: Paris, 1988.

Laessoe, Jorgen. "On the Fragments of the Hammurabi Code." *Journal of Cuneiform Studies* 4 (1950): 173–87.

Lafont, Bertrand and Raymond M. Westbrook. "Neo-Sumerian Period (Ur III)." Pages 183–226 in *A History of Ancient Near Eastern Law*. Edited by Raymond Westbrook. Vol. 1; Handbook of Oriental Studies 72/1. Leiden: Brill, 2003.

Lafont, Sophie. "Codification et Subsidiarité dans les Droits du Proche-Orient Ancien." Pages 49–64 in *La Codification Des Lois Dans L'Antiquité: Actes du Colloque de Strasbourg 27–29 novembre 1997*. Edited by Edmond Lévy. Université Marc Bloch de Strasbourg: travaux du centre de recherche sur le Proche-Orient et la Grèce antiques 16. Paris: De Boccard, 2000.

———. *Femmes, droit et justice dans l'antiquité orientale*. Orbis biblicus et orientalis 165. Fribourg: Editions Universitaires, 1999.

———. "Middle Assyrian Period." Pages 521–64 in *A History of Ancient Near Eastern Law*. Edited by Raymond Westbrook. Vol. 1; Handbook of Oriental Studies 72/1. Leiden: Brill, 2003.

Lambert, Maurice. "Les 'réformes' d'Urukagina." *Revue d'Assyriologie* 50 (1956): 169–184.

Lambert, Wilfried G. "Morals in Ancient Mesopotamia." *Jaarbericht Ex Oriente Lux* 15 (1958): 184–96.

———. "The Reign of Nebuchadnezzar I: A Turning Point in the History of Ancient Mesopotamian Religion." Pages 3–13 in *The Seed of Wisdom: Essays in Honor of T. J. Meek*. Edited by W. S. McCullough. Toronto: University of Toronto Press, 1964.

———. "Tukulti-Ninurta I and the Assyrian King List." *Iraq* 38 (1976): 85–94.

Landsberger, Benno. "Die babylonischen Termini für Gesetz und Recht." Pages 219–34 in *Symbolae Paulo Koschaker Dedicatae*. Edited by Johannes Friedrich, J. G. Lautner, and John C. Miles. Studia Documenta ad Iura Orientis Antiqui Pertinentia 2. Leiden: Brill, 1939.

———. "The Conceptual Autonomy of the Babylonian World." Pages 5–15 in *Monographs of the Ancient Near East*. Vol. 1, fasc. 4. Malibu: Undena, 1976. Translated by Thorkild Jacobson, Benjamin Foster, and H. von Siebenthal from "Die Eigenbegrifflichkeit der Babylonischen Welt." *Islamica* 2 (1926): 355–72.

Larsen, Mogens Trolle. "The 'Babel/Bible' Controversy and its Aftermath." Pages 95–106 in *Civilizations of the Ancient Near East*. Edited by Jack M. Sasson. Vol. 1. New York: Hendrickson, 1995.

———. *The Old Assyrian City-State and its Colonies*. Copenhagen Studies in Assyriology 4. Copenhagen: Akademisk, 1976.

Leemans, W. F. "King Hammurabi as Judge." Pages 107–29 in *Symbolae Iuridicae et Historicae Martino David Dedicatae.* Edited by J. A. Ankum, R. Feenstra, and W. F. Leemans. Studia Documenta ad Iura Orientis Antiqui Pertinentia 2. Leiden: Brill, 1968.

Lemche, Niels Peter. "Justice in Western Asia in Antiquity, or: Why No Laws Were Needed!" *Chicago-Kent Law Review* 70 (1995): 1695–1716.

Levinson, Bernard M. Review of M.T. Roth (with a contribution by H.A. Hoffner), *Law Collections from Mesopotamia and Asia Minor. Journal of Near Eastern Studies* 59 (2000): 119–21.

———, ed. *Theory and Method in Biblical and Cuneiform Law: Revision, Interpolation and Development.* Journal for the Study of the Old Testament Supplement 181. Sheffield: Sheffield Academic Press, 1994.

Lévy, Edmond, ed. *La Codification Des Lois Dans L'Antiquité: Actes du Colloque de Strasbourg 27–29 novembre 1997.* Université Marc Bloch de Strasbourg: travaux du centre de recherche sur le Proche-Orient et la Grèce antiques 16. Paris: De Boccard, 2000.

Lieberman, S. J. "Nippur: City of Decisions." Pages 127–36 in *Nippur at the Centennial.* Edited by Maria de Jong Ellis. Rencontre Assyriologique Internationale 35. Philadelphia: Occasional Publication of the Samuel Noah Kramer Fund, 1992.

———. "Royal 'Reforms' of the Amurrite Dynasty." *Bibliotheca Orientalis* 46 (1989): 241–59.

Liverani, Mario. *Three Amarna Essays.* Introduced and translated by Matthew L. Jaffe. Monographs on the Ancient Near East vol. 1, fasc. 5. Malibu, Ca.: Undena, 1979.

Loewenstamm, S. "The Law of Adultery and the Law of Murder in Biblical Law and Mesopotamian Law." *Beth Mikra* 13 (1962): 55–59.

Longman, Tremper III. "Form Criticism, Recent Developments in Genre Theory, and the Evangelical." *Westminster Theological Journal* 47 (1985): 46–67.

Luckenbill, Daniel David. *Historical Records of Assyria: from Sargon to the End.* Vol. 2 of *Ancient Records of Assyria and Babylonia.* New York: Greenwood, 1927.

Machinist, P. "The Question of Distinctiveness in Ancient Israel: An Essay." Pages 196–212 in *Ah, Assyria . . . Studies in Assyrian History and Ancient Near Eastern Historiography Presented to Hayim Tadmor.* Edited by M. Cogan and I. Eph`al. Scripta Hierosolymitana 33. Jerusalem: Magnes, 1991.

Mackenzie, R. A. F. "The Formal Aspects of Ancient Near Eastern Law." Pages 31–45 in *The Seed of Wisdom: Essays in Honor of T.J. Meek*. Edited by W. S. McCullogh. Toronto: University of Toronto, 1964.

Maine, Henry Sumner. *Ancient Law*. London: John Murray, 1864. Repr. Tucson: University of Arizona Press, 1986.

Malul, Meir. *The Comparative Method in Ancient Near Eastern and Biblical Legal Studies*. Alter Orient und Altes Testament 227. Kevelaer: Butzon & Bercker, 1990.

———. Review of Raymond Westbrook, *Studies in Biblical and Cuneiform Law*. *Orientalia* 59 (1990): 85–91.

McKeon, Richard P, ed. *The Basic Works of Aristotle*. New York: Random House, 1941.

Mendenhall, George E. "Ancient Oriental and Biblical Law." *Biblical Archaeologist* 17 (1954): 26–46.

Michalowski, Piotr and C. B. F. Walker. "A New Sumerian 'Law Code'." Pages 383–96 in *DUMU.E$_2$.DUB.BA.A: Studies in Honor of Åke W. Sjöberg*. Edited by Hermann Behrens, Darlene Loding and Martha Tobias Roth. Occasional Publications of the Samuel Noah Kramer Fund 11. Philadephia: University of Pennsylvania Museum, 1989.

Miles, John C. and O. R. Gurney. "The Laws of Eshnunna." *Archiv Orientalni* 17 (1949): 174–88.

Monroe, Christopher M. "Money and Trade." Pages 155–68 in *A Companion to the Ancient Near East*. Edited by Daniel C. Snell. Blackwell Companions to the Ancient World. Malden, Mass.: Blackwell, 2005.

Muhly, James David. *Copper and Tin: The Distribution of Mineral Resources and the Nature of the Metals Trade in the Bronze Age*. Hamden, Conn.: Archon, 1976. Repr. from *The Transactions of the Connecticut Academy of Arts and Sciences* 43 (1973): 155–535 and 46 (1976): 77–136.

Müller, D. H. *Die Gesetze Hammurabis und ihr Verhältnis zur mosaischen Gesetzgebung sowie zu den XII Tafeln*. Vienna: Hölder, 1903.

Murnane, William J. *Texts from the Amarna Period in Egypt*. Society of Biblical Literature Writings from the Ancient World 5. Atlanta, Ga.: Scholars Press, 1995.

Neufeld, E. *Hittite Laws*. London: Luzac & Co., 1951.

Oelsner, J. "Zweisprachige Gesetze Hammurabis oder sumerische Fluchformeln?" *Nouvelles Assyriologiques Breves et Utilitaires* 3 (1993): 55–56.

Olivier, H. "The Effectiveness of the Old Babylonian Mesharum Decree." *Journal of North-West Semitic Studies* 12 (1984): 107–13.

Oppenheim, A. Leo. *Ancient Mesopotamia: Portrait of a Dead Civilization*. Rev. ed. Chicago: University of Chicago Press, 1977.

———. *The Assyrian Dictionary of the Oriental Institute of the University of Chicago*. Vol. 6. Chicago: Oriental Institute, 1956.

Otto, Eckart. "Aspects of Legal Reforms and Reformulations in Ancient Cuneiform and Israelite Law." Pages 160–96 in *Theory and Method in Biblical and Cuneiform Law: Revision, Interpolation and Development*. Edited by Bernard M. Levinson. Journal for the Study of the Old Testament Supplement 181. Sheffield: Sheffield Academic Press, 1994.

———. "Auf dem Wege zu einer altorientalischen Rechtgeschichte." *Bibliotheca Orientalis* 48 (1991): 5–13.

———. "Die Bedeutung der altorientalischen Rechtgeschichte für das Verstandnis des Alten Testaments." *Zeitschrift für Theologie und Kirche* 88 (1991): 139–68.

———. "Kodifizierung und Kanonisierung von Rechtssatzen in Keilschriftlichen und Biblischen Rechtssammlungen." Pages 77–124 in *La Codification Des Lois Dans L'Antiquité: Actes du Colloque de Strasbourg 27–29 novembre 1997*. Edited by Edmond Lévy. Université Marc Bloch de Strasbourg: travaux du centre de recherche sur le Proche-Orient et la Grèce antiques 16. Paris: De Boccard, 2000.

———. "Korperverletzung im hethitischen und israelitischen Recht." Pages 391–426 in *Religionsgeschichtliche Beziehungen zwischen Kleinasien, Nordsyrien und dem Alten Testament*. Edited by B. Jankowski, K. Koch and G. Wilhelm. Orbis biblicus et orientalis 129. Göttingen: Vandenhoeck & Ruprecht, 1993.

———. *Korperverletzungen in den Keilschriften und im Alten Testament: Studien zun Rechtstransfer im Alten Testament*. Alter Orient und Altes Testament 226. Kevelaer: Butzon & Bercker, 1991.

———. "Prolegomena zur Frage der Gesetzgebung und Rechtsprechung in Ägypten." *Mitteilungen des Deutschen Archaologischen Instituts* 14 (1956): 150–9.

Paul, Shalom M. *Studies in the Book of the Covenant in the Light of Cuneiform and Biblical Law*. Vetus Testamentum Supplement 18. Leiden: Brill, 1970.

Pecchioli Daddi, Franca. "Il re, il padre del re, il nonno del re." *Orientis Antiqui Miscellanea* 1 (1994): 75–91.

Peet, T. Eric. *The Great Tomb-Robberies of the Twentieth Egyptian Dynasty: Being a Critical Study, with Translations and Commentaries, of the Papyri in which these are Recorded*. 2 vols. Oxford: Clarendon, 1930.

Petschow, Herbert. "Die §§ 45 und 46 des Codex Hammurapi. Ein Beitrag zum altbabylonischen Bodenpachtrecht und zum Problem: Was ist der Codex Hammurapi?" *Zeitschrift für Assyriologie* 74 (1984): 181–212.

———. "Beiträge zum Codex Hammurapi." *Zeitschrift für Assyriologie* 76 (1986): 17–75.

———. "Zu den Stillformen antiker Gesetze und Rechtssammlungen." *Zeitschrift der Savigny-Stiftung für Rechtsgeschichte* 82 (1965): 24–38.

———. "Zur 'Systematik' in den Gesetzen von Eschnunna." Pages 131–143 in *Symbolae Iuridicae et Historicae Martino David Dedicatae.* Edited by J. A. Ankum, R. Feenstra, and W. F. Leemans. Vol. 2. Iura Orientis Antiqui 2. Leiden: Brill, 1968.

———. "Zur Systematik und Gesetztechnik im Codex Hammurabi." *Zeitschrift für Assyriologie* 57 (1965): 146–72.

Pflüger, Kurt. "The Edict of Haremhab." *Journal of Near Eastern Studies* 5 (1946): 260–76.

Poebel, A. *Historical and Grammatical Texts.* Publications of the Babylonian Section, University of Pennsylvania Museum 5. Philadelphia: University Museum, 1914.

Postgate, Nicholas. *Early Mesopotamia: Society and Economy at the Dawn of History.* London: Routledge, 1992.

Preiser, W. F. "Zur rechtlichen Natur der altorientalischen 'Gesetze'." Pages 17–36 in *Festschrift für Karl Englisch.* Edited by P. Bockelmann, A. Kaufmann, and U. Klugg. Frankfurt: Main, 1969.

Pritchard, James B., ed. *Ancient Near Eastern Texts Relating to the Old Testament.* 3rd ed. Princeton: Princeton University Press, 1969.

Renger, Johannes. "Hammurapis Stele 'Konig der Gerichtigkeit': Zur Frage von Recht und Gesetz in der altbabylonischen Zeit." *Die Welt des Orients* 8 (1976): 228–35.

———. "Noch einmal: Was war der 'Kodex' Hammurapi-ein erlassenes Gesetz oder ein Rechtsbuch?" Pages 27–60 in *Rechtskodifizierung und soziale Normen im interkulturellen Vergleich.* Edited by Hans-Joachim Gehrke. Script Oralia 66: Series A: Altertumwissentschaftliche Reiche vol. 15. Tubingen: Gunter Narr, 1994.

———. "Wrongdoing and its Sanctions: On Criminal and Civil Law in the Old Babylonian Period." *Journal of the Economic and Social History of the Orient* 20 (1977): 65–77.

Richards, J., and M. van Buren, eds. *Order, Legitimacy and Wealth in Ancient States.* New Directions in Archaeology. Cambridge: Cambridge University Press, 2000.

Roth, Martha Tobias. "The Because Clause: Punishment Rationalization in Mesopotamian Laws." Pages 407–12 in *Veenhof Anniversary Volume: Studies Presented to Klaas R. Veenhof on the Occasion of his Sixty-Fifth Birthday.* Edited by W. H. van Soldt, J. G. Dercksen, N. J. C. Kouwenberg and Th. J. H. Krispijn. Publications de l'Institut historique-archéologique néerlandais de Stamboul 89. Leiden: Nederlands Institut voor het Nabije Oosten, 2001.

———. "Hammurabi's Wronged Man." *Journal of the American Oriental Society* 122 (2002):38–45.

———. "The Law Collection of King Hammurabi: Toward an Understanding of Codification and Text." Pages 9–31 in *La Codification Des Lois Dans L'Antiquité: Actes du Colloque de Strasbourg 27–29 novembre 1997.* Edited by Edmond Lévy. Université Marc Bloch de Strasbourg: travaux du centre de recherche sur le Proche-Orient et la Grèce antiques 16. Paris: De Boccard, 2000.

———. *Law Collections from Mesopotamia and Asia Minor.* (With a contribution by Harry Anger Hoffner, Jr.). Society of Biblical Literature Writings from the Ancient World 6. Atlanta, Ga.: Scholars Press, 1995.

———. "Mesopotamian Legal Traditions and the Laws of Hammurabi." *Chicago-Kent Law Review* 70 (1995): 13–39.

———. "Reading Mesopotamian Law Cases: PBS 5 100: A Question of Filiation." *Journal of the Economic and Social History of the Orient* 44 (2001): 243–91.

———. "The Scholastic Exercise 'Laws about Rented Oxen'." *Journal of Cuneiform Studies* 32/33 (1980): 127–46.

———. "Scholastic Tradition and Mesopotamian Law: A Study of FLP 1287, a Prism in the Collection of the Free Library of Philadelphia." Ph.D. diss. University of Pennsylvania. Ann Arbor: University Microfilms, 1979.

Rüster, Christel and Erich Neu. *Hethitisches Zeichenlexikon: Inventar und Interpretation der Keilschriftzeichen aus den Boğazköy-Texten.* Studien zu den Boğazköy-Texten 2. Wiesbaden: Harrassowitz, 1989.

San Nicolò, Marian. *Beiträge zur Rechtsgeschichte im Bereiche der keilschriftlichen Rechtsquellen.* Instituttet for Sammenlignende Kulturforskning 13. Oslo: Aschehoug & Co., 1931.

———. *Die Schlussklauseln der altbabylonsichen Kauf und Tauschverträge.* 2nd ed. New introduction and notes by Herbert Petschow. Munich: C. H. Beck, 1974 [1922].

———. "Die Stellung der Keilschrifturkunden in der vorderasiatischen Rechtsentwicklung." *Zeitschrift der Savigny-Stiftung für Rechtsgeschichte* 48 (1928): 21–50.

Sandmel, Samuel. "Parallelomania." *Journal of Biblical Literature* 81 (1962): 1–13.

Sauren, H. "Aufbau und Anordnung der babylonischen Kodizes." *Zeitschrift der Savigny-Stiftung für Rechtsgeschichte* 106 (1989): 1–55.

Scheil, V. *Textes élamites-sémitiques: deuxième série.* Mémoires de la Délégation en Perse 4. Paris: Libraire Ernest LeRoux, 1902.

Schuler, E. von. "Hethitische Königserlässe als Quellen der Rechtsfindung und ihr Verhältnis zum kodifizierten Recht." Pages 435–72 in *Festschrift Johannes Friedrich.* Edited by R. von Kienle, A. Moortgart, Heinrich Otten, E. von Schuler, and W. Zaumsell. Heidelberg: Carl Winter, 1959.

Selms, A. van. "The Goring Ox in Babylonian and Biblical Law." *Archiv Orientalni* 18 (1950): 321–30.

Siddall, Luis R. "A Re-examination of the Title *ša reši* in the Neo-Assyrian Period." Pages 225–40 in *Gilgameš and the World of Assyria: Proceedings of the Conference Held at Mandelbaum House, The University of Sydney, 21–23 July 2004.* Edited by J. J. Azize and N. K. Weeks; Ancient Near Eastern Studies Supplement 21. Louvain: Peeters, 2007.

Singer, Itamar. Review of Harry Angier Hoffner, *The Laws of the Hittites. Journal of Near Eastern Studies* 60 (2001): 286–89.

Sjöberg, Åke W. "Was There a Sumerian Version of the Laws of Hammurabi?" Pages 219–25 in *Velles Paraules: Ancient Near Eastern Studies in Honor of Miguel Civil.* Edited by Piotr Michalowski, P. Steinkeller, E. C. Stone and R. L. Zettler. Aula Orientalis 9. Barcelona: Ausa, 1991.

Smith, Morton. "East Mediterranean Law Codes of the Early Iron Age." *Eretz Israel* 14 (1978): 38–43.

Snell, Daniel C. "Methods of Exchange and Coinage in Ancient Western Asia." Pages 1487–1500 in *Civilizations of the Ancient Near East.* Edited by Jack M. Sasson. Vol. 3. New York: Hendrickson, 1995.

Sollberger, E. ed. "Aspects du Contact Suméro-Akkadien." *Genava* 8 (1960): 241–314.

Sonsino, Rifat. *Motive Clauses in the Old Testament and the Ancient Near East: Biblical Forms and Near Eastern Parallels.* SBL Dissertations Series 45. Chico, Ca.: Scholars Press, 1980.

Soss, Neil M. "Old Testament Law and Economic Society." *Journal of the History of Ideas* 34 (1973): 323–44.

Speiser, E. A. "Cuneiform Law and the History of Civilization." *Proceedings of the American Philosophical Society* 107 (1963): 536–41.

———. "Early Law and Civilization." *Canadian Bar Review* 31 (1953): 863–77.

Steinkeller, Piotr. "The Administrative and Economic Organization of the Ur III State: The Core and the Periphery." Pages 15–33 in *The Organization of Power: Aspects of Bureaucracy in the Ancient Near East.* Edited by McGuire Gibson, and Robert D. Biggs. 2nd ed. Studies in Ancient Oriental Civilizations 46. Chicago: Oriental Institute, 1991.

Stern, Fritz. *The Varieties of History: From Voltaire to the Present.* 2nd ed. Cleveland: Macmillan, 1970.

Stol, Martin. *Letters from Yale.* Altbabylonische Briefe 9. Leiden: Brill, 1981.

Sweet, R. F. G. "On Prices, Moneys, and Money Uses in the Old Babylonian Period." Ph.D. diss. University of Chicago, 1958.

Szlechter, Émile. "Le Code d'Ur-Nammu." *Revue d'Assyriologie* 49 (1955): 169–76.

———. "Le Code de Lipit-Ishtar (I)." *Revue d'Assyriologie* 51 (1957): 57–82.

———. "Le Code de Lipit-Ishtar (II)." *Revue d'Assyriologie* 51 (1957): 177–196.

———. "Le Code de Lipit-Ishtar (III)." *Revue d'Assyriologie* 52 (1958): 74–90.

———. "La "loi" dans la Mesopotamie ancienne." *Revue internationale des droits de l'antiquité* 12 (1965): 55–77.

———. *Les Lois d'Eshnunna.* Publications de l'Institut de Droit Romain 12. Paris: Université de Paris, 1954.

Talmon, Shemaryahu. "The 'Comparative Method' in Biblical Interpretation-Principles and Problems." *Vetus Testamentum Supplement* 29 (1977): 320–56.

Tetlow, E. M. *Women, Crime and Punishment in Ancient Law and Society.* Vol. 1. London: Continuum, 2005.

Theodorides, Aristide, Carlo Zaccagnini, Guillaume Cardascia, Alfonso Archi and Reuven Yaron, eds. *La Formazione del Diritto ne vicino oriente antico.* Rome: Edizioni Scientifiche Italiene, 1988.

Tigay, Jeffrey H. "On Evaluating Claims of Borrowing." Pages 250–55 in *The Tablet and the Scroll: Near Eastern Studies in Honor of William W. Hallo.* Edited by Mark E. Cohen, Daniel C. Snell, and David B. Weisberg. Bethesda, Md.: CDL, 1993.

Tsevat, M. "The Husband Veils a Wife." *Journal of Cuneiform Studies* 27 (1975): 235–40.

Van De Mieroop, Marc. *King Hammurabi of Babylon: A Biography*. Malden, Ma.: Blackwell, 2005.

Van Seters, John. *In Search of History: Historiography in the Ancient World and the Origins of Biblical History*. New Haven: Yale University Press, 1983.

Veenhof, Klaas R. "The Relation between Royal Decrees and 'Law Codes' of the Old Babylonian Period." *Jaarbericht Ex Oriente Lux* 35/36 (1997–2000): 49–83.

VerSteeg, Russ. *Early Mesopotamian Law*. Durham, N.C.: Carolina Academic, 2000.

———. *Law in Ancient Egypt*. Durham, N.C.: Carolina Academic, 2002.

Walton, John H. *Ancient Israelite Literature in its Cultural Context: A Survey of Parallels Between Biblical and Ancient Near Eastern Texts*. Grand Rapids, Mich.: Zondervan, 1989.

Wasserman, N. "CT 21, 40–42: A bilingual Report of an Oracle with a Royal Hymn of Hammurabi." *Revue d'Assyriologie* 86 (1992): 1–18.

Weeks, Noel. K. *Admonition and Curse: The Ancient Near Eastern Treaty/Covenant Form as a Problem in Inter-Cultural Relationships*. Journal for the Study of Old Testament Supplement 407. London: T.&T. Clark, 2004.

———. "Assyrian Imperialism and the Walls of Uruk." Pages 79–90 in *Gilgameš and the World of Assyria: Proceedings of the Conference Held at Mandelbaum House, The University of Sydney, 21–23 July 2004*. Edited by J. J. Azize and N. K. Weeks; Ancient Near Eastern Studies Supplement 21. Louvain: Peeters, 2007.

Weidner, Ernst. "Das Alter der mittelassyrischen Gesetzestexte." *Archiv für Orientforschung* 12 (1937/9): 46–54.

———. "Die Bibliothek Tiglatpilesers I." *Archiv für Orientforschung* 16 (1952/53): 197–215.

Weitenberg, Jos. "The Meaning of the Expression 'To Become a Wolf' in Hittite." Pages 189–98 in *Perspectives on Indo-European Language, Culture and Religion: Studies in Honor of Edgar C. Polomé*. Edited by Roger Pearson. Vol. 1. Journal of Indo-European Studies Monograph 7. McLean, Va. Institute for the Study of Man, 1991.

Westbrook, Raymond. "Adultery in Ancient Near Eastern Law." *Revue Biblique* 97 (1990): 542–80.

———. "Biblical and Cuneiform Law Codes and the Origins of Legislation." *Revue Biblique* 92 (1985): 247–64.

———. "The Character of Ancient Near Eastern Law." Pages 1–92 in *A History of Ancient Near Eastern Law*. Edited by Raymond Westbrook. Vol. 1; Handbook of Oriental Studies 72/1. Leiden: Brill, 2003.

———. "Codification and Canonization." Pages 33–47 in *La Codification Des Lois Dans L'Antiquité: Actes du Colloque de Strasbourg 27–29 novembre 1997*. Edited by Edmond Lévy. Université Marc Bloch de Strasbourg: travaux du centre de recherche sur le Proche-Orient et la Grèce antiques 16. Paris: De Boccard, 2000.

———. "Cuneiform Law Codes and the Origins of Legislation." *Zeitschrift für Assyriologie* 79 (1989): 201–22.

———. "A Death in the Family: Codex Eshnunna 17–18 Revisited." *Israel Law Review* 29 (1995): 32–42.

———, ed. *A History of Ancient Near Eastern Law*. 2 vols. Handbook of Oriental Studies 72/1. Leiden: Brill, 2003.

———. "The Nature and Origin of the Twelve Tables." *Zeitschrift der Savigny-Stiftung für Rechtgeschichte* 105 (1988): 74–121.

———. *Old Babylonian Marriage Law*. Archiv für Orientforschung, Beiheft 23. Horn: Ferdinand Berger & sons, 1988.

———. "Old Babylonian Period." Pages 361–430 in *A History of Ancient Near Eastern Law*. Edited by Raymond Westbrook. Vol. 1; Handbook of Oriental Studies 72/1. Leiden: Brill, 2003.

———. *Studies in Biblical and Cuneiform Law*. Cahiers de la Revue Biblique 26. Paris: J. Gabalda, 1988.

Westbrook, Raymond M. and Roger D. Woodard. "The Edict of Tudhaliya IV." *Journal of the American Oriental Society* 110 (1990): 641–59.

Wilcke, Claus. "Dieber, Räuber und Mörder." *Xenia* 32 (1992): 53–78.

———. *Early Ancient Near Eastern Law. A History of its Beginnings: The Early Dynastic and Sargonic Periods*. Sitzungberichte der bayerischen Akademie der Wissenschaften 2003/2. Munich: Bayerischen Akademie der Wissenschaften, 2003.

———. "Early Dynastic and Sargonic Periods." Pages 141–82 in *A History of Ancient Near Eastern Law*. Edited by Raymond Westbrook. Vol. 1; Handbook of Oriental Studies 72/1. Leiden: Brill, 2003.

———. "Der Kodex Urnamma (CU): Versuch einer Rekonstruktion." Pages 291–333 in *Riches Hidden in Secret Places: Ancient Near Eastern Studies in Memory of Thorkild Jacobsen*. Edited by Tsvi Abusch. Winona Lake, Ind.: Eisebrauns, 2002.

Wilson, John A. "Authority and Law in Ancient Egypt." *Supplement to Journal of the American Oriental Society* 17 (1954): 1–33.

Wiseman, Donald J. "The Laws of Hammurabi Again." *Journal of Semitic Studies* 7 (1962): 161–72.

Yaron, Reuven. "Enquire now about Hammurabi, Ruler of Babylon." *Tijdschrift voor Rechtsgeschiednis* 59 (1991): 223–38.

———. "Forms in the Laws of Eshnunna." *Revue internationale des droits de l'antiquité* 9 (1962): 137–53.

———. "The Goring Ox in Near Eastern Laws." *Israel Law Review* 1 (1996): 396–406.

———. *The Laws of Eshnunna.* 1st ed. Jerusalem: Magnes, 1969.

———. *The Laws of Eshnunna.* 2nd ed. Jerusalem: Magnes, 1988.

———. "The Nature of the Early Mesopotamian Collections of Laws: Another Approach." Pages 65–76 in *La Codification Des Lois Dans L'Antiquité: Actes du Colloque de Strasbourg 27–29 novembre 1997.* Edited by Edmond Lévy. Université Marc Bloch de Strasbourg: travaux du centre de recherche sur le Proche-Orient et la Grèce antiques 16. Paris: De Boccard, 2000.

Yoffee, Norman K. "Context and Authority in Early Mesopotamian Law." Pages 95–113 in *State Formation and Political Legitimacy.* Edited by R. Cohen, and J. D. Toland. New Brunswick: Transaction Books, 1988.

———. *The Economic Role of the Crown in the Old Babylonian Period.* Bibliotheca Mesopotamica 5. Malibu: Undena, 1977.

Zaccagnini, C. "La formazione del diritto in Mesopotamia. Codificazioni regie e consuetudine nel II Millenio a.C." Pages 35–50 in *La Formazione del Diritto ne vicino oriente antico.* Edited by Aristide Theodorides, Carlo Zaccagnini, Guillaume Cardascia, Alfonso Archi and Reuven Yaron. Rome: Edizioni Scientifiche Italiene, 1988.

Ziskind, J. R. "Incest Laws in the Ancient Near East." *Revue internationale des droits de l'antiquité* 35 (1988): 79–109.

INDEX OF REFERENCES

www.ingramcontent.com/pod-product-compliance
Lightning Source LLC
LaVergne TN
LVHW102008210926
848483LV00010B/168
9781593332211